PARLIAMENTS

A Comparative Study on the Structure and Functioning of Representative Institutions in Fifty-Five Countries

A NEW AND COMPLETELY REVISED EDITION
PREPARED BY
MICHEL AMELLER
*Doctor of Law, Graduate of l'Institut
d'Etudes Politiques de Paris*

Published for the
INTER-PARLIAMENTARY UNION
by
CASSELL *LONDON*

Publishers to the Hansard Society

CASSELL & COMPANY LTD 35 Red Lion Square, London WCI
Melbourne, Sydney, Toronto, Johannesburg, Cape Town, Auckland

© Union Interparliamentaire 1962, 1966
This translation © Inter-Parliamentary Union 1962, 1966
First published in Great Britain November 1962
Second edition (Revised and Enlarged) July 1966

328.3
I61p

66-10643

PRINTED IN ENGLAND BY
UNWIN BROTHERS LIMITED
WOKING AND LONDON
466

Contents

Introduction · ix

PART ONE · STRUCTURE OF PARLIAMENT

1 · THE NUMBER OF ASSEMBLIES · 3
1 · The Bicameral System in Federal States · 3
2 · The Bicameral System in Unitary States · 7
3 · The Unicameral System · 12

2 · THE ELECTORATE · 14
1 · The Right to Vote · 14
2 · Electoral Registers · 18
3 · Electoral Constituencies · 20

3 · THE BALLOT · 23
1 · Methods of Voting · 24
2 · Characteristics of the Vote · 28
3 · Organisation of the Ballot · 33

4 · MEMBERS OF PARLIAMENT · 40
1 · General Qualifications for Membership · 40
2 · Particular Ineligibilities · 43
3 · Candidates and Political Parties · 46
4 · The Election Campaign · 49
5 · The Mandate · 52

PART TWO · ORGANISATION OF PARLIAMENT

5 · STATUS OF MEMBERS · 59
1 · Immunities · 59
2 · Offences against Parliament · 64
3 · Incompatibility of Occupation · 66
4 · Parliamentary Remuneration · 71

CONTENTS

6 · ADMINISTRATION OF PARLIAMENT · 77

1 · The Directing Authority · 77
2 · The Administrative Services · 84

7 · INDEPENDENCE OF PARLIAMENT · 88

1 · Administrative Independence · 89
2 · Financial Independence · 91
3 · Procedural Independence · 94

8 · POLITICAL PARTIES AND GROUPS · 97

9 · COMMITTEES · 102

1 · Kinds of Committees · 102
2 · Composition and Organisation of Committees · 112

10 · SITTINGS OF PARLIAMENT · 122

1 · The Chamber · 122
2 · The Sessions · 125

PART THREE · LEGISLATIVE FUNCTION OF PARLIAMENT

11 · LIMITATIONS ON THE LEGISLATIVE POWER OF PARLIAMENT · 133

1 · The Sphere of Law · 133
2 · The Referendum · 135
3 · The State of Emergency · 136

12 · INTRODUCTION OF BILLS · 140

1 · The Right to Initiate Legislation · 141
2 · Procedure for Introducing Bills · 144
3 · The Declining Contribution of Individual Members · 149

13 · DELEGATED LEGISLATION · 151

CONTENTS

14 · THE MAKING OF LAW · 159

1 · The Role of Committees · 161
2 · Consultation with Outside Interests · 171
3 · Order of Business · 174
4 · Debate in the House · 180
5 · Methods of Voting · 196
6 · Constitutional Bills · 203
7 · Agreement between the Two Houses · 208

15 · THE PROMULGATION OF LAWS · 213

1 · Royal Assent · 213
2 · Promulgation and Publication · 215
3 · Request for a New Consideration · 216
4 · The Veto · 217

16 · THE CONSTITUTIONAL VALIDITY OF LAWS · 219

PART FOUR · POWERS OF PARLIAMENT OVER FINANCE

17 · NATURE OF THE BUDGET · 227

18 · PREPARATION AND PRESENTATION OF THE BUDGET · 230

19 · THE BUDGET AND PUBLIC CORPORATIONS · 234

20 · THE BUDGET AND BICAMERAL PARLIAMENTS · 237

21 · RIGHTS OF MEMBERS OF PARLIAMENT · 241

22 · TIMING OF THE BUDGET · 246

23 · PROCEDURE FOR CONSIDERING THE BUDGET · 253

1 · Committee and the Budget · 254
2 · Debate on the Budget · 257

CONTENTS

PART FIVE · CONTROL OF THE EXECUTIVE BY PARLIAMENT

24 · APPOINTMENT OF THE EXECUTIVE · 263

1 · The Head of State · 264
2 · The Head of Government and Ministers · 268
3 · High Officials · 274

25 · ACCOUNTABILITY OF THE GOVERNMENT TO PARLIAMENT · 276

1 · The Meaning of Ministerial Accountability · 276
2 · Forms of Ministerial Accountability · 279
3 · Ministerial Accountability and Dissolution · 285

26 · MACHINERY OF PARLIAMENTARY CONTROL · 288

1 · General Debate and Interpellations · 289
2 · Questions to Ministers · 294
3 · Committees of Investigation · 299
4 · The Ombudsman and Other Forms of Control · 302

27 · ACCOUNTING TO PARLIAMENT FOR PUBLIC EXPENDITURE · 304

28 · PARLIAMENT AND FOREIGN POLICY · 310

29 · JUDICIAL FUNCTION OF PARLIAMENT · 316

Index · 321

Introduction

Everywhere in the world today a crucial question must be faced: what is to be the role of Parliaments in modern States at a time when science has radically changed conditions of life and when it appears that only technocrats can master the problems of government?

The reform of Parliament, the strengthening of its control over the Executive, the adaptation of parliamentary procedure to cope with ever-growing legislation—these are only some of the many topical problems which are now the object of intensive discussion.

To provide a basis for the study of these questions the Inter-Parliamentary Union decided to publish a new and revised edition of the comparative study of the different types of Parliament in the world, first published in 1961.

In the interim, fundamental changes have taken place in many political regimes. New constitutions have been drawn up and put into practice; some legislative assemblies have disappeared while others have been newly created or reconstituted.

Changes such as these are not merely the reflection of an institutional instability within certain States in search of political equilibrium. Their significance goes much deeper. They are an expression of the imperative need for parliamentary institutions to adapt themselves to the requirements of a new world.

This book has been prepared by the International Centre for Parliamentary Documentation recently set up by the Union. The task of this Centre, which will include a specialized parliamentary library, will be to compile and keep up to date all such texts and documentation as are necessary for a systematic study of the structure, life and procedure of parliamentary assemblies in all countries.

Early in November 1965, in the very year of its inception, the Centre organized an international Symposium which provided an opportunity for active parliamentarians, specialists in constitutional law and Clerks of Parliament from all over the world, with widely differing political and ideological points of view, to debate some of the problems with which they are all concerned.

The basic information for this volume was obtained from an enquiry conducted among the National Groups of the Inter-Parlia-

INTRODUCTION

mentary Union, an organization which unites the representatives of the major political forces of the day in the common cause of the consolidation of peace and the strengthening of Parliament.

The first edition of *Parliaments* described conditions in forty-one countries. In the present edition, the figure has risen to fifty-five as follows: Albania, America (United States of), Argentina, Australia, Austria, Belgium, Brazil, Bulgaria, Cameroon, Canada, Central African Republic, Ceylon, Chile, Czechoslovakia, Denmark, Ethiopia, Finland, France, Germany (Federal Republic of), Ghana, Great Britain, Greece, Hungary, Iceland, India, Iran, Ireland, Israel, Italy, Japan, Laos, Lebanon, Liberia, Libya, Luxembourg, Monaco, Netherlands, New Zealand, Nigeria, Norway, Pakistan, Philippines, Poland, Rumania, Senegal, Sierra Leone, Somalia, Spain, Sweden, Switzerland, Tunisia, Turkey, United Arab Republic, U.S.S.R., Yugoslavia.

This increase is indeed a good illustration of the progress which the Union has made along the path to universality. Major alterations have been made to the text of the 1961 edition, with the result that the present volume is in reality an entirely new study which it is hoped will be of considerable assistance to all those who are interested in the development of representative democracy.

Naturally, a document of this kind cannot claim to be completely up to date at the time of publication since the institutions which it sets out to describe are in constant evolution. It would obviously have been impracticable to follow the changes which have occurred by means of successive addenda to the original material.

Indeed, to modify the details relevant to any given country, as a consequence of constitutional changes that may have occurred there, would have destroyed the comparative basis on which the whole work rests.

It was therefore decided to approach the matter scientifically so that the study would describe the parliamentary institutions of the countries in question as at a certain date, namely July 1, 1963, and no mention has been made of events which have taken place since then.

The text, which was compiled by Mr. Michel Ameller during the course of 1964 on the basis of information supplied by National Groups, was approved in its final form by the Governing Board of the International Centre for Parliamentary Documentation in July 1965. Presided over by Mr. G. Codacci-Pisanelli (Italy), Deputy, former Minister, the Board includes the following: Mr. André Chandernagor (France), Deputy; Mr. Christian Dominicé (Switzerland), Professor of Constitutional Law at the University of Geneva; Sir Edward Fellowes (Great Britain), former Clerk of the House of

INTRODUCTION

Commons, Chairman of the Council of the Hansard Society; Mr. A. F. Gorkine (U.S.S.R.), Deputy, President of the Supreme Court of the U.S.S.R.; Mr. Matthew T. Mbu (Nigeria), Member of the House of Representatives, Minister of State; Mr. A. F. Schepel (Netherlands), Clerk of the Second Chamber of the States General, representing the Association of Secretaries-General of Parliament. This English translation is the work of Mr. Kenneth Bradshaw, Senior Clerk of the House of Commons.

Given the diversity of legislative bodies there could naturally be no question of taking any one form of Parliament as a model. The aim has been to provide readers, and especially those who are themselves parliamentarians, with an opportunity to view their own system in the light of others, while maintaining the utmost objectivity throughout.

Assemblies of longer standing might themselves well profit from such a comparison. For they should not be content to rest complacently on their past achievements: in politics, as in other fields, the search for truth must be unremitting. The institutions best fitted to represent a people and serve its true interests are not necessarily those developed in a particular period of history. On the contrary, their effectiveness may depend on their ability to adapt themselves to changing circumstances in the light of experience.

For new Parliaments the comparisons provided in the present study may even be of greater value. It is important that their members see how other peoples have solved problems similar to those which they in their turn must face, not for the purpose of imitation but to help them find their own solutions. These should both take into account practices existing elsewhere and ensure that parliamentary institutions be adapted to the actual conditions in each country.

It is because of its unremitting faith in the future of the representative system that the Inter-Parliamentary Union now places increasing emphasis on the study of the problems involved.

Its efforts to extend its activities may for a while be checked in certain countries by circumstances which are detrimental to constitutional order. Some Parliaments are dissolved, others are suspended, while others again may suffer grievous limitations to their prerogatives.

Experience shows, however, that the concept of democracy as the legitimate basis of power is nowadays so firmly embedded in people's minds that sooner or later representative assemblies arise again, even in those States where Parliament and its methods seem to have failed.

INTRODUCTION

This may be the reason why the Inter-Parliamentary Union, which celebrated its seventy-fifth anniversary in 1964, has withstood the upheavals of the first half of the twentieth century. Empires have collapsed, dictatorial regimes have ended in disaster; yet the fundamental idea of "Government of the people, by the people and for the people" remains intact. To this day, no lasting substitute has been found for the principle of representation of the people as the basis of political power.

With members in the Parliaments of seventy-six countries the Inter-Parliamentary Union is a progressive force in the world of today. For it serves a democratic ideal which, in one form or another, is present in the minds of all men.

André de Blonay	G. Codacci-Pisanelli
Secretary General	President
Inter-Parliamentary Union	International Centre for Parliamentary Documentation

Geneva, December 1965

PART ONE

Structure of Parliament

1. The Number of Assemblies

THE BICAMERAL SYSTEM IN FEDERAL STATES – THE BICAMERAL SYSTEM IN UNITARY STATES – THE UNICAMERAL SYSTEM

How many Chambers should Parliament comprise? This question has proved one of the most controversial in constitutional law and the answers given to it reflect the diversity of parliamentary institutions. This is no mere matter for academic political scientists. The solution adopted in each country is the result of a political choice which goes to the heart of the regime.

Yet the choice seems simple enough. Generally it is limited to the alternative: should there be one chamber or two, a unicameral or a bicameral system? While federal states without exception are spared this choice by reason of their peculiar constitutional structure, unitary states—and this means the majority—are wholly free to choose the system they prefer. The widely differing factors which account for the existing unicameral and bicameral systems are analysed in this Chapter.

1. THE BICAMERAL SYSTEM IN FEDERAL STATES

In federal states no choice of system is open because they are by definition two-tier in structure. On the one side there is the nation as a complete entity; on the other the several states of the federation with their particular circumstances.

Within the Federation's Parliament this two-tier structure is inevitably translated into two separate chambers, the one emanating from the people as a whole the other made up of members representing each state.

This tidy explanation of the bicameral nature of the federal state derives from entirely fortuitous historical circumstances. Federal bicameralism came about as the result of a compromise between two schools of thought in the Philadelphia Convention of 1787 which, starting from the hypothesis that there was to be only one chamber had disagreed upon the number of members that each state should have.

STRUCTURE OF PARLIAMENT

Usage transformed this compromise into a generally accepted rule dictating one of the stock features of a federal Parliament. For the strictest application of this rule two conditions relating to the structure and powers of the Chamber representing the states of the Federation have to be met: first it must be made up of an equal number of representatives from each state, irrespective of size or population; secondly its powers must be equal to the powers of the Chamber representing the people as a whole. In few Federations are both these conditions met.

The Congress of the United States comprises two separate Assemblies. The House of Representatives has 435 members, each being elected for two years. The number of Representatives is determined by the population of the state, being not less than one for each state and each member representing a given proportion of the population of that state. The Senate is so composed as to ensure an equal representation of all the states: each state elects two senators for six years.

The two Houses have the same power to legislate, except that only the House of Representatives may initiate bills dealing with taxes. In practice the Senate's right to amend a bill offsets this difference. With one vote for each state the House of Representatives has the duty of electing the President of the United States when none of the candidates obtains a majority of the votes cast by the Electoral College. In similar circumstances the Senate has to elect the Vice-President. The power to impeach belongs to the House, while the power to adjudge an impeachment is vested in the Senate. The Senate has the exclusive right to confirm or reject official appointments and to take part in the drafting and ratification of international treaties. In general the Senate appears to enjoy a measure of political advantage which itself underlines the federal character of the Constitution of the United States.

The same features are to be found in Brazil where the powers of the Senate, which consists of three members from each state, are broadly comparable with those of the Chamber of Deputies.

In Switzerland the structure of the Federal Assembly is comparable with that of the Congress of the United States. But the two Chambers, the National Council and the Council of States, are on a footing of equality except in the rare instances of joint sittings where the National Council enjoys the advantage of having five times as many members as the Council of States. The National Council consists of 200 members elected for four years; each Canton must return at least one member. The Council of States comprises forty-four members; each canton returns two and in the sub-divided cantons each subdivision returns one.

THE NUMBER OF ASSEMBLIES

The suggested criteria for a federal Parliament are equally respected by the Supreme Soviet of the Union of Soviet Socialist Republics whose two Chambers have equal powers. The Soviet of the Union is elected on a basis of population and represents the general interests of all the people regardless of their nationality. The Soviet of Nationalities represents the specific interests of the various kinds of national state included in the Union and is composed as follows: twenty-five members for each of the fifteen federated Republics; eleven members for each of the twenty autonomous Republics; five members for each of the eight autonomous Regions and one member for each of the ten national Territories. The autonomous Republics and Regions and the national Territories make up the federated Republics.

The Australian Parliament comes close to the two criteria of the stock Federal Parliament given above. First the equal representation of each of the states in the composition of the upper House is strictly observed. While the House of Representatives consists of 124 members elected by constituencies drawn in terms of population, each of the six states is entitled to ten seats in the Senate. Senators, like members of the House, are elected by universal suffrage; but while members are elected for three years only, senators are elected for six.

Secondly the powers of the Senate are analogous to those of the House except in matters of finance where the right to introduce bills and to make amendments is subject to certain restrictions.

In other countries the growing centralisation of power has weakened the hold of the federal idea. In terms of the structure of Parliament this decline has meant that the principle of equal representation of the several states is no longer regarded as sacrosanct and that the lower House claims a preponderance of authority over the upper House. The difference in the powers of the two Houses is often accompanied by the suppression of direct universal suffrage as the means of designating members of the upper Houses. These features may be observed in the countries described below.

In the Federal Republic of Germany each of the Länder is represented in the Bundesrat (Federal Council). But the number of members to which each Land is entitled varies with the size of the population: each Land has at least three members; those with over two million inhabitants are entitled to four; and those with over six million inhabitants have five. These seats are filled by members of the governing bodies of the Länder. The Bundesrat plays no part in the appointment of the Chancellor. It cannot bring down the Federal

STRUCTURE OF PARLIAMENT

Government and it has not the same legislative powers as the Bundestag (Federal Diet) which is elected by universal suffrage.

In Austria the Diets of the various Länder return to the Council of the Länder (Federal Council) of fifty members a number of delegates which varies between three and twelve according to size of population. The powers of the Federal Council are notably less than those of the lower House (National Council) both in legislative matters and in its relations with the executive.

The position is comparable in India. Besides the twelve members appointed by the President, the Council of States (Rajya Sabha) has 238 members elected by the legislatures of the states of the union, not on a basis of equality but in relation to the size of the population of each state. The House of the People (Lok Sabha) appointed essentially by universal suffrage also contains fifteen members representing the territories of the union and the Anglo-Indian community. It has greater powers than the House of the States especially in financial matters and in the control which it can exercise over the executive.

So the principles inspiring the organisation of a Federal Parliament have lost much of their force.

In India this may be attributed to the influence of British institutions which has also been felt in two other federal states, Canada and Nigeria, where the bicameral system owes as much to the example of the Parliament in London as to the needs of federation.

The Canadian Senate consists of 102 members appointed for life by the Governor General on the recommendation of the Prime Minister. Senators are supposed to represent the province for which they are nominated, and in order to safeguard the principal of equal representation the provinces are grouped into four divisions which are each entitled to the same number of senators. The role of the Canadian Senate is primarily legislative. Although it has the same powers as the House of Commons except for the right to introduce bills with financial implications, it is by virtue of its method of recruitment essentially a House of reflection.

The Senate of Nigeria has a similar role. Its members unlike those of the House of Representatives are not elected. Each region is represented by 12 senators chosen by the local legislatures from persons nominated by the Governor. Four senators represent the federal territory and four others are appointed by the Governor General in agreement with the Prime Minister.

Finally, in some states the federal structure has not led to a bicameral system. The most striking examples are Yugoslavia on the one hand and Cameroon and Pakistan on the other.

Since the Constitution of 7 April 1963 the Federal Assembly of Yugoslavia consists of five Councils, namely, the Federal Council and four Councils of working communities, which are the Economic Council, the Council for Education and Culture, the Council for Health and Social Affairs and the Council for Political Organisation. These four Councils take part in the legislation so far as each is concerned. They have the same rights as the Federal Council. But the Federal Council has exclusive powers in certain matters such as international treaties, national defence and the exercise of the electoral functions of the Assembly.

The federal structure of the state is represented not by the existence of a separate Chamber representing the federated territories but by the presence in the Federal Council itself of a certain number of members elected by the assemblies of peoples' republics and autonomous provinces. There are seventy of these members who together constitute a council of nationalities. It is their duty to secure 'the protection of equal rights for the peoples and republics of Yugoslavia'. With the same object this council has to take part in the consideration of proposals to revise the constitution. It may also meet at the request of a majority of the members from any republic, of ten of its own members or of the President of the Federal Assembly. Despite these special functions the council of nationalities does not have the status of a separate Chamber within the Yugoslav Parliament.

In Pakistan and in Cameroon provision is made for the federal system within a single Assembly. In both countries members of the Assembly are appointed by indirect suffrage through the intermediary of 'the basic democracies' in Pakistan, and in Cameroon by the legislatures of the federation. The next Assembly in Cameroon will however be elected by direct universal suffrage, with one member for every 80,000 inhabitants. At that moment all reference to the federal concept will have disappeared from the parliamentary organisation of the Cameroon Republic.

The solutions adopted by these last three countries show that a bicameral system is not an inescapable element in the structure of a federal state. Other factors relevant to unitary as well as to federal states may be equally important.

2. THE BICAMERAL SYSTEM IN UNITARY STATES

The bicameral system evolved long before the emergence of federal states. It has its roots deep in past history. Over a long period of time

STRUCTURE OF PARLIAMENT

it has developed new and varied facets as a result of theoretical and practical rationalizations. In the end these developments have supplanted the original intention which has long been forgotten.

The earliest example of the bicameral system is to be found in England towards the end of the thirteenth century. It began with the institution of a Chamber for the high aristocracy, bringing together the King's vassals, the Lords Spiritual and Temporal. In this House there are still 872 hereditary peers making it a unique phenomenon in contemporary constitutional law. Besides the Lords of Appeal in Ordinary and the 26 Lords Spiritual, there have been Life peers since 1958. In that year the Life Peerage Act authorised the Crown to appoint life peers; and by July 1963 47 had been appointed. But although the non-democratic composition of the second Chamber has managed to survive through the ages, the aristocratic character of the House has been attenuated and its powers have been greatly restricted in favour of the lower House, the House of Commons. Since 1911 the House of Lords has had no power to amend or reject money bills. Since 1949 it can only delay the passage of other kinds of bill for two sessions or for at least one year. While the House of Lords retains an important jurisdiction as the highest Court of Appeal, politically it has no power to bring down the government.

In democratic regimes the bicameral system is no longer explained by the need for a separate, aristocratic representation. Nowadays the theoretical arguments for a bicameral system are of two kinds: first the concern for a more stable balance between the Executive and the Legislature, the unbridled power of a single chamber being restrained by the creation of a second Chamber recruited on a different basis; secondly the desire to make the parliamentary machine run if not more efficiently at any rate more smoothly by having a so-called 'revising' chamber to maintain a careful check on the sometimes hasty decisions of a first Chamber.

In practice these arguments have not always by themselves explained the preference for the bicameral system. Its true nature can only be understood in many countries by reference to specific political motivation, an explanation of which would go beyond a mere description of parliamentary institutions.

In unitary states the nature of the second Chamber in some cases reflects the desire, conscious or unconscious, of those who framed the Constitution to temper the democratic aggressiveness of the first Chamber with a representational body of a more conservative character. On the assumption that the aim of democracy is to enable the sovereign will of the people to express itself as directly as possible,

THE NUMBER OF ASSEMBLIES

and that the evolution of man towards democratic ideas is linked historically with the growth of universal suffrage, the strength of the conservative elements in question may be assessed by applying two complementary criteria to the nature and structure of the second Chamber. First how are its members appointed? Secondly how do its powers compare with those of the lower Chamber?

These two criteria which are themselves pointers to the complex and varied character of parliamentary bodies suggest a basis for classifying bicameral systems, ranging as they do from 'conservative' bicameralism to a largely formal bicameralism that comes close to a unicameral system.

At one extreme would be a system in which the second Chamber was recruited by non-democratic means, but had powers equal to or greater than those of the first Chamber. The best example used to be the House of Lords in Great Britain before it became inferior in status to the House of Commons. But Parliament in the following countries shows varying degrees of kinship to this type of system.

In Ethiopia members of the Senate are appointed for six years by the Emperor from among the princes, high dignitaries, eminent civil servants and in general from persons who have gained the confidence and esteem of the people and have served their country and government with distinction. The Senate has the same power as the Chamber of Deputies. The only difference appears in joint sittings where the number of senators is less than half the number of members.

The twenty-four members of the Senate of Libya are also appointed by the King. Until recently half of them were elected by provincial legislatures. But these bodies were suppressed together with the federal system when the Constitution was reformed on 25 April 1963. The Senate has no initiative in financial matters nor is the government responsible to it.

In three other countries members of the upper House are also in large measure nominated.

In Laos the National Assembly and the Council of the King have equivalent powers. All the members of the upper House are nominated by the King but half their number are recommended by resolution of the National Assembly. Thus in the selection of the King's Councillors universal suffrage is partially and indirectly applied.

The bicameral system in Ceylon is similar. Of the thirty members of the Senate fifteen are appointed by the Governor-General on the recommendation of the Prime Minister, the other fifteen being elected by the House of Representatives. But the upper House's powers in Ceylon are more restricted than those of the lower: it may

STRUCTURE OF PARLIAMENT

not delay the passage of a bill for more than one year and it has less authority in financial matters.

In Iran thirty senators are chosen by the Shah-in-Shah. The other thirty are elected by the people. The two Chambers have equal rights except in financial matters where the Chamber of Deputies has primacy.

The Senate of the Turkish Republic is also composed of some members who are appointed and some who are members *ex officio*. While 150 senators are elected by universal suffrage, fifteen are directly appointed by the President of the Republic and twenty-one life members are appointed under the Constitution. These are the former members of the Committee of National Union which resulted from the revolution of 27 May 1960. Former Presidents of the Republic are also members of the Senate. The Government is responsible only to the National Assembly which also enjoys primacy in legislative matters.

This restriction of the powers of the upper House is also a feature of the Irish bicameral system. Here too the method of appointing members of the Senate (Seanad) does not altogether comply with the principles of universal direct suffrage. Eleven members out of sixty are appointed by the Prime Minister and six are elected by the universities. The remaining forty-three are elected by members of the lower House (Dail), by outgoing senators and by local authorities. This indirect method of appointment is a characteristic feature of bicameralism in several countries of Western Europe where the object has been to apply a form of brake to the accelerating tendencies of the lower House. France, the Netherlands and Sweden are examples.

The French Senate, which according to the Constitution allows the representation of the local communities of the Republic and of Frenchmen living outside France, is elected by an electoral college consisting of members of the National Assembly, Councillors General of Departments and delegates from municipal councils who have themselves been elected by universal suffrage.

The upper House (First Chamber) of the Netherlands is also elected by an electoral college consisting solely of members of Provincial councils.

In Sweden the system is analogous: the upper House is elected by county and city councils.

In other countries the appointment of members of the upper House is affected by different kinds of conservative practice. There are for example vestiges of autocracy in Belgium where the King's sons, or if there is no male issue the heirs presumptive to the throne, are *de jure* members of the Senate at the age of eighteen. In Italy the President of the Republic can nominate as life senators five citizens who have rendered distinguished service to their country; in addition, former Presidents of the Republic are *ex officio* members of the Senate. The raising of the age limit either for electors and candidates as in Italy, or for candidates as in France and Belgium, is another step in the same conservative direction.

These varying conservative elements in the method of appointing members of the upper House are frequently complemented in some degree by a reduction in powers. In France the Senate has not the same power as the National Assembly especially in matters of legislation and government responsibility. The same is true of the Netherlands. Bills may not be introduced in the First Chamber; it may only adopt or reject a bill as a whole, it may not amend it. In Sweden the inequality of powers can be seen only in the decisions of a joint sitting of the two Chambers to settle differences on legislative matters: members of the lower Chamber outnumber those of the upper Chamber.

By contrast where the methods of recruiting the upper House approximate to direct universal suffrage, its powers are often correspondingly greater and may even be the same as those of the lower House. This is the position in Belgium and in Italy where both Houses have the same powers in matters of legislation and government responsibility; either can bring the government down.

A similar regime is found in Japan. Both the House of Representatives and the House of Councillors are elected by the people. But the House of Representatives has greater power in legislative proceedings (it has the final voice), in considering the budget, in ratifying treaties and in appointing the prime minister and calling the government to account. On the other hand the House of Councillors may not be dissolved.

In the Philippines and in Chile the House of Representatives and the Senate are parts of presidential constitutions on the American pattern. The essential elements of these two bicameral systems are the representative character of both Houses and equivalent powers.

The method of appointing members of the second House and the powers accorded to that House when taken to their logical democratic extremes result in bicameral systems which paradoxical as it may sound can fairly be called 'unicameral bicameral systems'. Here the existence of a Second Chamber is not based on political considerations as in the other countries. The underlying motive is simply one of practical convenience. Examples are to be found in Norway and Iceland. In these two countries every member of Parliament is elected directly by the people in the same way. The separation into two Houses takes place only after the elections. Members of Parliament themselves appoint a proportion of their number (in Iceland one-third, in Norway a quarter) to sit in the upper House. Since political composition of the two Houses is the same, as are their methods of recruitment and their powers, this theoretically bicameral system is in truth a unicameral system. The belief of these countries is that the work of legislation is done more thoroughly if it has to be done twice in two separate Houses. Many unitary states do not consider this reason enough to justify dividing Parliament into two Houses.

3. THE UNICAMERAL SYSTEM

According to contemporary constitutional theory the unicameral system is more appropriate to democracy, bicameral systems being regarded as essentially designed to restrain and moderate the ebullience of popular sovereignty which would operate in too ruthless a manner if there were only a single chamber. The single chamber should, then, be elected by direct universal suffrage. But this is not by itself a sure enough clue to the nature of the unicameral system because here more than anywhere else allowance has to be made for the spirit, the traditions and the economic and social evolution of the particular nation concerned.

Thus although many countries have a Parliament with a single chamber, any attempt to classify them according to the reasons which led them to make this choice is bound to be somewhat arbitrary. Two of these countries, Monaco and Luxemburg, have been able in all probability to cut out one chamber simply because of their small geographical size and because the problem of the balance of political power is less difficult for small than for bigger countries to solve. The eighteen members of the Monaco National Council are enough to scrutinise the administration of the Principality, and the fifty-two members of the Luxemburg Parliament are enough for the purposes of the Grand Duchy. (In Luxemburg it must be remembered that the Council of State whose members are appointed has some legislative responsibilities.)

The fact that Denmark is small in size was probably one of the reasons for its change in 1953 to the unicameral system. A more fundamental cause lay in the deliberate movement of all the Scandinavian countries except Sweden towards the institution of a single chamber within the framework of the parliamentary system. The original constitutional practices of Iceland and Norway have already been noted, though Finland since 1906 has been the forerunner and is still the best example of this movement towards a single Chamber. There are some signs of the same tendency in other parts of the world.

New Zealand dispensed with an upper House (or Legislative Council) on 31 December 1950. The Chamber of Deputies in Greece and in Lebanon and the Knesset in Israel are other examples of single Chambers operating in a constitutional system of the western type.

With the exception of Yugoslavia whose peculiar institutions have already been considered all the People's Democracies of Europe, namely, Albania, Bulgaria, Czechoslovakia, Hungary, Poland and Rumania, have one Chamber only. The bicameral system is regarded in those countries as leading to complications, delays and expense without any compensating advantage for the regime.

Finally the unicameral system is found in a number of countries which have either recently achieved independence or where the current trends bearing on an ancient political structure do not suit the political temper that is supposed to favour the bicameral system. This is especially the position in African countries where a single Chamber responds more easily to the search for efficiency and to the need for the right balance of authority between the various institutions of government. Examples are the Central African Republic, Ghana, Senegal, Sierra Leone, Somalia and the United Arab Republic.

This short survey of the institutions of different countries from the narrow standpoint of the number of Chambers in their Parliaments shows clearly the importance of the choice between the bicameral and unicameral systems. Frequently it has its roots deep in the country's history, its peculiar characteristics and national spirit; in the main it involves a fundamental political choice which goes far beyond the sphere of day-to-day parliamentary practice.

Even from the narrow standpoint of this survey it is evident that a bicameral Parliament is better suited to federal states with their two-tier structure whatever the nature of their political system; that in unitary states the bicameral system endures above all in those countries with a strongly implanted parliamentary tradition; that the bicameral system generally loses ground in countries where the thrust of democracy has affected the nature of the upper House and deprived it of value; and finally that a unicameral system is better suited to the needs of younger countries which are evolving politically in circumstances very different from those obtaining in Western Europe where parliamentary government was born.

2. The Electorate

THE RIGHT TO VOTE – ELECTORAL REGISTERS – ELECTORAL CONSTITUENCIES

In the previous chapter special reference was made to the upper Chamber, especially to its powers and the way in which its members are recruited. Membership of Parliament relates more particularly to popular chambers because it touches the question of suffrage. In representative systems the consent of the people from whom authority emanates is signified by elections.

Democracies incline naturally towards universal suffrage. All popular chambers, that is, those of unicameral Parliaments and the lower chambers of bicameral Parliaments, follow this system. In an absolute sense there is no satisfactory definition of universal suffrage. The only way to grasp what it implies is by comparison with suffrage limited by qualifications of property or ability or sex. Those limitations were used to slow up the transition from autocratic government to democratic government and today are merely of historical interest.

During the twentieth century universal suffrage has become the accepted medium for popular authority. In practice however problems arise. An initial difficulty is how to define an elector. A definition is necessary because the vote cannot be granted to everyone indiscriminately. The selection of legislators is too important a matter to be left even partly in the hands of irresponsible elements. So electoral theory tends to disqualify these elements by praying in aid specific factors such as nationality, age, or good conduct. The degree of encroachment upon what is theoretically universal suffrage can be measured by the severity of the disqualifications which are imposed.

1. THE RIGHT TO VOTE

For a long time the vote was restricted to men, political affairs being regarded as an exclusively male domain. Since the turn of the century the progress of democracy and the campaign in favour of equal rights for women have prevailed over the efforts of men to maintain their exclusive rights. The most important exception is Switzerland where women may not vote in federal elections, though they are able to vote in some cantonal elections. In the Northern Province of

Nigeria women do not enjoy the right to vote. In Monaco it was accorded to them by the constitution of 17 December 1962 and in Libya by the reforms of 25 April 1963.

The delimitation of universal suffrage on grounds of sex is no longer significant. But other conditions remain.

The primary condition for the exercise of the franchise embodied in all codes of electoral law is that of nationality. Before a person can vote he must be a national of the country; for this reason the vote is nowhere given to aliens. The only practical problem is to decide what to do about aliens who have become nationals through naturalisation. This problem is particularly important in countries where there is large-scale immigration and where the influence of the immigrants could have a decisive impact on the conduct of public affairs. The general rule is to grant the franchise only after a certain length of time or where the persons concerned can show that they are well enough assimilated to their new surroundings. In France and the United Arab Republic for example naturalised persons may vote only after they have been naturalised for five years. In Belgium they must have acquired so-called 'full naturalisation' which is more difficult to obtain than ordinary naturalisation.

It is not always enough to hold the qualification of nationality. In most countries a period of residence in the same place is also required. This period is usually short and its purpose is partly to ensure as strict a check as possible on the regularity of the elections, for account has to be taken of the fact that citizens may have to move from place to place, but should not lose their civic rights by doing so. Where the period is long its purpose is to establish the attachment of the elector to his country as a prerequisite of his taking part in political life. In practice however it may have the result of disfranchising a relatively large number of people. In Iceland for example the minimum period is five years, in Ethiopia one year. Similarly in the United States, where the movement of population takes place on a fairly large scale, the qualification of residence required by most of the states has the effect of cutting down the number of electors. The same qualification is to be found in several countries of the Commonwealth. The period of residence required is one year in New Zealand and six months in Australia. In Canada where it applies only to British subjects who are not Canadian citizens the period is one year.

By contrast the electoral laws in other countries carry the theory of universal suffrage to its logical conclusion: no qualifications relating to domicile or residence are required. In Israel the explanation is that there is only one electoral constituency which comprises the whole country. In Czechoslovakia in order to ensure the universality of the

STRUCTURE OF PARLIAMENT

suffrage, electors' cards are issued which enable electors who change their place of residence after the electoral registers have been published and to vote in a constituency other than that in which they were registered. Similar methods are used in Bulgaria, Poland, Rumania and the U.S.S.R. In Finland if an elector presents a certificate that he is on the electoral register, he may vote in any polling station.

The franchise requires that male and female electors should have reached an age at which they are fully aware of their civic duties and are capable of expressing a reasonable opinion on political matters. As a rule this age coincides with that of legal majority. In other words it varies very little from one country to another, ranging from a minimum of eighteen to a maximum of twenty-three years, though exceptionally for elections to the upper House of some countries such as Iran or Italy it is as much as twenty-five. The age adopted in most codes of electoral law is twenty-one. New governments or governments of a revolutionary type are the most apt to grant the franchise at an early age, as in the People's Democracies and the nations which have attained independence relatively recently.*

Age is not the only criterion of the elector's intelligence. To qualify for participation in the political life of the country, a citizen must also be of sound mind. This is a principle which every country recognises. The difficulty is to determine precisely at what point an individual is to be regarded as insane or mentally deficient. In most instances the disqualification is not insanity or mental deficiency, even where the cases are clear, but their legal recognition, in the form of certification or committal to an asylum. The rights of every citizen are protected by the power of the courts to intervene.

In some countries other infirmities are treated in the same way. In Laos deaf mutes and blind persons and in Chile those with any physical defects that prevents them acting freely are disqualified. By contrast in Albania, Czechoslovakia, Rumania, Austria, The Netherlands and the United Arab Republic the blind and other invalids who can vote without assistance may be accompanied by another elector to the polling station and even into the polling booth.

---

* *23 years:* Denmark.
21 years: Australia, Belgium, Cameroon, Canada, Chile, Ethiopia, the Federal Republic of Germany, Finland, France, Ghana, Great Britain, Greece, India, Iceland, Ireland, Italy, Lebanon, Libya, Luxemburg, Monaco, Nigeria, Norway, New Zealand, Pakistan, Netherlands, Philippines, Sierre Leone, Sweden, Turkey, and the United States (except in the states of Georgia and Kentucky (18 years)).
20 years: Austria, Iran, Japan and Switzerland.
18 years: Albania, Bulgaria, the Central African Federation, Ceylon, Czechoslovakia, Hungary, Israel, Laos, Poland, Rumania, Somalia, the United Arab Republic, the U.S.S.R. and Yugoslavia.

In Albania this right is extended to the illiterate. In some instances the mental ability required of electors is measured in terms of a certain level of education. In Chile and in the Philippines an elector must be able to read and write; in the United States he must be able to give proof of some basic knowledge by reading a passage from the Constitution, by presenting a certificate of primary studies, or in any other way laid down in the electoral laws of each state. In Denmark and in some Swiss cantons persons who are a charge on public funds are disqualified. So are beggars in Iran.

In general however the loose nature of the rules governing the intellectual aptitudes of the electors is a measure of the desire to avoid any serious encroachment upon the principle of universal suffrage. The standard of conduct required of the elector is marked by the same concern. The conduct is defined in a negative way: a person is considered fit to be a voter provided he has not incurred a conviction entailing disqualification. The courts ensure an impartial application of the laws which in each country list these convictions. Generally a middle course is sought by which persons who are really depraved can be kept off the electoral registers without extending the list of disqualifications in a way that would strike at the principle of universal suffrage.

For this reason the offence committed or the penalty imposed must be of a certain gravity before it entails confiscation of the right to vote. Most often the duration of the term of imprisonment is the determining factor. In some legal systems an important factor is the nature of the offence committed—treason in Australia, Brazil, the Federal Republic of Germany, Ireland and Turkey; matrimonial and domestic misdemeanour in Belgium; electoral corruption in Australia, Canada, Ceylon, Finland, the Federal Republic of Germany, Ireland, Japan, Lebanon, Nigeria, New Zealand and the United Arab Republic.

In the Soviet Union conviction by the courts never entails disqualification from voting. Generally in the People's Democracies only serious crime would entail disqualification.

In some countries persons found guilty of dishonourable conduct in business may be disqualified. For example persons declared insolvent or bankrupt are liable to disqualification in Cameroon, the Central African Republic, France, Iran, Lebanon, Luxemburg, Monaco and the United Arab Republic. In all countries a judicial sentence is necessary to enforce disqualification. In order to preserve fully the theory of universal suffrage, that sentence should only be pronounced in respect of the crimes and misdemeanours known to common law. To deprive electors of their vote following a sentence

STRUCTURE OF PARLIAMENT

for political offence would be to pursue the opposite objective. Deprivation of voting rights is seldom permanent. It is often made concurrent with the length of the sentence or related to the duration of loss of civic rights; and it can be annulled by the process of rehabilitation or amnesty. These varying practices mitigate the severity of the laws governing the disqualification of persons for offences committed and help to maintain the principle of universal suffrage.

This relaxation is in step with other moves towards the extension of the suffrage which have already been noted as features of the many different codes of electoral law, namely, the virtual abolition of qualifications of property or ability, votes for women and the lowering of the age limit for voting.

In some countries however there are provisions designed to restrict the franchise in respect of membership of particular social groups by virtue of the work they do. In most instances the motive underlying these restrictions on the suffrage is to safeguard electoral freedom. They bear essentially on persons subject to particular disciplines; the aim is to prevent professional discipline from jeopardizing the genuineness of the voter's choice and to ensure that electioneering does not make for a slackening of discipline. The following do not have the right to vote: members of the armed forces and the police in Iran and Libya; members of the armed forces in Brazil and Turkey; under-officers, corporals and troopers in Belgium during their military service, though members of the regular army may vote after three years' service. Members of religious orders and students who do not pay taxes are excluded in Laos, peers in Great Britain, and public servants responsible for the conduct of elections and judges appointed by the Governor-General in Canada.

2. ELECTORAL REGISTERS

Once the qualifications of the electorate have been established, the next step is to determine which electors are to be called upon to take part in the voting. This is the purpose of the electoral registers. The establishment of registers serves a two-fold purpose: it enables every elector to vote and it ensures that those who are not qualified electors do not take part in the elections. It is a matter of the utmost practical importance that the registers should reflect as closely as possible the alterations in the composition of the electorate. It demands the strictest impartiality on the part of both the authorities compiling the registers and of those who decide the issue if the results are contested.

THE ELECTORATE

The electoral registers are generally drawn up in territorial units which are small enough to make practicable a rapid and efficient check of the population. Usually the names of the electors are included in the register as a matter of course provided that they fulfil the necessary conditions, and in particular that they have reached the required age. In some countries however such as Great Britain, Greece, New Zealand, Libya, Ghana and Somalia, the electors themselves must take steps to be placed on the register. In some states of the United States they must do so for each election.

In Western Europe the preparation of the electoral registers is most frequently entrusted to the local authorities who possess civil registers giving at a glance full particulars of the local residents. This is the system in Australia, Belgium, Denmark, France, the Federal Republic of Germany, Italy, Luxemburg, Monaco, the Netherlands and Switzerland. In Cameroon, Chile and Laos also, this duty is discharged by local authorities.

In Great Britain the task is entrusted to public officials with special knowledge of elections, known as registration officers. In practice they are the clerks of the county, borough or district who act independently, but under the guidance of the Home Secretary. The arrangements in Australia, Canada, Ceylon, Ireland, Nigeria and Sierra Leone are similar. In India and Ceylon special officials known as commissioners for elections prepare the registers. In Israel, with its single constituency comprising the whole country the register is prepared directly by the Ministry of the Interior.

A different method of seeking to secure that the difficult and complex regulations governing the franchise will be applied impartially is seen in countries such as Brazil where the responsibility is placed on judicial bodies.

In the U.S.S.R. and the People's Democracies the responsibility for drawing up the electoral registers rests with the executive committees of the local people's councils. The methods used in Albania may be cited as typical of those used in Bulgaria, Czechoslovakia, Hungary, Poland, Rumania and the U.S.S.R. In the thirty days before each vote the electoral registers are exhibited in the polling stations so that every voter may check that they are correct. Any complaint has to be addressed to the competent executive committee and in the event of a dispute, the matter comes before a people's court. This court must give a decision within three days; and its decision is final. This procedure together with the simplicity of the voting system and the civic enthusiasm which characterises elections in these countries enables the purpose of universal suffrage to be achieved. The negligible number of abstentions and the absence of complaints suggests that the electoral registers embrace virtually the whole of the electorate.

In the so-called classical democracies the problem of revising the lists is not solved so expeditiously. French legislation may be cited as an example because many countries in Europe and Africa follow similar practices. Normally the revision is annual. It is made between 1 and 10 January by a committee of three members comprising the mayor, a representative of the municipal council and a representative of the prefect. When the list has been revised it is made public, and during the next 20 days a complaint may be made by any elector or by the prefecture. Complaints are considered by a municipal committee with a further appeal from their decision to a Justice of the Peace. On 31 March the list is finally closed except for the deletion of electors who are either deceased or deprived of their vote for misconduct or incapacity.

In addition to the annual revisions the lists are revised as an exceptional measure before certain elections. This is the system authorised by law in Austria, the Federal Republic of Germany, Iceland and Turkey.

The principle that the lists should be revised is recognised in all countries, even if they are in fact revised only every two years as in Sierra Leone or every three years as in Ghana.

Where mistakes are made or unfairness is alleged, the electors have invariably the right of appeal to higher authority. This authority may sometimes be purely administrative but as a rule it is a judicial authority because a court of law is the ideal body to settle a conflict in accordance with the Constitution and the law. In spite of the many different methods used for drawing up and keeping the electoral registers, the purpose intended is perfectly clear: it is to ensure that the largest possible number of citizens exercise their right to vote.

3. ELECTORAL CONSTITUENCIES

Electoral constituencies are the territorial divisions within which the electors have to elect either a specific number of members of Parliament or one only where voting is for a single candidate or several where voting is for a list of candidates.

It is generally speaking impracticable for the entire nation to form a single electoral college and elect *en bloc* all the members of Parliament. Such a system would be perfectly in keeping with the theory of national sovereignty according to which members of Parliament do not represent their particular constituency but the country as a whole. In practice it is only feasible in small states such as Monaco which is no larger than a medium-sized town. Nevertheless there are no constituencies in some countries, the best example being Israel where the 120 members are elected *en bloc* from national lists. The same system is to be found together with the single list of candidates in the Central African Republic. The Netherlands constitutes in practice a single constituency for members of the Second Chamber by virtue of the method of voting that is used. The same applies to the election of one hundred members of the House of Councillors in Japan.

The division into constituencies also serves to bring the elected Member of Parliament into closer contact with the elector and it helps the electorate first to exercise a choice between candidates and secondly to influence the member once he has been chosen. But this justification for constituencies on practical grounds is less important than the principle which is fundamental to the equality of the suffrage: every elected member should represent an equal portion of the population. The size of constituencies in some countries is tabulated below:

Albania	8,000 inhabitants
Bulgaria	25,000 ,,
Hungary	32,000 ,,
Belgium	43,000 ,,
Laos	50,000 ,,
Great Britain	60,000 ,,
Cameroon	80,000 ,,
France	93,000 ,,
Brazil	150,000 ,,
Nigeria	170,000 ,,
U.S.S.R.	300,000 ,,

Once a figure has been established, whether voting is for a list of candidates or for a single candidate, the next question is to determine the geographic boundaries of the constituency itself. This requires very precise figures of the local population based on a census and absolute impartiality. The operation of dividing up the population may comply with the strict letter of the law and yet do outrage to its spirit if there is any political influence at work.

In many countries the electoral constituencies are the same as the administrative or political divisions of the country, especially where the drawing of boundaries is expressly provided for by the constitution as in Chile, Iceland, Luxemburg, Norway and Switzerland. But

STRUCTURE OF PARLIAMENT

this method cannot take a swift enough account of the movements of population, and its rigidity may affect the accuracy of the people's representation. In Iceland a system of 'compensating seats' has been developed to meet this deficiency.

In general the redrawing of boundaries happens periodically in accordance with a procedure in which Parliament itself takes part to a greater or lesser extent.

The procedure in most general use is to pass an electoral law. In the United States the power resides in the legislatures of each state. After each decennial census the President sends to Congress a report on the number of members to which each state is entitled on the principle of proportional representation. With this number in mind the state legislatures proceed to redraw the electoral boundaries. The methods by which this is done have recently been called in question by a decision of the Supreme Court.

In Albania, Bulgaria, Czechoslovakia, and the U.S.S.R., the Presidium of Parliament and in Poland and Rumania the Council of State redraw the boundaries at least two months before the date of the elections.

In several other countries this duty is carried out by independent specialised bodies drawn both from the executive and the legislature; under the name 'Representation Commission', 'Election Commission' or 'Boundary Commission' this body of experts can be found in Great Britain, Australia, Canada, the Lebanon, India, Nigeria, New Zealand, Pakistan, and Sierra Leone.

The procedure followed in Australia gives some idea of the method used by these experts.

The size and population of constituencies in each state are determined by three commissioners nominated by the Governor-General. One of them has to be the federal director of elections. In carrying out their task the commissioners are required by law to take into consideration the ideal electoral quota for each constituency, the community or diversity of territorial interests, means of communication, geographical characteristics and the boundaries already set. The population of each constituency must not be greater or less than the quota by more than one fifth.

The new boundaries proposed by the expert body are published in every post office. Any person may submit objections within 30 days of publication. The commissioners then make a report to the Government which takes account of these objections, and the Government submit it to the two Houses of Parliament. If the scheme is approved, it is promulgated. If either House disagrees with the scheme, the Government may invite the commissioners to reconsider their work.

In the Federal Republic of Germany there is a permanent committee on constituencies consisting of the President of the Federal Bureau of Statistics, a judge of the Federal Administrative Court and five other members appointed by the President of the Republic. This committee also makes a report to the Government and to the Bundestag.

The fact that experts and judges are taking part in this work means that it will be competent and objective. Without these conditions the electors are unlikely to be able to play an equal part in choosing their government.

The representation of dependent territories generally follows different rules. Few of them are left today, and most of these have reached the status of internal autonomy which allows them their own institutions but excludes them from the processes of metropolitan legislation. Porto Rico does, however, take part to some extent in the work of the House of Representatives of the United States through a resident commissioner who has all the powers of a member except the right to vote.

France has a special practice. It is the only country to allow the representation of its overseas territories (Comoro, French Somaliland, New Caledonia, French Polynesia, Saint-Pierre and Miquelon, Wallis and Futuna) in its national Parliament. Overseas members sit in the National Assembly and the Senate with the same rights as their metropolitan colleagues.

3. The Ballot

METHODS OF VOTING – CHARACTERISTICS OF THE VOTE – ORGANISATION OF THE BALLOT

The electorate selects its representatives in accordance with legal provisions and practical arrangements governing the methods of voting, the characteristics of the vote and the organisation of the ballot.

1. METHODS OF VOTING

The choice of an electoral system seems at first sight to raise only one technical problem: how are the parliamentary seats to be allotted to reflect the voting expressed by the electors? There are two main voting systems: the majority vote, with one or two ballots in which the candidate or candidates obtaining most votes are elected; and proportional representation, by which the seats are divided up among the lists or parties in proportion to the number of votes obtained by each.

The common feature of the various majority systems is that they give minorities only an indirect and approximate representation and even so only when minorities at national level become the majority in certain constituencies. Proportional representation on the other hand is considered to guarantee in principle to minorities and to the true electoral majority a representation corresponding to their precise strength as shown by the elections. Thus the choice between these two systems far from being purely technical is frequently made on political grounds, so that the significance of the election may be open to question.

For a long time methods of voting were not a matter of controversy. Parliamentary tradition especially in the Anglo-Saxon countries managed perfectly well with the simplest system of all, namely, election in a single ballot by a majority vote—summed up in the phrase 'the first past the post'. But in the second half of the nineteenth century the efforts of the supporters of proportional representation began to show results. By 1891 and 1892 it had been adopted in some of the Swiss cantons. In 1893 it was adopted by Belgium, in 1906 by Finland and in 1908 by Sweden. Gradually it spread through Europe as political systems changed following two world wars. Outside Europe the system has not achieved anything like the same success, and some European countries which adopted it have returned to the majority system.

This brief historical outline largely explains the geographical distribution of the various methods of voting.

The majority system with a single ballot has always been used in Great Britain. Each constituency has to return one member. The candidate is declared elected who obtains the largest number of votes cast regardless of the percentage of the total votes cast that that number represents. Not surprisingly this system is found also in most of the countries which have systems based on that of Great Britain especially among members of the Commonwealth such as Canada, Ceylon, Ghana, India, New Zealand, Nigeria and Sierra Leone. The same system is in force in Libya, the United States and the Philippines and in Brazil for elections to the Senate.

The method of voting for elections to the House of Representatives in Australia appears to perfect the British system. Each constituency is entitled to one member only. The elector votes for a single candidate, but he indicates in decreasing order his preferences for the others. If no candidate obtains an absolute majority at the first count, the candidate who has received the smallest number of votes is eliminated, and the votes which he has obtained are distributed among the other candidates. The process of eliminating candidates who obtain the smallest number of votes is then continued and the preferences reallocated until one of the candidates obtains an absolute majority whatever the number of those remaining. This system has the advantage of showing this result with one ballot instead of two.

With majority voting for a single candidate in two ballots a candidate must obtain an absolute majority of the votes cast in order to be elected at the first ballot. If a second ballot is necessary, the 'first past the post' is declared the successful candidate. This method of voting was frequently used in France under the Third Republic. After its eclipse under the Fourth Republic when it was replaced by proportional representation, it was restored in a slightly different form in 1958.

In the U.S.S.R. and several of the People's Democracies (Bulgaria, Czechoslovakia, Poland and Rumania) the law provides for a second ballot within fourteen days if at the first ballot a candidate does not obtain an absolute majority of the votes cast or if the number of votes cast is less than half the number of the electors on the register. The significance of the second ballot in the countries of Eastern Europe with their institution of the single candidature is however very different from that in countries like France which have many different parties.

Majority voting can also be used with a list of candidates when each constituency has to elect several members, but there are few examples of this system. It is found in Cameroon, Hungary, Poland and the Lebanon, where only one ballot is held; in the principality of Monaco where two ballots are held; and in some instances in the United Arab Republic. French senators are elected in the same way in departments which are entitled to four seats or less.

Throughout Western Europe proportional representation has gradually become the rule. In different forms and with variations too extensive to detail, it is to be found in Denmark, Finland, Iceland, Norway and Sweden; in Belgium, Luxemburg and the Netherlands; and in Austria, Greece, Italy and Switzerland. In France it is used only for the election of senators for departments which are entitled to more than four seats.

Outside Europe proportional representation is found in Israel and Turkey, in Australia for the Senate and in Brazil for the House of Representatives.

The many variations of method testify to the difficulty of putting into practice a system which is very simple in principle. The purest application of proportional representation is found in countries like Israel or the Netherlands where it works on a nation-wide scale. Nevertheless the allocation in each constituency of the votes over and above the quota raises complex if not insoluble problems in spite of the ingeniousness of the theoretical exponents of electoral law. In Denmark and Iceland it is provided that in such instances a certain number of supplementary seats are to be distributed according to a national plan when the result of the election shows a flagrant injustice in the allocation of seats between the parties.

The Federal Republic of Germany has an original system, comprising both proportional representation and majority voting, which could be described as a personal form of proportional representation. Half of the seats in the Bundestag (248) are elected by constituency on a majority vote for a single candidate and the other half by proportional representation on a list of candidates within each Land. The elector has two voting papers. On one he casts a vote for a candidate for the constituency, on the other a vote for a list of candidates for the Land. The seats are disposed of in such a way that each party has a total number of members due to it after the vote by proportional representation. If however as a result of the majority vote for a single candidate a party obtains a number of seats greater than that to which it would have been entitled by proportional representation, it may retain them, though the total number of seats in the Bundestag is increased to that extent.

The system known as the single transferable vote, which is found in Ireland and in India for electing the House of the States, is an attempt to combine proportional representation and voting for individual candidates. Under this system the elector casts his vote for a particular candidate and then indicates his preferences for the others, where the constituency comprises several seats. Once a candidate has obtained the electoral quota, he is elected. The additional votes he obtains are passed on to the second-choice candidate and so on. This complicated system in effect adapts proportional representation to allow votes to be cast for individuals.

Not unlike this system is the one practised in Japan which is more unusual although it derives from the British system of the single candidate. The constituencies are required to elect several members in a single ballot, but each of the electors votes for a single candidate only, the candidates at the head being elected. Thus the problem for each party is to calculate precisely how many candidates to present. If they put forward too many, the votes may be split up among them in such a way that none is elected. If they put up too few, each candidate elected will have a number of extra votes which might well have elected another candidate of the same party.

These two examples show how far the imagination of legislators has gone in devising electoral systems to safeguard the principle of the equality of suffrage. All electoral systems, whether based on majority vote or on proportional representation, have the effect ultimately of weighting the election by giving the votes cast by the electors an influence which does not correspond exactly to their numerical strength. In the United Arab Republic for example each constituency has two members, at least one of whom must be a worker or a peasant. If two candidates head the poll neither of whom has this qualification, only the one with the most votes is declared elected. Another election must be held for the second seat in which only candidates who are workers or peasants in that constituency may take part.

In general however it is rare for parliamentary representation not to reflect approximately the main currents of opinion in the electoral body. The electoral system reflects each country's politics of which it is both cause and effect. The system of majority voting suits the countries with a single party. When majority voting is combined with a single ballot, the two party system is generally to be found. Proportional representation on the other hand is the system characteristic of countries with a large number of parties. But the object of all electoral systems should be to ensure the best representation possible and in particular to safeguard the representation of minorities.

Allied to the problem of voting methods is the question what happens to seats which become vacant during the lifetime of a legislature. In practice the solution differs according to whether in general elections majority voting or proportional representation is used. In the latter instance the seat is most often filled without a by-election's being held: it is automatically filled by the candidate of the same party on the list who is next in order; or it is filled by a substitute who was included in the list together with the titular candidate, as in Belgium and in Sweden; or lastly the parties themselves choose between these two methods.

In countries which rely on a majority vote, the seat is generally filled in a by-election. In that event the electoral law in most countries lays down the time within which the election must be held. It rarely exceeds three months. In the United States it is provided that within this period a vacancy in the Senate may be filled pending elections by a person nominated by the executive of a state and confirmed by the legislature. In Poland the electors are only called upon to vote if the number of seats vacant in their constituency exceeds one-third of the total number of seats for that constituency. In Turkey by-elections for any reason are only held every two years.

In Cameroon members who die or resign can only be replaced when there are two vacancies. They are replaced during the twelve months following the second vacancy. If the second vacancy occurs within a year of the end of the Parliament, an election for the first vacancy is not held.

The mixed system in Japan reflects an electoral regime which as has been seen combines voting for a list of candidates and voting for a single candidate. If it occurs in the three months following the general elections the vacancy is filled by the candidate who came closest to the successful candidate. When this period has elapsed by-elections are held. In a system of majority voting by-elections can still be avoided if substitutes are elected at the same time as titular members at the general elections. This system is found in Hungary where it is helped by the use of a single list. It was introduced in France by the constitution of 1958. Members and senators elected by majority vote whose seat becomes vacant through death, acceptance of office as a member of the government or as a member of the constitutional council or an absence prolonged for more than six months on a temporary mission requested by the government are replaced by persons elected at the same time for this kind of emergency. By-elections are held only to fill vacancies arising for other reasons, that is to say, after a resignation, if an election is declared null and void or in cases of misdemeanour.

In practice the French system which resembles in this respect the system in force in the Netherlands, Norway and Sweden is an attempt to soften the impact of the principle that ministerial duties are incompatible with membership of Parliament.

2. CHARACTERISTICS OF THE VOTE

(*a*) *Compulsory Voting*

Theoretically there are two ways of regarding the franchise: as a right or as a duty.

The first is bound up with the theory of the sovereignty of the people; every citizen is entitled to the vote on the strength of his share in that sovereignty. The second way of regarding the franchise is linked with the theory of national sovereignty: the nation not the people who compose it is the repository of sovereignty. The nation needs organs through which to express its sovereign will, and the elector is one such organ. In other words he is performing a duty.

If the franchise is a right, voting is optional because no one can be forced to exercise a right. If it is a duty, voting may be made compulsory. Few legal codes reflect the second belief and those which do so have been inspired by practical rather than doctrinal considerations: the main object has been to prevent part of the electorate from staying away from the polls and to ensure that the selection of legislators is not exclusively in the hands of the professional politicians.

In Austria voting is compulsory in one or two of the federal Länder, and in Switzerland in certain cantons. Compulsory voting is general in Belgium, Greece, Italy and Luxemburg. Outside Europe it is found in Australia, Brazil, Chile and the United Arab Republic. In the Netherlands attendance at the polling station is enough.

The trickiest question is to decide what sanctions shall apply to reinforce the obligation to vote. If severe they are intolerable; if light they are ineffectual. The golden mean which might be described as 'encouragement' to exercise the right to vote consists mostly of the payment of a fine. This fine imposed for failure to vote is never very high: it is five guilders in the Netherlands, £2 in Australia and 100 piastres in the United Arab Republic. In Italy failure to vote is noted in the public record of convictions; it is only deleted after five years. The electoral code of Chile provides for committal to prison which can however be avoided by paying a fine related to the prison sentence. But everywhere the severity of the sanction is mitigated by the acceptance of reasonable excuses for a failure to vote.

Some indication of the effectiveness of compulsion can be gained from the size of the poll recorded in elections in the various countries. The figures would appear to support compulsory voting. In Australia, Austria, Belgium, Greece, Italy, Luxemburg, the Netherlands the proportion of non-voters to the total electorate is not higher than 10 per cent or 12 per cent in the United Arab Republic. In Chile (20 per cent) and Brazil (30 per cent) however little improvement is shown on the performance in countries where voting is optional. Apart from Iceland (8 per cent non-voters) and New Zealand (10 per cent) where the electorate gives evidence of a particularly strong sense of public duty, a substantial proportion of the electorate in the

Western type of democracy do not vote. On average that proportion is about 20 per cent, ranging from the Federal Republic of Germany with about 14 per cent to France and Switzerland with 30 per cent at their last general elections.

Failure to vote is a serious problem in Ghana, India, Lebanon and Sierra Leone where nearly half the population does not vote. It suggests that the electors are not yet aware enough of their political responsibilities. In the U.S.S.R. on the other hand and in the People's Democracies, even though voting is not compulsory, failure to vote is practically non-existent: it is generally less than 1 per cent, except in Hungary (3 per cent) Yugoslavia (4·5 per cent) and Poland (5 per cent).

(b) Voting by Proxy and by Post

If an election is to be truly free, the act of voting must be a personal act. It calls for the physical presence of the voter at the polling station; no one should come between the elector and the ballot box. But while this rule is necessary to ensure that voting is genuine, it may if rigorously applied militate against the universality of the suffrage by depriving of their right to vote those who are unable by virtue of sickness, professional commitment or other reason to attend personally at the polling stations.

This difficulty is largely avoided in those countries such as the U.S.S.R. and some of the People's Democracies which allow persons who are absent from their constituency to cast their vote wherever they may be after establishing their right to vote. In Rumania special arrangements are made for voters who are sick or immobilised: special ballot boxes are taken round, and these voters can cast votes at their own homes. In the U.S.S.R. comparable arrangements are made in trains, ships, hospitals, maternity homes and thermal stations. In all circumstances the vote may be cast personally.

In countries where the ballot boxes are not circulated or where the polling booths are strictly prescribed for every elector steps are taken to allow those who are unable to go to their polling stations to exercise their right to vote. These methods are voting by proxy and voting by correspondence.

Voting by proxy entails serious risks: electors may be subjected to pressure, and fraud is more probable. These risks explain why proxy voting has not been generally adopted and where it has been adopted why the electoral law lays down stringent controls designed to safeguard the freedom and secrecy of the vote.

Voting by proxy is authorised in few countries. France, Great

THE BALLOT

Britain and the Netherlands are examples. In France the classes of persons who are permitted to vote by proxy are relatively numerous: members of the armed forces and civil servants stationed outside metropolitan France, staff of civil airlines, Frenchmen domiciled abroad and military and police who have to move about during the time of an election period. In Great Britain voting by proxy is in principle confined to members of the armed forces. In the Netherlands the person who is delegating his vote is subject to legal restrictions: he may only appoint as proxy one of his own family or one of his household. In Sweden although there is no proxy voting one spouse may take the voting paper of the other to the polling booth if a witness certifies that the secrecy of the ballot has been observed.

Postal voting raises fewer practical problems. It is used by many countries and by many electors in those countries. In Australia, Denmark, the Federal Republic of Germany, Japan, Sweden, and the United States there are virtually no restrictions on postal voting. A reasoned explanation for his absence, provided that it is given in due time, is enough to enable an elector to vote by post. In Sweden since 1940 anyone may vote by post. Before an election he has only to obtain a certificate that he is on the electoral register. On presentation of that certificate his vote is accepted by any post office or in any foreign legation or consulate during the eighteen days before an election.

In Germany postal voting was instituted by the electoral law of 7 May 1956. An elector using this procedure has to send his electoral card and his voting paper to the director of elections in his constituency by not later than 6 p.m. on the day of the ballot. The elector has to certify in writing on his card that he has himself marked the voting paper. This correspondence is admissible as a postal vote provided that the official electoral envelopes are used.

Electors in Great Britain may under certain conditions have themselves registered on a list of postal voters. They then receive a voting paper and a declaration of identity, which when completed they must send back to the returning officer in a special envelope. These envelopes are placed in a special ballot box and are not opened and checked until the time for counting the votes. In Australia postal voting requires the presence of a witness.

Absence is only recognised as valid for certain categories of electors such as members of the armed forces or diplomats in Canada, the Central African Republic, Ceylon, India, Ireland and Sierra Leone and sometimes for the police as in Ireland.

The recognised categories are most numerous in France where

under a complicated procedure, the following may vote by post: members of the armed forces, pregnant women, the sick, civil servants on mission, certain old or infirm persons, journalists, commercial travellers, transport drivers, business men concerned with exports, seasonal agricultural workers, the staff of thermal centres, students, artists, sportsmen, ministers of religion who are away from their flock and others. This list does not necessarily mean that postal voting is widespread. In fact electors hesitate to make use of this concession because the formalities are so complicated. The formalities are however essential if the secrecy of the vote is to be preserved.

(c) *Secrecy of the Vote*

It is generally agreed that a public ballot hampers the freedom of the elector making him more vulnerable to official and social pressure or to reprisals from his political adversaries. The secrecy of the vote is the corollary to freedom of the vote. It is largely a matter of practical arrangement, and most countries have taken ample legal steps in this direction.

In the first place with the introduction of the individual polling booth, a small space enclosed on at least three sides, the elector can choose whichever ballot paper he wishes or mark his paper with no possibility of being spied on. As a rule it is compulsory to go into a polling booth and each person must of course go there alone. In Albania, Czechoslovakia, Poland, Rumania and the U.S.S.R. as well as in Austria, the Netherlands and New Zealand however persons incapacitated by blindness or other physical deficiency and illiterates may be assisted by another elector who may accompany them into the polling booth. In the United States an elector may seek the help of a third party in the same way. In Japan this responsibility is discharged by the director of the election who on request will designate two persons one to write down the name of the chosen candidate and the other to act as a witness. The United Arab Republic even provides for a vote to be cast orally in such a way that only the officials responsible for the election can hear.

In several African countries where (as will be seen later) one or more ballot boxes are allotted to each candidate the room in which the boxes are located is isolated from the rest of the polling station and the electors enter it one by one to cast their vote in whichever ballot box they choose.

The second safeguard of the secrecy of the vote is the use of ballot papers with the same format and of official envelopes. In several countries notably Belgium, Great Britain, Luxemburg and the

Netherlands the ballot papers are simply folded so that the elector's choice cannot be seen. In addition the paper must not bear any writing or any special mark by which the person using it could be identified; if it does, it is liable to be treated as a spoilt paper. This provision is in practice a difficult one to enforce. Perhaps the most satisfactory system in this respect is that used in Belgium. The ballot paper gives a list of candidates; at the top of the list and also opposite each name is a black square with a white dot in the centre. The elector votes by blacking in completely either the square at the top if he wishes to vote for the entire list, or one or more of the squares opposite the names if he wishes to split his vote. This method is used in several other countries such as Austria and the Netherlands where the officials give each elector a single ballot paper carrying the names of all the candidates. He then has to fill in with a pencil which is found in the polling booth the circle against the name of the candidate he chooses. In theory the use of voting papers which are numbered and extracted from a book of papers with counterfoils as in Great Britain might allow unauthorised persons to know how individual electors have voted. In that instance the secret character of the vote depends entirely on the integrity of the public servants who are responsible for directing and controlling the election. In fact that integrity has never been doubted. Extremely severe penalties are provided in case of irregularity.

The secrecy of the vote is often guaranteed by the requirement that every elector should himself put his voting paper in the ballot box which is so constructed as to allow only one ballot paper to be put in at a time. With this object control is sometimes ensured by the official in charge of the polling station himself placing in the ballot box the envelope handed to him by the elector. This is the practice in Austria, Sweden and the United Arab Republic.

A final point of importance is that everywhere the ballot boxes are sealed until the time comes for counting the votes.

The principle of the secret vote is thus recognised by most countries. In its application some countries are stricter than others. One of the most effective safeguards is the use of computer voting machines which are becoming more common in the United States.

3. ORGANISATION OF THE BALLOT

(a) Voting Papers

To enable the elector to cast his vote voting papers carrying a list of the candidates are placed at his disposal. He makes his choice by marking the chosen names. That is the procedure as has been seen in Austria and the Netherlands as well as in the Federal Republic of Germany, Great Britain and Canada.

Another procedure is to have different ballot papers for each candidate or list of candidates. The voter chooses one or the other and then puts it in the ballot box.

In both instances the ballot papers carry the names of the candidates. They often carry other indications such as the political party of the candidate or the name of the party or organisation which is presenting him or his profession or address. Other details are sometimes added in order to assist the elector and avoid confusion. For example in Iceland and Israel a letter of the alphabet and in Belgium, Chile and Finland a number is put on each list. Use is also made of symbols or emblems. The Italians use them for elections of the House of Representatives; and in Poland their use is voluntary. But they have greater importance as a means of ensuring that the vote is genuine in countries with numerous illiterate electors. In Ceylon, India, Pakistan and the United Arab Republic candidates are identified by different symbols on the ballot papers and their use is very strictly regulated. In Ceylon the use of emblems for each party was authorised by an electoral law of 1956. Independent candidates may be allotted others if the President of the electoral Commission agrees; if several candidates ask for the same emblem, lots must be drawn. In Nigeria provisions governing the allocation of symbols are specially detailed and in particular require the payment of a registration tax of £20.

Different colours for each candidate are used in the Central African Republic, Turkey and the United Arab Republic. In Laos there is a particular method of distinguishing candidates: each one is given a number represented by points set in a rectangular picture like a domino. This picture is exhibited in the polling booths below a photograph of the candidate. The object of all these colourful details is to ensure that the processes of election are as genuine as possible. They allow any elector whatever his intellectual capacity to take part fairly in the voting.

This is why some African countries such as Ethiopia, Ghana, Libya, Nigeria, Sierra Leone and Somalia allot a special ballot box to each candidate instead of using voting papers carrying the names of the candidates. Use is also made of visual aids such as colour (Libya), emblems (Ethiopia, Ghana, Nigeria, Sierra Leone and Northern Somalia) and photography (Nigeria and Sierra Leone). While this system clarifies the choice to be made by the electors, it does require that the ballot boxes should be completely isolated from public view if the secrecy of the ballot is to be preserved. It raises a problem of how the voting processes can be supervised.

(b) *Counting the Votes*

After a ballot has taken place, the ballot papers are collected and the votes counted. This proceeding culminates in the announcement of the successful candidates. The way in which this announcement is made depends on the methods of voting: it varies so considerably from one country to another that it is impossible to go into details. However all countries provide for a series of measures designed to safeguard the validity of the election. The measures relate mainly to the keeping of order at the polling stations, to the supervision of the polling operation, to the counting of the votes and to the announcement of the results.

Responsibility at each polling station rests on authorities who may be referred to collectively as the 'electoral Bureau'. The Bureau's task is to ensure that the poll is conducted as efficiently as possible, and it is vital that their impartiality should be beyond reproach.

This may be the reason why in some countries a number of electors work jointly with locally elected officials such as mayors and councillors. This happens for example in the Central African Republic, France, Laos, Lebanon and Monaco. In Switzerland the Bureau consists of members of different political parties; and the electoral committees of Denmark, Finland, Norway and Sweden are composed in the same way.

In the U.S.S.R. and the People's Democracies at every level —ward, constituency, district, region, state—the supervision of operations is entrusted to electoral committees composed of electors whose choice is approved by the appropriate people's councils. Israel's Central Electoral Committee on which all parties are represented proportionally under the chairmanship of a judge of the supreme court is a comparable organisation; while in Norway and Iceland Parliament itself appoints a national committee to oversee electoral operations.

In many countries that follow the example of Great Britain the administration of elections is confined to public servants with special knowledge of electoral procedure known as 'returning officers'. This important person whose authority may extend over several constituencies himself appoints the electoral officers and in particular the presiding officers of each voting station and their assistants who are known as polling clerks and who under his orders and responsibility ensure that the processes of voting are smoothly carried out. Every

STRUCTURE OF PARLIAMENT

electoral officer is bound by professional secrecy, and any infraction is punished by extremely severe penalties. This organisation or something like it is found in Ceylon, Ghana, Nigeria, Pakistan and Sierra Leone, as well as in Australia, New Zealand and Canada where the entire electoral administration comes under the authority of 'a director general of elections' appointed by the lower House and enjoying the same security and status as a judge of the supreme court. In the Philippines there is a 'commission on elections' set up under the constitution consisting of 3 members appointed for 9 years by the President. In this country as in the United States the administration of elections is carried on by officers under the direct supervision of 'inspectors of elections' appointed by the parties.

This double control, by the administration and by the political organisations, is also to be found in the Federal Republic of Germany: at every level—voting station, constituency, Land, federation—a director of elections who is an appointed officer is associated with a committee consisting of representatives of the different parties.

Impartiality at elections is sometimes secured by bringing in members of the judiciary. In Belgium the officers at each voting station are appointed by justices of the peace, members of the district courts, barristers and solicitors; in Greece a magistrate supervises every part of the process of voting. In Turkey electoral commissions in which representatives of the parties take part are presided over by the senior judge in the constituency. In the United Arab Republic the president of each electoral Bureau must be appointed from among the judges, the staff of the public prosecutor, members of the Council of State, civil servants belonging to the department responsible for settling official disputes or other civil servants of a certain category.

Whatever its composition the electoral Bureau constitutes a real administrative authority and sometimes also has judicial powers (in Canada the returning officer has the powers of a justice of the peace). It is responsible for the maintenance of order at the premises where the balloting takes place and for seeing that the often complex rules governing the procedure for casting votes are observed. In particular there must be no suggestion of partisanship likely to interfere with the results of the election. As a rule the police can only intervene at the express request of the administrative authorities, who are in sole charge of the polling stations.

Incidents are rare because the polling operation takes place under the watchful eye not only of the electors who are voting but also of the representatives of the candidates themselves who have the right to be in the polling station throughout the proceedings. Most systems allow representatives of the candidates to be present in this way as an additional safeguard of fairness in the elections.

The counting and checking of the votes are carried out as a rule under one and the same control, and the announcement of the results is a mere formality. Accordng to the polling procedure used and the size of the constituency this is the responsibility either of the local authorities in charge of the count or of regional authorities or of a central state authority which collects the returns sent in by the polling officers for the different polling stations. Magistrates sometimes take part in checking the votes as in France and Italy.

Voting for a single candidate allows the immediate declaration of the result of the election. A certificate establishing his status as a member may be handed to him at once as it is in the U.S.S.R. and in the People's Democracies; or a formal statement may be made by the returning officer as in countries which have followed the British system. In any event as soon as they are definite the results of the voting are made public by the authorities who advertise the result and have the details set out in official bulletins and gazettes and above all by the press, radio and television. Representatives of these organs are generally invited to follow the progress of the election.

The scale of this publicity underlines the concern which is felt for the freedom and regularity of the voting whatever may be the systems employed.

(c) *Fraud at Elections*

Despite stringent precautions during the processes of elections there is always the risk that the true result will be falsified by some form of fraud. Some devices such as the taking of ballot boxes, the impersonation of voters and the falsification of results have been made virtually impossible by the controls which operate under the scrutiny of the public and of the candidates' own representatives. When they are not part of the electoral bureau, those representatives have official status in some countries, as for example election inspectors in the United States and the Philippines and witnesses in Belgium and Austria.

Other less direct forms of fraud—such as gifts in money or in kind, promises of employment, payment of debts, and various forms of pressure and intimidation—are more difficult to penalise, though special provision to deal with them is made in most countries. All these frauds are of course universally forbidden. If candidates and electors know that they are being perpetrated it is their business as well as that of the electoral authorities to expose them. The special procedure of election petitions is provided in Great Britain and Ireland for this purpose: the courts may be called upon to give judgment as quickly as possible and check the fraud even if it means calling in question the result of a particular election.

The penalties for corruption and illegal practices at elections may range from a simple fine to a term of imprisonment. The maximum term provided is 15 years in Italy, 5 years in Poland, Rumania and Turkey, 3 years in Czechoslovakia, Hungary and the U.S.S.R. and 2 years in Finland. These penalties often carry loss of civic rights for a specified period, and in particular the right to vote or to stand for election.

Today most countries by efficient prevention and by effective sanctions are on the way to the elimination of fraud from the electoral process.

(d) Contested Elections

However rare it may be the possibility of fraud or error in the electoral process means that there must be an opportunity to question, within a specified period, the regularity of an election. That is why the announcement of the results is never final: the electors or the unsuccessful candidates always have the right to contest the election and obtain an award which either confirms the result or declares it null and authorises another election, or provides for the direct replacement of the candidate who has irregularly been declared elected. The importance of these decisions raises the question which authority or body should have the power to decide them.

One possibility is that Parliament itself should decide these disputes. Parliament is the sovereign body and its Houses are first in the hierarchy of public bodies, and therefore no interference by those bodies, and especially the Executive, in the designation of members of Parliament can be proper.

On this principle the verification of the credentials of members is done by the House itself in the People's Democracies of Albania, Bulgaria, Czechoslovakia, Poland, Rumania, U.S.S.R. and Yugoslavia. The state's electoral committee brings together the records of all the elections, checks them and hands them over to Parliament which finally determines its own membership on a report from some kind of committee on credentials.

A comparable system is to be found in several countries of Western Europe such as Belgium, Denmark, Italy, Luxemburg, the Netherlands, Sweden and Switzerland. In Norway the validity of the elections is verified in turn by two credentials committees, one set up by the outgoing Parliament and the other by the newly elected Parliament.

Similarly Cameroon, Iceland, Iran, Israel, Laos, Lebanon and the United States leave it entirely to their assemblies to satisfy themselves that the credentials of their own members are in order. In the Lebanon a majority of two-thirds of the members of the House is needed to declare a member's credentials invalid. This provision draws attention to the dangers inherent in this system: although it guarantees the independence of Parliament, it does not offer members any protection against lack of impartiality on the part of their political opponents if they are in the majority.

For this reason many countries prefer to entrust the settlement of contested elections to those persons whose business it is to settle disputes equitably, namely, the judges. This is the procedure in most states (Australia, Ceylon, Ghana, Ireland, Nigeria, New Zealand, Sierra Leone and Somalia) which have followed the example of Great Britain where disputes in the form of 'election petitions' are judged according to common law by the courts which for this purpose become election courts. Their decision may be that the contested election is valid; or that another candidate is elected; or that the election is null and void and that a new election should be held. Except in Great Britain an appeal lies from the court of first instance to the higher courts and even to the Privy Council.

The removal of these disputes from Parliament's jurisdiction is interesting from other aspects. The special nature of contested elections has led some countries to set up a special judicial body which alone has power to deal with these matters. Examples are the electoral high court in Turkey and the court of elections in Greece. The second of these bodies consists of members of the court of appeal and councillors of state. A contested election may also be submitted to what is sometimes known as a political jurisdiction, that is a body whose role is to judge the matter but whose composition recognises the political nature of the subject. For example in Austria the constitutional court whose members are named by the Federal President on the advice of the Government, the National Council and the Federal Council is competent in this matter. In France it is the constitutional council which comprises in addition to *ex officio* members (who are former Presidents of the Republic) nine members, three of whom are nominated by the President of the Republic, three by the President of the National Assembly and three by the President of the Senate. Some countries have instituted a mixed system in which both Parliament and the courts play their part, thus reflecting both the respect for parliamentary sovereignty and the need for legal, impartial decisions. In the Philippines for example both the Senate and the House of Representatives have electoral courts. Each court consists of nine members of whom three are justices of the Supreme Court and the other six are members of Parliament, three being from the majority and three from the minority parties. The senior justice presides over the courts. The Federal Republic of Germany and the United Arab Republic also have mixed systems. The Federal German Diet decides in the first instance as to the validity of elections but its decisions may be challenged by appeal to the federal constitutional court. In the United Arab Republic disputes are settled in the first instance by the court of appeal, subject to ratification by a two-thirds majority of the members of the National Assembly within two months of the date on which the documents are referred to it.

The range of procedures for the verification of credentials shows that the real problem is to prevent political proclivities from prevailing over strictly judicial considerations and so to safeguard the dignity as well as the independence of Parliament.

4. Members of Parliament

GENERAL QUALIFICATIONS FOR MEMBERSHIP – PARTICULAR INELIGIBILITIES – CANDIDATES AND POLITICAL PARTIES – THE ELECTION CAMPAIGN – THE MANDATE

If he wishes to become a member of Parliament, a citizen must consider first the laws determining the principles of disqualification and secondly the practical difficulties of becoming a candidate and conducting an electoral campaign.

1. GENERAL QUALIFICATIONS FOR MEMBERSHIP

By qualification for membership is meant the personal eligibility of a candidate to be chosen by the electors to sit in Parliament. In countries which have parliamentary government eligibility like the franchise should be as wide as possible. Limitations on eligibility should not strike at the free choice of the elector but should be dictated by practical considerations and be empty of political motive.

In theory every elector should be eligible for election to Parliament. This is the practice in Albania, Bulgaria and Hungary. Yet if the purpose of an election is to select an assembly representing the best elements of the population and capable of looking after the affairs of the nation, it is reasonable to ask for a minimum of qualifications which hardly seem necessary for the ordinary elector. In most countries the conditions for qualification for membership of Parliament are more stringent than those required for the right to vote. The difference applies mainly to age, nationality and conduct.

Of these three eligibility is most often restricted by age. Practice varies greatly; and indeed there are countries besides the three cited above in which the age for the prospective members of Parliament is the same as for electors—for example Yugoslavia (18), Switzerland (20), Australia, Canada, Chile, Finland, Great Britain, Ireland, Iceland, Nigeria, New Zealand, Norway (21) and Denmark (23). Elsewhere some experience of life is felt to be indispensable. In most bicameral Parliaments that experience has to be relatively long for members of the second Chamber. It is 30 years in the United States, India and Japan, 35 years in Brazil, Ceylon, Chile, France and the Philippines and 40 in Belgium, Libya and Turkey. Sometimes the required age of members has been raised at the same time as the required age for electors; this is the position for example in Iran and Italy where senators must be 40 years of age and electors 25 years.

For lower Houses of Parliament in bicameral systems or single Chambers the difference between the age of electors and that of elected members is generally small; but it has been clearly established by several countries. It is significant for example that the eligible age for membership is 21 years in Poland and Czechoslovakia and at 23 years in Rumania and the U.S.S.R. although the age for an elector is 18 years. 23 years has also been chosen by Cameroon, the Central African Republic, France and Sweden but the most usual age is 25 years as in Belgium, Ethiopia, the Federal Republic of Germany, Ghana, Greece, India, Italy, Japan, Lebanon, Luxemburg, Monaco, the Netherlands, Pakistan, the Philippines, Sierra Leone and the United States.

It has been brought down to 21 years in Brazil, Ceylon and Israel but it has been raised to 26 years in Austria and 30 years in Iran, Libya, Turkey and the United Arab Republic

The second restriction upon eligibility is nationality. Prospective

STRUCTURE OF PARLIAMENT

members of Parliament must show that they belong to the country whose destiny will be in their hands. For this reason many states apply stricter conditions of nationality to candidates for Parliament than to mere electors. Often citizenship from birth is required; and where naturalisation is not an absolute bar, a relatively long period of citizenship has to be shown, for example, 10 years in France and the United Arab Republic, 7 years for Representatives and 9 for Senators in the United States and 5 years in Cameroon.

The qualification of nationality is frequently supplemented by a condition of residence such as that in the United States where members must live in the state which has elected them. In other countries such as France the civic qualities of candidates are not regarded as established until they have completed their military service.

In addition to other qualifications candidates must be morally beyond reproach or at any rate a higher degree of rectitude is required of them than of electors. In general apart from convictions entailing the loss of civic rights those which are likely to disqualify a candidate are less serious than those which prevent an elector from casting a vote. In some countries such as Australia, Canada, France, Great Britain, India, Ireland, Laos, New Zealand, Sweden and Turkey the law is severe on electoral corruption and on insolvency or bankruptcy.

It is interesting to observe that in the Netherlands a sentence of more than one year's imprisonment prevents an elector from casting a vote but does not affect his eligibility for membership. On this reasoning a crime is seen to have a political consequence, and even if the crime is serious, it should not be allowed to interfere with the election of a candidate. This care for the principle of equity is significant. It illustrates the determination in most countries that the principle of universality should in no way be damaged. The conditions of eligibility for membership usually reflect a legitimate concern to select suitable candidates democratically.

In some countries however parliamentary candidates have to pass tests of intellectual, moral or financial fitness and the choice of the electors is limited to that extent. In Laos only persons who have certain degrees or diplomas or who have held a public post or who pay taxes at a specified rate may become members of the National Assembly. A somewhat similar principle is applied to the Upper Houses of three countries. In Turkey senators must have a diploma of higher education. In Iran they must either have been members of the Lower House for the duration of at least three Parliaments or they must have been ministers, ambassadors, presidents, procurators general, presidents of the court of appeal, retired generals, professors or lawyers with a practice of 15 to 20 years or businessmen or property owners paying taxes amounting to 500,000 rials (about £2,400). In Belgium senators must belong to similar though more numerous categories, namely, ministers, members, holders of diplomas of higher education, heads of important businesses, former presidents of professional societies and associations or persons paying taxes of more than 3,000 Belgian francs (about £500) a year.

2. PARTICULAR INELIGIBILITIES

Besides requiring certain general qualifications most Parliaments regard particular categories of persons as ineligible usually because the posts that they hold are thought to be incompatible with the office of Member of Parliament.

Ineligibility must be distinguished from incompatibility, a subject which is treated in Part Two of this book. The two are often confused because the rules governing them have the same object which is to ensure that Members of Parliament are not subject to pressures either from the Executive power or from private interests.

But this common object is achieved in different ways. Ineligibility constitutes an absolute legal bar to membership. It nullifies the election of a candidate. Incompatibility of occupation on the other hand does not affect the validity of the election; all it does is require the member once elected to choose between his occupation and his new office. It is therefore important to know whether this choice has to be made before or after an election. For the candidate it is crucial: if he has to choose before the election, he must resign his existing office before standing for election often with no guarantee of recovering it if he loses; but if he need not choose until after the election he incurs no risk. So more candidates are likely to be ruled out on grounds of ineligibility than of incompatibility.

Except in Yugoslavia no citizen is ineligible for membership in the People's Democracies or in the U.S.S.R.

Everywhere else it seems necessary to protect the independence of members either by drawing up a list of persons who are ineligible or by making rules governing incompatibility. Following the British system most countries have chosen the first method. The problem is then to determine the extent of the ineligibility. As a general rule ineligibility relates mainly to the holding of public office. The starting point is that an assembly ought not to consist of members who are at the same time subordinated to the government because that would mean the end of any separation of powers and parliamentary control would cease to have effect.

On this footing in the many countries which follow British practice such as Australia, Canada, Ceylon, Ghana, India, Ireland, Nigeria, New Zealand, Pakistan, Sierra Leone and Somalia civil servants and all other persons remunerated from public funds on the active list are declared ineligible for membership. The Australian constitution provides for a very heavy financial penalty for contravening this provision and also for the laying of information by an informer: any person declared ineligible would have to pay to any person prosecuting him a sum of £100 for every day on which he had occupied a seat as a member or a senator.

Civil servants in Greece and Yugoslavia and federal officers in the United States are also ineligible.

In the Central African Republic and in Libya a candidate holding an incompatible office must resign at least six months before the date of an election. In Israel this period is 100 days and the rule applies only to civil servants of a certain grade. The same applies in Brazil where only the state governors and prefects of police are ineligible if they have not resigned within three months of an election. In Norway only persons who are serving or have served in the secretariat of state, the royal court or the diplomatic or consular services are ineligible. In Cameroon officials of the prefectoral body, directors of financial administration and of the treasury, officers, police, the sûreté and factory and health inspectors are ineligible while they hold their posts and for six months after that.

The second category generally declared ineligible are members of the armed forces. The reasons are the same as for civil servants. This rule is found in most of the countries cited above and also in others such as Finland, Turkey and the United Arab Republic. In Israel only officers and in Brazil only chiefs of staff are affected by it.

Apart from civil servants and members of the armed forces the office holders most often regarded as ineligible are judges or magistrates. There is an additional reason here: the impartiality of a judge who has taken part in an election as a candidate might be open to question. This is the motive in countries like Brazil, Cameroon, Canada, Ceylon, Great Britain, the Lebanon, Turkey, the United Arab Republic and Yugoslavia.

In other countries only the most exalted judges are ineligible. For example in Iceland ineligibility is confined to judges of the supreme court, in Finland to members of the supreme court of justice or the supreme administrative court and to the Chancellor of Justice and the parliamentary commissioner (ombudsman). Returning officers and members of the electoral bureaus in those countries which have these officials are naturally ineligible. In Israel however professors of higher education are eligible because their status is supposed to ensure their total independence.

There are also particular instances of ineligibility: in Great Britain clergy of the Church of England, ministers of the Scottish Church and Catholic priests, in Israel all rabbis and clergy of different persuasions and in Greece lawyers and holders of mortgages are ineligible. Finally in several countries especially Canada, Ceylon, New Zealand and Sierra Leone and Somalia contractors, that is to say, persons who benefit from public contracts are not admissible as candidates. In the same spirit directors of nationalised industries in Great Britain, India and Ireland are in some instances ineligible.

The ineligibility of all these categories of persons may be termed absolute in the sense that it prevents them being elected throughout the national territory.

In some countries there is also a relative ineligibility which forbids election in certain constituencies only. While absolute ineligibility aims to ensure the independence of the member, relative ineligibility seeks to guarantee the freedom of the elector by preventing certain persons profiting from the influence which they have acquired through the positions they hold in particular constituencies. This kind of ineligibility may be superimposed on the more general standards of ineligibility. In Greece for example officers of the armed forces and the security corps who have resigned their posts in order to stand for election are ineligible in a constituency if they served there for more than six months during the two years preceding the election. Similarly a civil servant is ineligible to stand for a constituency in which he served for three years before the election.

By contrast in France ineligibility is only relative for important civil servants: they may not be candidates for constituencies where they were previously in post for a certain period after they have left it. According to the category of civil servant—there is a long list—this period varies from six months to three years. On the same principle members of the armed forces, magistrates and civil servants in Iran are ineligible in the areas in which they were in post.

Finally the object of the rules governing ineligibility may be to secure the independence of members of Parliament from private interests. In practice this concern raises the difficult problem of how to judge whether a given influence upon a given individual is too great. There is also the risk that particularly well qualified people who would be useful to the country may be prevented from standing for election.

3. CANDIDATES AND POLITICAL PARTIES

The general conditions for membership and the particular kinds of ineligibility impose formal and legal limitations on a prospective candidate for Parliament. These limitations are not however broad in scope. Far more important seem to be the practical difficulties which he must face. Any citizen who complies with the legal requirements is qualified to stand for Parliament. But if he is to have any chance of being elected he must at any rate within his own constituency have the backing of an organisation which will enable him not only to bring his view to the notice of public opinion but also to put up a fight against the opposing political forces. Generally speaking to meet these two conditions together is beyond the resources of a candidate who stands for Parliament as an independent; and the task is greatly simplified for a candidate who enjoys the support of a political party. Although the position accorded to them varies from country to country, political parties are generally associations of citizens who share the same views on certain issues and policies which they endeavour to promote by presenting candidates to the electorate. This is the significance of the provision in the French constitution of 1958 that parties and political groups may take part in elections. In the same way the fundamental law of the Federal Republic of Germany provides that parties may help the people to express their political will. The same is true of regimes which recognise only one party or a single front.

A close link between the candidate and his party is more often a matter of fact than of law. Few constitutions expressly approve the existence of parties. On the contrary in many countries standing for Parliament is regarded as an individual action which bears no reference to the political context in which it is undertaken. One might even say that in most of the classical democracies an individual candidature is the ordinary legal procedure. In Great Britain for example a country with the two-party system political parties are not officially recognised in electoral procedure; everything is expressed in terms of the candidates who are treated as individuals.

At the same time some countries have felt the need for a certain degree of formality in order to emphasise the serious character of an election.

In countries which have been influenced by Great Britain this need is reflected in the stipulation that the candidate must be backed by a certain number of electors ranging from two in New Zealand and three in Sierra Leone to six in Libya and ten in the United Kingdom and Ireland (for the Dail). In Ireland one elector must propose the candidate, another must second the proposal and eight others must support it. A still more precise practice is found in Canada where there must be twenty-five electors supporting a candidature, and among other formalities, an oath must be taken by one of them, the consent of the candidate submitted in writing and a deposit paid.

The support of a given number of electors is also required in some of the northern countries: between 25 and 50 in Denmark, 30 in Finland, 50 or 100 in Norway, depending on whether the constituency is rural or urban, between 50 and 200 in Iceland depending again on the constituency, and 300, 400 and 500 in Belgium according to the size of the constituency.

In these instances the requirement of electoral support is rooted in the belief that a candidate should represent a definite current of opinion rather than a mere personal impulse. As currents of opinion are most often reflected by the political parties, their role is obvious to all. The support they give to the candidates takes on an official character which is recognised by the electoral laws of the countries concerned.

Some countries carry this *de facto* state of affairs to the extreme of withholding legal recognition from individual candidatures, only the political parties having the right to put forward candidates. In Sweden although individual candidates are not expressly forbidden, no list of candidates is acceptable unless it is related to a political party. The same applies in the Federal Republic of Germany at any rate to the national lists which must be formally sanctioned by the national executive committees of the parties. Lists of new parties must also be supported by at least 1 per cent of the electors of the Land who took part in the last Federal election. In Austria in the same way only the party lists or 'proposals for election' signed by 100 electors are valid. In Italy there must be from 500 to 1,000 signatures for elections to the Chamber, depending on the nature of the constituency, and from 300 to 500 for elections to the Senate. In Israel 750 electors must be found to support a party list and in Chile 2,000 are necessary for elections to the Chamber and 5,000 to the Senate.

Whether the candidate stands for Parliament on his own account or is backed by a group of electors or a political organisation, it is hard to conceive of an election without the intervention of parties. They are essential to the functioning of the democratic system because they express in public life the various political views of the electorate.

The status accorded to the political party varies however according to the different kinds of regime. In most countries they are allowed to form freely as an extension of the right of assembly and the right of

STRUCTURE OF PARLIAMENT

association which are fundamental rights of all citizens. In some they must be formally authorised and may therefore if necessary be prohibited. In Norway for example to obtain authorisation a party must comprise at least 100 members. In some countries parties must respect specific principles laid down in the constitution. If they do not do so they are banned usually by decision of the supreme court of the state. This is the position in Brazil, the Lebanon, Somalia and Turkey as well as in the Federal Republic of Germany where two parties have been declared unconstitutional by the federal constitutional court. In the same spirit the law of 1954 passed by the Congress of the United States may be mentioned. According to this law, the communist party 'cannot lay claim to any of the rights, privileges or immunities that attach to legal organisation'. It is not, however, illegal to belong to the party.

In the U.S.S.R. and the People's Democracies, the historical nature of the regime requires that there is only one party or one front comprising various political and social organisations which are not in any sense mutually antagonistic.

This one-party system is also found in the Central African Republic and in the United Arab Republic where the Arab Socialist Union which is not strictly speaking a party is defined as the association of all the active popular forces of the nation.

Whatever the system the role of the parties in choosing candidates seems to be essential. But the danger is that the electors' choice will be too greatly restricted especially when candidates are nominated by the party executive or 'caucus'. The choice is left to a few leading figures or politicians and is made in secret without consulting the electors or even the party members. This method is open to criticism. But other more democratic methods are tending to become more generally accepted.

There is first the procedure by convention as known in Belgium, the Federal Republic of Germany, the Netherlands, Norway and Sweden and some of the United States. Party members nominate candidates either directly by the party convention or through the appointment of delegates at regional congresses. This is a more democratic system than the preceding one but its effect is to impose on those who vote for the parties' candidates the candidates chosen by the party members only.

This defect is supposed to be avoided in most of the United States where the system of 'primaries' is used. Here the electors themselves hold a preliminary ballot at which they choose one of several candidates to run for office on behalf of the party at the congressional elections.

Pre-election activity is also crucially important in the U.S.S.R. and the People's Democracies. Like the party the electors have the right to present candidates. Grouped in their social and cultural organisations, workers, employees, peasant and military come to terms on the choice of a single candidate or on the drawing up of a single list. The best candidates are thus selected and presented to the electorate by the party and the organisations working together. Past experience shows that candidates are then assured of massive popular support.

4. THE ELECTION CAMPAIGN

The electoral campaign generally opens after the submission of candidatures which may be several weeks before the election. Its official beginning is usually signified by a special formal decision or as in Great Britain by a statement of the Prime Minister announcing the dissolution of Parliament. The purpose of the electoral campaign is to make known the personalities of the candidates and the opinions they hold so that the electors can vote in full knowledge of the issues at stake. It constitutes an indispensable part of the electoral procedure.

It does however raise one difficult problem: how is it possible to make sure that the various candidates are assured of an equal opportunity to win the support of the electors? For a long time this was the candidates' own affair and in some countries it still is. But the publicity required today for an effective campaign is a costly item: it can create inequalities between candidates and expose the electoral battle to the power of money. For this reason in many countries nowadays the electoral campaign is carefully regulated by law.

These measures are of course applied only in countries where rival candidates or lists are competing. In countries where a single list is presented to the electorate the campaign no longer consists of a competition between various candidates; its purpose is to ensure the largest possible attendance at the polls on election day. Its effectiveness is inversely proportional to the number of abstentions and as has been seen this proportion is for the most part negligible. This publicity is a joint effort with the help of the state by all the organisations whether party, trade, economic, social or cultural which at an earlier stage have collaborated to choose the candidates or to draw up the single list proposed to the electors.

In the western type of democracy however the problem of fairness among the candidates is of vital significance. Some countries have come to the conclusion that the best way of solving the problem is still to pretend that it does not exist. For example in the Scandinavian countries—Denmark, Iceland, Finland, Norway and Sweden—and most of the democracies of continental Europe—Austria, Belgium, the Federal Republic of Germany, Greece, Luxembourg, the Netherlands and Switzerland—there are no regulations governing election campaigns. The freedom of action of the candidates is limited only by the ordinary rules of law, especially those relating to the maintenance of public order and to defamation of character.

This non-interference by the authorities in the electoral campaign is explained largely by the desire to show a strict neutrality towards all the candidates and partly by the existence of organised and stable parties which in practice run the electoral campaign and bear the resulting costs; so that the inequalities between the personal resources of candidates are not significant.

Other countries do not regard these practical considerations as enough. To enable every candidate to conduct an effective campaign they have preferred either to limit the amount which each candidate may spend or in various ways to subsidise each candidate to the same extent.

Limitations on spending by candidates is frequently to be found in countries influenced by the British system. In Australia, Ceylon, Great Britain, India, Ireland (as well as in the Philippines and Japan) the law fixes a ceiling for election expenses. In Australia it is £250 for Members of the House and £500 for Senators; and in New Zealand it is also £500. In Great Britain and Ceylon the sum is related to the number of electors in each constituency. In Japan the rules are similar; the incidence of expenditure is fixed by the Government. In the Philippines, it is fixed at the same level as the annual salary of a member or senator.

For these systems to be effective the accounts have to be carefully audited and this is often by no means easy.

Provision may however be made for other kinds of control. In Canada candidates must furnish to the returning officer after every election a report on the subventions which they have obtained and the expenses which they have incurred. The position is the same in the United States though there the report is made as appropriate to the Secretary of the Senate or the Clerk of the House of Representatives. The activities of the parties are thus brought under control during the period of elections.

These rules effectively govern expenditure at elections. Their object is to ensure equal opportunity to candidates and also to eliminate corruption or illegal practices.

MEMBERS OF PARLIAMENT

The electoral law in Australia, Canada and Ireland devotes special attention to the definition and repression of various methods of corruption. Two of these methods are particularly worth mentioning: one consists of providing the electors with free transport to the polling stations, the other is the direct distribution of money, food or drink. In Canada as in Japan it is however provided that during election meetings sandwiches or non-alcoholic drinks may be served to those taking part.

Controls over the methods of propaganda during the election campaign further the object of giving every candidate an equal chance. In Japan the rules are particularly detailed. They forbid canvassing or door to door propaganda at the homes of electors which is one of the features of the electoral campaign in Great Britain; on the other hand they allow the use of vehicles and loudspeakers and they define the number of postcards which may be sent out to electors, the number of posters, the size and frequency of announcements in the press and the number of electoral meetings. Methods of propaganda such as mobile caravans and luminous or aerial posters are generally forbidden.

In France electoral posters are also controlled. Municipal authorities are required by law to earmark special sites for posters and to forbid them anywhere else during the period of the election. Many other measures are enforced to ensure equality between candidates: hoardings numbered in advance and allocated as demands arise; prohibition on the exchange of sites for posters; and penalisation for failure to use the hoardings allocated or to use them for purposes unrelated to the election.

These limitations on electoral propaganda are often complemented as in France by the facilities granted to all the candidates by public authorities. Here again the object is to enable less rich candidates to inform the electors of their views and so ensure that all candidates face the polls on equal terms. Candidates may enjoy various monetary concessions which are substantial inasmuch as they spare the candidate considerable expense, for example, free postage for their election addresses, free printing of a certain number of posters and circulars, exemption from taxes on publications.

The use of radio and television, those most important instruments of propaganda, is also generally provided for and controlled for the duration of the electoral campaign.

All these efforts to equalise the advantages of candidates whether poor or rich and to ensure that everyone has his say in complete freedom are only partially successful. In practice abuses are frequent, and the complexity of the regulations does not make it easy to

STRUCTURE OF PARLIAMENT

enforce them when they are infringed. Disputes arising out of the election campaign are generally dealt with as part of the control exercised over the elections themselves: it is the responsibility either of Parliament, in countries where Parliament itself verifies the credentials of its members, or of the courts which after taking into account the seriousness of the penalty that can be incurred, namely that the election should be declared null and void, may be disinclined to give these matters of detail the attention they deserve.

5. THE MANDATE

The representative function of a member of Parliament is often described as a mandate.

The full implication of this term is that a member is bound on pain of dismissal to carry out the mandate given him by the electorate. In this sense the mandate is imperative, and it is the key to the relationship between members of Parliament and the electorate in the People's Democracies. If a member loses the confidence of his electors or if his behaviour proves unworthy of a member he is likely to be 'recalled', that is, dismissed. This procedure is provided for in Albania, Bulgaria, Czechoslovakia, Hungary, Poland, Rumania, the U.S.S.R. and Yugloslavia. In Czechoslovakia it works as follows: first it is the duty of the National Front to inform the member that the procedure is being set in motion, giving reasons why they are doing so. The member is then given an opportunity of defending himself. If his defence is not acceptable, the proposal to recall him is forwarded to the Bureau of the National Assembly and the electors for that constituency have to elect a new member. In Bulgaria the decision to recall a member is taken by the National Assembly itself on the proposal of the electors. In practice the power to unseat members of Parliament is very rarely used because the law requires members to give an account at regular intervals of how they have carried out their mandate.

In other countries there is no constraint of this kind on members of Parliament. The term mandate does not correspond to reality because members are not bound to their constituents by any legal obligation. They are considered to be representatives of the nation as a whole and not as delegates of the electorate in their particular constituencies. Their independence is reflected in the absence of any procedure for recall and in the fact that the imperative mandate has no validity. Their position is sometimes safeguarded by constitutional or legal provisions as in Denmark, the Federal Republic of Germany, Finland and Laos. In Germany for example the fundamental law provides that members of the Diet represent the whole of the people, that they are not bound by instructions or orders and that they must obey only their own conscience. The Danish Constitution also stipulates that members must be guided only by their own convictions. In Finland the law relating to Parliament expressly provides that every member must act in accordance with justice and truth and that in carrying out his duties his sole obligation is to respect the constitution.

In Israel the possibility of an imperative mandate or a recall by the electorate is made impossible by the nature of the electoral system of proportional representation on a national level.

The absence of any procedure for recall or recognition of imperative mandates does not mean that there is no link between the elected member and his constituents. In fact close contact is invariably maintained; visits, correspondence and periodic reports take up much of a member's time. He does so not because it is required by law but because he is concerned to keep his constituents informed and to preserve their confidence. The penalty which a member risks by not keeping in close touch with his constituency is that he will not be re-elected. Between this sanction and the recall the only difference is how soon the penalty has to be paid. This depends on the length of the period for which the member is elected. Democratic theory calls for short Parliaments and frequent appeals to the electorate but longer Parliaments promote stable government. Parliamentary experience and practice have succeeded in reconciling this contradiction. Most countries have made the lifetime of a legislature four or five years which has been long enough for carrying out major schemes without losing contact with the electorate. In the United States elections to the House of Representatives take place every two years and in Australia and New Zealand elections are held every three years.

Upper Houses in bicameral Parliaments are generally re-elected at longer intervals and often by sections in order to avoid too blunt an impact of representative opinion.

However long the legislature members may lose their seats before the time appointed for its end. All members may do so if a Parliament is empowered to dissolve itself as in the majority of the People's Democracies and in Israel or if the Executive is entitled to dissolve it (this matter is directly bound up with the relationship between Government and Parliament which will be discussed later). Individual seats can be vacated by death, resignation or expulsion.

With the exception of Norway all countries give the members of their Parliaments the option of resigning. In some countries however a resignation must be accepted by Parliament itself or by one of its directing bodies before it can become effective. This is the position in Finland, Italy, Japan, Laos, Sweden, the United Arab Republic and Yugoslavia. The object of this formality is to allow the House to consider the reasons why the member is resigning and if necessary to refuse to accept his resignation if the reasons are of an improper nature.

Where the formal acceptance by the House is not required steps may be taken to ensure that resignation results from the will of the member and not from exterior pressures or from a blank cheque signed during the elections and upheld by the party. In Germany for example a resignation is not considered valid unless a member makes an express declaration either to the President of the Federal Diet or before a lawyer to this effect.

Resignation may also come about automatically through an incompatibility of occupation. A member of Parliament who accepts offices that are incompatible with membership is presumed to be tacitly resigning his seat. The important point is that there should be a procedure by which the authority responsible for ensuring that the rules are obeyed should be given the fullest information on which its decisions can be grounded. The rules governing incompatible offices are often complex and difficult to apply.

Finally a member may be expelled. Expulsion differs from resignation because it derives from the rules governing ineligibility whereas resignation results from the principle of incompatibility. Parliament may not expel a member except in pursuance of a judicial decision or for incapacity or misconduct during his term of office. The power to decide the matter generally rests with the same authorities that are responsible for deciding contested elections, namely, the courts or the House of Parliament concerned. If the decision is for the House expulsion, like the checking of credentials, might in the absence of any judicial safeguard become a dangerous weapon in the hands of an unscrupulous majority. It depends entirely on the political wisdom of the House concerned, especially in cases which do not arise directly from the rules governing ineligibility. In Great Britain as in Australia, Canada, Ghana, India and New Zealand improper conduct is reason enough for expulsion. Sometimes the decision to expel has to be taken by a special majority which limits the possibility that power will be abused. In the United States, Japan and the United Arab Republic a majority of two-thirds of the members of the Chamber is required. In the Federal Republic of Germany expulsion may take on a political aspect when used against members who are found to have misused their rights in order to try to upset the liberal, democratic constitutional order or who belong to an unconstitutional party. The Bundestag, the Bundesrat or the Federal Government however merely lodges the petition. The sentence of expulsion is pronounced by the federal constitutional court.

In some countries expulsion is used as a penalty for absenteeism. The period of absence varies: one session in New Zealand, two in Nigeria, two months of one session in Australia, three months in Ceylon. Expulsion is also used as a penalty in Ghana and Sierra Leone.

In practice whether the grounds are ineligibility, improper conduct or absenteeism expulsion is an exceptional procedure. If it were not, serious damage could be done to the principle of universal suffrage and in consequence to Parliament itself.

PART TWO
Organisation of Parliament

5. Status of Members

IMMUNITIES – OFFENCES AGAINST PARLIAMENT – INCOMPATIBILITY OF OCCUPATION – PARLIAMENTARY REMUNERATION

Once his fellow citizens have expressed their confidence in him by sending him to Parliament, a member is faced with heavy responsibilities. He ought to have assumed them freely: if he is to carry them out conscientiously, he must have complete moral and material independence both of the government and of other persons. To help him carry out his duties a member enjoys a special status of which the main features are first that he has certain privileges or immunities, secondly that he may not accept some other offices, and thirdly that he receives parliamentary emoluments.

1. IMMUNITIES

The object of parliamentary immunities is to protect members from repressive measures or from legal actions by the government or by private persons. Immunities derogate from the principle that citizens are equal before the law. Originally their purpose was to secure the precarious position of elective assemblies in the face of powerful governments. With Parliament at the stage of development it has reached today, they are less obviously justifiable. The public tends to regard them as privileges which benefit unduly the parties most directly interested. Nevertheless their object is the same as it always has been, to ensure the smooth running and complete independence of Parliament.

For this reason immunities relate primarily to the exercise of parliamentary duties. Here the independence of the elected member is guaranteed by the provision to be found in most constitutions that he is not accountable at law. Immunity applies to anything spoken or written or any act committed by a member of a parliamentary assembly in the ordinary course of his official duties such as a speech delivered in the House or in committee, interruptions in debate, bills or motions put forward, reports, oral or written questions, in short any action which presupposes that the person carrying it out is doing so in the course of his parliamentary duties and which no person other than a member could do. Immunity applies to these special actions only. But within this field it is quite categorical: the protection afforded is absolute and lifelong. A member cannot have any criminal charge or civil action brought against him for these actions, even after he has ceased to be a member.

All countries without exception endorse the principle of non-accountability defined in this way. Even where the term itself is unknown as in British law, the concept exists in the form of privilege or more precisely as the privilege of freedom of speech whose effects are the same as those produced by the law in other European countries: no action for defamation may lie nor may a member be prosecuted for words spoken in the House or a committee or for parliamentary papers which he has originated. Some constitutions however set limits to the principle of non-accountability in order to prevent its abuse: under the constitution of the Federal Republic of Germany for example immunity does not cover defamation of character and insult even when committed in the course of parliamentary duties. Similarly in Denmark and Iceland members may be held accountable for their actions if the assembly to which they belong so authorises. In Finland and Sweden the authority to prosecute requires a favourable majority of five-sixths of the votes cast.

These are the few exceptions to the principle of non-accountability. The immunity of course governs a member's relationship with the outside world and does not release him from obedience to the rules and orders of the House. Nor does it derogate from his practical responsibility to the public. This is a matter for the voters to assess and if need be breaches can be checked by not re-electing an offender. In the final analysis this democratic check on parliamentary activity is what gives immunity its proper significance in the political field. Apart from this check members of Parliament must be granted the utmost freedom and independence.

Besides non-accountability members may benefit from 'inviolability' or protection from legal process which ensures that members of Parliament are protected against legal actions brought against them for acts committed outside the orbit of their office, in other words, acts which the ordinary citizen might commit. On the face of it this seems too great a privilege with less obvious justification than non-accountability; so it does not meet with the same unanimous approval in all constitutions. Canada and the Netherlands for example consider that members are well enough protected in criminal and civil matters by the ordinary law. In Great Britain there has never been

STATUS OF MEMBERS

any suggestion that 'inviolability' could interfere with the workings of penal law. It applies only in civil matters and its only effect is to prevent the arrest of members during sessions and for forty days before and after the session. This was of some significance when debtors could be imprisoned for not paying their debts; but since 1869 when imprisonment for debt was abolished members have for practical purposes come under the ordinary law subject to the ruling of the Speaker. His authority and the independence of the British judiciary from the executive are regarded as constituting an adequate safeguard against threats from outside. Evolved in the British Parliament this system has been adopted with slight variations by countries like Australia, India, New Zealand and Nigeria which thus do not grant any real privileges of this kind to members of their Parliaments.

In most countries fear of encroachment by the executive upon the liberty of members of Parliament is much more manifest. Although arrest for civil offences has been abolished in most legal systems, imprisonment has nevertheless been made the subject of specific provision in Belgium and Luxemburg. In Greece no member may be imprisoned in the lifetime of a Parliament or during the four weeks following its dissolution; and if a member is in prison, he must be released four weeks before Parliament is opened.

It is in the criminal matters that inviolability takes on its fullest significance: here the problem is to protect members of Parliament against governments. It has been solved in two ways, the one according to practical considerations and the other according to more strictly legal principles.

Some countries regard the main object as being to ensure that members are able to take part in the work of the House in spite of possible action or manœuvre by the government. They think it enough to prohibit the arrest of members while they are travelling to and from Parliament or while they are attending Parliament. This is roughly the course adopted in Ireland, the United States and the Philippines. In some countries moreover 'inviolability' so defined does not cover what are regarded as the major offences such as treason, felony and sedition nor does it apply to offenders discovered *in flagrante delicto*. A similar system is in force in Ceylon, Norway and Sierra Leone. In Ghana an arrest may not be made without the authority of the Speaker.

Similarly in Sweden inviolability has a significance which is limited to arrest or detention. Except in cases of *flagrante delicto*, a member of the Riksdag may not be arrested or detained until a judge after a preliminary investigation decides that it is necessary. While that

ORGANISATION OF PARLIAMENT

process is going forward, no administrative or police action against the member is permitted.

Other countries however regard it as desirable that their members should as far as possible be subject to the ordinary law. As long as due respect is paid to the provisions of the constitution and the law, Parliament should not in this view be called upon to intervene. The principle of immunity from arrest in criminal cases gives rise to a more complicated procedure which reflects both the desire to safeguard the liberty of members against any improper attack and the fear of giving them excessive privileges that might be open to criticism. In Chile, as a result, the court of appeal sitting in plenary assembly and when necessary the supreme court, have been made responsible for deciding in the first instance whether the grounds for an indictment, prosecution or arrest of a member of either House are well-founded.

In most countries this task falls to the Chambers themselves who are in some measure guardians of the freedom of their own members. This is the general rule in Europe as well as in the U.S.S.R. and the People's Democracies (Albania, Bulgaria, Czechoslovakia, Hungary, Poland, Rumania and Yugoslavia) as in Austria, Belgium, Denmark, the Federal Republic of Germany, Finland, France, Greece, Iceland, Italy, Luxembourg, Monaco and Switzerland. Outside Europe the authorisation of Parliament is necessary for a criminal prosecution in Brazil, Cameroon, the Central African Republic, Ethiopia, Iran, Israel, Japan, Laos, the Lebanon, Libya, Senegal, Somalia, Turkey and the United Arab Republic.

In all these countries a member of Parliament who has committed a crime or misdemeanour may not be prosecuted, arrested or detained unless authorisation is given by the Chamber of which he is a member, after it has considered the case put forward by the petitioners, whether they are administrative or judicial authorities or private persons. The task of determining whether the action is straightforward and serious and does not bear the character of political persecution is entrusted to a committee which has to report to the House; it may be either the committee concerned with questions of immunity or as in Belgium and France a special, temporary committee appointed to deal with each particular case.

Since immunity is instituted in the interests of Parliament and not for the personal benefits of its members, it has a public character which precludes a member from waiving it if Parliament considers that it should not be waived. Personal waiver of immunity is permitted only in Switzerland.

There are two important exceptions to the general rule of

prior authorisation by the responsible assembly. One is the case of *flagrante delicto*; the other relates to the duration of the immunity.

Constitutions in general provide that cases of *flagrante delicto* fall outside the reach of immunity. The immediate arrest and prosecution of the member against whom the charge is made is possible without recourse to any other form of proceedings. The essential feature of *flagrante delicto* is that the person committing the offence can be identified unequivocally, ruling out any risk of mistaken identity or tendentious interpretation of the facts. The concept of *flagrante delicto* does however vary: in the Federal Republic of Germany for example it extends in all its consequences until the day after the commission of the offence; and in Yugoslavia immunity would only be lost if the act were such as to attract a punishment of at least five years' imprisonment.

The second exception relates to the duration of the immunity. In practice the immunity in most countries is co-terminous with the parliamentary session. This means that between sessions the member reverts to the rule of ordinary law. The only formality imposed on the authorities is that Parliament must be kept informed of a proposed prosecution or of the arrest of a member. This requirement allows Parliament when the session begins to request, if it thinks fit, that the prosecution or arrest should be suspended.

Some constitutions require a different procedure to be followed for prosecutions and arrests out of session. In France when Parliament is not sitting no member may be arrested for purposes already authorised or for definitive sentence without the authorisation of the Bureau of the Assembly to which he belongs, except, of course, in case of *flagrante delicto*. A similar position is found in Senegal.

In several countries, especially those which do not have the sessional system, 'inviolability' is permanent so that members are protected by their assemblies for the whole term of their office. This is the position in Austria, the Central African Republic, Denmark, the Federal Republic of Germany, Greece, Iran, Israel, Italy, Somalia and Turkey. The position is the same in the U.S.S.R. and the People's Democracies. Throughout a legislature a prosection or arrest has to be authorised. During a session it is given by the Assembly itself and between sessions by its presidium in Albania, Bulgaria, Hungary and the U.S.S.R., the Presidential Bureau in Czechoslovakia, or the council of state in Poland and Rumania.

Parliamentary immunities can be very extensive. But however necessary they may be, they still represent a definite derogation from the principle of equality before the law which lies at the root of parliamentary sovereignty. It is for Parliament to avoid the natural tendency of all institutions to place a broad interpretation upon the provisions from which they benefit and so transform their immunities into personal prerogatives.

2. OFFENCES AGAINST PARLIAMENT

Among the privileges enjoyed by Parliaments and their members protection from 'offences against Parliament' is in many countries included. Parliament itself may give this protection and does so in Great Britain. For this purpose there is a special procedure by which the House itself acts virtually as a court of law. When a formal complaint is made to the House by one of its members, it is usually referred to the Committee of Privileges which is set up at the beginning of each session. The committee inquires into the matter and on its report the House decides what measures should be taken. The punishments are either an admonishment formally pronounced by the Speaker at a sitting of the House; or a reprimand addressed in the same way; or imprisonment in which case the offender is entrusted to the Serjeant at Arms or transferred to one of Her Majesty's prisons. Besides these penalties if an offender is a member of Parliament, he may, on a motion by the House, be suspended for a specific period or permanently expelled.

This curious procedure in which the distinction between judge and plaintiff is blurred is also found in Australia, Canada, India, Ireland and New Zealand. In Ceylon the judicial authority is the supreme court except for minor offences which are dealt with by a reprimand from the Speaker. Jurisdiction is also shared in the United States and the Philippines. A person who has committed an offence against one House may be formally indicted on a vote by that House. The indictment is then referred to the judiciary and an ordinary trial is held. But each House has the right to summon an offender to appear before it and to sentence him to the penalty of a fine or imprisonment if he is found guilty. Straightforward criticism however never constitutes an offence.

Many other countries, while regarding offences against Parliament as being in a special category, have not thought it desirable for Parliament itself to take cognisance of them. They are dealt with exclusively by the ordinary courts who may according to the circumstances impose fines upon or imprison the offender. Imprisonment for up to one year is possible in Hungary, two years in Czechoslovakia, Israel and Poland and three years in Italy and

Yugoslavia. Parliament intervenes only to initiate the prosecution. It does so at the request of the President or the Bureau of the Chamber or, as in Austria or Italy, on the decision of the Chamber itself. A procedure of this kind is followed in Belgium, Chile, Denmark, the Federal Republic of Germany, Finland, Iceland, Norway, the Netherlands, Sweden and the United States as well as in Ghana, Iran, Nigeria, Turkey and the United Arab Republic.

Whatever the practice followed, the essential problem is to determine the gravity of the offence. It is difficult enough to discuss the principle underlying the action to be taken on, say, open revolution or physical violence against Parliament or one of its members; but to decide what in Great Britain is termed 'contempt to any member of the House or to the House collectively' must be still more complex. As in practice it is usually the newspapers of the more controversially political kind that are guilty of contempt, the whole problem of the freedom of the press and so of freedom of speech is thrown up. This large subject goes beyond the scope of this study. But to keep to concrete facts, the main point at issue is where the right to criticise ends and where defamation begins. In the opinion of an Australian Speaker 'newspaper criticism is not a breach of privilege unless something is done to coerce or impede members, or bring Parliament into contempt'. There is no doubt that the existence and cohesion of a society implies a respect for certain collective values which in democratic countries include Parliament. On the other hand criticism is as much the lifeblood of democracy as it is of scientific progress. The application of harsh laws may well jeopardise the rights of the minority. In these circumstances the offence must be dealt with carefully.

Offences against Parliament are sometimes treated in the same way as offences against public authorities. Parliament is not protected for its own sake but because it is part of the machinery of government which has in all circumstances to preserve its dignity. This solution has been adopted in several of the People's Democracies, notably Albania, Hungary and Rumania. Similarly in Scandinavia and especially in Sweden persons offering injury or violence to a member of Parliament in his professional capacity are liable to the same penalties as those provided for offences against civil servants in the course of their duties. In Finland the fact that an offence has been committed against a member must be considered by the courts as simply an aggravating circumstance.

Finally offences against Parliament may be dealt with by the ordinary rule of law: that is to say, the offence is not punishable unless it would be punishable if committed against any individual or any other organisation. In France, Japan, Luxemburg, Monaco and Switzerland, the concept of an offence against Parliament is unknown: no special law has been passed. This application of the ordinary rule of law is open to abuse and may give rein to irresponsible anti-parliamentary activity; but it is the outcome of a desire to avoid any encroachment upon free speech which is the basic principle of democracy.

3. INCOMPATIBILITY OF OCCUPATION

Incompatibility is the rule which forbids a member of Parliament to carry on certain occupations while he is a member. Like ineligibility its object is to prevent members from becoming dependent upon either public authorities or private interests. But the rule operates in a less direct way: it does not prevent a member from being a candidate, nor can the validity of his election be questioned on its account. But a member must choose within a predetermined period, which is generally short, between his membership and the occupation which is held to be incompatible with it.

Most countries have rules on one or other of these subjects and some countries have them on both. Exceptions are Iceland, Sweden, the U.S.S.R., and the People's Democracies other than Yugoslavia which do not recognise any incapacity resulting from a member's profession or occupation. In Sweden members who hold public office must however be officially on leave during sittings of Parliament. In Poland each member of the Diet has a right to continue his profession or occupation whatever its nature for the whole period of his membership though there is no obligation upon him to do so. In Hungary any activity or political, economic or social policy which is contrary to the interest of the workers is declared incompatible with Parliamentary membership. The matter is decided by the Assembly itself on the proposal of its committee on immunities and incompatibilities. The procedure is similar to that followed when a resignation of a member is submitted upon a recall by the electorate.

The first object of the rules governing incompatibility as with the rules governing ineligibility is to protect the member as far as possible from subordination to the government.

The scope of the rules may be limited to the posts of directors as in Monaco; to posts in the public treasury or army as in Luxembourg; or to the federal administration as in Switzerland. But in general the criterion used is nomination by the government or payment from public funds which in practice takes in the whole of the civil service. In France for example incompatibility in this field has the widest application. It covers virtually the whole field of the non-elective public service. This principle is also observed in Cameroon, the Central African Republic and Senegal. In the same way members may not belong to the public administration for as long as they are members in Belgium, Brazil, Chile, the Federal Republic of Germany, Iran, Italy, the Netherlands, Turkey and the United Arab Republic.

The principle of incompatibility which applies to office held before an election naturally applies also to those which might be offered to a member once he has been elected. Nevertheless the fear that the executive may influence members of Parliament after their election by appointing them to certain offices can be seen to be the reason for measures taken in various countries. In the United States for example no member of Congress may be appointed to an administrative office which has been created or for which the salary has been provided during his term of office as a member. The same prohibition exists in the Philippines. In the Argentine such an appointment would only be possible if the Chamber concerned authorises it. In Japan it would have to be approved by both Houses. In France, as in the Central African Republic and Cameroon, a member may accept the appointment but only for a limited period (six months in the first two countries and two years in Cameroon). On the other hand any of the directorships of nationalised industries or public national institutions or in any advisory body to these industries or institutions are incompatible with membership.

An exception to the principle of incompatibility with public office are teachers, particularly professors of higher education. This is the position in Chile, the Federal Republic of Germany, Senegal and the United Arab Republic. In France this concession applies only to professors who at the date of their election held chairs awarded to them by the university authorities when a vacancy occurred or who are responsible for directing research.

In several countries steps have been taken to ensure that incompatibility does not harm the careers of civil servants who are elected to Parliament. One solution is to authorise the retention of their status as civil servants and simply to suspend them from carrying on their duties during their term of office as members. They are placed in some kind of special position such as leave or secondment or detachment which has the effect of safeguarding their rights especially in respect of promotion and superannuation. This is the position in France, the Federal Republic of Germany, the Netherlands, Cameroon and Senegal. In these countries civil servants are replaced in the posts they occupy within the administration and as a result they cannot be sure of coming back to the same post when they rejoin the service. In Belgium a more severe procedure is followed. A fresh nomination is necessary, and it may not be put forward for one year after its subject has ceased to be a member.

Generally speaking the rules governing incompatibility are less severe than those governing ineligibility so far as they affect civil servants.

At the same time it has seemed necessary to extend the field of incompatibility to certain professions and to certain activities of a private character partly to safeguard the independence of members from financial and economic influence and partly to prevent them from deriving advantage from their membership in carrying out their profession.

It is for this reason that in Iran a member may not take part in any commercial transaction of which one of the parties is the state. In the Philippines a member may not benefit directly or indirectly from any business negotiation with the state or any public authorities. In the United Arab Republic no member of the National Assembly may acquire or rent property belonging to the state or sell or buy any goods whatsoever from the state. At the same time members are forbidden to conclude directly or indirectly with the state or any other public authority or any related society or institution any kind of business contract.

In Brazil, France, Greece, Italy, Japan, Senegal, Turkey and the Central African Republic membership is declared incompatible with specific appointments in private business. In France for example this applies particularly to management of enterprises which are exclusively concerned with public savings and credit; which receive public subventions, interest guarantees or analogous advantages; or which carry out programmes of public works or furnish supplies to public authorities.

Similar provision is made in the Central African Republic, Italy and Senegal. In Japan and Turkey the rules apply particularly to businesses in which the state has a controlling interest. In Brazil and Greece the criterion is the privileges and subventions which are accorded to certain businesses. It is worth noting that in Greece incompatibility extends not only to the posts of management but to any employment in such businesses.

In a growing number of countries the rules governing incompatibility are being extended to the profession of lawyer or at least to certain actions which are carried out by that profession when the public interest is at stake. In France and the Central African Republic for example lawyers who have become members of Parliament are forbidden to take part in cases in which prosecutions have been laid for crimes or misdemeanours against the public interest. Nor may they accept a brief on behalf of establishments whose managing offices are incompatible with parliamentary membership. Finally they may not either accept a brief nor give an opinion against the state or any public authority or enterprise. Such provisions with variations of detail are also found in Belgium, Brazil, Iran, Italy and the Philippines.

Few people think that the rules governing incompatibility in the private professions are so rigorous that they do not allow the talent available within Parliament to be used as fully as necessary. In applying these rules however numerous difficulties arise in determining jurisdictions and a procedure suitable for particular cases. The ultimate sanction which is resignation from office does not help to solve these problems.

An important aspect of the rules of incompatibility is that affecting certain public offices. In bicameral systems for example it is forbidden to be a member of both chambers at the same time. But members are generally allowed to be elected representatives of local authorities. There are some exceptions: in Brazil incompatibility is total and embraces any office at federal, state or municipal level; in Chile a member may not be a municipal councillor; in Italy he may not be a member of a regional council, in Belgium of a provincial council or in the United Arab Republic of a local council.

More interesting is the extent to which members of Parliament can be ministers. This goes beyond the strict problem of incompatibility and raises constitutional problems which go to the heart of the regime.

Incompatibility between ministerial office and membership of Parliament is the rule for regimes which have a formal separation of powers. It is particularly a feature of presidential regimes like those in the United States, the Philippines, Argentina, Chile and Pakistan. In the same way members of the government may not be members of Parliament in Ethiopia, Iran and Switzerland. In Laos the position of minister is incompatible only with membership of the Upper Chamber or the Royal Council.

On the other hand this kind of incompatibility is generally not recognised in parliamentary regimes whose essence is the closest collaboration between the legislature and the executive. Here the holding of both offices is not only authorised but is positively desirable in order to strengthen the bonds between Parliament and the government. For instance in Great Britain for many years members who were appointed ministers had to submit themselves for re-election in order that their position as a member should be confirmed. The point of this provision which was repealed in 1926 was that the electors were considered to be entitled to approve (or disapprove) the election of any member of Parliament who was appointed to a ministerial post and so to bless officially the principle of holding both offices. Although this provision has not survived, there is a statutory limit on the total number of ministers who may sit in the House of Commons. In several countries such as Ceylon, Ireland, Ghana and Nigeria ministers must be members of Parliament, a provision which emphasises the concept of collaboration between the legislature and the executive. In Australia a person who is not a member and is appointed a minister may hold that office for three months only unless he becomes a member of Parliament. Such measures however are exceptional even in the parliamentary regime. The general rule is that ministers are normally members of Parliament but they do not have to be members. Conversely a provision that these two offices are incompatible would not necessarily mean that parliamentary government had been thrust aside, because the motive might be a desire to improve its operation. This is the position in Luxembourg and the Netherlands; and it has been so in France since the constitution of 1958 where this provision was considered to be a method of re-establishing if not the separation of powers at least the separation of functions.

In these last three countries the principle of incompatibility is tempered by a system of substitutes: a substitute may occupy a seat which becomes vacant when a member is made a minister. In Norway a member who is made a minister would regain his position in Parliament if he resigned from the government. On the other hand in France the substitution is definitive for the whole of that legislature: even if the ministry falls, those of its members who were originally in Parliament do not regain their seats. Incompatibility however only takes effect after one month from the date on which a member is appointed minister. In the Netherlands a member who becomes a minister loses his seat and is succeeded by the candidate who came immediately after him on the electoral list. Conversely, if a minister is elected a member he has three months in which to decide between his seat as a member and his post as a minister.

In spite of this variety of procedures incompatibility is often criticised by the upholders of Parliament who fear that it makes collaboration between the executive and the legislature more difficult by creating a gap between the representatives of the nation and the government.

4. PARLIAMENTARY REMUNERATION

A seat in Parliament is everywhere rightly considered as a vocation and not a livelihood, though paradoxically the principle of unpaid service which would seem to be the logical corollary has been abandoned everywhere except in Yugoslavia. In theory if a member's parliamentary work prevents him from obtaining the rewards which he would otherwise earn in his own calling he should have the right to equivalent compensation; and only those members who carry out certain specific duties of a permanent character in the House obtain fixed, monthly emoluments.

Today in virtually all countries parliamentary emoluments are an essential part of the status of a member. That being so, the old controversy as to whether members of Parliament should be paid is merely academic. Instead there is the knotty problem of the nature and rate of members' emoluments, a topic most apt to arouse the indignation of the public which more often than not is ill-informed. 'No pay means that the poor have no say.' Aphorisms of this kind, rooted as they are in democratic principles, mean that the electors must have full liberty to choose the man in whom they place their confidence whether or not he happens to be rich.

A member of Parliament has to incur much expense in the course of his duties. He has to bear the cost of accommodation; he must pay for a secretary and for his correspondence; and he has to pay other official subscriptions and contributions. Nor can he continue to look after his own affairs in the normal way.

In these circumstances some emoluments are generally paid though the forms vary greatly. A few countries rely solely on a system of daily allowances, under which members receive a relatively small sum for each day of the session. In Switzerland they receive 65 francs a day during sessions and sittings of committees together with allowances for travel and accommodation.

The idea that emoluments are supposed only to cover the day to day expenses of membership is found in the U.S.S.R. and in the People's Democracies where members generally continue to carry on their profession and to receive their ordinary salaries. Compensation for loss of income is provided only for those who in their particular trades enjoy a fixed monthly salary. In the U.S.S.R. members of the Supreme Soviet receive emoluments amounting to 100 roubles a month to cover day to day expenses, to which is added 15 roubles a day during the sessions of the Supreme Soviet, permanent committees and other parliamentary bodies. In Albania, Czechoslovakia, Bulgaria, Hungary, Poland and Rumania parliamentary emoluments are calculated in a similar way, though a supplement is payable to the holders of important posts such as chairmen of committees in recognition of the special expenses which they may incur. In Albania and in the U.S.S.R. members who live in the capital are not entitled to the daily living allowance.

The growing claims of parliamentary life and the increasing frequency and duration of sessions have led to the introduction in many countries of annual emoluments designed to provide members of Parliament with the means of livelihood which they can no longer earn from their former occupation, especially where it proves incompatible with membership. As a result the nature of parliamentary remuneration has gradually changed: instead of being a mere reimbursement of expenses it has become to some extent at least a salary. Apart from the consequences for taxation the change carries the implication that members of Parliament are paid for the services they render and increases the temptation to consider membership of Parliament as just another job. Eventually it may come to be referred to as the parliamentary profession.

This change in the character of the payment made to members is especially notable in countries which have linked parliamentary remuneration directly with the salaries of certain grades of civil servants. This procedure ensures that the parliamentary salary remains satisfactory for members and also has the advantage of avoiding public debate when circumstances, especially a rise in the cost of living, make it necessary to adjust that salary. In Austria members of the National Council receive emoluments equivalent to 50 per cent of the salary of the Federal Chancellor which is 11,000 schillings a month. In Finland emoluments are fixed by reference to the same salaries and come out at 20,400 Finnish marks a year to which is added 19 marks for each sitting day for members not resident in the capital. In Laos parliamentary emoluments are completely assimilated to the salaries of the highest rank of the civil servants. The same applies in the Central African Republic, Senegal and Turkey. It is also the position in France where emoluments are calculated by reference to the salary of civil servants occupying posts classified as outside the ordinary scales (*hors échelle*), that is to say, equal to the average of the lowest and the highest salaries in this category. In

STATUS OF MEMBERS

addition a member may receive expenses whose total sum amounts to a quarter of the basic emolument but varies according to the extent of a member's participation in the work of the Chamber to which he belongs. From these two sources a member may expect to receive between 5,500 and 6,000 francs a month.

In Japan it is also provided that the basic parliamentary emoluments shall not be less than the remuneration of the highest rank of civil servants. The President of the Diet receives 260,000 yen a month, the vice-presidents 190,000 yen and the members of the Diet 180,000 yen. To these sums are added two special allowances namely, a subsistence allowance of 3,000 yen a sitting day and a correspondence allowance of 50,000 yen a month. For members who live more than 12 kilometres from the Diet a travel allowance is paid. The position of the Japanese member seems specially enviable, especially when it is remembered that each of them is entitled to an office and two secretaries.

In some countries fixed annual emoluments are supplemented by a daily subsistence allowance, the chief advantage of which is to stress the special nature of membership by specifically tying the allowance to the work done by members in Parliament. It also has the further advantages of allowing the fixed emoluments to be reduced and of discouraging absenteeism about which public opinion is often particularly sensitive.

The first example of this method is Great Britain where a member of the House of Commons receives £3,250 a year. In Ireland the basic salary is only £1,000. A similar system is found in countries where the influence of British institutions remains important such as India, Pakistan and Somalia. In Norway and Sweden the method of remuneration is similar as the following figures show:—

> Norway: 32,000 crowns a year plus 20 crowns for each sitting day.
> Sweden: 32,000 crowns a year plus 700 crowns for each month of sittings.

The daily allowance is sometimes replaced by an allowance to cover the cost of travelling. This is done in Bulgaria, Liberia and Libya. The travelling allowance may vary according to where a member lives as in Denmark, or members may receive between 20,000 and 26,000 crowns as appropriate. Travelling expenses are also reimbursed by the Second Chamber in the Netherlands to a total of 2,400 florins, which has to be added to the 15,000 florins, the basic emolument, and to the daily allowance varying from 3,000 to 6,000 florins. All this amounts to only a modest total sum. Members of the first chamber receive only 1,200 florins a year and 30 to 60 florins for each sitting day depending on their place of residence. Travelling expenses are also an element in the remuneration of members of Parliament in the Federal Republic of Germany. Essentially that remuneration comprises a monthly payment amounting to 22·5 per cent of the salary of a federal minister, a lump sum payment for out of pocket expenses determined annually in the finance bill and a daily subsistence allowance related to attendance.

In Italy the daily allowance is the essential part of a member's remuneration. Despite a fixed sum of 65,000 liras a month an Italian member may receive a daily allowance of up to a maximum of 370,000 liras; but it may be reduced in proportion to the number of absences, the amount of reduction varying according to whether the member lives in Rome or the provinces, whether sittings take place in the morning or afternoon, during the summer vacation or during the rest of the year. An analogous system is found in Luxembourg: a maximum payment of 60,000 francs a year may be reduced according to the number of meetings which the member has failed to attend.

It is worth noting the practical difficulties of checking the attendance of members. Many different methods are employed. The most common is the keeping of a daily register of attendance. In France votes cast in the Chambers and work done in permanent committees is taken as a basis for calculations. In the National Assembly if a member takes part in not less than two-thirds of the votes during a session, one-third of the working allowance for a period equivalent to that of the session is deducted. If a member has taken part in not less than half the votes, the deduction is doubled.

In most other countries members are paid irrespective of whether they attend sittings. But although it is a single payment, it consists of two parts—salary and reimbursement of out of pocket expenses—and it is difficult to determine the proportion of each. The way in which the remuneration is regarded for purposes of taxation throws some light on the question. In general compensation for out of pocket expenses is not taxable. In Australia a member receives a salary of £2,750 of which £850 to £1,050 is free of tax. In Canada these sums are respectively 12,000 and 6,000 dollars and in New Zealand £1,550 and £375 to £675.

In the United States members of Congress receive a fixed salary of 22,500 dollars of which not more than 3,000 dollars may be treated as expenses. The emoluments of the Speaker of the House of Representatives and of the President of the Senate amount to 35,000 dollars. In other countries parliamentary emoluments vary, as the following figures show:—

STATUS OF MEMBERS

Argentina	75,000 pesos a month
Chile	1,000 escudos a month
Iran	25,000 rials a year
Lebanon	1,750 Lebanon pounds a month
Philippines	7,200 Philippine pesos a year
Sierra Leone	920 pounds a year
United Arab Republic	75 Egyptian pounds a month

In Ethiopia members receive the equivalent of 200 United States dollars a month. Under the constitution a bill to increase the parliamentary emoluments may not apply until the beginning of the next legislature.

The variety and complexity of the methods used in calculating parliamentary emoluments makes generalisation very difficult. The rate of pay cannot be taken as a valid criterion because of the differences in the economic and social conditions in different countries and the varying obligations which parliamentary duties entail. Furthermore within each country there may be differences between the members themselves even though they all receive the same remuneration. It may also be affected by the length of sessions and the distance which they have to travel. Due weight is given to this inequality in several countries. But inequality stems above all from legal or practical incompatibility of occupation which may make it impossible for some members after their election to engage in any gainful occupation outside their parliamentary duties, whereas others may be able to carry on their profession or enjoy private means. So apart from countries like the U.S.S.R. and the People's Democracies where all members are able to continue with their profession or trade, these considerations explain why it is imperative to ensure whatever the circumstances that members of Parliament are able to live in a manner in keeping with the dignity of their high office.

The same considerations justify the award of retirement pensions. This innovation is becoming frequent. It emphasises the transformation, which is evident in many countries, of parliamentary membership into a profession. The question of a parliamentary pension does not arise in countries which have no rules governing incompatible offices because members benefit from the pensions paid by their own business or trade and the remuneration which they receive as members is taken into account in calculating the pension. This is the position in the U.S.S.R. and the People's Democracies where pensions for members are unknown.

In most western countries on the other hand some system of pensions has been instituted. The most important exceptions are the Federal Republic of Germany, Luxembourg and Switzerland. In Great Britain the right to a pension is reserved to those members who have had to relinquish all other sources of income during their term of office. Elsewhere no such restriction applies and any member who has sat for a certain number of years, most often varying from eight to ten, and has reached an age varying from forty-five to sixty-five, is entitled to a pension. This is the practice in Austria, Belgium, Denmark, Finland, France, Iceland, Ireland, Italy, Norway and Sweden.

Outside Europe few countries provide a special system of pensions for their members. Among them are Australia, Canada, Chile, Japan and New Zealand. In the United States it is open to members of Congress to subscribe to a pension fund provided for holders of public offices. If they do, they must pay 7·5 per cent of their monthly salary to the fund. Similar provision at varying rates and supplemented by a grant from the parliamentary budget is made by all countries that wish to guarantee a minimum income to former members. In Ghana provision for pensions is partly replaced by a special payment to every member after five years' unbroken service.

Besides emoluments and pensions there are various benefits attaching to a seat in Parliament which are designed to help the member to perform his duties efficiently.

It is a general practice to grant members of Parliament facilities for transport. These take various forms from reduced fares exclusively for journeys between a member's constituency and Parliament to free travel anywhere. In several countries travelling expenses are charged to the members who, as has been seen, receive a lump sum for this purpose.

The high cost of correspondence has led the authorities in most countries to allow members of Parliament free postage at least for the part of their correspondence directly connected with their parliamentary duties. Special allowance is also made for the use of the telephone and cable services. Exceptions to this rule are those countries which believe that this type of expense ought to be met by the member himself out of his emoluments. The same assumption is made almost everywhere in respect of private secretaries and office premises. Few countries can emulate Japan and the United States in providing each member with an office and a secretariat.

This impressive list of the perquisites enjoyed by members of Parliament may be misleading. In practice their financial status is not always enviable. It is difficult to assess the full extent of their obligations, but these must be taken into account if it is to be made possible for any person, whatever his social position, to hold a seat in Parliament. Only in this way can a member be kept free from the influence of political or financial groups which would inevitably be brought to bear if the official remuneration is inadequate. At the same time that remuneration ought not to be too great if the danger is to be avoided of turning the office of member of Parliament into a lucrative business and thus robbing it of much of its honour and prestige.

6. Administration of Parliament

THE DIRECTING AUTHORITY – THE ADMINISTRATIVE SERVICES

Parliament as an institution can be the subject of innumerable theories of constitutional law. But it is also something much more concrete. Beneath the constitutional edifice is a substructure which is often complex and which in practice has tended to follow a more or less uniform pattern. To ensure that their work runs smoothly, Parliaments have appointed a directing authority, set up an administration and laid claim to an independent organisation, the nature and individual features of which reflect a common purpose however much the systems vary.

1. THE DIRECTING AUTHORITY OF PARLIAMENT

In spite of the special nature of the recruitment and legal status of its members, Parliament 'is after all only an assembly of men which like any other body must be directed by some authority'. This authority can be traced back to the very origin of Parliament. Since 1376 members of the British House of Commons had felt the need to designate one of their number to speak in their name: this is the origin of the office of Speaker. Over the centuries the duties of this high dignitary have gradually evolved after many vicissitudes until today the office of Speaker is one of high prestige, a model admired and copied but, when all is said and done, inimitable.

For a long time it was the Crown's nomination that mattered in the election of a Speaker. Nowadays it is the election that matters. This victory for democracy subsequently won by most of the world's Parliaments has not extended from the House of Commons to its neighbour, the House of Lords which is still presided over by a member of the executive, the Lord Chancellor. But his role is limited to putting questions to the vote; he does not intervene to regulate the conduct of debates. Fortunate indeed is a House that can successfully impose its own rules of discipline. In some countries the President is appointed by the executive; for example in Spain he is nominated by decree of the Head of State. In Ethiopia the President of the Senate is appointed by the Emperor and in Libya by the King. Similarly in the Netherlands the Queen appoints the President of the First Chamber from a list of three names which the Chamber submits after a vote by secret ballot. The first name is always automatically appointed; in other words, the effective choice of its President lies with the Chamber.

The constitution of certain federal states provide that the Vice-President of the Union is President of the Upper House *ex officio*. This is the position in Argentina, Liberia and the United States of America. In India the Vice-President of the Union, President *ex officio* of the Council of States, may not be a member of Parliament. He is however elected by the two Houses in joint session.

The principle of an elected President is recognised in all other Parliaments; in many an absolute majority of votes cast is required at least for the first ballot in order to broaden the bases of the presidential authority. In Turkey a presidential candidate must obtain a majority of two-thirds, and in Sierra Leone a candidate for Speaker must obtain three-quarters, of the votes cast. The ballot is also secret in most instances, an essential feature in view of the impartiality demanded by the office. The successful candidate is presumed not to know who has voted for him so that he will not be under any obligation towards them. While the election is responsive to the movement of political opinion, due weight can be given to the personality and competence of the candidate because the ballot is secret.

The prestige which has come to be attached to the office of Speaker of the British House of Commons absolves the House from these precautions. The election is usually unanimous after the majority party and the opposition have reached an understanding. The agreed candidate is then proposed and seconded by one member from each side of the House. It is traditional to re-elect the Speaker of the previous Parliament. This is the pledge of his impartiality, the essential characteristic of his office. From the day of his election, the Speaker severs all links with his own party, even going so far as to avoid personal contacts, which might give grounds for suspicion of partiality. He has an official residence and a high salary. Upon retirement he is raised to the peerage and he enjoys a substantial pension. The pomp and ceremony surrounding his official actions help to create around him the aura of a judge. In the House itself he possesses comparable power and he wields it with sovereign authority. 'The Speaker like the Pope is infallible', were the words of Mr. Speaker Lowther on one occasion. He regulates the conduct of debate at his own discretion, and there is no appeal from his decisions. He tries to ensure that the rights of minorities are respected while parliamentary business is despatched according to the will of the majority. He gives rulings on matters of parliamentary procedure in accordance with custom subject naturally to the consent of Parliament which is rarely withheld because, as Jennings says, 'the Speaker's authority is greater than his power'. To the world he represents the unity of the House of Commons and within the House he ensures that debate is productive and dignified. In presiding over debates he is helped by two deputy speakers. These two members are also the Chairman of Ways and Means, and the Deputy Chairman who take the chair when the House sits as a Committee of the whole House.

Apart from his numerous duties in taking the chair the Speaker is concerned with the administration of the House so far as it falls within his competence. The chief officers of the House are appointed by the Crown, and Parliament sits in a royal palace for which responsibility does not belong entirely to him. This duty though not spectacular demands energy and application. Several committees are set up to deal with purely administrative matters; they advise the Speaker without encroaching upon his authority or his prestige.

This office patiently moulded by centuries of experience, has naturally been both admired and copied. In all the countries which have been influenced by Great Britain and especially in Australia, Canada and New Zealand there is a Speaker as the chief officer in the Lower House. As in Great Britain he holds office for the lifetime of a Parliament; he represents Parliament in its relations with the outside world and his authority extends both to procedure and to the administration of Parliament.

In Australia some departments, namely, the library, the official report of debates, and administration common to both Houses are administered jointly by the Speaker of the House of Representatives and the President of the Senate. Special committees assist them in this task.

Ceylon, Ghana, India, Nigeria and Pakistan have also followed the example of Great Britain but without always being equally successful; it is difficult to create overnight an institution which has taken centuries to evolve.

The Speaker of the House of Representatives in the United States, like the Speaker of the Commons, has the casting vote; but that does not mean that he fulfils all the same functions. Above all he is elected by one party and he must often take account of the advice of the Chairman of the powerful Rules Committee, the Chairman of the Ways and Means Committee, the floor leaders and party policy committees.

The Presidents of the Irish Dail and Senate resemble the British Speaker in their exercise of the casting vote; they preside over sittings, represent their House in its external relations and are responsible for its administration. They are at the same time chairmen of the committees on procedure and privileges. They also have important constitutional prerogatives, such as membership of the Council of State, and of the committee which may be set up to exercise the powers of the Head of State if he is absent or prevented from exercising them himself. The Speaker of the Knesset in Israel must also act as Head of State if the President is indisposed or absent. Within the House he holds office for the duration of a legislature and he is assisted in the procedure and administration of the House by seven deputy speakers who are also elected and who form with him the nucleus of a presiding group, which is found elsewhere in the form of a Bureau. In Japan the direction of each House is also laid upon its President who is helped in his administrative duties by the administrative committee of the two Houses.

As in the House of Commons the common characteristics of these different Parliaments is the establishment of a single authority covering all aspects of parliamentary activity usually with a term of office for the whole life of the Parliament. It is not the duration of the Speaker's term of office which distinguishes the British system from that of other countries, for there are many Parliaments which elect their President for the duration of the Parliament: they do so in the U.S.S.R. and in the People's Democracies as well as in Austria, the Central African Republic, the Federal Republic of Germany, France, Italy, Somalia and the United Arab Republic. But elsewhere and notably in most of the countries of Western Europe Presidents are elected for the session. This is the position in Belgium, Denmark, Finland, Greece, Iceland, Luxembourg, the Netherlands, Sweden and

Switzerland. It is often the custom, as in Sweden, to re-elect the President until he retires. Outside Europe he is elected for one year in the Cameroons, Ethiopia, Iran and Libya. In Liberia and Turkey he is elected for two years.

The essential feature in Britain is the concentration of authority in the hands of a single individual. By contrast in many other Parliaments the President is surrounded by a collegiate body which under various names shares with him the responsibility for the working of Parliament. Except in Spain this directing body is always elected. It may be very small: in Austria, Denmark, Iceland, Norway, Sweden or equally in Bulgaria, Poland, Rumania and the U.S.S.R. it consists only of the President and Vice-Presidents. In Norway for instance it comprises six members, namely, the President and Vice-President of the Storting and a President and Vice-President for each of its two major parties who appoint their own secretaries. In Yugoslavia the Presidents of the Federal Assembly and the Presidents of the various Chambers composing the Assembly meet together for the same purpose. There may be many members of the directing body: in Czechoslovakia the Presidential Bureau has 30 members and in the French National Assembly the Bureau comprises in addition to the President six Vice-Presidents, three questeurs and twelve secretaries. In the French Senate there are eight Vice-Presidents and six secretaries. In Italy the Bureau of each House consists of the President, four Vice-Presidents, three questeurs and eight secretaries. This composition is found in several other countries such as Belgium, Cameroon, the Central African Republic, Greece, Iran, Libya, Somalia and Turkey. The fact that there are so many is explained partly by the importance and variety of duties to be performed, for which the President regards himself as specially responsible, and partly also by the desire to associate representatives of all political groups in its major decisions. The Bureau or its equivalent is often regarded merely as a consultative body like the committees which advise the British Speaker. It is designed solely to assist the President in his difficult task and not to act as a check on his work nor to take decisions in his stead. This is the role of the Council of Elders, both in the Federal Republic of Germany, where it is elected by proportional representation from the political groups, and in the U.S.S.R. where it is made up of representatives of groups of members from the Republics, territories and regions.

The role of the Bureau is generally confined to administrative and financial questions with the President himself bearing the entire responsibility for the conduct of parliamentary business. In France however the Bureau has the duty as a body of directing the work of

Parliament: according to the procedure of the National Assembly and the Senate, it has full power to supervise their deliberations and to administer and direct all the services. The same position is found in the Central African Republic, Cameroon, Iran, Luxembourg and Turkey.

In Finland the Bureau is sub-divided into the presidential council (comprising the President, the two Vice-Presidents and the chairmen of committees) which handles procedural matters and the chancellery committee in which the President, the Vice-Presidents and four elected members deal with administrative questions.

Whatever the Bureau's powers they are generally procedural or administrative and rarely political in character. In Czechoslovakia however the Bureau has an unusually important role. Besides directing parliamentary business it exercises most of the National Assembly's powers when the Assembly is not sitting; only its powers in relation to the election of the President of the Republic and the revision of the constitution are outside the Bureau's competence. It may take any step, by legislation if necessary, subject only to the Assembly's approval in the next session. In certain circumstances it may declare war or be called upon to appoint or dismiss the government. These powers are exceptional. As a rule the Bureau is a subsidiary body of an Assembly even when it represents the Assembly in formal ceremonies. It is worth noting however that in France no member may be arrested out of session without the Bureau's permission except in case of *flagrante delicto*.

In practice the work of the Bureau even within an Assembly is mainly carried out by its individual members according to the posts they hold, President, Vice-Presidents, Secretaries and Questeurs.

Like the Speaker in Great Britain the President has in all countries first and foremost the responsibility of conducting debates as impartially as possible. This duty is all important because debate is the lifeblood of a parliament. The President has to see to it that the rules of procedure are observed, that order is maintained in the House and that his own rulings are enforced, when necessary, by appropriate measures. Impartiality demands that he should not take part in debates or in some countries vote, even if he has the right to do so. For the same reason in the Netherlands he is the last to vote in order to preclude the possibility of influencing his colleagues. His signature validates legislative enactments; and either in his own right or as President of the Bureau he assumes direct responsibility for the administrative services or controls the expenditure which is incidental to the working of the Chamber.

There are a few countries where the President has an important role to play outside Parliament. For instance he has to take the place of the President of the Republic in his absence. This is the position in Ireland and Israel, as has been seen. In Iceland the President of the Parliament exercises the powers of the Head of State, together with the prime minister and the President of the supreme court, if the Head of State dies or is prevented from exercising these powers. In Turkey this duty is discharged by the President of the Senate. The French constitution provides that if the Presidency of the Republic is vacant or if the incapacity of the President has been confirmed by the constitutional council, the President of the Senate shall carry out the duties of the President of the Republic. The Presidents of the two French Chambers each nominate three members of the constitutional council. Moreover they have to be consulted by the President of the Republic before the National Assembly is dissolved, a procedure that has also to be applied in Turkey.

The Vice-Presidents' only function as a rule is to take the chair in the event of the President's absence. In the Belgian House of Representatives and the National Assembly of the United Arab Republic the Vice-Presidents preside by right over one of the permanent committees of which they are members. Their members vary from country to country according to the number of meetings held and sometimes to the number of political groups which must be represented in the Bureau. This explains why there is only one Vice-President in Albania, Chile (the Senate), Denmark, Laos, Libya, Monaco and Switzerland. More frequently there are two, as in Brazil, Chile (Chamber of Deputies), Finland, Hungary, Iceland, Iran, Luxembourg, the Netherlands (Second Chamber), Poland, Spain, Sweden and the United Arab Republic. There are three in the Belgian Senate, Bulgaria, Cameroon, Greece, Somalia and Turkey, four in the Federal Republic of Germany, in the French Senate and the U.S.S.R.; five in the Belgian House of Representatives and six in the French National Assembly.

The Bureau may also include officers known as secretaries whose main function is to assist the President in the servicing of meetings. They check the number of members present and oversee the preparation of the minutes of proceedings and reports of debates. They also receive the names of members who wish to speak, maintain order, supervise the counting of the votes, call the roll for a vote by that method and read out proposals which have to be communicated to the Assembly. Their number varies: there are fifteen in the Bundestag, twelve in the French National Assembly, eight in the French Senate and the United Arab Republic, six in Belgium, Iran and Turkey and only one in Albania. In Bulgaria, Poland and Rumania there are six, ten and four secretaries respectively all carrying duties analogous to those in other Parliaments but they are not members of the Bureau. In Austria besides five secretaries the Bureau contains three members who are specially responsible for keeping order. In Switzerland only scrutineers of ballots are provided for.

Questeurs are a less common institution and there are fewer of them. Usually there are three as in France, Iran, Italy, Lebanon, Somalia and Turkey or two as in Greece where they are known as commissioners and Libya where they are known as controllers. Only one Questeur is appointed in the Central African Federation, Cameroon and Laos. Questeurs deal mainly with practical financial and administrative matters. In France, Laos and Turkey for example they deal with terms of employment and promotion of parliamentary officials, and in Belgium, Italy and Turkey with problems of protocol and the organisation of ceremonies. The peculiar nature of those responsibilities often entitles them to such benefits as official quarters or special allowances.

In every country various factors—the power of tradition, the interests of efficiency, the prestige of office, the concern for objectivity—have helped in varying degrees to fashion an authority which is responsible for the smooth running of Parliaments. These examples of some of the systems existing in various countries have shown the great importance of the role played by the President. His is the dominant personality because, even where his appointment is annual, he is seldom replaced. He must possess a large measure of personal authority, objectivity and flexibility, and the ability to make prompt judgments, qualities which are seldom all found in one man. The worth of an institution depends in large measure upon the men at its head. Parliament itself must always have the last word, even though smooth running demands that the President should be given the utmost latitude.

2. THE ADMINISTRATIVE SERVICES OF PARLIAMENT

Every Parliament must have at its disposal a wide range of resources, both intellectual and material, to enable it to carry out its work and exercise its powers. It is the function of the administrative services of Parliament to provide these resources under a director who is responsible to the President or to the Bureau.

ADMINISTRATION OF PARLIAMENT

(a) The Secretary-General

Whatever his title happens to be—Secretary-General, Clerk, Greffier, Director-General— this senior official is responsible for a series of tasks the mere enumeration of which shows his importance. First he is the technical adviser to the President who draws continually upon his experience and thorough knowledge of parliamentary practice especially during sittings of the House when difficult procedural problems may arise. He directs the work of the assembly services which together ensure the smooth flow of parliamentary debate. He controls the administrative services—library, staff, supplies, accommodation, accounts—unless as sometimes happens this is made the responsibility of a second high official, an administrative director or Serjeant at Arms. In other words the task of the Secretary-General is to see that all members have at their disposal every facility to help them to carry out their parliamentary duties. The abilities required for the performance of this task make it essential for special care to be exercised in making an appointment to this post.

In some countries the Secretary-General is appointed by the executive. In Monaco the head of the Secretariat is appointed by the Prince, in Ethiopia by the Emperor and in Ghana by the Head of State. In Great Britain although Parliament is notoriously jealous of its privileges it is the Crown who appoints the Clerk of the Parliaments (as the Clerk of the House of Lords is historically known) and his opposite number in the House of Commons. But the fact that they are appointed for life ensures their independence of the executive. The influence of the executive is also apparent in most Parliaments which have been influenced by the British Model. In New Zealand and Ceylon the Governor-General appoints the Clerk of the House though in Ceylon the House may request his dismissal. In Australia the Clerks of each House are also appointed by the Governor-General but on the recommendation of the President of each House. In Pakistan the appointment is made by the Head of State on the Speaker's recommendation. In Ireland the Prime Minister nominates him on the recommendation of the President of each House and of the minister for finance. Comparable with this system is that followed in Nigeria and Sierra Leone where the Clerk is appointed by the body responsible for appointing all civil servants, the public service commission.

The practice of allowing Parliament to choose its own Secretary-General would seem more consistent with the nature of the office. Nevertheless the system of election although democratic in conception carries with it the risk of transforming what is in essence a technical office into a political office subject to the vagaries of successive majorities. In the United States the Clerk of the House of Representatives is elected at the beginning of each Congress on the proposal of a caucus or party conference. An election to the Clerkship of the Senate takes place on each change of majority. So these officers are dependent on the parties. Certain provisions may lessen this disadvantage. In Luxembourg the official is elected for three years. In Norway candidates are proposed by the President of the Storting and in Finland by the chancellery committee and only when the post becomes vacant. In Belgium the Greffier is elected for life but can be dismissed by the House he serves. In Sweden, the secretary is elected annually but it is customary to re-elect him each year. Chile, the Netherlands, the Philippines and Yugoslavia are other countries in which each Assembly elects the head of its own secretariat.

Several countries have preferred to entrust the appointment of the Secretary-General to the person or body who seems best placed to appreciate the requirements of Parliament and to make a choice based essentially upon technical competence. For this reason it is the duty of the President in Austria, the Federal Republic of Germany, Greece, Hungary, India, Ireland, Iceland, Israel, Laos, Lebanon and Poland; of the executive committee of the Bureau, on the proposal of the President of the Assembly in the United Arab Republic; and of the Bureau in Brazil, Cameroon, the Central African Republic, Czechoslovakia, France, Italy, Libya, Somalia, Spain and Turkey.

However the appointment is made, whether by the executive, the Chamber, the President or the Bureau, it is the general practice that the person chosen should be drawn from among officials qualified in the parliamentary administration. This is in itself a guarantee of independence and technical competence.

(b) *Assembly Services*

The services which enable an assembly to do its work as a legislature efficiently are usually manned by public servants recruited from an open competition. Their number varies from country to country according to the amount of work to be done by Parliament and the place it occupies in the machinery of government. In some instances, too, civil servants from other branches of the public administration who do not strictly speaking belong to the body of servants of Parliament are placed at its disposal.

In Switzerland and Monaco the Assembly's secretariat comprises a

ADMINISTRATION OF PARLIAMENT

mere handful of staff, while in Brazil, Czechoslovakia, the Netherlands, New Zealand and Spain there are a mere twenty or thirty. Without counting junior employees the usual figure seems to be about one hundred, though it is greatly exceeded in several countries such as the Federal Republic of Germany, France, Italy, Turkey, the United Arab Republic and the United States. In Japan each House employs a staff of more than one thousand. A detailed study carried out some years ago by the Association of Secretaries-General of Parliaments shows that there is a direct relation between the number of members of Parliament and its total staff. This conclusion has to be modified today to take account of the practice of many newly independent states which have not thought it useful to set up a separate administration for their Parliaments. Nevertheless in every Parliament there are certain services concerned directly with parliamentary business or with administration and finance which have to be provided and which call for an effective minimum staff. It has also to be remembered that such services as libraries, establishments, accounts, buildings, equipment and transport, though not directly concerned with parliamentary business, indirectly help its despatch.

Unquestionably the hub of parliamentary activity is debate in the House. In order to make the proceedings available to the public, there is a service of an official records in every Parliament. One of its duties is to reproduce the entire debate; and it thus constitutes the only authentic record of debates. But its preparation takes time; and to provide a more rapid publication, especially for the press, a summary report is sometimes made. A summary report can be published immediately if need be during a sitting. This is the practice in Belgium, Ceylon, France, Luxembourg, Rumania, and the United States. In Sweden there is no summary report but only a verbatim report which appears in two editions only the second of which is regarded as official.

In Parliaments where two or more languages are used provision often has to be made for simultaneous or consecutive interpretation, unless the languages being used are supposed to be generally known as with Laotian and French in Laos, Hindi and English in India, or English and Spanish in the Philippines. Countries which have to use interpreters and translators are Belgium, Cameroon, Canada, Finland, Israel, Pakistan, Somalia and Switzerland. In Albania, Hungary, Rumania, the U.S.S.R. and Yugoslavia representatives of national minorities may speak in their own languages; their speeches are then interpreted. Czech and Slovak are used equally in Czechoslovakia but all members understand both languages. As the U.S.S.R.

is a multi-national state, reports of the sittings of Supreme Soviet are published in at least fifteen languages.

Sittings are of course never arranged casually. They must be prepared down to the last detail by the officers of the House in accordance with the orders of the House and the rules of procedure. In particular they prepare the President's 'dossier', which enables him to conduct debates in full knowledge and to deal with any procedural problem that may be posed. Members are supplied with the documentary material they need by several services especially the library, the home and foreign information services, and by the committee clerks who give members of committees much help and information while preparing reports to the House. Other officers take charge of the publication and distribution of parliamentary papers and the keeping of the archives.

All these tasks have to be carried out for the benefit of all the members in a spirit of strict neutrality and without any outside interference. This can only be achieved in so far as the administrative services are provided by an independent organisation operating exclusively for the benefit of the House.

7. Independence of Parliament

ADMINISTRATIVE INDEPENDENCE – FINANCIAL INDEPENDENCE – PROCEDURAL INDEPENDENCE

The independence normally enjoyed by Parliaments is natural because the power of self-organisation is inherent in every constituted body. But it also stems from the progressive development of parliamentary powers rooted in popular suffrage. It is a recognition that Parliament is pre-eminent among public authorities and that as far as possible it should not be subject to control by any other authority. Under some constitutions the independence of Parliament follows from the principle of the separation of powers which keeps the legislative power distinct from the executive.

INDEPENDENCE OF PARLIAMENT

In practice this independence is not always absolute. Depending on the form of government it is encroached upon to a greater or less degree. Nevertheless such is the strength of the principle that in practice it is possible to find evidence of it in most branches of parliamentary life. Its impact on the character of the administrative services has already been noted. It also affects the question of appeals against decisions made by parliamentary bodies; but its consequences are particularly noticeable in settling the grant of funds to be made to cover expenditure on Parliament and in the rules of procedure which Parliament has adopted.

1. ADMINISTRATIVE INDEPENDENCE

To say that the administrative services of Parliament are independent means that they come exclusively under the authority of Parliament's own directing body whether President or Bureau; and in particular that this directing body is exclusively responsible for the composition, organisation and powers of the various services.

Absolute independence means that the staff are not only completely independent of governmental authority but are free of all control by the civil service through recruitment, salary scales, promotion and discipline. These conditions are realised in some countries where the parliamentary officials comprise a special corps with special terms of employment worked out by the Assembly or its Bureau in terms of the peculiar requirements of parliamentary work. Those countries are Argentina, Belgium, Brazil, Cameroon, Denmark, Greece, Italy, Lebanon, Libya, Luxembourg, New Zealand, Spain, Turkey and the United Arab Republic. Among the People's Democracies only Czechoslovakia grants parliamentary staff special terms of employment.

The staff of Parliament is a separate body in Austria, Ceylon, Great Britain, Japan and the United States; in these countries their special status is conferred by law not by any kind of interior regulation. In the Central African Republic and Finland staff are employed on a contract of service. A special status for parliamentary staff is also found in Australia, Canada, India, Iran, Israel and Sierra Leone although these staffs are integral parts of their public services. Similarly in France the staff of Parliament are considered to be civil servants whose status is however determined by the Bureaux of the two Assemblies.

It should be stressed that special terms of employment does not mean privileged employment. Generally speaking the rules governing employment are practically identical to those in the civil service. Autonomy and the special conditions of employment that result raise questions of principle rather than practical problems. This explains why, apart from distinctions of form, there is a kind of compounding of the parliamentary staff and the civil service which is reflected if not in the interchangeability of staff at least in similarity of terms of employment.

Moreover many Parliaments employ staff directly from the civil service who remain subject to the ordinary regulations that apply to that service. In the Federal Republic of Germany for example the administration of Parliament is not considered to be autonomous. It is an integral part of the federal administration; the only difference is that the power to appoint staff belongs to the presidents of the two Chambers rather than to the Federal President. The position is similar in the Netherlands. In the U.S.S.R. and in the People's democracies, with the exception of Czechoslovakia, the staff of Parliament are not autonomous; they are subject to the ordinary regulations governing the public service. The same applies in Ethiopia, Ghana, Monaco, Norway, Pakistan, the Philippines, Sweden, Somalia and Switzerland.

In short, the only special feature of the staff of parliamentary assemblies in contrast to the staff of government departments is the nature of the work they do and the special obligations entailed by the service of Parliament.

The administrative autonomy enjoyed by the directing bodies of Parliaments leads to the question of appeals against their decisions, more particularly from the standpoint that damage may be caused to individual persons. This particular aspect of the principle of independence usually passes unnoticed because it is rarely embodied in law and is seldom tested. It is not a matter of political action which could ultimately be supported by reference to constitutional powers; it is a matter of administration which by its nature does not differ from what may be done under the ordinary law. But should the fact that these are the actions of a sovereign body make them unassailable? Many countries would reply in the affirmative on the grounds that the sovereignty of Parliament extends to everything done in its name or on its behalf. In Great Britain for example to initiate legal proceedings against the Speaker would certainly constitute a breach of privilege and would be punishable.

The problem hardly ever seems to have been considered from this aspect because there have been few concrete cases. Two kinds of decision could be tested: first decisions affecting the staffs of parliaments and secondly decisions affecting persons not connected with Parliament.

The application of the ordinary law appears to be adequate to deal with the second category of cases because it is always open to third parties to claim reparation for injury, whoever was responsible for it. But despite the force of this principle the position is not always as clear as in the Federal Republic of Germany where anyone may challenge the decision of the Presidents of both Houses in their capacity as heads of the administration before the ordinary civil, administrative, industrial or disciplinary courts, depending on the nature of the case. Similar opportunities seem to be given to injured parties in the Argentine, Brazil, Ceylon, Ethiopia, Greece, Iran, Luxembourg, the Netherlands, Nigeria, Norway, the Philippines, Somalia and Sweden. In Turkey and the United Arab Republic decisions of parliamentary Bureaux are considered to be administrative acts and as such can be challenged before the Council of State.

The first category of cases in which the staff of Parliament challenge a decision of the directing authority are as a rule settled in accordance with an internal procedure which excludes reference to the courts. In some countries however an appeal is provided for where a member of the parliamentary staff feels aggrieved by a decision which affects him personally. This is the position in India and the Netherlands while in France only the administrative courts are competent to decide these matters.

The decided vagueness which surrounds this particular aspect of the independence of Parliament may be chiefly attributed to the lack of case-law. There have probably been no appeals because of the practical impossibility of making an appeal rather than because of well-established principles.

2. FINANCIAL INDEPENDENCE

The financial independence of Parliament, one of the more important corollaries of the sovereignty of Parliament, raises few problems. If Parliament is to be completely independent it must have at its disposal means adequate to ensure its freedom of action, that is to say, enough funds to meet all its needs. To achieve this result the financial autonomy of Parliament should be reflected first in the preparation of the estimates and secondly in control over expenditure.

As a general rule each Chamber itself decides upon its own total expenditure. The estimates are drawn up either by the President or by the Bureau or some of its members such as the questeurs or by a special committee on the basis of figures prepared by the administrative services. The only problem is how far the executive is to have a hand in the estimates of expenditure by Parliament because at one stage or another they must be included in the national estimates.

The system in force in Belgium, Denmark, Italy, the United Arab Republic and the United States allows the maximum degree of independence to Parliament. After separate discussions without interference from the government, the minister of finance is informed of the total sums required, the figure then being entered as a matter of form in the national estimates without awaiting approval; in fact the Government is not even consulted. In the U.S.S.R. and the People's Democracies each Chamber has the power to decide its own estimates, though in Yugoslavia they are subject to general budgetary policy and in Albania the assistance of experts in the ministry of finance and of the director general of the national bank may be sought in preparing them. In many countries such as Australia, Austria, Finland, Ghana, Great Britain, Israel, Lebanon, Luxembourg, the Netherlands, Norway and Switzerland the estimate for Parliament goes through the same channels as the estimates for any ministerial department; before it can form part of the national estimates, it must have the approval of the Treasury, the Minister of Finance or some other equivalent part of the executive. In practice however it is not modified by these authorities. Here Sweden has an unusual practice: it is for the Commissioners of the National Office for Public Debt to draw up the estimate for the Riksdag; they submit their proposals to the Government for inclusion in the general estimates. This practice conforms to the principle of the financial independence of Parliament, for the commissioners are elected by and are solely responsible to the Riksdag itself.

In France there is also a special procedure which dates from the constitution of 1958. While the financial autonomy of the Chambers is still formally recognised, an administrative control now applies when the estimates are being prepared. The necessary expenditure for the two Chambers is decided by a committee composed of questeurs of each Chamber, but the chairman of this committee is the President of the Court of Accounts. Moreover two members of the Court of Accounts attend the committee in a consultative capacity.

The executive sometimes takes a more positive hand. In Monaco the Royal government must approve the estimates drawn up by the National Council; in Ireland the ceiling is fixed by the minister of finance; and in Ceylon the estimate for each House is prepared by the

INDEPENDENCE OF PARLIAMENT

Speaker assisted by an advisory committee which includes the leaders of the political parties and the minister of finance or his deputy. In the Federal Republic of Germany the estimates for Parliament must be submitted to the Cabinet which may withhold its approval. If it does so, it must put forward amendments which may be accepted or rejected by Parliament. Japan goes a step further: the task of deciding what the total sum is to be is the responsibility of the Government after consulting the Presidents of both Houses. As in Germany if there is disagreement, the Diet decides the matter. The practice of including parliamentary expenditure in the national estimate is found in all countries. It enables the figure to be debated in Parliament in the same way as the expenditure of a ministerial department. In practice this seldom happens because the estimates will have been drawn up by a parliamentary body where any objections will have already been discussed and settled.

It is clear that Parliaments with few exceptions enjoy real and demonstrable independence in drawing up the estimates for expenditure; but control over the expenditure is rather different. Parliament should not be afraid of having its accounts audited. Just as it is reasonable that Parliament should be allowed to decide without let or hindrance what expenditure will be necessary, so it is to be expected that like any other funds those allocated to Parliament will be audited to ensure that they have been used for their proper purpose and administered wisely and efficiently. This at least is the theory in a number of countries which draw the logical conclusion that Parliament's expenditure should follow the ordinary rules. It should, they contend, be scrutinised not only by a special parliamentary body, whether bureau or committee, but also by some authority with experience in financial matters which is both unconnected with Parliament and independent of the executive. In systems which follow the British model the authority is the Comptroller and Auditor General, who is appointed by the Crown or Head of State (but can only be dismissed by Parliament) and is often, as in Great Britain and Ireland, associated with a Committee of Public Accounts. This high officer also exercises control in Ceylon, Ghana and India; in Norway he is elected by the Storting. In the Argentine, Austria, Japan, the Netherlands and the Lebanon the duty of control is discharged by the Court of Accounts, in the Federal Republic of Germany by the Federal Office of Control, in Sweden by the National Debt Office and in the United States by the General Accounts Officer on the authority of the Controller General who is an independent magistrate.

In other countries however the sovereignty of Parliament is more vigorously upheld, and no other authority is permitted to interfere in its financial affairs. This does not imply a complete lack of control; it means that control is exercised by a qualified body within Parliament itself. This duty is carried out by the Presidents of the two Chambers in the U.S.S.R. and in Bulgaria by the President of the Praesidium, but more often it is done by a committee which is either a special committee as in Belgium, France and the United Arab Republic, or the finance committee as in Cameroon, the Central African Republic and Liberia. In Ceylon it is the task of the advisory committee assisted by the Clerk and in Finland by controllers elected by the chancellery committee. In Chile, Iran, Libya, the Philippines, Somalia and Turkey, it is the business of the Chambers themselves or one of their subsidiary bodies.

In practice the significance of these procedures lessens when it is remembered that Parliament's own expenditure is small and its accounts straightforward. Nevertheless public money is being spent and the principle that its expenditure should be scrutinised remains fundamental.

3. PROCEDURAL INDEPENDENCE

The autonomy of Parliament is also evident in the control it exercises over its own rules of procedure. It is important that this control should be real if it is to retain its freedom of action. This kind of autonomy means that an assembly is able within the framework of its constitutional functions to decide its own method of working. The rules of procedure ensure that Parliament works smoothly. But they also have great political significance: their impact on the progress of public business can be even more important than that of the constitution when experience has shown that the constitution itself has lacunae.

This explains why efforts have often been made to limit the power of Parliament in this field. The advent of the Fifth Republic in France provided a good illustration. The freedom of each Chamber was limited in two ways. First a whole series of matters which had formerly been regulated solely by the rules of procedure of each Chamber were embodied in the constitution and in organic laws. The same situation was reproduced in Senegal. In Japan also provisions governing the business of Parliament are found in the constitution and in the law relating to the Diet. The same applies in Sweden where the chief provisions are to be found in the constitution and in the law relating to the Riksdag. There are also separate rules of procedure in the Riksdag dealing with matters common to both Chambers and adopted jointly by them. The rules of procedure of each Chamber deal only with secondary matters.

Secondly, and this is the more important aspect of the problem, the constitution provides that before they are put into force the rules of procedure of the two French Chambers must be submitted to the constitutional council which has to consider whether they conform to the constitution. An intrusion of this kind into the internal affairs of a parliamentary assembly is extremely rare. It is however found in Monaco where the supreme court has a similar jurisdiction and in Turkey where the rules of procedure may be referred to the constitutional court if any parliamentary party so requests.

Besides being a kind of manual of parliamentary practice, the rules of procedure give direct and concrete effect to the most important constitutional principles on which the machinery of government is founded. They reflect the special character of each assembly, though they reveal several features common to many assemblies. In the first place each rule consists of a resolution or a series of resolutions adopted by the House itself without any government interference. In this way it differs from a statute which, as will be seen later, is ordinarily the product of the combination of the executive and legislative powers. There are certain exceptions however. In Iceland and Spain the rules of procedure are laid down by law in agreement with the government. To a small extent this is also true of Great Britain where among other sources of parliamentary procedure are the Parliament Act 1911 as amended by the Parliament Act 1949 and the Statutory Orders (Special Procedure) Act 1945. The main body of rules however are to be found in the hundred or so standing orders which fit into the classic category of rules of procedure. There is also a vast body of tradition and precedent accumulated over several centuries in part brought together in certain special collections. Without being formally codified these traditions and precedents are observed through regular application by members and officials of Parliament. Except for the Australian Senate where since 1903 precedents have been systematically collected to make a code of rules, they nowhere have codified authority.

The reason for this is that in most countries the rules of procedure are not founded upon decisions made on particular incidents as they occur but on a detailed study conducted by specialist bodies which endeavour to foresee and settle all procedural problems. The Secretary General or Clerk or Greffier is by virtue of his special knowledge often called upon to take part in this study which is most usually

ORGANISATION OF PARLIAMENT

made by a committee of the House on the constitution, on procedure or on administration; it may be either a permanent committee or a committee appointed for the purpose. The task of drawing up the rules of procedure is entrusted to various bodies as for example the Bureau of Cameroon, the Central African Republic and Czechoslovakia, the Presidential Council in Finland and the council of Elders in the U.S.S.R. In the Netherlands it is done by a committee of which the leaders of political groups are members and whose proposals are then considered in detail by the Chamber. In Laos the proposals of the competent committee are sent to the Bureau which submits them to the Chamber for consideration. In New Zealand it falls to the Prime Minister as Leader of the House to propose that the recommendations of the committee should be accepted.

Whoever prepares the draft of the rules of procedure, it is always debated and if necessary amended by the House itself. Israel is an exception: the rules of procedure need not be passed by the Knesset before they can come into force; they merely have to be laid on the table of the Knesset by the House Committee.

Once the House has adopted its rules of procedure it is bound to observe them. Moreover it must observe every provision of the rules especially where as in France they have been approved by a judicial body in accordance with the constitution. It has been shown that the duty of the President, sometimes with the assistance of the Bureau, is to ensure with the utmost impartiality that the rules are observed. In the Federal Republic of Germany however there is a specific provision under which in exceptional circumstances the Bundestag, if it sees fit, may depart from its rules of procedure in certain respects with the approval of two thirds of the members present. This provision is found in few Parliaments. Generally speaking when a rule no longer answers its purpose, the members must move to amend it under a procedure similar to that by which the rules originally were made. Draft amendments are studied by a committee or whatever body is competent to deal with the subject, and then placed before the House which makes the final decision to accept or reject them.

In some countries motions to amend the rules of procedure are regarded as a serious enough matter to warrant additional safeguards. In France the constitutional council must approve any change in the rules of procedure of the two Chambers. In Poland only the Presidium, the committee on offices and rules, or at least fifteen members may propose amendments to the rules. In Austria bills relating to the rules of procedure may be passed only if at least half the members are present and if two thirds of them vote in favour. In Japan although motions to amend the rules are drafted by the House

INDEPENDENCE OF PARLIAMENT

Management Committee, they are not submitted to the House until they are accepted by representatives of all parties so that the final decision is unanimous. In the United States any matter touching the rules of procedure is given priority in both Houses of Congress if the Rules Committees think fit.

The rules of procedure have a continuing force: in most countries they retain their validity from one Parliament to the next. In a few such as Albania, Bulgaria and Norway their duration is limited to a single Parliament. In the United States a different practice is followed in each House: the House is called upon to adopt its rules of procedure at the beginning of each Congress, while the Senate applies the rules that originated in 1884 and have been amended several times since that year. The Senate is regarded as a permanent body by virtue of the fact that only one third of its membership is subject to election at one time.

Whether the rules of procedure retain their validity beyond the lifetime of a single Parliament is not of great importance because in practice a newly elected Parliament simply takes over the existing orders which have stood the test of time. This practice is yet another manifestation of the sovereignty of Parliament because it emphasises its absolute right to define its own working rules. Where rules of procedure have a more lasting validity, that right is implicit in the power of each House to revise the standing orders if it so desires.

The procedural independence of Parliament is no empty phrase. With rare exceptions such as France it is the duty of each House to determine the limits of its own powers. The only safeguards lie in the control and restraint of members of Parliament and in the continuous watch kept by public opinion.

8. Political Parties and Groups

Under representative forms of government parties have become the instruments for the expression of the people's will. In the liberal democracies the most easily observable aspect of their activity is that they send as many representatives as they can to Parliament. This is what gives an election its meaning, and the contest is carried on inside Parliament through political groupings which bring together members belonging to the same party or holding the same views, making so many units to be thrown into the battle for political supremacy.

For a long time official recognition of political parties, or the groups which within Parliament reflect the parties fairly accurately, lagged considerably behind the important contribution made to public affairs by these organisations; in many countries this is still the position. Only recently have they been accorded any constitutional status and then for their part in elections rather than for their activities in Parliament. According to certain theorists the representative system has no room for political groups because each member represents the whole nation, not a faction. If he is to contribute to the expression of the nation's will he can do so only as an individual, and his speeches and votes ought to be guided solely by his conscience.

But although ignored by constitutions, laws, and even by the rules of procedure of Parliaments, political groups have gradually become an inseparable part of modern parliamentary practice. The idea of the group derives in the first instance from man's natural tendency to consort with those who hold the same views as himself. It has gained ground for historical reasons because political groups have often played a major part in all the movements which have brought about constitutional changes and the emergence of new states. It has profited from the theoretical arguments which have led many countries to adopt proportional representation, a system favourable to the formation and growth of political groups, and it reflects a psychological feature of modern life, namely the predilection for collective activity and the sense of discipline that goes with it. All these reasons explain why the position of political groups within Parliament, even in the classical democracies, is marked by great diversity.

Bound up as they are with the nature and development of every regime, political groups have no *raison d'être* in countries where only one party is recognised. In Albania and the U.S.S.R. members who are also members of the communist party form a single group. In Yugoslavia the 'club for federal members' has the same purpose. There are no political groups in the Parliaments of Czechoslovakia, Hungary or Roumania. But in Bulgaria the National Assembly comprises groups made up of the communist party and the national agrarian union. Similarly groups of the united workers' party, the united peasants' party and the democratic party figure in the Polish Diet in the form of 'clubs'. There are also 'circles' which reflect particular opinion in the Diet such as the catholic members, the social christian association and the association of pax. The Parliaments of certain socialist states such as Albania, Czechoslovakia, Hungary and the U.S.S.R contain regional groups who, like political groups in the classical democracies, have a hand in the setting up of subsidiary bodies of Parliament and in the arrangement of business. In the Lebanon also, members are drawn together by regional affinity; there are no political groups. In other countries the nature of the regime militates against political splintering. For example there are no political groups in Ethiopia, Iran, Libya, Monaco and Spain while the single party system is found in the Central African Republic, Ghana and the United Arab Republic.

Yet the political group is closely bound up with the development and functioning of parliamentary democracy. It provides the backbone of parliamentary activities or at any rate those which are most in the public eye. Paradoxically the majority of long-established European democracies such as Belgium, Finland, Iceland, Luxembourg, the Netherlands and Norway fight shy of according official recognition to political groups. Allusion to their existence is made only in so far as they figure in the composition of certain parliamentary bodies. In the same way the British Parliament does not recognise them as such. The only official bodies are Her Majesty's Government and Her Majesty's Opposition. It is a practical and realistic system of majority and minority which combines efficiency with a high degree of flexibility by compelling all sections of opinion to concentrate behind one side or the other. This dualistic system based on a government and an opposition is also found in Australia, Canada, Ireland and New Zealand. More often than not it is found alongside the single ballot for a single candidate which reduces differences of opinion to a blunt 'for' and 'against'. Under this system the opposition which may tomorrow become the government has official standing in the machinery of government and above all in Parliament. The function of the leader of the opposition is essential to the working of those Parliaments. His post corresponds to that of the Prime Minister and like him he draws an official salary.

In most countries the existence of a government and an opposition does not denote a two-party system. It generally conceals a wide range of political groups, and the fluid nature of these groups can have serious repercussions on the stability of government. To limit the harm thought to be done in many respects to parliamentary business by the fragmentation of parties, minimum size of membership is placed on them so that not all Parliamentarians have the same rights. In the French National Assembly a political group must have at least thirty members and in the Senate eleven before it can officially participate in the business of Parliament. In Italy groups in the House must have at least twenty members, in the Senate ten. In the Bundestag of the Federal Republic of Germany groups of less than fifteen members do not enjoy the privileges granted to recognised groups, and the consent of the Bundestag is required for the formation of groups consisting of members who do not belong to the same party. The position is similar in the Austrian National Council where a group must have at least five members as in the Swiss National Council. The minimum number is three in Belgium, seven in Cameroon, ten in Somalia and Turkey and one tenth of the number of members in the Brazilian House of Representatives.

The question of remuneration for leaders of the opposition may have a direct bearing on this matter. In Canada no payment is made to leaders unless their group consists of at least twelve members, in Australia ten and in the Irish Dail seven.

The role of political groups is bound up with their internal organisation. The bigger the group the more powerful it will be; but its power demands a considerable degree of discipline. Once more the British House of Commons provides the most striking example. In Great Britain parliamentary group and political party merge into one another; the members direct the party but are themselves directed by leaders and 'whips' who are drawn from their own number. The whips of the majority hold official posts either in the Treasury or the Royal Household but their main function is the marshalling of party forces. At the time when the office was created in the first half of the nineteenth century the task was made easier by an open-handed distribution of posts, titles, decorations and patronage. Today the chief whip and his assistants under the direction of the cabinet draw up plans for the parliamentary session in consultation with the whips of the other parties, allot tasks within the party, prepare a timetable and forecast possible opposition tactics. He also has the task of smoothing out differences between the leaders of the various shades of opinion within the party. Most important of all he has to marshal his troops so that in the event of a division there will at all times be enough of them present to ensure a majority. In short, he plays the part of a liaison officer between the government and the back-benchers: he needs to be an energetic and skilful tactician, explaining points of procedure, passing on instructions and at the same time keeping an ear cocked to the trend of public opinion.

The opposition chief whip has similar duties to perform though he is more concerned with his extra-parliamentary duty of preparing a victory at the next election. The office of whip is a purely British institution; it is found in Ceylon and Ireland and as far as one can see in all Commonwealth countries which have based their Parliaments on that of the United Kingdom.

In the United States the power of the whips is very much more restricted. All that is expected of them is to see that members are present when their party needs them. In other words the whips perform duties which in other parliaments devolve upon party officers. Those officers are responsible for calling meetings and for developing a consistent policy to inform all the party's activities. The party may also have an administrative secretariat which with very few exceptions is independent of the staff of Parliament, because that staff is governed by the principle of neutrality. Generally speaking Parliament provides political groups with the necessary material facilities, namely, places for their meetings and office accommodation.

The function of parties or groups is mainly political. It is to decide the measures necessary for the carrying on of responsible government, and it becomes of special importance in moments of crisis. Political parties or groups may be rarely mentioned in the purest statements of parliamentary procedure but in practice their activity is considerable. They keep an eye on important issues, study government or individual members' bills before they come up for debate in the House or in committee and decide which of their members shall speak in debate on behalf of the whole group. Sometimes this decision gives the representatives of groups the right to speak first in the debate as for example in the Federal Republic of Germany. Other members may express their personal views and record their disagreement by voting contrary to the line taken by the group. Few groups are so well integrated that their discipline is perfect. That standard is only achieved where the members are entirely under the control of the party; and while it may not be consonant with the principle of national representation, there is a trend towards it in present-day parliamentary practice.

The rules of procedure of Parliaments sometimes recognise the existence of political groups, if only to ensure that they are fairly represented on the more important parliamentary bodies such as the Bureau, the Conferences of Presidents, the House Management Committee or the Council of Elders. In most Parliaments too committees are composed on the principle of proportional representation, and all political groups are represented in proprtion to their numbers. In Ceylon, France, Israel, Japan and the Netherlands the speaking time allotted to each group also depends on its size.

The recognition of political groups in textbooks on parliamentary business appears to be overdue. The combined importance in politics of the groups in Parliament and the parties in the country as a whole is such that today it is impossible to leave them out of account. For practical as well as political reasons there is a growing tendency towards cohesion and consolidation of the groups. Whether this is a good thing or not will depend upon what the purpose of a seat in Parliament is considered to be—individual action involving individual conscience only or organised, disciplined, collective action in which the personal contribution takes second place to the party line. In any event political groups today are much better equipped than a single, isolated member to fulfil the purposes for which members are elected, namely, to serve as a permanent link between the government and public opinion.

9. Committees

KINDS OF COMMITTEES – COMPOSITION AND ORGANISATION OF COMMITTEES

Unlike political groups committees are recognised in the rules of procedure of all Parliaments. They meet a practical need: the House as a whole is too unwieldy a body to deliberate efficiently on the problems put before it unless they have first been considered by a smaller body. Pressure of circumstances and in particular the growing range of matters with which Parliament is concerned has led to the steady development of parliamentary committees until today they are essential to the efficient despatch of parliamentary business. But the division of labour, the principle underlying specialisation, must not be used by the committee as a pretext for taking to itself powers which properly belong to the House.

1. KINDS OF COMMITTEES

For many years the British House of Commons in its concern to retain its powers used the procedure of sitting as a 'Committee of the whole House' and so did not follow the trend towards the greater use of committees. This committee is simply and solely a working body which comprises all the members of the House who wish to take part and in which the more stringent rules of debate are laid aside; for example, in this committee members may speak more than once on the same subject. The Committee of the whole House is presided over by the Chairman of Ways and Means or his deputy. The Speaker is not present, partly in recognition of the committee's status as a subordinate body of the House and partly as a remembrance of the days when his duty was to the Crown and his taking the chair might be awkward if delicate questions were being discussed by the Commons. The institution of standing committees was found necessary towards the end of the nineteenth century to deal with the larger number of bills which were at once more complex and technical. But the Committee of the whole House remains today an essential part of British parliamentary practice: it still regularly examines major issues. In particular it meets to consider matters relating to expenditure and taxation; for this purpose it becomes either the Committee of Supply or the Committee of Ways and Means. It also considers bills the main object of which is to authorise expenditure; to do this it becomes an *ad hoc* committee to approve or disapprove the expenditure and it ceases to exist when it has reported to the House. As a purely legislative body it considers and if necessary amends resolutions on which some bills are based, thus deciding the essential principles which bind any subsequent committee appointed to consider the detailed clauses. But the Committee of the whole House has no power of decision: it reports to the House which itself remains the sole authority. As it is composed of all the members of the House, the committee's sittings are inseparable from those of the House itself. Its sittings can be held only within a sitting of the House: it could not for example sit when the House was adjourned or prorogued. For these reasons it has no power to adjourn its sittings or its debates to a future day. This complex machinery which involves a large number of successive stages for every measure was originally designed to prevent hasty decisions being taken at the instance of the government. Today, though it is an anachronism, the system continues to give satisfactory results especially in allowing every member of Parliament to take part in debate on problems of a general nature which it would not seem right to hand over for study to a few members.

The fact that this system works satisfactorily has caused it to be adopted in its general lines by a number of countries such as Ireland and Pakistan. Something like it is also found in the Parliaments of Denmark and Iceland. It reflects the notion that committees are subordinate bodies of the House itself, and that both their powers and terms of reference must be circumscribed.

This same notion is inherent in the so-called system of 'sections'. Under this system the House as a whole remains the only body with the power of decision, but for convenience of debate it is divided into a number of sections drawn by lot which study one particular problem simultaneously. All members of Parliament theoretically take part in the debate on every topic which makes the system similar to that of the Committee of the whole House. It is used in Belgium though only to consider proposals for expenditure which have been approved by the Senate. These sections comprise all the titular and substitute members of the committee concerned and any other member of the House who wishes to take part. They hold a general debate and a debate on the clauses and amendments proposed thereto, but voting is reserved to the House itself. The use of sections is also common in the First Chamber of the Netherlands where it gives rise to a somewhat complex procedure: each of the five sections appoints rapporteurs who form a committee of rapporteurs which alone is entitled to submit conclusions to the House. This procedure is also available in the Second Chamber. But because of its ponderousness, it has become obsolete. It makes almost impossible demands on members of Parliament who are expected to have a hand in everything that is going on. Moreover the method of drawing names by lot to set up the sections has the effect of giving them more often than not a different political balance from that of the House as a whole and is bound to impair the value of the section as a deliberative body.

For all these reasons a purely arithmetical division of members has given way increasingly to a division of labour based on the special qualifications, knowledge, and even the likes and dislikes of individual members. It is better policy to leave nothing to chance and to employ each member of Parliament where his services can be most useful, at the same time making due allowance for the relative strength of the various shades of political opinion. This method improves the handling of Parliamentary business by reflecting the primacy of the majority but with the minority acting as a check. These are the various considerations that have led to the committee system as found nowadays in all Parliaments even those which still operate on the principle of the Committee of the whole House or use the device of sections. It has become the rule that no issue should be submitted to the House which has not been previously discussed in committee, that is to say, by a body small enough to enable the work to be dispatched rapidly and thoroughly.

An essential distinction must be made between temporary or *ad hoc* committees and permanent committees. *Ad hoc* committees are set up to deal with a particular matter and cease to exist as soon as they have made a report to the House. The brief existence of these committees makes it impossible for them to impinge upon the powers of the House. There is for practical purposes no Parliament which applies this system exclusively. However it is the regular method of drafting bills in Denmark where, apart from certain special committees specified in the rules of procedure, all committees are *ad hoc*, and cease to exist when the matter referred to them has been dealt with by the House as a whole. Temporary committees are found alongside permanent committees in most countries of which France since the Constitution of 1958 is an example. Under that constitution bills introduced by the government or by an individual member are referred to a special committee if the government or the Assembly so request. In the absence of a request it is referred to one of the six permanent committees in each Assembly.

The standing committees of the House of Commons are in effect *ad hoc* committees in that they are appointed to consider a single bill. With the exception of the Scottish Standing Committee their terms of reference are not specialised, that is to say, they have no exclusive fields to work in; they are simply designated by the letters of the alphabet—A, B, C, D, and so on. There is no limit to the number of these committees that may be set up, though in practice the number has never exceeded six. Each committee considers any bill allocated to it by the Speaker after second reading that is not referred by the House to a Committee of the whole House, a select committee or a joint committee of both Houses. Private members' bills are allocated to one of the standing committees designated by the Committee of Selection as that on which government bills do not have priority.

Standing committees consist of between twenty and fifty members. These members are appointed by the Committee of Selection who take into account the qualifications of members to consider each bill and also ensure that the composition of the standing committee reflects the balance of parties in the House. So much changing membership is involved in this process that it is difficult to give the word 'standing' anything like the sense of 'permanent'.

Standing committees are found in several countries which have been influenced by the British type of Parliament. But some of these countries unlike the British model have specific terms of reference. In Australia there are standing committees on administration, the rules of procedure and library; in Ceylon and India on the rules, petitions and public accounts; and in Ireland on procedure, privileges and public accounts. To consider bills two standing committees are set up in Ceylon, three in Nigeria and a larger number in Ghana, India and Pakistan. These committees are sometimes allotted a special field of work as in Sierra Leone.

In addition to standing committees and varying from country to country, the British type of committee system always comprises either *ad hoc* committees or select committees. Strictly speaking the term select committee is used in Great Britain to describe any committee consisting of a small number of members in contrast to the Committee of the whole House. The term does not apply either to standing committees or to committees which consider the committee stage of private bills. Select committees consider among other matters bills described as hybrid bills and even on occasion some public bills. But as a general rule they are appointed to enquire into a particular subject, and they make recommendations to the House. In some instances their terms of reference may be extended for the duration of a session to various matters falling into the same category so that they tend to resemble permanent committees more especially because the same members tend to be reappointed automatically at the beginning of every session.

The distinction between the duties of the various committees of the House of Commons is relatively complex. In fact the House proceeds on a pragmatic basis which has proved its value during the gradual development of British institutions.

The position is much more straightforward in countries where there is a system of permanent specialised committees. These committees are described as permanent because they are appointed once and for all for the duration of the session or of the Parliament and not to deal with a particular problem. In most Parliaments the life of these committees is the length of the session; but some Parliaments depart from this rule and make the life of the committee the same as that of the Parliament. This is the rule for example in the Austrian National Council, the Belgian Parliament, the Federal German Bundestag, the Israeli Knesset, the Japanese Diet, the Swiss Federal Assembly and the United States Congress. The long lifetime of the committee gives its members a chance to acquire real knowledge of their subject, but at the same time there is the danger of increasing its powers unduly to the detriment of those of the House itself. In practice there is little or no difference between lasting for the session and lasting for the Parliament because re-appointment at the beginning of each session does not usually mean many changes in the composition of committees. It does however provide an opportunity to make changes which may not be possible in the course of the session.

COMMITTEES

Permanent committees are as a general rule specialised: each is concerned with one particular branch of activity such as finance, economic affairs, foreign affairs, social affairs, education or national defence and are entrusted with the study of all bills or other matters relating to that particular field. The degree of specialisation differs according to the country. The most convenient system as far as the work of Parliament is concerned is where the special subjects of the committees correspond to the responsibility of the various ministerial departments. This is the position in Belgium, in the Japanese Diet and in the Spanish Cortes which each have sixteen committees. A relationship between the number of ministries and the number of permanent committees can be distinguished at least in countries where the committees are relatively numerous. There are 19 in Poland, 17 in Yugoslavia, 13 in Chile and Norway, 10 in Bulgaria and Sweden, 9 in Hungary and Rumania and 8 in Czechslovakia. The principle of specialisation is most fully developed in the United Arab Republic where there are at least 25 and in the Federal German Bundestag where there are as many as 28. The number varies with each legislature: in the United States of America the House of Representatives and the Senate each have some 20 permanent committees while in the Argentine the figures are respectively 22 and 18. Committees in the French Parliament have been more severely restricted since 1958. Because of the effect of the proliferation of committees on the equilibrium and efficiency of the executive, the new constitution has restricted to 6 the number of permanent committees in each Assembly. A similar figure is found in many other countries, notably the U.S.S.R. and some of the People's Republics where the number of committees corresponds approximately to the number of major fields of public administration. In Bulgaria however development has been in the opposite direction, that is to say, more committees have been appointed in order to allow a stricter control over administration. In Finland there are five 'statutory' committees to deal with constitutional law, legislation, foreign affairs, finance and banking as well as so-called 'extraordinary committees' set up regularly to deal with economic, cultural, agricultural and social affairs, communications and defence, and the 'Grand Committee' which considers all plans. The Austrian National Council which makes liberal use of the permanent committee system attaches special importance to one of them known as the main committee whose function is not only to deal with matters referred to it but also to co-operate directly with the executive in drafting certain federal decrees which must have its approval before effect can be given to them. It also elects a standing sub-committee whose function is to act as substitute for the National Council in its relations with the government in the event of dissolution or when the National Council is unable to meet. The powers of committee of this kind go beyond the scope of legislation and enter that of government control. This example when considered along with the procedure in Italy where committees have genuine legislative powers, and the position in the United States, illustrates very clearly the natural tendency of permanent committees of the specialised kind to encroach upon the functions of the House and even of the executive.

There is no such danger in the system of standing committees in Great Britain because their subject matter varies greatly, their powers are limited and their composition is fluid. These bodies simply carry out the duty laid upon them: to relieve the House of a burden and to speed up work on legislation.

That is the difference between the British system and other committee systems. It is universally recognised that the British standing committees even though their powers are limited do a sound job; and they are certainly less open to criticism than permanent committees of the specialised kind the abuse of which may lead to a root and branch overhaul of their organisation and powers as it has done in France.

In most countries some flexibility can be given to a system of permanent committees by the power to set up *ad hoc* committees with strictly limited powers and length of life. But in practice they are seldom appointed because the area not covered by the permanent committee is very small. The position in France may be taken as typical: not more than a dozen special committees were set up in the first legislature after its first two years of life. In the Netherlands however *ad hoc* committees are set up to consider bills presented by several ministers so that they are resorted to fairly frequently.

The committee of inquiry (*commission d'enquête*) is a special type of *ad hoc* committee; and like other *ad hoc* committees it deals with one matter only. Its peculiar feature is the power of investigation given to it in the resolution of the House which sets it up. Exceptional powers of this kind, which sometimes make the committee a quasi-judicial body especially in its capacity to summon witnesses to give evidence, explain why these committees are temporary and why in practice they are seldom used, though there is provision for them in all Parliaments except in Sweden and Switzerland. Sometimes the constitution and powers of committees of inquiry contain restrictive provisions whose object is to safeguard the separation of the legislature and the judiciary. In France for example while committees of inquiry have to collect information on specific acts and report their conclusions to the Assembly which has set them up, they may not pursue a matter when those acts have caused a prosecution to be set on foot or for as long as it is going forward. Moreover if a committee of inquiry has already been set up, it must conclude its work as soon as an information relating to its subject matter has been laid in the courts.

In Great Britain, Ireland and other countries which have adopted similar institutions such as Australia, Ceylon, Nigeria, Pakistan and Sierra Leone there are on committees of inquiry in this sense. In these countries select committees carry out this kind of duty especially by summoning witnesses under powers given them by the House.

A parliamentary inquiry does not always mean setting up a 'specialised committee'; powers of investigation may be given to existing committees. For example in the Federal German Bundestag a committee of inquiry must be set up if at least one quarter of its members so request; but in addition the fundamental law has vested permanent powers of investigation in the committee set up to watch over the rights of the Bundestag in its relationship with the federal government and in the defence committee. In Japan and the Central African Republic any committee may easily obtain such powers from the Assembly or its President. In the United States inquiries may also be held by permanent committees of the Senate and sub-committees appointed by them. In the House of Representatives select committees may be set up for this purpose: they are then known as investigating committees. The powers of these committees are extremely wide: they may summon any person whom they think it necessary to hear and they have the right not only to impose a penalty on anyone who fails to appear but also to compel him to appear by issuing a warrant for his attendance.

Committees of inquiry come close to 'committees of control' which are set up as a particular kind of committee in certain Parliaments. In France they consider administrative, financial and technical progress in the public service and in nationalised industries, and report to the Assembly the results of their scrutiny. These are temporary committees. Committees of this kind are also found in Poland and Rumania but as a general rule in other Parliaments they cannot be distinguished from either select committees or from committees of inquiry.

The allocation of work between committees is not necessarily inflexible. Committees are often empowered to meet together to study particular problems affecting two or more of them. But the use of this procedure is limited because of the practice of referring the substance of a matter to one committee and of requesting an opinion from one or more others, as is done in Belgium, Finland, France, Libya, Rumania and the United Arab Republic. Moreover the system of referring complex problems to *ad hoc* or special committees, especially in countries where this is the usual practice, has the merit of avoiding procedural complications because committees sitting together are not generally empowered to take decisions. It is otherwise in Sweden where meetings composed of different committees constitute independent bodies which may report the results of their deliberations directly to the Assembly concerned. In the Central African Republic similar committees known as committees of coordination with special powers are appointed. So they are in Somalia where several committees may meet to consider matters on which each is interested or where the views of the committee on finance does not agree with that of the committee primarily concerned.

In Brazil committees have the right to make a joint report when a matter falls within the terms of reference of both of them. In Rumania, the committees are entitled to make either a joint report or separate reports in those circumstances. In the Lebanon, when several committees hold a joint sitting, the President of the Chamber takes the chair.

In several countries such as Austria, Finland, Libya, New Zealand, Pakistan and Sierra Leone meetings of two or more committees together are prohibited, if not formally at any rate by established practice. In Great Britain such meetings would require the express authorisation of the House. In most Parliaments there is nothing to prevent them taking place but the need seems rarely to have been felt The only countries in which this procedure is used are on the one hand the U.S.S.R. and the People's Democracies and on the other Australia, Belgium, Chile, Israel and Luxembourg. As these meetings are little more than fact-finding and do not significantly forward the work of legislation, the question arises whether they serve any really useful purpose.

Bicameral Parliaments may need to set up joint committees of both Houses in order to function properly. Their value will depend on the terms of reference given to them.

In parliaments which are bicameral in name only joint committees are inherent in the special nature of that form of government. For instance the thirteen committees of the Norwegian Storting are permanent joint committees with the exception of the protocol committee which comes under the Odelsting. The same applies to the Icelandic Althing which regularly appoints three joint committees and empowers the other eight committees of each House to sit jointly if they so desire. In Australia and Sweden although the two Houses are more definitely separated joint committees are the rule.

The usefulness of setting up permanent joint committees may be seen in certain Parliaments where they are used to consider internal matters common to both Houses. In the Netherlands a joint committee controls the stenographic services and arranges delegations for international and supranational assemblies. In India joint committees consider parliamentary emoluments; in Ireland the library, the restaurant and the rules of procedure; and in the Argentine the library and public accounts. In the Congress of the United States eight joint committees out of ten have simply administrative duties.

Joint committees can make a contribution of special value to the process of legislation. They provide suitable machinery for making joint decisions on bills which have to be passed by both Houses. If the two Houses disagree, a joint committee may be set up to consider the matter in dispute. This is a temporary committee which ceases to exist when its task of finding a compromise or reporting failure to agree is done. It may come into being either by a joint meeting of the competent committee set up by each House or more frequently by the appointment of an equal number of members of each House. This procedure is found in Great Britain, Canada, Ceylon and the United States; and provision for it exists in Chile, Iran, Libya, Nigeria, the U.S.S.R. and Yugoslavia. In Ireland the committees of the two Houses meet jointly to consider consolidation and private bills. In France a system of joint committees composed of an equal number of members of each Chamber was introduced in the constitution of 1958. When a Government or an individual member's bill is not agreed to in the same terms by the two Chambers, the prime minister may after two considerations, or only one if there is urgency, convene a meeting of a joint committee to propose a draft of the provisions still to be debated. This committee consists for each bill of seven titular and seven substitute members of each Chamber. In Turkey the members of joint committees appointed to settle disagreements between the two Chambers are elected by the competent committees of each Chamber.

In some Parliaments a permanent joint committee is set up to assure a harmonious relationship between the two Houses. The best example is in the Federal Republic of Germany. The Bundestag and the Bundesrat have set up a permanent arbitration committee consisting of eleven members of each House. Its task is to consider and report on any disagreement arising between the two Houses when requested to do so by the Bundesrat. A similar committee functions in Austria but only for financial matters or when the federal government opposes a bill approved by the Diet. In the same way the committee on the budget in Turkey is a permanent joint committee of both Houses, an arrangement which reflects the special nature of the procedure for approving the balance of revenue and expenditure. In the United States there are also two joint committees which are permanent and can consider bills: one deals with atomic energy, the other with taxation. The recommendations of the second of these committees are however only examined by the two Houses through the Committees of Ways and Means.

Joint committees may be set up to inquire into matters other than legislation as they sometimes are in Great Britain. In Italy joint committees are set up for purposes of scrutiny or inquiry or to give an opinion on delegated legislation. In Switzerland two permanent joint committees scrutinise in detail the Federal expenditure and revenue and the liquor trade.

So far the part played by the many different kinds of parliamentary committees in the work of Parliament and in scrutinising the actions of the executive have been described. Who compose these committees and how they are chosen must now be considered.

2. COMPOSITION AND ORGANISATION OF COMMITTEES

Although committees are generally regarded simply as working parties, an obligation is laid upon members of Parliament in many countries either by law or custom or by the rules of procedure to take part in the work of committees. It is difficult to discover the grounds for this principle because the practice of countries which have the same kind of regime varies: for example in Albania, Bulgaria, Poland, Rumania and the U.S.S.R. service on committees is compulsory whereas in Czechoslovakia and Hungary it is optional. There is a similar variation in Western Europe. In Belgium, Italy, the Netherlands, Norway and Sweden every member is required to take part in committee work whereas in Austria, the Federal Republic of Germany, France, Great Britain, Luxemburg and Switzerland they are not bound to do so. In practice the distinction is not important because members in all countries regard it as valuable experience to belong to committees. The real problem is to limit the number of committees to which anyone may belong at the same time. It is not wise policy to disperse the special knowledge and ability of a member over too many different fields or to establish definite privileges for the more influential, let alone to fail to take advantage of the contribution that each member can make. Moreover the fact that the meetings of committees are frequently held simultaneously may make it physically impossible to take part in all of them. In most Parliaments however members may sit on several committees. But in the Central African Republic, France, Norway, Pakistan, Sweden and Turkey members may belong to only one committee. Membership of two committees is allowed in Cameroon, Italy, Lebanon, Rumania, Switzerland and Yugoslavia; and the number is three in Libya. In the Congress of the United States the rules have been changed: every member may now belong to several committees.

There are three methods of appointing members to serve on committees: by the President or the Speaker; by a committee specially set up for the purpose; or by the House itself. In some Parliaments appointments may be made by a combination of these methods. In practice however with all three methods the most important influence in most countries is the political parties or groups, at least wherever their existence is recognised.

Appointment is the responsibility of the President alone in the Spanish Cortes. He also acts in Ghana on the recommendation of the Leader of the House and in Greece and Japan after consulting the leaders of the political groups. In the Netherlands the Second Chamber has made a practice of leaving its President to deal with appointments. The President endeavours to fulfil this task with the utmost impartiality, taking into account the relative size and importance of the various groups and the special knowledge and expressed wishes of particular members. In Argentina and India the Chambers also entrust to their Presidents the duty of appointing the members of all committees or some of them, though he must have regard to the composition of the Chamber in making appointments.

The practice in Libya comes close to this system. Here the delegated authority is not to the President himself but to the whole Bureau. The Bureaux of the Assemblies are also competent in Switzerland where they consider not only the size of each political party but also the representation of the three official languages and the different regions of the confederation.

In some Parliaments the appointment of members of committees or some of them is the duty of a committee of selection set up for this purpose. The committee of selection in the British House of Commons has eleven members. They are responsible for appointing members of all standing committees, of select committees on hybrid bills and committees on private bills and bills for confirming orders of local application made by the government. In the House of Lords nominations made by the committee of selection are formally approved by the House itself. A committee of selection carries out analogous duties in the Parliament of Ireland, Ceylon, Nigeria and Sierra Leone. In the Norwegian Storting there is a 'Committee on Elections', consisting of 37 members and in Finland a similar body of 45 'electors'. In Israel candidates chosen by the steering committee have to be approved by the House.

Generally speaking appointments are made by the House itself which as a rule does no more than ratify the choice made by the political groups. The composition of committees follows the same principle everywhere, namely proportional representation of party political views. This means that either by agreement between the party leaders or whips or as a result of an arithmetical calculation, the seats in each committee are allocated to the parties in proportion to their numbers in the House. Whatever the procedure used, this rule, which is sometimes embodied in standing orders and always respected in actual practice, makes each committee a miniature of the House. It is more suitable than the House itself for studying particular matters fully and reflects the preponderance of the majority and the check exercised by the minority.

There are some instances of special interest. In the Congress of the United States nominations are made by the committee on committees of each party and election by the House is a pure formality. The exception is the Rules Committee of the House of Representatives. Here the majority party takes most of the fifteen seats chiefly because of the powers of this committee over the business of the House.

Appointments are made by the Chambers on the proposal of the President in Chile and Somalia and on the proposal of the Bureau in the United Arab Republic and the Central African Republic. In the U.S.S.R. and the People's Democracies members of committees are effectively appointed by the Chambers which have regard to their specialised knowledge and personal preferences. In Poland candidates are proposed by the Council of Elders and in Yugoslavia in each federal Chamber by a group of at least ten members.

The concept of the committee as a faithful reproduction of the House itself may be upset if some of its members are absent from meetings. To correct this deficiency some Parliaments have instituted a system of substitutes. A number of substitute members are chosen at the same time as the titular members and sit on the committees if the titular members are absent or unable to attend. This system seems to be confined to a few countries in Western Europe such as Austria, Belgium, the Federal Republic of Germany, Finland, Iceland,

Luxembourg, the Netherlands and Sweden. Moreover the system is sometimes restricted to the more important committees in Luxembourg or to the Committee on Foreign Affairs as in Iceland. Nor is the number of substitutes always the same as that of the titular members. In Finland it is only one third of the membership and in Belgium half. In some Parliaments a member of a committee is entitled as an exceptional circumstance to ask one of his fellow-members to replace him at a particular meeting.

With the exception of these few devices enabling committees to keep their original complexion at critical moments, the replacement of members of committees can only take place by the ordinary process of nomination, that is, by the President, Bureau, Committee of Selection or House on the proposal of the political party which is entitled to the seat. Despite the delay, there is much to be said for a formal, official appointment which may constrain members of committees to take part in the work of committees not only by voting when occasion arises but also by following all the items through from beginning to end and contributing personally to the decisions reached.

Seniority as well as special knowledge and personal preference is often the ground for nominating members to committees. This criterion is never officially formulated but arises naturally in practice because in making nominations to committees political parties are bound to take into consideration the experience acquired by the senior members in certain specific fields. In Ceylon, Great Britain, Greece, New Zealand, Sierra Leone, Spain and Sweden these members are given some advantage both in choosing the committee which they wish to join and in being put forward for the chairmanship or vice-chairmanship. This has become virtually the rule in the United States: a member is appointed for the duration of his term of office; and as long as he is re-elected, he may continue to be a member of the committee. In this way he acquires the experience and seniority which lead ultimately to the chairmanship. In every committee the chairman is in practice the oldest member.

Should committee meetings be held in public? Those in favour argue that no aspect of parliamentary activity should be withheld from public knowledge. On this reasoning the public are admitted to meetings of committees in the U.S.S.R., Albania, Bulgaria, Czechoslovakia and Yugoslavia. The same is broadly true in the Argentine, Australia, Canada, Japan and the Philippines. In the United States Congress meetings of committees are as a general rule public, and those present can be asked to give their views; but committees may decide on a majority vote to hold them in private, especially when

ORGANISATION OF PARLIAMENT

hearings of certain witnesses such as cabinet ministers or high officers of the armed forces are judged to be confidential or when a vote is to be taken on matters which are to be reported to the House. In the House of Commons meetings of the Committee of the whole House are by definition public. So too are meetings of standing committees and committees on private bills. Select committees on the other hand usually sit in private.

Those who are against meeting in public point out that the work of committees is provisional in character and should not commit any of the members taking part. It is for the House as a whole to take the final decisions and to do so publicly. Moreover the way in which an individual behaves in private is not the same as it is in public. Frankness and mutual trust are affected by the presence of an audience, and there is no doubt that off-the-record discussions tend to prevent playing to the gallery, encourage a spirit of compromise, and make for quicker and more satisfactory results. These arguments would appear to have been given weight in most Parliaments, and strangers are not allowed to attend the meetings of committees. This does not mean that the work is necessarily kept secret. As a general rule a certain amount of publicity is given in the form of short press releases.

Another question is whether the privacy of a committee meeting applies to members of Parliament who are not members of a committee. Only in Ceylon, Ethiopia, Finland, Iceland, Nigeria, Spain and Switzerland is there a total prohibition on their attendance. In Denmark, Ghana, Ireland, Israel and Norway this prohibition may be raised by a special decision of committees. In Sierra Leone it would need the authorisation of the House. In other Parliaments members of the House are entitled to attend meetings of committees of which they are not members but on certain conditions. In Belgium (House of Representatives), Cameroon, France, Luxembourg, Pakistan, Sweden and the United Arab Republic, only proposers of bills, motions or amendments that are being considered by the committee may attend, and if they do so they may take part in the proceedings in a consultative capacity. As a general rule the presence of strangers in a committee does not give them any right to take part in its work nor *a fortiori* to vote. They attend meetings simply as observers. In the Belgian House and in Israel a member of a party that is not represented on a committee always has the right to attend in that capacity. In the Belgian Senate all members can attend meetings of committees of which they are not members but they have no right to speak or vote. It is sometimes contended that any member may take part in discussions of a committee. This is accepted in the

Second Chamber of the Netherlands when bills are being considered. In the U.S.S.R. and the People's Democracies, as well as in Argentina, Canada, Chile, the Federal Republic of Germany, Laos, Monaco and the United States this is also the position. While every member of those assemblies may have the right to take part in a committee's discussions, he may only do so in a consultative capacity and if necessary he may be invited to withdraw when decisions are being taken. In Great Britain where any member of the House may attend though not speak in meetings of committees, committees do not have the power to exclude him from their proceedings without special authority of the House.

Like the Assembly to which they belong, committees are subject to a directing authority in the conduct of their work. The directing authority of a committee, known as the Bureau, consists of a chairman who is usually assisted by the vice-chairman and sometimes secretaries. In some Parliaments this directing body also includes a permanent rapporteur, as in the Lebanon, Turkey and the United Arab Republic, who acts as a spokesman for the committee on all legislative matters. In Cameroon and France a permanent rapporteur is appointed only in the finance committees. But apart from the Polish committees which are headed by a Presidium, the main figure is as a rule the chairman of the committee, though the rules of procedure usually have nothing to say on the extent of his powers. They are more or less the same in all Parliaments, that is to say, for the handling of debates they correspond *mutatis mutandis* to those of the President in the House. In the British Parliament and those modelled on it the chairmen of committees have no disciplinary powers except in committees of the whole House; but they perform an important political function both by their work on the committee and by their participation in the work of certain parliamentary bodies such as the President's Council in Finland or the Conference of Presidents in France.

On democratic principles it would seem reasonable that the chairmen of committees like the President of the Chamber should be elected to office. This is what usually happens.

Election may be the prerogative of the Chamber itself as in Albania, Bulgaria, Czechoslovakia, the U.S.S.R., and Yugoslavia, though in the first three of these countries vice-chairmen are elected by committees. The same rule is followed in Japan, though in practice the President himself makes the appointments.

The general rule is that the committee elects its own chairman from among its members. This is true of most Parliaments including those of Hungary, Poland and Rumania. It applies even in Australia and

Ireland, although these countries belong to a family which tends to fight shy of the election procedure in favour of other systems that put more stress on personal ability than on political allegiance. This tendency is rooted in the principle that committees are technical bodies set up for the convenience of the House, and that political strife and personal rivalry are out of place there.

This principle is found regularly in Parliaments of the British type which find it preferable to give the Speaker a fairly free hand in nominating persons to direct the work of committees. He has the exclusive responsibility in India. In Nigeria he is advised by a committee of selection. In Great Britain and Ceylon the chairmen of standing committees are chosen by the Speaker from a list drawn up in advance and known as the chairmen's panel. This is a list of members who are regarded as specially qualified to act as chairmen. In the House of Commons the committee of selection appoints the chairmen of committees on opposed private bills. In Sierra Leone the chairmen of all committees are appointed in this way. A parallel is found in the Swiss Federal Assembly where the Bureau appoints the chairmen of all committees except for the finance committee which elects its own chairman.

The *ex officio* chairmanship of committees is another peculiarity of the parliamentary system based on the British model. In the House of Commons the Committee of the whole House is presided over by the Chairman of Ways and Means who is also chairman of the Standing Orders Committee and is responsible for the procedure on private bills. In Nigeria the Speaker or his deputy, except in cases of objection, takes the chair of special committees. In India if the Deputy Speaker is a member of a committee, he is always the chairman. The same applies to the President of the Senate in Australia who also presides *ex officio* over the three committees of the House dealing with its internal matters. The *ex officio* chairmanship of committees is also the general rule in the Belgian Parliament. The President of the House or a Vice-President chosen by him directs the business of the permanent committees of which they are members. The other permanent committees name a chairman from their number for the duration of the session in accordance with the advice of the President of the House who distributes these positions among the parties in relation to their numerical strength. In Pakistan the chairmen of permanent committees are named by the Speaker who gives to the opposition parties the number of posts corresponding to their importance in the House.

The various procedures which limit the committees' right to choose their own chairmen are important in that they prevent the majority party from monopolising the chairmanship of committees. The preponderance given to the majority by the proportional rule would inevitably lead to a monopoly if a curb of rule or custom were not put upon it. Chairmanships are sometimes allocated between parties by a simple official agreement as happens in Finland, the Netherlands, Sweden and Turkey, or the recommendation of a higher body like the Knesset committee in Israel, or the application of cut-and-dried rules as in the Federal Republic of Germany where before the committee chairmen are elected the Council of Elders lays down the strict proportions to which the committees must conform. There is a similar system in the Polish Parliament, although party fragmentation in this case does not show the same characteristics as in the Western type of democracy. The allocation of chairmanships between majority and minority obviously does not apply in Parliaments where the concept of majority and minority has no meaning as in the U.S.S.R. and the People's Democracies, Monaco, Spain and the United Arab Republic. Conversely where this concept is an essential part of the political system, the majority ought logically to hold the reins in all committees. The most striking example is the United States Congress where the chairmanship of every committee vests automatically in the eldest member of the majority party. Only in certain unofficial sub-committees may a member of the minority if the need arises take the chair.

The preponderance of the majority party is to be found in most of the Western democracies, subject to the modifications already referred to which derive from institutions like the chairmen's panel in the British type of Parliament and ensure that the opposition is fairly represented. In the Japanese Diet too the President endeavours to bear the rights of the opposition in mind. There are also traditional exceptions like the Public Accounts Committee in the House of Commons where the chairmanship is invariably given to a member of the opposition.

Apart from these few instances the allocation of chairmanships among the various parliamentary groups does not appear to follow definite rules. The powers of a chairman are too important for the majority party to be readily prepared to hand over any chairmanships to the opposition. But in the final analysis parliamentary systems rest on certain tacitly accepted conventions of which the rights accorded to an opposition is one. Those rights are fully honoured in the composition of parliamentary committees, but they have not extended to the chairmanship of committees to the same extent. Nevertheless the majority and the minority, or government and opposition which taken together represent the whole country do find that the present method of allocating chairmanships allow them to work together satisfactorily.

Once they are set up, with a chairman at their head, committees work according to a variety of methods which are seldom laid down precisely and obviously cannot be examined in detail in this kind of book. In practically all Parliaments the rules followed by committees are founded on the rules governing debates in the House itself though they are less formal. If committee work is to be fruitful the rules must be flexible enough to allow a constant interplay between the various points of view. As the number of members is small, disputes are rare and are generally settled by common agreement. There are a few special rules governing such matters as the order of speakers, the submission of amendments, or the quorum required for meetings and especially for voting; but these rules are mere exceptions or departures from the general provisions governing debates in the House which apply to discussions in committee even though in theory the committee is master of its own proceedings. However some Parliaments in for example Austria, Belgium, Czechoslovakia, India, Japan, Libya, Pakistan, Poland and Turkey have adopted detailed rules governing procedure in committees; and in Yugoslavia the rules adopted by each committee have to be approved by Parliament.

In theory and practice, proceedings in committee follow from those in the House: a general debate takes place followed by a debate and vote on each clause and amendment thereto. In the committees of the House of Commons there is no general debate on the principle of a bill because that has already been decided by the House. The committee's duty is to consider the clauses within the ambit of that acceptance of principle.

The deliberations of a committee logically culminate in the preparation of a report designed to inform the House of the opinions and findings of the committee. Most often a report on each item is drawn up by a member chosen by the committee from among the majority for or against the bill under discussion, which is not necessarily the same as the government majority. In some Parliaments the rapporteur is one of the officers of the committee and is appointed to deal with all items. This is the position in the Lebanon and Turkey and in the finance committees of Cameroon and France.

In the House of Commons and several other Parliaments of the same kind it is for the chairman of each committee to submit a draft report which is generally accepted as the committee's report. In the Knesset of Israel the chairman of the committee can give the task of drawing up the report to another member of the committee. In the Congress of the United States it is habitually the chairman who presents the report to the House. In the Netherlands the report is drawn up by the Clerk or one of his assistants under the supervision of the committee who must approve each item before it is submitted to the Chamber.

There is one final question on the conduct of business in committee: are committees bound by the rules applying to sittings of Parliament as a whole? As a general rule they are not, because the flexibility which characterises the working methods of committees extends to their timetable. In a few countries such as Belgium, Cameroon, Iran and Libya, committees are not allowed to meet when the House is not sitting. But this prohibition which stems from the belief that a tight rein should be kept on committees is sometimes modified in important respects. For example authority for committees to meet during adjournments of the House may be given by the House itself in Great Britain or by the Presidential body in Norway. Again this authority may be given to certain committees only, such as public accounts committees or select committees in Nigeria, the finance committee and the committee on internal affairs in the Central African Republic or committees of inquiry in New Zealand. In Israel a committee may sit during adjournments of the Knesset only if the government or one third of the members so request.

With these exceptions there is nothing to stop committees sitting whenever they like and if necessary notwithstanding the adjournment of the House. The advantage of this is that it spreads the work demanded of committee members over a longer period, lightens the programme and yet makes it possible to study problems more thoroughly in an atmosphere free from the haste imposed by the closing date of a session. In practice however committees make little use of this power except in the Federal Republic of Germany, Japan and above all in the U.S.S.R. and the People's Democracies where the plenary session is relatively short and most of the work is done in committees.

The committee system has two essential characteristics: in the first place it meets a need which has been felt everywhere because of the increase in the amount of parliamentary business; secondly it is governed by flexible rules in keeping with its purpose which is to render services of a technical rather than a political kind. But the need for committees and the latitude given to them must be duly circumscribed. The sovereignty of Parliament is indivisible; and committees must not seek to encroach upon it. The organisational freedom which they now enjoy must not develop into independent action. The function of the committee, important and effective though it is, must be exercised with restraint so that it does not usurp functions which properly belong to Parliament itself.

10. Sittings of Parliament

THE CHAMBER – SESSIONS

In spite of a certain similarity in organisation and structure all Parliaments, whatever the form of government of the country, have their own individuality, and the peculiarities of each are seen most clearly in their sittings. This suggests two questions, and the answers to them may determine the essential feature of a Parliament: where does it sit, and when does it sit?

1. THE CHAMBER

The relationship between the shape and arrangement of the Chamber and the form of government of a country is interesting. The architecture of the Chamber may result from the historical circumstance that led to the choice of a seat for Parliament. But it is not always a mere legacy from the past. It may also reflect a state of mind, a particular outlook or an unusual political situation. Many countries have found it necessary to construct or reconstruct their Houses of Parliament, and the design has undoubtedly been influenced by political considerations peculiar to each country. The most important question is how the seating is arranged within the Chamber whatever the shape may be. For example in the Federal Republic of Germany and in the United States' Congress the Chamber is rectangular but the seats are arranged in a semicircle.

The seating arrangement most commonly found is semicircular. The members' seats are spread out fan-wise, facing the presidential tribune. This allows the space allocated for seating to be split up into any number of segments which can expand or contract with the movement of the various political groups. This arrangement is especially appropriate to multi-party systems because the political strength of the parties at any given moment can be seen, however fluid the groups and relative numbers. It also has such practical advantages in the way of visibility and acoustics that it has been adopted by most Parliaments including those of Hungary, Poland, Rumania and Yugoslavia where the differentiation of political colour is not as important as in Western Parliaments.

In the Parliaments of Albania, Bulgaria and Czechoslovakia and the U.S.S.R. the seating arrangement is different: the Chamber is rectangular and the seats are arranged in parallel rows facing the presidential tribune. A similar arrangement is found in Ethiopia and in the Turkish National Assembly.

The Chamber in which the British House of Commons sits is also rectangular, but the seating plan has an entirely different purpose. The Chamber is divided down the middle for the whole of its length so that the two series of parallel benches face each other, on either side of the Speaker. This arrangement is admirably suited to the two-party system, or at any rate to a strict observance of the principle of government and opposition which could be applied even if a number of splinter parties appeared. The example of the House of Commons has been followed in the Parliaments of Canada, Ceylon, Nigeria and New Zealand, and it is also found in Cameroon. The Second Chamber in the Netherlands is divided into two across its width and not down its length.

The natural tendency of members to form into groups according to their political leanings is reflected in the allocation of seats within the Chamber. But in some countries the seats are allocated on a different system, either alphabetically as in Cameroon and Spain or by constituency or region as in Ethiopia and Liberia and also Czechoslovakia, Hungary, Rumania and the U.S.S.R.

Another system is to allow members to choose their own places and to change places if they wish at each sitting. Under this system seats are not allocated to individual members. Albania, Bulgaria and Yugoslavia as well as the Central African Republic, Ghana, Iran, Laos, Monaco and Somalia follow this practice. In Libya every member may choose where he wishes to sit, though priority is given to supporters of the government. In the United States House of Representatives seats are not assigned to individual members but by practice democrats always sit on the Speaker's right and republicans on his left.

Where there is a two-party system or a government and opposition, the practice is simply to divide the Chamber in two. In the

ORGANISATION OF PARLIAMENT

British House of Commons members of the government party and the opposition party face each other. No member has an individual seat assigned to him for the very good reason that there are only enough seats for about half the number of members. The arrangement is clear and straightforward, especially as the front benches on either side above the gangway (dividing the blocks of seats on either side of the Speaker into two) are reserved for the leaders of the parties. The rest of the seats both behind the leaders and below the gangway are for 'backbench' members. Every Parliament has its traditions of this kind which sometimes give it its particular character. Where the Chamber is semicircular, the distinction between government and opposition is less emphatic. Differences are expressed in terms of 'right' and 'left' which derive from the French political tradition. After the Revolution the conservatives acquired the habit of sitting on the right of the President and the degree of progressiveness of political thought was indicated by moving along the benches towards the left. This tradition has become so strong that it has taken on a symbolic meaning so that the terms right and left are used today to describe political groupings even in countries where the seating arrangement is not the same as in the French Parliament. Nevertheless the identification of political thought and seating in a semicircular Chamber has been criticised as inflexible in that it prevents the natural processes of political realignment which are essential to the vitality of parliamentary government.

An attempt has been made in some countries to remedy this defect either by breaking up the political groupings or by refusing to attribute a precise political connotation to the terms right and left. In Norway and Sweden political groups are split up: members sit in the alphabetical order of their constituencies. In Sweden within constituencies seats are distributed in accordance with electoral rank in the Upper House and seniority in the Lower. In the United States Senate seats are all allotted by seniority. In Iceland and the Philippines they are drawn by lot. The Knesset in Israel and the Japanese Diet have adopted systems of their own based on the number of members in each group. In the Knesset the political groupings are placed in descending order of size from left to right. In the House of Counsellors of Japan the largest party occupies the centre of the Chamber, and the other parties are located on either side in order of size. This method has been partially followed in France where in practice the majority party occupies the centre and part of each wing of the Chamber. The other parties are seated on both sides of the majority party according to the traditional concepts of right and left. In the Second Chamber of the Netherlands the terms left and right have a very special meaning. The members continue to arrange themselves according to their political affiliations, but the parties based on religious principles, especially the catholic and protestant parties, sit on the President's right and all the others on his left. In the Swiss National Council the language question plays a part in the allocation of seats: as a general rule the French and Italian-speaking members sit on the left and the German-speaking members on the right.

The best way of escaping from the notions of right and left is to seat parties or groups according to whether they belong to the government or the opposition. This is the custom in most Parliaments which have been influenced by the British practice. Except in Ireland the government parties traditionally sit on the Speaker's right and opposition parties on his left. While the character of a House may be affected by the way in which the members are seated, it depends to a greater degree on the length of time for which it sits.

2. SESSIONS

Should the independence of Parliament give it the option of deciding for itself how and when sittings should take place and how long it should continue to sit? Or should sittings be delimited by some constitutional provision or decided by some authority other than Parliament? The question is pertinent because the answer to it largely determines the function of Parliament and its influence on the political life of the country.

It is important first and foremost to define carefully the terms used. A session is the period during the year when Parliament has the legal right to meet and to transact its business. There may be more than one session in a year and its length may vary. A sitting is the effective meeting of members on a given day; sittings take place within the framework of the session. How far parliamentary assemblies are empowered to fix their own sittings within the session will be considered later. The question treated here is the length of the session and the legal principles which govern it.

There are two contradictory constitutional approaches to this problem: first the 'monarchist' or authoritarian tendency to curb the action of Parliament by making the frequency and length of sessions a matter for the government to decide; and secondly the democratic or republican tendency to vindicate the sovereignty of Parliament, jealously guarding its independence and giving its a free hand to choose the period in which its sittings are held.

ORGANISATION OF PARLIAMENT

The second of these two methods is sometimes called the 'permanent assembly' system. The implication is not that sittings are uninterrupted but that there is power to sit for an unlimited duration. On this view there are legally no sessions, but only a legislature, that is, the lifetime for which a Parliament is elected. This is the system in force in the Federal German Bundestag which except for the recess it allows itself in summer and a few public holidays is in permanent session in cycles of four weeks: two weeks are devoted to plenary sittings of the Bundestag and to committee meetings, the third week to committee meetings only and the fourth is a free week. The annual average of plenary sittings is not more than fifty, each sitting lasting about five hours; in the light of the Bundestag's powers of control, this average figure does not seem excessive.

The permanent assembly system is often combined with the use of annual sessions. In that event the close of one session is determined by the opening of the next session. In Denmark under constitutional law the Folketing convenes each year on the first Tuesday of October and remains officially in session throughout the entire year, even though ordinarily it does not meet at all during the summer. In practice the session lasts for eight months. In Iceland, Luxembourg and Norway the session is also annual but its effective length is six or seven months. In the Netherlands the session officially opens on the third Tuesday in September and closes on the Saturday preceding the third Tuesday of September of the following year. Each Chamber decides of its own accord on what days it will sit during that period. Neither Chamber appears to take unfair advantage of its permanent character: the first Chamber sits on an average fifty days a year, and the Second Chamber eighty days. The Belgian Parliament which, subject to a royal right to dissolve it after forty days, has an annual session beginning on the second Tuesday in November only sits for eighty days out of the eight effective months of the session.

Provided that it is not abused, the practice of permanent session enables Parliament to devote as much time as it chooses to the effective performance of its duties, and ensures that it remains independent of the executive. But a danger arises if it puts no limit on its sittings. A Parliament which sits permanently is likely to be muddle-headed and over-excited; party bickering becomes rife. Political problems give rise to artificial feuds which do not necessarily reflect the country's real feelings; antagonisms are aggravated and embittered; and, what is worse in a parliamentary system, a government is hamstrung by constant battery of questions and motions of censure which leave no time for steady administration and can have unfortunate consequences for ministerial stability.

SITTINGS OF PARLIAMENT

At the other end of the scale from the permanent session is the system under which sessions are fixed by the executive. This system is monarchical in origin, and the underlying principle is that the assemblies should meet only when necessary in order to transact legislative business and approve the national budget. The Monarch, or in his name the government, summons Parliament and brings the session to an end.

This idea is hardly compatible with the parliamentary principle that Parliament should scrutinise the actions of the government and be free to do so without the government's permission. That is why specific provision is made to ensure regular meetings of the Parliaments of countries in which the opening and closing of sessions is the prerogative of the Crown. In Ghana, Laos and Libya the constitutions provide that Parliament shall meet at least once a year. The interval between sessions may be laid down; it is a maximum of six months in India and Pakistan, twelve months in Nigeria. In Libya and the United Arab Republic when the Head of State fails to convene Parliament, it may meet as of right. In Greece the King must convene the Chamber once a year; and he may suspend a session only once for not less than thirty days, unless the Chamber agrees to a longer period.

In Great Britain the power to convene Parliament resides in the Crown. The only condition laid down by statute is that a new Parliament must be summoned within three years of the dissolution of the last one. In practice however the need to grant supply to renew each year the authorisation to maintain a standing army and to prolong each year the Army Act (the statute securing the discipline of the military) meant that sessions of the British Parliament became regular at an early date. At the same time there is no constitutional provision governing their maximum length so that sometimes a session may last for more than a year. The British system is marked by the absence of rules and regulations; in their place is the concept and tradition of the public interest. For all that the British Parliament does normally hold a session each year from October or November to the end of July, amounting to an average of 160 sitting days a session. Without meeting for so long or so often the Parliaments of Australia, Canada, Ireland and New Zealand use the session in a way similar to that of the British House of Commons.

Between the permanent session at the one end of the scale and the session fixed by the executive at the other there is room for any number of systems which attempt to strike a balance between two contradictory ideas; the principle of the sovereignty of Parliament and the exigencies of practical government, parliamentary scrutiny and the exigencies of the public service. A method most frequently used is to lay down in the constitution periods during which Parliament may meet and transact business. These provisions bind the executive as well as Parliament itself. As a rule these periods are known as ordinary sessions which means first that they open each year as a matter of course on a fixed date but more important that their closing date is also fixed so that it is impossible for an assembly to sit permanently. This kind of session is being adopted more and more as the general practice; and there seems to be a growing tendency to shorten markedly its length. In Cameroon Parliament may only meet twice for 30 days. In Somalia and Tunisia the constitution provides for two ordinary sessions of at least three months and of at least two months in the Central African Republic, Monaco and Senegal. In France there are also two sessions a year, one of 24 days and the other of 90 days. In Libya sessions last for more or less the same time.

The two sessions may be much longer as in Sweden where the first session lasts from 10 January to 31 May, and the second from 15 October to 15 December. The same applies in Israel: the first session is from October to April and the second from May to August. In Finland, although the session must end after 120 days with or without interruption, Parliament may decide to extend it. In practice it sits from the beginning of February to the end of May and from the beginning of September to the end of December. In Austria the Constitution provides for a minimum length for sessions, two months for the spring session and four for the autumn session.

It is also possible to have only one session of varying length. In the United States a session lasts from 3 January to 31 July though it may be extended if circumstances require. During a session neither House may adjourn for more than three days without the consent of the other. In Brazil there is one session lasting from 15 March to 15 December, in the Argentine from 1 May to 30 December, and in Chile from 21 May to 19 September. In the Philippines the session opens on the fourth Monday in January; it may not last for more than 100 days.

Neither sessions described as annual nor ordinary sessions—as has been seen—cover an entire year. There are long periods when Parliament is in recess usually for vacations, whether summer or winter. In these periods events grave enough to justify recalling Parliament may occur. To cater for this eventuality most constitutions allow for the possibility of extraordinary sessions.

These sessions may begin on the initiative of the executive, Head of State, Sovereign or President of the Republic, or Government (in

SITTINGS OF PARLIAMENT

Argentina, Austria, Belgium, Brazil, Cameroon, the Central African Republic, Chile, Finland, France, Greece, Iceland, Israel, Italy, Japan, Laos, Libya, Monaco, the Philippines, Senegal, Somalia, Sweden, Tunisia, Turkey and the United Arab Republic). In the United States the President can convene each House in special session but can only bring them to an end in the unlikely event of disagreement between them on the date of the adjournment. This is a reasonable practice because the executive is in the best position to judge whether a meeting of Parliament, other than in ordinary circumstances, is desirable. This right ought not to be refused to it because the efficient working of the machinery of government depends upon it.

How far should Parliament itself be at liberty to call for an extraordinary session? This is an incontestable right of Parliament, though one which needs qualification if the drawbacks of the permanent assembly system are to be avoided. Many constitutions have saving clauses for this purpose, though their nature varies considerably. Only in Italy, Somalia and Turkey is the President of the Chamber alone empowered to convene an extraordinary session. In Israel the House committee takes this decision. As a general rule a request has to be made by a given number of members, a provision designed to emphasise the serious nature of an extraordinary session. The number is two thirds of members of the Assembly in Cameroon, Monaco and the Central African Republic and at least half in France, Laos, Lebanon, Senegal, Tunisia and the United Arab Republic. In Chile and Libya a majority of each of the two Chambers is necessary. Several countries pay heed to the rights of minorities. In Sweden a request for an extraordinary session must be presented by 65 members of the upper House or 100 members of the lower House. One third of the members is enough in Austria, Brazil and Italy as well as in Czechoslovakia, Poland, Hungary and Rumania, a quarter in Japan and Somalia, one fifth in Bulgaria and 25 members in Israel. The Supreme Soviet of the U.S.S.R. may be convened if only one republic of the union requests it. But in practice an extraordinary session is rarely requested by an individual member. On the one hand it is superfluous in Parliaments where ordinary sessions last relatively long and on the other it raises its own problems because in some instances its length is limited and in others the order of business has to be determined in advance or the executive may be empowered to refuse requests made by members. This is particularly the position in France and Japan.

While the regulations governing parliamentary sessions are definitely important, the length of the sessions themselves is a good deal

ORGANISATION OF PARLIAMENT

more important because it is a revealing indication of the relative importance of Parliament in any country. There is often a wide discrepancy between the letter of the law and what happens in practice; it was shown above for example that in Great Britain Parliament sits for a lengthy period each year, though there is no written statute requiring it to do so. In some other countries clear constitutional requirements as to the number and length of sessions are not always applied. The number of sitting days of each Parliament gives an idea, if not of the amount of work done, at least of that Parliament's place in its machinery of government. More than 150 sitting days seems to be the maximum. This is the average total in Great Britain, Italy, the United States and Chile. In most countries Parliament sits for about 100 days corresponding to a session of five or six months. This is the average in Finland, France, Greece, India, Israel, the Netherlands, Pakistan and Turkey.

The Parliaments of Belgium, Ireland, Japan, New Zealand and Switzerland sit for an average of 80 sitting days. If it sits for fewer days, Parliament would appear to make a relatively small contribution. This is the position in the Lebanon, Monaco and Liberia in which Parliament sits for no more than 40 days.

There remains the U.S.S.R. and the countries of Eastern Europe where two ordinary sessions a year is normal. Their duration is particularly brief: they sit depending on the circumstances from two to seven days, which corresponds approximately to about a dozen sittings a year, though the sittings are usually long. In Poland where the annual average of sittings is more than a dozen and in Yugoslavia where since the new constitution the Federal Assembly meets from ten to fifteen days are exceptions to the general rule. But it should be remembered that in these Parliaments the basic work of legislation is done by committees which sit frequently between sessions. The nature and character of the parliamentary session shows how the scope of Parliament varies from one country to another. But however the status of Parliament varies the work of Parliament generally falls into three main categories, namely legislation, the control of finance and the scrutiny of the administration.

PART THREE

Legislative Function of Parliament

According to the classical tradition of representative government, the power to legislate resides in Parliament. The making of laws is the business of Parliament and only of Parliament. To this statement of principle there are a number of exceptions which are considered before the process of law-making in different Parliaments is described.

11. Limitations on the Legislative Power of Parliament

THE SPHERE OF LAW – THE REFERENDUM – THE STATE OF EMERGENCY

The legislative power of Parliament may be limited for three reasons. First there is the concept of the proper sphere for law-making; secondly there is the infringement that arises when public opinion can express itself directly during the legislative process; and thirdly there is the 'state of emergency' which is recognised in a growing number of countries.

1. THE SPHERE OF LAW

The concept of law, like that of the budget which is treated in Part IV of this book, has been shaped by the events that marked the emergence of Parliaments in the teeth of royal power which gradually lost its absolute character.

Since the seventeenth century political scientists have frequently attempted to delimit precisely the field of action of the various institutions of the state. A theory known as the separation of powers has been evolved according to which the sum total of a state's authority is divided into three spheres—legislative, executive and judicial. Even today this division serves as a framework for many constitutions and treatises on law; but it owes more to a confused understanding of what ought to be the democratic tradition than to a grasp of the facts on which that tradition is actually based. Within the principle of separate powers however the legislature is most important. It lays down basic principles which the executive has to apply and which the judiciary has to use as its frame of reference. The legislative body takes precedence over the other two. In a democratic system this legislative body is Parliament. It represents the sovereign people, and it alone is competent to express the will of the people in the form of law.

Despite this theoretical division the sphere of law remains imprecise. Those who frame constitutions have seldom taken the trouble to define the legislative function as opposed to, say, the executive function which is the province of the government or to determine Parliament's proper scope. But the idea of reserving certain functions for Parliament while relieving it of less important matters is not new. For a long time now, confronted with the apparatus of regulation that is necessary for the modern state, political theorists have suggested drawing up a list of subjects which are proper for a statute and another list of subjects which are proper for regulations which can come into force without direct action by Parliament. This kind of '*a priori*' classification of legislative matters appears attractive; unfortunately it does not always correspond to reality because the importance of any particular matter may depend on the circumstances. This classification could also prevent Parliament from debating a serious political matter at a given moment for the sole reason that it was said to be outside its proper field. If that happened the rights and duties of the nation's representatives would be seriously traversed. On the other hand some such classification would relieve Parliament of subsidiary matters and allow it to concentrate on matters of national interest.

The strictest application of this idea of shared authority is to be seen in France under the constitution of 1958. The principle that the actions of the executive must be within the law is of course maintained. In making law Parliament continues to lay down the framework within which the activity of public authorities unfolds but its own actions are bounded by predetermined limits. It may no longer legislate on the matters listed in Article 34 of the Constitution. For some of these matters Parliament may 'define the rules', for others it may only 'determine the fundamental principles', a distinction which is not easy to grasp. In contrast to the previous regime however Parliament's powers have been radically altered. Before 1958 every matter fell within the authority of Parliament; the two Chambers defined as they wished the proper scope for government regulations. Now regulation has become the norm and legislation the exception: the constitution delimits Parliament's power to make laws and what is left is for the executive. Moreover a strict control is exercised over the constitutional validity of laws in order to prevent Parliament from extending its jurisdiction.

Outside France constitutions rarely define what is proper for a statute. In Cameroon, the Central African Republic and Senegal however the French example has been closely followed. But it is important not to confuse the sharing of authority between the sphere of law and the sphere of regulation with the solution adopted in the Netherlands of listing the matters which may be treated only by law.

LIMITATIONS ON THE LEGISLATIVE POWER OF PARLIAMENT

This list is not intended to prevent Parliament from taking up other problems; its purpose is to ensure that some important matters are dealt with by the representatives of the nation and not by anyone else. Reference must also be made to regimes of a federal type where, as in the United States, the authority of the Central Parliament is limited to a certain number of matters which are specified in the Constitution.

2. THE REFERENDUM

Parliament's legislative monopoly may also be infringed when the task of making laws is entrusted at least in part to the sovereign people on the principle of direct or semi-direct democracy. Under this procedure public opinion can in certain instances express itself during the legislative process.

The most widely adopted form of popular expression is the referendum. It is most often used on constitutional matters because in democracies the constituent, sovereign power resides in the people, although they may wish to delegate it to elected representatives.

The legislative referendum under which ordinary bills are submitted for approval is more restricted in its use. For that reason the criteria for recourse to the referendum are fairly stringent. In Switzerland it requires a petition by 30,000 electors or eight cantonal governments. Moreover financial bills and bills declared urgent by both Chambers on a vote by an absolute majority of their memberships may not be submitted to a referendum.

In France the legislative referendum was introduced by the constitution of 1958. The right to call for a referendum is vested in the President of the Republic on the proposal of the government during a session or on a joint resolution of the two Chambers. The intention was first to avoid the referendum's being used to legislate when Parliament is not sitting and secondly to allow Parliament to call the government to account when it initiates a proposal for a referendum. The objects of the referendum are also limited: it may only be used for bills dealing with the machinery of government and bills embodying a community agreement or ratifying a treaty which though within the scope of the constitution do affect the balance of public authority. In Spain the Head of State also has the power to submit bills to a popular vote if he thinks them of first importance or interest.

There is also a particular form of referendum which allows the people to express opposition to the enforcement of an Act of Parliament. In Italy for example the partial or complete repeal of an Act of Parliament may be submitted to referendum if requested by 500,000 electors or five small regional councils. The repeal of an Act requires a majority of votes cast and a majority of the electors to have taken part in the vote. But this 'popular veto' does not extend to Acts of Parliament relating to finance, to amnesty or cancellation of sentence, or to the ratification of international treaties. In Denmark a referendum to repeal an Act of Parliament can be initiated only by the members of the Folketing: one third of the members may request it.

In the U.S.S.R. popular consultation or referendum on any matter takes place if proposed by the Presidium of the Supreme Soviet or if requested by a union republic. But it is rarely used; and this is the position in other countries either because of the difficulties inherent in a referendum or because of the restricted scope for its use.

3. THE STATE OF EMERGENCY

Nowadays a more and more important place in written constitutions is being given to the state of emergency. It is frequently invoked as a justification for lapses from constitutional regularity. At first sight it seems unnecessary to make special rules for this contingency because the existing authorities are equipped to deal with it, and the legislature can itself take exceptional steps to deal with exceptional events. But recent historical experience has shown that the ordinary processes may be inadequate in times of crises when it is most necessary for the machinery of government to work. To deal with these circumstances certain procedures have been developed which have the effect of relieving Parliament of its legislative power and of placing it in the hands of an authority which can take decisions at the necessary speed.

There are essentially two kinds of procedure for a state of emergency. In one Parliament does take part; in the other it does not.

France provides the most striking example of a Parliament which for this purpose is entirely relieved of its legislative authority. The constitution provides that in exceptional circumstances the President of the Republic shall take the place of the government, the two Chambers and all other public authorities. He may take any step that he thinks necessary. He acts alone in the name of the nation and to safeguard its interests. Two conditions have to be fulfilled. First the institutions, independence or territorial integrity of the Republic or its ability to carry out its international commitments must be threatened in a serious and immediate way. Secondly the ordinary working of the central authorities set up by the constitution must be interrupted. When these two conditions are fulfilled, the Head of State may take special powers after officially consulting the Prime Minister, the Presidents of the two Chambers and the constitutional council. He informs the nation in a message of what has occurred. The steps he takes must be designed to enable the central authorities to resume normal working as quickly as possible. The constitution provides that Parliament shall meet automatically and that the National Assembly may not be dissolved. These are the only provisions which in practice limit the extent of the exceptional powers conferred on the President of the Republic; and in particular it is possible for Parliament to impeach the Head of State before the High Court for high treason. But the two Chambers are not empowered to take any part in decisions of a legislative character taken under the exceptional powers.

The position is analogous in Cameroon where there are however degrees of emergency. The President of the Republic may when circumstances require proclaim a state of emergency by decree, and special powers provided by federal law then vest in him. If there is a serious threat to the life, independence, or territorial integrity of the nation or its public authorities, the President of the Republic, after consulting the prime ministers of the federal states, may proclaim a state of emergency by decree and take any steps that he thinks necessary. The nation is informed by message and the national federal assembly meets automatically.

In Tunisia if there is an imminent threat to the institutions, security or independence of the Republic or if the normal working of the central authorities is interrupted, the President of the Republic may take the exceptional measures that the circumstances require. These measures cease to have effect when the circumstances which gave rise to them have come to an end. The President of the Republic sends a message to the National Assembly explaining his actions.

The constitution of Ghana also provides for special powers of the same kind to be exercised by the Head of State who may alter the existing law but not the Constitution itself.

In Senegal circumstances may enable exceptional powers to be exercised in the same way as in France. But the constitution is specific that these powers may not be used to alter the constitution itself and, a difference of great importance, the National Assembly which meets automatically must be informed within fifteen days in a message from the President of all the legislative measures which have been taken by the President. These measures become null and void if a bill to ratify them is not introduced in good time; and the Assembly has the power to amend them. This *a posteriori* control by Parliament is the only method of ensuring that the exceptional powers are not used for purposes other than those for which they were destined. This kind of control is also found in several countries where it has been thought useful to maintain the principle of legality while at the same time authorising a state of emergency.

It often happens that the use of exceptional powers is only authorised when Parliament is not sitting. This is the position in the United Arab Republic. If circumstances require and if the National Assembly is not sitting the President of the Republic may make decrees carrying the force of law and take decisions which would normally fall within the competence of the National Assembly. provided that he submits them to the Assembly at its next sitting They may then be rejected by the Assembly if a majority of two thirds of its members is forthcoming. They cease to have effect from the date on which they are rejected.

In India if the Head of State thinks it necessary he may promulgate ordinances having the force of law. This action may only be taken when Parliament is not sitting. These ordinances must be laid before each House, and they cease to have effect after six weeks from the meeting of Parliament unless Parliament decides to annul them during that period or to ratify them.

A similar position is found in Somalia. The government may make temporary measures carrying the force of law, and they are promulgated as such by the President of the Republic and must be laid before the National Assembly in order to be ratified as part of the ordinary law. The constitution of the Central African Republic also provides for a state of emergency when Parliament is not sitting. Decrees made by the President of the Republic come into force immediately but must be laid before the Assembly on the first day of its next session. Otherwise they become null and void.

The Yugoslav constitution of 1963 has provisions on the same subject. In the event of war or danger of immediate war the President of the Republic may promulgate decrees carrying the force of law if the Assembly is not sitting. These decrees must be submitted to the Assembly for ratification as soon as it can meet. During the state of war and if the interests of national defence require, the provisions of the constitution relating to specific rights and liberties of citizens, the rights of self-governing bodies and the powers of political and administrative organisations may be suspended.

In some western European countries a state of emergency does not prevent Parliament from taking decisive action. In Iceland the Head of State may make provisional decrees between sessions if they are necessary. They must all be submitted to Parliament as soon as it meets. Their promulgation depends on their confirmation by the Assembly and they become null and void automatically if the Assembly passes a bill under the ordinary procedure. The President of the Austrian Federation may in exceptional circumstances make provisional decrees amending the ordinary law. But a series of precautions are built in to avoid the abuse of this power. First the President may only act on the proposal of the federal government with the sole object of saving the country from irreparable harm at a time when the National Council is not sitting. Moreover before making a proposal the government has to secure the agreement of the permanent sub-committee of the principal committee of the National Council. Finally the decrees must be countersigned by every member of the government and immediately laid before Parliament which shall decide in the last resort whether they should be upheld. In any event decrees may not traverse constitutional provisions, financial legislation nor certain basic social rights such as freedom to form trade unions or the protection of tenants.

The Greek constitution makes provision for a similar procedure. When the House is not sitting, the King may promulgate decrees on matters of extreme urgency but he must do so on the advice of a special committee of members appointed at the beginning of each session. The number of members of that committee may not be less than one fifth of the total number of members, and royal decisions have to be approved by relative majority but with two thirds of the members present. Bills to modify repeal or annul these decrees presented by members during the first three months after the Chamber reassembles must be given priority in the order of legislative business provided that they are supported by fifteen members.

In Italy the rights of Parliament are more effectively secured. If urgent action is necessary, the government may adopt on its own responsibility measures having the provisional force of law. But it must submit them on the same day to the two Chambers for ratification; and even if Parliament is dissolved the two Chambers must be convened for this purpose and must sit within five days. The decrees lose their force as from their date of origin if they have not been ratified within sixty days of their publication.

The need for urgent action can sometimes be used as a kind of rebuff to the legislative power of Parliament. In the Lebanon by making a decree after consulting the Council of Ministers the President of the Republic may give the force of law to any bill declared

LEGISLATIVE FUNCTION OF PARLIAMENT

urgent which the Assembly has not passed within forty days of its introduction.

Comparable with this procedure are the time limit and other conditions with which the Federal Republic of Germany hedges the concept of 'legislative necessity'. This position arises when a vote of confidence has been requested by the Chancellor, an absolute majority has not been obtained and yet the Diet has not been dissolved. If the Diet has rejected a bill declared urgent by the government, the President may proclaim a state of legislative necessity if requested to do so by the Chancellor and if the federal council agrees. The effect of this declaration is to give the bill the force of law after a second reading and a second rejection by the Diet provided that it has been agreed to by the federal council. During his term of office the federal Chancellor may apply this procedure to any bill rejected under these conditions by the Diet provided that he does so within the six months of his proclamation of a state of legislative necessity. When this period has expired, the same federal Chancellor may not have recourse to this exceptional procedure during his term of office. So far it has never been used.

It has been shown that more and more countries are adopting constitutional provisions, some of them absolutist in character, which have the effect of withdrawing from Parliament its essential function of making laws.

Moreover where Parliament retains full possession of this function, it does not always play a decisive part in the various stages of the complex proceedings which result in an Act of Parliament.

12. Introduction of Bills

THE RIGHT TO INITIATE LEGISLATION – PROCEDURE FOR INTRODUCING BILLS – THE DECLINING CONTRIBUTION OF INDIVIDUAL MEMBERS

The first stage of the legislative process is the introduction of a bill. A bill proposes either a change in the existing law or makes new proposals; it is the first draft of what will ultimately become a statute. The power to take the step from which a statute emerges and without which it would not exist is of the utmost importance.

From this stage onwards the legislative monopoly of Parliament is markedly encroached upon. Even if the type of system—hardly compatible with democratic government—where the executive has exclusive powers is left on one side, comparative law makes it clear that the right to introduce bills is usually shared between the government and Parliament. Indeed this theoretical division of labour tends to give way to a system under which the government definitely takes the lead in introducing bills. This is what emerges from the study of the right to initiate legislation, the various methods of exercising that right in Parliament and the procedure of the message from the Head of State used in some countries.

1. THE RIGHT TO INITIATE LEGISLATION

It is implicit in the concept of democracy that the initiative in law-making should rest with the elected Parliament. At the same time it is understood in fact and in law that this right is always shared with the executive.

The function of the government is to apply a given policy. The government is better acquainted than anyone else with the needs of the country, and because of the more and more complex nature of the problems that have to be solved, it is technically better equipped than individual members of Parliament to draft bills which are acceptable from the legal standpoint. In most countries therefore the government has the right to introduce bills whether its ministers are members of Parliament or not. Where they are, it can be argued that Parliament has the exclusive right to initiate legislation.

In countries where there is strict separation of powers as in the United States, members of the legislative assemblies alone have the right to introduce bills. Even when the President either personally or through his executive officials recommends to Congress a given measure as part of his general policy, the bill embodying it must be sponsored by a member of Congress. In practice however the exercise of this right amounts to initiating legislation because the President does not merely outline the general gist of legislation he would like to see enacted; he sends to Congress a complete draft. This draft is enclosed in a message to the Speaker of the House and the President of the Senate. It is noticed in the Journal and referred to the competent committee. No provision of the constitution or rule of procedure requires this bill to be taken up; but it is customary, even when the President's own party does not have a majority, for the chairman of the committee to which the bill is is referred to present it in his own name. He presents it either in its original form or as amended to suit his own views. A similar procedure is followed in the Philippines and Liberia.

In the Western parliamentary democracies the separation of powers is not so strict, and the Head of State's message, where that institution exists, has not the same importance because governments have the right to initiate legislation directly. In most of the Parliaments influenced by the British model messages are sent from the Crown when it is desired to introduce a bill on certain specific subjects. When the House of Commons receives a message, it considers it immediately and if necessary makes a reply in the form of an address, at the same time ordering the preparation of the bill referred to in the message. In the Netherlands and Sweden it is the practice for every government bill to be accompanied by a message recommending that it should be passed.

This system of messages designed to set in motion the legislative process should not be confused with the 'speech from the throne' made at the opening of a parliamentary session nor with formal statements on matters of policy made by the Head of State on the occasion of important national or international events. The first of these procedures is provided for in some European monarchies such as Great Britain, Luxembourg, the Netherlands and most of the countries in the Commonwealth. The royal speech normally sets out the government's programme for the year and ministers are entirely responsible for it. The Assembly replies with an address. Provision for messages of a political character by the Head of State is made in many constitutions. This is usually one of the methods by which Parliament is kept informed so that it can follow and scrutinise the activities of the executive. While in some countries such as Cameroon, the Central African Republic, Czechoslovakia, the Netherlands and Nigeria messages may give rise to debate—they never do so in France, Spain or Italy—they are never formally voted upon by Parliament.

In bicameral Parliaments the right to initiate legislation raises a special problem where the two Houses are not on an equal footing. The two Houses have equal rights in Belgium, Italy, Japan, Laos, Sweden and Switzerland. Although the five councils comprising the Federal Assembly of Yugoslavia have specific fields of competence,

INTRODUCTION OF BILLS

each may introduce a bill on a matter within the competence of another council.

By contrast in the Netherlands a bill may not be introduced in the first chamber, the upper House. The same is true in Norway of the Lagting. This last example may seem particularly strange seeing that the two Houses are the product of the same election and can be regarded on the same footing as Houses elected by universal suffrage; in fact the difference in treatment is merely the outcome of a desire to improve the effectiveness of the work of Parliament. In Austria and the Federal Republic of Germany the difference between the two Houses is less marked, but there is a distinct suggestion of hierarchy. In Austria bills can be put before the Federal Council, but a bill may only be sent to the lower House through the intermediary of the federal government. In the Federal Republic of Germany government bills are submitted first to the Federal Council which has three weeks in which to express its views. After this period the bill is laid before the Bundestag together with a statement of the Federal Council's views (if they have been expressed) and the government's reply.

In most other bicameral Parliaments the difference can be seen most clearly in financial matters. It is based on the belief that the authorisation of expenditure and the imposition of taxation must be the preserve of the House elected by universal suffrage, on the principle that the people must give their consent to the financial burdens which they will have to bear. The Parliament Act 1911 took from the House of Lords any power over money bills other than the power to delay them for one month. The position is similar in Australia, Canada, Ceylon, India, Ireland, Libya and Nigeria, as well as in Argentina, Brazil, the Philippines and the United States, where financial legislation can only be introduced in the popular House, although the Senate keeps the power to amend.

Some other restrictions on the powers of the second chamber though less interesting are worth noting. In the Philippines, bills of a local or private nature can only be introduced in the lower House; and the same applies in Argentina and Brazil to legislation relating to the recruitment and strength of the armed forces.

While the right to initiate bills is generally exercised only by Parliament and by governments, it can also be granted to other bodies. In the People's Democracies specific parliamentary bodies are so empowered such as the Presidium in Albania, Hungary and the U.S.S.R.; the Council of State in Poland and Rumania; and the Presidential Bureau in Czechoslovakia where the right to initiate bills is also accorded to the President of the Republic and the Slovak National Council. In Italy the national council on the economy and on labour may if the appropriate majority agrees submit bills to Parliament on matters within its competence. More unusual is the right to initiate legislation enjoyed in the United Kingdom, Finland and Sweden by the church, though it applies only to laws on ecclesiastical matters.

Apart from the procedure by petition for a private bill in the British Parliament, the direct initiation of legislation by the people is rare. It derives from a strict construction of the people's sovereignty, the object being to offset any tendency by members to be lazy by inviting them to legislate on particular topics. Among Western democracies only Italy has a procedure of this kind. Regional councils can submit bills to Parliament in accordance with the same procedure as is followed for government or other bills. In addition, a body of 50,000 electors can introduce a bill in a fully drafted form. In Somalia 10,000 electors are enough to set in motion a similar procedure which however excludes financial legislation.

In the U.S.S.R. this principle has been broadened and altered in character. The right to initiate legislation is given not only to the Government, the Presidium and the Chambers of the Supreme Soviet but also to the federal Republics through their supreme organs, to the permanent parliamentary committees, to the procurator general, to the supreme court and in general to any other public body represented by its central agency. The Yugoslavian Constitution of 1963 takes the principle a step further by extending it to every citizen as well as to social, political and commercial organisations and associations of citizens whatever their object.

The variety of forms which the initiative in legislation can take must not blind us to the fact that it is first and foremost an inherent right of a member of Parliament. How is this right exercised?

2. PROCEDURE FOR INTRODUCING BILLS

(a) *Individual or Collective Presentation*

According to traditional parliamentary practice every member of Parliament in his individual capacity has the right to introduce bills. Similarly there is as a general rule nothing to prevent several members from concerting their efforts where they agree upon a particular proposal and wish to make what amounts to a collective presentation of a bill.

INTRODUCTION OF BILLS

Some Parliaments cling firmly to the right of the individual. In the House of Representatives of the United States (though not in the Senate) if several members wish to put forward a particular proposal, each must present a bill in his own name. In Great Britain the rule on individual presentation of bills is regarded as so important that when a bill has been passed by one House, it will only be considered by the other House if it is taken up by one of its members. In other countries the number of members who may back a bill is limited. The number is five in Luxembourg, six in Belgium and the Lebanon and ten in Libya and Norway.

Some countries disregard traditional parliamentary practice and do not allow an individual member to introduce a bill; members of Parliament are obliged to combine for this purpose. The principle underlying this requirement is no doubt the desire for bills to be sifted at the outset so that only those supported by a considerable weight of opinion go forward.

Collective presentation is the rule in some of the People's Democracies. In Bulgaria a bill must be signed by at least one fifth of the total number of members, in Rumania by at least thirty members and in Poland by at least fifteen.

There is a similar obligation in the Bundestag of the Federal Republic of Germany. Here the minimum number of fifteen members who must sign a bill corresponds to the minimum number necessary to form a political group. In practice the signature of the president of the group constitutes an adequate surety. Eight signatures are required in the Austrian National Council, ten in Ethiopia and fifteen in Iran. In the Spanish Cortes a bill must have the support of fifty signatories. In Japan twenty names are required in the House of Representatives and ten in the House of Councillors, or fifty and twenty respectively for bills imposing a financial charge.

(b) Methods of Presentation

Whether the right to introduce a bill is individual or collective, the method of presenting bills follows well defined practices. In those parliamentary systems which are most jealous of the individual right of members of Parliament in legislative matters, the introduction of a bill is simply an expression of will on the part of a member which he expresses by handing it in to the office responsible for receiving it. In the House of Representatives of the United States bills are put in a box known as 'the hopper' at the side of the presidential tribunes. In the Senate the bill must be authorised in plenary session before being sent to the bureau. If objection is raised, the author of the bill must wait at least one day before it is sent there. In the U.S.S.R. and in some of the People's Democracies members can introduce bills orally, and the introduction is then recorded in the minutes of proceedings of the House. Sometimes a bill has to be submitted for an expression of view by the president of the chamber before it can be received. This is the position in Japan; here a bill must also be accompanied by an explanatory memorandum and a special note on its financial implications. This intimation of expenditure is also required in Czechoslovakia. In the United Arab Republic every bill introduced by one or more members is referred to a committee which recommends whether or not it should be proceeded with. No further stages may be taken until the Chamber decides the matter. A similar committee is found in Libya; it has to make a report on each bill within fifteen days. The bill is referred to the competent permanent committee only if the Chamber approves it after considering the first committee's report. In Spain the first consideration is entrusted to the permanent committee. In Belgium the House itself may be consulted by the President at the request of the author of the bill and after its inclusion in the orders of the day. The House may either take up the bill and send it to the competent committee, or adjourn its further consideration, or resolve not to proceed with it.

In Parliaments of the British type presentation of a bill is often preceded by a request by the author of the bill for leave to introduce it, after the title indicating the purpose of the bill has been placed on the order paper. In Great Britain the right of members to introduce legislation is based as always on practical considerations which pays little heed to legal theory.

The procedure for introducing a bill in the House of Commons is for its long and short title to be placed on the order paper. The short title is then read out in the House. This constitutes the first reading of bills whose main purpose is to impose a financial charge. The House after approving a resolution adopted by a Committee of the whole House may order a bill founded on that resolution to be brought in. Particular members are specified to prepare and bring it in. There is also the introduction of bills preceded by a motion. This procedure, a survival from the past, enables a member who has been unable to have a bill in which he is especially interested placed on the order paper as a result of the ballot; so he can still set the legislative process in motion. At the beginning of public business on two days a week a short period may be set aside for the purpose. This is known as the 'ten minute rule'. After hearing one speaker for the bill and one against, the House may if it sees fit give leave for the bill to be introduced. This is also a regular practice in Israel.

INTRODUCTION OF BILLS

A distinction has to be made between motions accompanied by a complete bill and motions which do not submit the terms of a bill but merely request the government to introduce a bill on a particular subject. Only the presentation of motions accompanied by a complete bill can be said to constitute the introduction of a bill. Both forms are used in Finland where the first form has led to the enactment of many important statutes. But it is significant that several other European democracies of long standing, Sweden and Switzerland in particular, only make use of the second, which amounts in practice to giving the government a monopoly in the presentation of bills. The second form is gradually gaining ground. Given the complex character of most subjects of legislation, this development is to be expected. In Norway the abandoning of a constitutional right is particularly noteworthy. A member first submits his bill to the government which may amend it or advise against introducing it. The advice does not necessarily have to be followed, but in practice it always is. In the Central African Republic too a member has to send his bill to the government before being considered by the Assembly or its committees. In Monaco the procedure represents a blend of contributions by the Assembly and the government. When a bill has been passed by the Assembly, it is sent to the government. If the government approves of the bill, it will prepare and send to the Assembly a bill whose objects correspond to those of the bill which the Assembly has passed.

Besides these limitations imposed by the executive power on the rights of private members, there are limitations arising from the rules of procedure. Some are confined to specific matters, others result from the time limits laid down for presenting bills. In countries where the sphere of law is defined in detail in the constitution, a member may not deal with any other matter. In France for example the government may claim that a bill is inadmissible if during its progress through the Chamber it appears to transgress these constitutional limits. If the President of the Chamber concerned does not accept the government's claim, the Constitutional Council must decide the matter within eight days if either party requests that it should be referred to them.

The strictest limitations are placed in many countries on a member's power to introduce bills with financial implications. In most countries influenced by British practice these bills have to be accompanied by a message or recommendation from the executive if they are to be admissible. They are out of order unless founded on a message or a 'recommendation' from the executive. In Canada a member may not introduce a bill if it has any financial incidence.

This is also the position in France and Greece. Bills cannot be introduced by members of the French Parliament if their effect is either to diminish public revenue or to create or increase a charge on the people. The Greek constitution provides that no bill may be introduced by a member if it involves a charge on public expenditure or on the expenditure of local authorities or other bodies or a reduction in their revenue if its object is to grant an appointment or a pension or in general to benefit an individual. The removal of a member's power in matters of expenditure which is tending to become more general may have the object of preventing members from succumbing to the temptations of demagogy; but it may also have the effect of emptying of all its meaning their right to introduce bills because it is rare for a bill not to have any financial implication.

There are also countries in which no provision is made for members to introduce bills of any kind because the government exercises a complete control over legislation.

As a general rule bills may be introduced throughout the session. However some Parliaments have taken the precaution of laying down a terminal date for the presentation of bills to ensure that the programme of business is reasonable. In Iceland unless waived by a vote of the House the time limit is eight weeks from the beginning of the session. In Finland the rule is still more stringent: no bill may be presented later than noon on the fourteenth day after opening of the first session following a general election or later than noon on the tenth day in other sessions. But there is an important exception: a bill may be introduced after that date if it is consequential upon an important parliamentary event such as the presentation or withdrawal of a government bill provided that the bill is introduced within seven days of that event. In Norway the time limit applies not only to bills introduced by private members but also to government bills. Unless authorised by the President a bill may not be presented after 10 January, the session opening at the beginning of October. Sweden has a similar system: the government has ninety days from the opening of the annual session in which to present its bills. Other members have only fifteen days.

(c) Introduction of Bills by Committees

It was shown above that the main purpose of committees is to help Parliament to expedite its business especially by examining bills submitted to them. But should they be granted the right to introduce bills themselves? According to the principle that they are nothing more than working parties without the power to legislate, the answer would be definitely not. Where committees occupy a preponderant influence in a Parliament, the answer would be affirmative. An affirmative answer would be given in Argentina, Brazil, the Philippines and the United States, as well as in Austria, Iceland, Japan and Luxembourg where parliamentary committees may initiate bills on subjects within their terms of reference. This is also the position in Czechoslovakia, Hungary, Rumania, Yugoslavia and in the U.S.S.R. where the permanent committees of the Supreme Soviet and of its Chambers have the right to introduce all types of bills including those concerned with the normal economic plan and the state budget. In Israel, committees have on paper the right to initiate bills on certain subjects such as parliamentary indemnities or the powers of the state controller. In the Netherlands committees, like individual members, are entitled to ask the government to bring in bills which they think desirable.

In other Parliaments committees have the right to introduce bills but only in exceptional circumstances and more particularly in financial matters. In Finland the finance committee and the committee on the bank have this power. In Sweden the committee of ways and means, the bank committee and the constitutional committee have the right to introduce bills on matters within their terms of reference. The practice in the British House of Commons under which bills whose main object is to authorise expenditure or to impose a charge must originate in a Committee of the whole House has already been noted. This committee is entitled to pass resolutions. If they are approved by the House, a bill founded on them is prepared and introduced by a member of the House. In the House of Representatives of the United States the Budget Committee takes the initiative in introducing bills on expenses, the Committee of Ways and Means for bills on financial and the Committee on the Judiciary for consolidation bills.

As a general rule however committees are not empowered to initiate bills as they are to amend bills. But there is nothing to prevent their members from taking action either separately or together to achieve the same result. The ban has the effect of putting a brake on attempts by committees to embark on independent action.

3. THE DECLINING CONTRIBUTION OF INDIVIDUAL MEMBERS

Although the power to legislate is regarded everywhere as belonging absolutely to Parliament, the essential phase in which the legislative process is set in motion appears under modern constitutional practice to concern the executive as well as the legislature. The division between the two powers established by constitutions evolves constantly in favour of the government and to the disadvantage of Parliament. This is a palpable fact which can be observed in most countries.

Why should the contribution made by members to the introduction of bills be declining? In the first place it is the consequence of the complexity of modern laws which, as one commentator has put it, require not only the creative imagination of a political brain but the combined knowledge of an economist and a specialist in a whole series of cognate sciences. The technical resources available to a member of Parliament are greatly inferior to those enjoyed by the government, and his bill bears the marks of this inferiority when contrasted to bills coming from government departments. It has been shown that members may not propose to increase expenditure or reduce revenue. This rule which is being adopted in more and more countries prevents members from bringing in bills on many important topics. It must also be remembered that in some countries only the government is entitled to raise the question of altering the rules.

Even when a bill is forthcoming from an individual member, it is often impossible to find an opportunity to debate it because the time given by Parliament to legislation is largely taken up in considering bills proposed by the government to carry out its policy. It is rare for the government to agree to debate such a bill because its own policy is seen as a unity which requires neither addition nor subtraction. If an idea put forward in a bill by a member seems to the government to be sound, the government will itself take it over and introduce a bill of its own on the same subject. At best it will allow members to legislate only on public matters which do not interfere with the exposition of its own policy.

Theoretically even if a member is convinced that his bill has little chance of being taken up, there is nothing to prevent him from introducing it. In practice if he belongs to the majority party, he will seldom exercise his right. If his bill is worthwhile, the government itself will sponsor it unless it wishes to reward the proposer by allowing him to show publicly his interest in a particular subject. In Western parliamentary practice bills are for this reason most often introduced from the opposition benches. These bills have a special significance which is far removed from the normal one, its main purpose being to embarrass the government by directing attention to weak points in its general policy.

In most Parliaments the right to introduce bills tends more and more to be used by the minority party only. Nothing could explain more clearly the meagre showing of bills deriving from ordinary members. Those which are finally passed are extremely few in number and represent only a small proportion of the laws enacted. About one-third of the total in Great Britain are private members' bills. In France the figures were seven private members' bills out of the fifty-three passed in 1962. In 1963 the figures were thirteen and ninety-eight.

The government is by no means simply the executive agent which implements legislation enacted by Parliament; it is the dominating authority in formative stages of legislation. Parliament has a safeguard in the fact that it is still the deliberating body, and it alone has the right of decision in the last resort. But it loses this protection, at any rate in part, where it has occasion to delegate to the government its own legislative power.

13. Delegated Legislation

Delegated legislation in its ordinary sense has two basic ingredients: Parliament itself must authorise some other body to legislate in its place; and this authority must be some branch of the executive power.

Two kinds of delegated authority that fall outside this delimitation are not discussed in this chapter. These are first the powers to act in a state of emergency which have already been considered. Here the power to legislate is not delegated under a specific decision of Parliament; it is directly conferred either upon the Head of State or on the government through the constitution.

Secondly there is a procedure found in the U.S.S.R. and the People's Democracies under which directing bodies set up by Parliament are authorised to perform certain acts of a legislative character when Parliament itself is not sitting. This power is specially important because the sessions of those Parliaments are usually short. Power is given to the Presidium of the Supreme Soviet in the U.S.S.R., to the Presidium of the Parliaments of Albania, Bulgaria and Hungary, to the Council of State in Rumania and to the Presidential Bureau in Czechoslovakia. The decrees made by these bodies must be submitted to Parliament for approval at its next session. In Poland the most important political and economical matters and in particular the revision of the constitution, the budget and the national plan are excluded from the province of the Council of State. But even in other matters the Council of State has not made use of this procedure since 1957 and so has left intact the legislative authority of the Diet. Nevertheless there is here a genuine delegation of power in which the beneficiary is a body belonging to Parliament and not to the executive.

Delegated legislation in the strict sense of power given to the executive by Parliament to legislate raises one of the most complex problems of contemporary constitutional law. Its complexity arises essentially from the difficulty of determining exactly where to draw the line between what is law and what are regulations, the two spheres according to classic theory being the preserves of Parliament and government respectively. Generations of writers have pondered over this question of the division of power which those who have drafted constitutions have at least until recently left vague more often than not. The accidental vicissitudes of history have thrown up empirical and piecemeal solutions; but the general tendency has been an encroachment upon the exclusive rights of Parliament in legislative matters. This tendency has been officially blessed in some recent constitutions notably the constitution of the fifth French Republic of 1958.

The problem arises in most countries. Ideally in a democratic country all laws should emanate from the direct representatives of the people. But the legal authority of those representatives does not necessarily imply a practical capacity to make laws. Technical intricacies, the ever increasing number of problems to be solved and the urgency of the decisions to be taken fit less and less easily into the traditional pattern of law-making which is not readily adaptable to circumstances and functions that constitutions of the past never contemplated. This discrepancy between the function which Parliament has to discharge and the means at its disposal has been well illustrated since the first World War, and it was aggravated by the economic crises which followed the war and affected many countries. The delegation of legislative power took on a permanent aspect after the second World War when it was officially recognised in some constitutions. But in whatever way power is delegated, the act of delegating does give rise to a serious dilemma: should a country respect the democratic techniques of legislation and accept the risk of dangerously reducing the speed at which laws can be made in times of

DELEGATED LEGISLATION

crisis; or is it better to ensure that this work is done as and when it is required, even if the bounds of democratic government are overstepped in doing so? Both alternatives can be justified in democratic terms. The first is founded on the traditional idea that there should invariably be a measure of national representation; the second is based on the more modern concept that the first concern of parliamentary government should be to produce legislation which will meet the wishes of the people.

Whatever the reasons adduced in its favour, delegated legislation has become current practice in most countries. As a general rule it is authorised by the constitution or by established usage, though there are still a few countries which refuse to admit the principle. Among them are Argentina, Brazil, Ethiopia, Libya, Tunisia, Turkey, the United Arab Republic and Yugoslavia. In the same category are the U.S.S.R. and the People's Democracies. But it has to be remembered that in these countries the absence of delegated legislation is explained by the power given to the directing bodies of Parliament to legislate between sessions subject to later ratification by the parent assemblies.

The delegation of power to the executive can be considered a threat to the supremacy of Parliament if the government tends to abuse that power. This applies with special force in countries where delegated legislation does not appear to conform to the strict letter of the constitution.

This hazard is easily avoided in countries in which Parliament is supreme in all fields—constitutional, legislative and administrative. One result is that the right of Parliament to delegate the power to make laws as and when it wishes has no limit. This is how the delegation of legislative power is viewed in Great Britain. It does not seem to cause difficulty though a glance at the legislation described as delegated makes it clear that most of it consists of regulations of a kind which in other countries would be handled by the executive without any need for delegated power. So the primary effect of the system of delegated legislation has been to invest the government with real power to make regulations in the absence of any other written authority to do so. But this power has developed to a point where the pressure of circumstances and the application of various enabling statutes have made it a substitute in certain instances for Acts of Parliament. Since 1946 the members of the British Parliament have felt it desirable under the Statutory Instruments Act to have a uniform procedure for delegating power, which previously had not followed any principle, and at the same time to keep a more effective control on the legislation delegated. As a result statutory instruments, that is to say, the rules and regulations issued in pursuance of the enabling statute, are divided for practical purposes into two categories. First there are instruments which come into force only after a resolution approving them has been passed in both Houses. This is known as the 'affirmative procedure'. Secondly there are instruments which take effect immediately but can be annulled by a resolution of either House. This is the 'negative procedure'. The annulment must take place within forty days of the date of laying the instruments in the House, less any periods of adjournment for more than four days.

In view of the mass of statutory instruments which are necessary to give effect to the statutes but which might easily escape the notice of the members of Parliament, the House of Commons has had since 1944 a select committee of eleven members whose task is to examine these instruments and to draw the attention of Parliament particularly to all those which they feel warrant a more careful scrutiny, such as instruments with financial implications or with retrospective effect or which have been delayed or are incomplete or obscure. This committee known as the Statutory Instruments Committee was originally set up for one session but it has been re-appointed in every session since. It has no power to pass judgment on the expediency of a statutory instrument; its task is merely to make sure that the exercise of delegated powers is a proper one, and in particular to see to it that matters on which Parliament must maintain the upper hand such as finance and individual liberty do not slip from its grasp through the effect of a statutory instrument. The mere existence of this committee has undoubtedly had a salutary effect because only a small proportion of the total number of instruments examined has had to be drawn to the attention of the House. Most of the instruments put before the committee are in the nature of regulations. Therein lies the remarkable feature of the system. Its purpose is to put a curb on the delegation of legislative power, but in fact it amounts to a means of exercising a greater degree of parliamentary control over the power to issue regulations.

A comparable control is exercised in Australia under the Acts Interpretation Act. All regulations must be published and laid before both Houses. They may be annulled by either House within fifteen days. The position is the same in New Zealand. An Act of Parliament as a rule contains a section authorising the government to make regulations to give effect to its provisions. As soon as they are published these regulations are laid on the table of the House. They can be debated and if necessary considered by the statutes revision committee which may meet even when the House is not sitting in order to draw attention to any abuse of power. In India where in general 'every principal Act of Parliament' contains provisions delegating to the executive power to make rules for the practical working of the Act. These rules must be submitted to both Houses where they may be amended within time limits specified in the original statute. Moreover all regulations emanating from the executive are automatically examined by the committee on subordinate legislation set up within the House of the People to make sure that they do not go beyond the powers conferred by the enabling Act. In Ireland regulations made under delegated powers may be challenged within twenty-one days of the day on which they were laid before Parliament. In addition the ordinary courts have the power to declare void any regulation that violates the enabling statute; and the constitutional validity of regulations may be challenged in the same way as an Act of Parliament. As in most of the countries which have come under British influence, it would appear that in Israel most of the delegated legislation consists of instruments with the character of regulations.

Because of this uncertainty as to where the law ends and the sphere of regulations begins, in Sweden legislation enacted by the Riksdag is so detailed that there is little room for the exercise of the power to make regulations. Sweden offers a unique example in contemporary constitutional law of a limitation of executive powers. Everywhere else the tendency is for the executive to encroach upon the legislative function whether by practice or by constitutional prerogative.

In countries with rigid constitutions the problem of delegating the legislative function presents major legal difficulties because the right to legislate is vested in Parliament, and it cannot be turned over to the executive without infringing the constitution. A bill which confers full powers on the government in effect removes the ensuing measures from the control of the representatives of the people. This step would be a serious challenge to the principle of national sovereignty which is inherent in democratic institutions. The logical solution would be to amend the constitution before the powers are delegated.

Finland has adopted a procedure based on this concept. The power to delegate is exercised in the same way as in Great Britain but in addition whenever the need arises to confer on the government a legal right to make regulations, an enabling statute must be passed under the same procedure as that followed when the constitution is to be amended. Such a system is obviously inapplicable in countries where constitutional revision requires many formalities and imposes significant delays. Equally where delegation of powers is formally forbidden, it is found convenient to stretch the constitutional provisions to their limits by a practice for which the theoretical justification is left to the jurists.

The example of the United States is particularly significant. There is no doubt that on a strict interpretation of the constitution and the principle of the separation of powers the delegation of legislative powers to the President is impossible. But this has not prevented Congress in the last thirty years from delegating to the President the right to legislate in numerous spheres previously reserved for formal Acts of Congress. However the existence of the Supreme Court before which questions of constitutional validity can be raised ensures that these delegated powers are duly limited. In principle it does not admit that Congress can delegate powers which are strictly and exclusively legislative.

France under the Fourth Republic was still more striking an example than the United States, because the constitution provided categorically that 'The National Assembly alone shall pass legislation. It may not delegate that right'. Under the pressure of events the legislature had recourse to certain practices which evaded this provision and which could only be justified by the administrative courts and by constitutional theorists on somewhat tenuous grounds. The constitution of 1958 remedied the matter by formally authorising the delegation of powers.

Belgium has been troubled by the same misgivings for the same reasons. Many theories have been worked out to make it possible in exceptional circumstances to enact a variety of laws known as 'special powers' or 'extraordinary powers', giving the Head of State the right to adopt measures normally coming within the sphere of the legislature. It is recognised that these enabling statutes delimit the scope of the delegated powers and the duration of their validity. As a general rule regulations made under these laws must be submitted to Parliament for approval.

The same might be said of Switzerland, with the difference that the constitution does not specifically refer to the matter. However all the writers on the subject agree that the grant of full powers to the government cannot be justified on constitutional grounds. According to Swiss theory the delegation of power is legitimate on the unwritten principle of urgent necessity. These circumstances are likely to arise at any time, and they pose a special problem for countries like Chile, Denmark, Iran and the Lebanon, as well as Switzerland, where delegated legislation is not authorised by the constitution. In other words the concern for the safety of the state must take precedence over respect for constitutional procedure. 'Necessity knows no law', says the proverb. Here is the perfect illustration of it.

It is no longer necessary to rely on this kind of justification because more and more countries have formally approved the delegation of powers. Two of the first countries to do so after the second World War were Italy and the Federal Republic of Germany. Article 76 of the Italian constitution authorises the delegation of powers provided that the general principles and policy have been laid down by Parliament and that the delegation is for a limited time and for specific purposes. But this safeguard of Parliament's powers may be little more than academic, because it is always possible for Parliament to lay down principles and policies which are so vague that the government has ample latitude. The same provision is found in the constitution of Somalia.

In the Federal Republic of Germany Article 80 of the fundamental law provides that the federal government, a federal minister, or the governments of the Länder may be authorised by law to issue 'regulations having the force of law'. The law must determine the content, purpose and the scope of the delegation, and the legal authority for the regulations must be plainly indicated; if it is not they are liable to be declared null and void.

The French constitution of 1958 put an end to the widespread misconception that the delegation of powers was in some way unconstitutional. Today in order to carry out its programme the government may ask Parliament for authority to make ordinances for a limited period on matters which normally fall within the field of the law as defined in the constitution. These ordinances come into force on publication, but they become null and void if a bill to confirm them is not introduced in Parliament before the date fixed by the enabling statute. On the expiry of that period the ordinances may only be altered by bill if their subject matter falls within the field of the law.

The same provisions are found in the Central African Republic although here powers are delegated to the President of the Republic and not the government, and the enabling statute becomes null and void if Parliament is dissolved. In Tunisia the National Assembly may also authorise the President of the Republic to make decrees for a limited period and for a specific purpose. They must be ratified before the period laid down in the statute has expired. The President also has the power to make decrees between sessions provided that he obtains the agreement of the Assembly's permanent committee concerned and that the decrees are submitted to the Assembly for confirmation during its next ordinary session.

The constitution of Senegal has a more original provision: it inaugurates in favour of the President of the Republic a procedure for delegation that compares with those of France and the Central African Republic and yet has something in common with the methods used in the People's Democracies and with the Italian procedure of granting legislative powers to permanent committees. The Assembly of Senegal can delegate the right of legislation to one of its committees known as the Committee on Delegated Powers. It does so by resolution which has to be made known immediately to the President of the Republic. The committee can then agree to resolutions, and provided that the periods and scope laid down by the Assembly's own resolution have been observed, those resolutions may be promulgated as laws. These laws are laid before the Assembly not later than the first day of the ordinary session following promulgation. If they are not altered by the Assembly in the first fifteen days of the session, they become definitive.

In the Netherlands a compromise solution has been found for the problem of delegated legislation which appears to be satisfactory. The constitution specifies the subjects which must be governed by law; so that in this field there can be no delegation at least on matters of principle. But powers may be freely delegated on all other matters provided that an enabling statute has laid down the general principles to be observed by the government and in some instances that a bill to ratify the delegated legislation is presented in the shortest possible time. So fastidious a concern to safeguard Parliament's right to legislate is rare nowadays.

In the U.S.S.R. and the People's Democracies full power rests with Parliament, the supreme authority within the machinery of government. But in most other countries the government has become a legislator. In the opinion of some jurists this is not an alarming development. It merely indicates a changed concept of parliamentary democracy to which current pressures led inevitably. They argue that in view of the urgent economic and political problems in certain countries Parliament has admitted that it is frequently incapable of fulfilling its legislative function; so the delegation of power tends to become a normal method of government. At the same time there is a shifting of emphasis in the role of Parliament so that its legislative function diminishes but instead a wider and more detailed control over the actions of the government grows up. Against this view it has always to be remembered that while legislation emanating from government departments has the advantage of being more rapid, it is

DELEGATED LEGISLATION

not necessarily of higher quality than that produced by Parliament in accordance with a procedure which, though at times it may be more complex, is calculated to ensure the free expression of all shades of opinion.

14. The Making of Law

THE ROLE OF COMMITTEES – CONSULTATION WITH OUTSIDE INTERESTS – ORDER OF BUSINESS – DEBATE IN THE HOUSE – METHODS OF VOTING – CONSTITUTIONAL BILLS – AGREEMENT BETWEEN THE TWO HOUSES

Whether a bill is introduced by an individual member or at the instance of the government, the process of law-making is set in motion. Members of Parliament are informed of the bill in a variety of ways—by the posting of notices, by announcements in the chamber, by an entry in the minutes of proceedings or the report of debates, and in some countries by a purely formal first reading. If it complies with the rules of order, the bill is then printed and distributed. It has been noted for instance that in the United Arab Republic bills must first be submitted to a committee whose duty it is to sift proposals and decide which should go forward. At this stage before publication bills tabled by individual members in France are examined by the Bureau of the Assembly to ensure that they have no financial implications. In Cameroon this check is made by the Conference of Presidents. In Brazil the Bureau of each Chamber is given forty-eight hours before sending bills to the appropriate committee which is responsible for printing them. Occasionally a bill is published before it has been examined to see whether it is in order. In Great Britain a bill may be withdrawn after it has been presented and printed. The officials of the public bill office check to ensure that it conforms to the standing orders of the House. In particular they consider whether the contents of the bill are covered by the terms of its title and whether the rules dealing with public money have been observed. In Yugoslavia before any debate takes place in the

Chambers, every bill is considered by the Assembly's legislative and judicial committee which sees that it conforms to the constitution and the existing law and that it is in correct form.

If they are in order, government and other bills are distributed, a practice to which there is virtually no exception. Once published or at least distributed to members of Parliament and to the government, a bill follows a procedure the details of which may take a vast variety of forms according to the different countries. But in almost all countries two essential phases can be distinguished. First there is the preparatory phase, generally entrusted to committees whether committees of the whole House, permanent committees or *ad hoc* committees. Secondly there is the phase of debate and decision which is generally a matter for the House.

In some countries this division of labour is subject to variations of greater or less importance, ranging from the exclusive jurisdiction of the House itself to the less orthodox practice of handing over that jurisdiction to committees. The tendency of committees to increase their powers has already been noted; and in some countries such as Italy this increase has been approved by law.

Article 72 of the Italian constitution specifies that the two Chambers may entrust to committees not merely the examination of bills, but also their final enactment. In practice the President of the Chamber designates the bills which follow the ordinary course and those which are treated according to the unusual procedure by which the Chambers divest themselves as it were of their legislative prerogatives and hand them over to committees who then act in the name of the Chamber with full powers. It is true that even up to the final enactment of the statute the Chamber has the power to recall a bill from a committee; and in practice it must be referred to the Chamber if the government, one tenth of the members, or one fifth of the members of the committee so request. This is known as 'automatic return'. It is also true that this procedure cannot apply to certain kinds of bills such as bills on constitutional and electoral matters, bills delegating legislative power, bills to ratify treaties, or bills relating to taxation or public expenditure. The fact remains that this novel procedure is well established and that it applies to bills of ever-growing importance. Even though its task may be lighter, the Chamber itself has given up the function of passing bills which touch several important aspects of the life of the country.

In the same spirit the constitution of Senegal authorises committees to make law when this power is expressly delegated to them by the Assembly.

By contrast in several countries Parliament may decide to debate a bill in the House without referring it to a committee. This procedure is mostly used to consider bills that are urgently needed. It is used in Albania, Czechoslovakia, and the U.S.S.R. In Iran and the Lebanon a bill must be given status of extreme urgency by the Assembly in order to be debated straightaway. An analogous procedure is found in the Chamber of Deputies in Ethiopia and in Japan. In the Argentine a decision to debate the bill must be taken by a majority of two-thirds of the votes cast; even so this can only be done if the bill has no financial implications. It has to be remembered that in the Argentine the House cannot resolve itself into committee as is done in Assemblies on the British model. This is what is done in the Congress of the United States where in order to gain time and to evade the formalities of procedure the two Houses deliberate in committee of the whole House.

Between two extremes of giving full power to committees and making no use of them whatever is the more usual procedure under which the work is shared between House and committee. In many countries which follow the example of Great Britain the activities of committees are under the permanent control of the House, while others apply the continental or American type of procedure which leaves the final decision to the House but grants the committee considerable powers over the content of a bill. The role of committees can thus be regarded as the touchstone in distinguishing various forms of legislative procedure.

1. THE ROLE OF COMMITTEES

The importance of the part played by committees can be determined first by the stage at which bills are referred to them and secondly by the extent of the powers conferred on them to consider bills.

(a) Reference to Committees

The stage at which a bill is referred to a committee is of fundamental importance. Which should consider the bill first—the House itself or the appropriate committee? If it is the House, its decisions of principle will explicitly or implicitly bind the committee and so limit its powers. If it is the committee, the likelihood is that its report will have a profound effect on the decision taken finally by the House.

Most Parliaments have adopted the second alternative. In practice direct reference to a committee as a rule goes hand in hand with the existence of permanent specialised committees. In most of the Western European countries such as Belgium, France, Italy, the Netherlands (Second Chamber), Norway, Spain and Switzerland the President refers the bill directly to a committee. The House does not come into the picture unless there is a dispute between several committees when according to French practice a given number of members may request the appointment of a special committee. The same system applies in Laos, Turkey, Brazil and Japan. In Sweden, the United States and the Philippines the reference of a bill to a committee is announced in the House at the first reading. This stage consists of reading aloud the title of the bill and the names of its proposers without debate.

The countries where bills are first debated by the House before being referred to committee may be divided into two groups. The first comprises Denmark, the Federal Republic of Germany, Iceland and Israel. Committal is ordered after the first reading which is not a pure formality; it can give rise to a general debate during which the general principles of the bill are made clear. The second group consists of Great Britain, Australia, Canada, Ceylon, Ghana, India, Ireland, Nigeria, New Zealand and Sierra Leone. Committal takes place only after the second reading, as a result of which the main principles of the bill are defined. The first reading is merely a formal presentation of the bill except in Australia, India and Ireland where the procedure can be interrupted at this stage if the motion for the presentation of the bill is rejected. In the Australian Senate a motion for the first reading of bills which the Senate may not amend is debatable and requests for amendment may be made to the House of Representatives at that stage.

In the Austrian National Council either of these procedures may be followed. As a general rule bills are committed without a preliminary reading to the appropriate committees; but the government or the sponsor of the bill may ask for an immediate first reading at which its general principles are debated. Then the bill is referred to a committee.

Finland has an unusual system, a sort of compromise between a first examination in committee and a first debate in the House. The main feature is a double committal. Every bill is referred by the House sometimes following a general debate to a special committee, on the proposal of the presidential committee. When the bill has been examined by the special committee, it is given a first reading at which the committee's report is introduced and a general debate on the bill takes place. This is concluded by referring the bill to the grand committee. That committee's report gives rise to the second reading at which the bill is considered in detail and if necessary amended. This stage may end in re-committal to the grand committee which must then make a new report. Only at the third reading is the bill finally passed.

In the U.S.S.R. and several of the People's Democracies there are no strict and uniform rules governing reference to committees: it largely depends on the nature and importance of the bill. It is for the House itself, or for the appropriate committee if a bill has been presented when the House was not sitting, to decide whether the bill is first to be debated in the House or in committee. A report made by a committee must be distributed twenty-four hours before the sitting in which it is to be debated. In Bulgaria and the U.S.S.R. committees consider the principle of a bill before it is debated by the Assembly. In Czechoslovakia the government must inform the committee of the broad principles of any bill it is intending to present. This information is considered by the committee who report their conclusions to the responsible minister. He must take them into account in drafting the bill and some of the committee are called upon to help him at the drafting stage.

In Poland bills which the Presidium decides are important enough are first debated in the Diet. This first reading comprises a statement by the proposer of the bill, a debate on its general principles and a decision to reject it or refer it to the appropriate committee. The practice of referring bills to committees reveals two different concepts of legislative procedure: on the one hand in Parliaments where permanent specialist committees exist, they consider the bill before it is debated in the House; on the other hand in Parliaments where bills are considered by a committee of the whole House or by *ad hoc* committees, the House itself plays the main role.

This conclusion is confirmed by evidence drawn from the study of the powers of committees in the making of law.

(*b*) *Powers of Committees*

The powers of committees vary considerably according to the Parliaments which appoint them. The wide powers of the Italian committees have been noted. With this exception committees so far as their powers are concerned are of two kinds.

In Great Britain and countries which have been influenced by British institutions committees have relatively little power. The exception is the Committee of the whole House, a body which is only distinguishable from the House itself by its title and greater informality. But it is the House itself that is regarded as the essential working unit. The task of committees is to consider matters of detail, especially when a bill is complex. Although they can amend a bill, the latitude given them is limited by the fact that the main principles of the bill have already been laid down before it is referred to them. As the bill has been approved by the House on second reading, no amendment conflicting with the main purpose of the bill is admissible; and a committee must confine its consideration within those purposes unless it is specially instructed by the House to do otherwise. It might be wondered in the circumstances whether committees perform any useful function. In fact they give invaluable help to Parliament. They relieve the House of all questions of detail, and they fulfil precisely the task entrusted to them, which is the minute scrutiny of both the form and substance of every clause in the bill.

At the opposite end of the scale are the committees of the United States Congress. Their purpose was originally the same as that of British committees; but they have become the nerve centres of congressional activity. In the first place they can amend or transform as they wish any bill, including those which derive from the President. More important, the fact that they are entirely independent of the House and the Senate, which have no way of controlling their activity, means that the future of a bill depends in large measure on their will. In practice the key part is played by the chairman of a committee. If he is personally hostile to the bill and the majority in the committee is favourable, he can apply a whole series of delaying tactics to prevent the bill from being considered. Whatever its origin the bill has no chance of success unless he is personally in favour of it. Only one factor may limit his authority: on important bills he has to take account of the policies and pressures of the two political parties.

Similar to the American committees are all those committees which have the power to recast a government or other bill referred to them as they think fit even to the point of totally altering their contents. In the opinion of some writers this power is tantamount to giving committees the right to initiate legislation, though they may be formally denied this right in constitutional law. In many Parliaments on the European continent committees have this power. The permanent committees in France had it until 1958. Today their powers are much more restricted. They can no longer play a decisive role in their Assemblies; there are now only six in number and each one is too large to allow it to work as an effective unit of political control. When a special committee is appointed, it is only to consider a single bill and it disappears when its work is done. In the Assembly itself the bill as introduced is debated and not the bill as amended by the committee. These constitutional alterations have eliminated serious abuses because the bills used often to be mutilated by committees and debate in consequence became distorted.

The procedure known as 'voting without debate', which is somewhat analogous to the Italian system of granting legislative powers to committees, is still in the rules of procedure of both French Chambers although it is now used much less frequently. Under this procedure debate on the floor is waived; all that remains is the voting. The power of deliberation disappears and is replaced by the mere power to vote. The unanimous agreement of all the interested parties—government, committee and members of the Assembly—is an essential condition for the use of this procedure because any one of them can challenge it, in particular by putting down an amendment. If a 'vote without debate' is opposed, the government or the committee may request a 'short debate' in which only the proposers of amendments, the government and the chairman and rapporteur of the committees concerned may speak. Before a vote is taken one speaker for each group can speak for five minutes in explanation of their votes.

Such procedures are used only in committees within the limits of their powers, the Assembly being restricted to approving or disapproving decisions taken elsewhere. But they are used very little, even in Parliaments which have permanent specialist committees. The important work done by these committees is the most characteristic feature of those Parliaments and one that distinguishes them most clearly from Parliaments of the British pattern.

Whatever the extent of their powers committees work in much the same way. Procedure in committee is more often than not modelled on that of the House. But there is much less formality in the conduct of debate so that a committee is free to exploit to the full the sources of information at its disposal and to carry out a thorough inquiry. In the U.S.S.R. and the People's Democracies as well as in Austria, the Federal Republic of Germany and the United States it is current practice to set up sub-committees, small in size and circumscribed in their powers, with instructions to make a preliminary study of the work of the committee, especially on the more delicate or complex points. These sub-committees add a stage to the procedure but the addition is to a great extent offset by the value of the work they do. Because a sub-committee is small and can hold frequent meetings it can go into matters more thoroughly and collect the necessary data more rapidly than the committees themselves.

The data in question are furnished primarily by the minister who is in charge of the bill under consideration. As a general rule if a committee requests a member of the government to appear before it, he will almost invariably accept the invitation. In Austria, Chile, the Federal Republic of Germany and Japan he is obliged to appear. Requests for appearances are most frequently sent direct to the ministers. In Austria, Brazil, Libya, the Philippines and Spain requests must be made through the President of the House. This is also the practice in France where in addition a minister's appearance must be authorised by the prime minister. In the Netherlands a committee first exchanges views in writing with the minister concerned. A paper of their preliminary observations is sent to him, and he sends a memorandum in reply. The object of this exchange is to allow the government to clear away any misapprehension which members may be under as a result of their first impressions of the bill. Only when these papers have been exchanged and published can the bill be debated in the Chamber.

In the Lebanon, Switzerland, the United Arab Republic and Yugoslavia it is the normal practice for representatives of the government to attend committee meetings at which government bills are considered.

The problem of ministers appearing before committees does not arise when a bill is examined by the Committee of the whole House, as in the countries on the British model where this is the regular practice. As ministers are also members of Parliament they attend sittings as required and also where necessary belong to the standing committees and to special committees. So the government is in practice represented at every stage of the legislative process without any need for a written rule.

Conversely where ministers have no right either by rule or in practice to attend the meetings of committees, they may be anxious to be heard. As a general rule even if committees do not make use of it, they have the right to turn down such a request except in a few countries such as Argentina, Austria, the Central African Federation, France, Greece, Japan and Switzerland where the constitution or the rules of procedure specify that ministers must be heard if they so request.

The data sought by committees do not necessarily come from the ministers personally. They are often furnished by civil servants on the authorisation of the head of the department to which they belong. In this respect the powers of committees are particularly wide in the U.S.S.R. and the People's Democracies. They extend to every branch of public life; and representatives of every public body are required to give committees information about their activities if requested to do so. Between sessions committees act in the name of the Assembly and are frequently required in concert with the executive to consider regulations made during this period which is often prolonged.

Another means of obtaining information is the hearing of private individuals, whether they are interested parties in the subject matter of the committee's inquiry or persons with special knowledge. As a general rule the object of these hearings is to help the committee to understand the problem; they are not quasi-judicial proceedings nor do those who take part incur any obligation. But in some Parliaments private persons may be heard by committees as 'witnesses', their function being as it were to give evidence for or against the bill under consideration. In the British system witnesses are examined by select committees. They no longer give evidence before the Committee of the whole House nor before standing committees. In Ceylon the scope of evidence by witnesses is unusually wide: any organisation or any person outside Parliament may ask to give evidence. But it is for the committee alone to decide who should give evidence. Witnesses are also examined in committees of the United States Congress. In the House of Representatives three of the twenty permanent committees have the power to summon witnesses. The others require special authorisation from the House. In the Senate all committees are given this power which is backed up with penalties for those who do not comply. A feature of the legislative work of Congress is the system of public hearings which are usually conducted in subcommittees. Members of the administration and any other person interested in the bill can be heard. This method in part replaces the procedure of questions to ministers and even of interpellations neither of which are possible in Congress because of the separation of powers.

The complex nature of certain problems occasionally makes the committees highly dependent on experts, and the importance of the interests touched by some bills frequently gives rise to pressure groups who seek especially at the level of committees to obtain favourable decisions from Parliament. Activity by these groups within Parliament is as a general rule forbidden, but their influence is often hard to pin down, and it is resisted with varying degrees of success. In some countries committees have experts permanently attached to them with instructions to furnish them with any clarification they need on the matters within their field. This is the practice in the United States Congress where each committee may engage permanent staff with special qualifications to work alongside the committee's own secretariat. But this method is only effective if these experts are independent of other bodies and in particular of the executive which would not overlook this means of influencing Parliamentary decisions. The administrative staff of committees on the other hand, being trained in economics and law, is most often best placed to provide impartially information for members in general and committee members in particular.

Committee procedure is notable for the wide measure of freedom allowed in its deliberations. Any member of the committee may express his views, speak more than once, or put forward and defend amendments on which the committee decides, if necessary by voting. From the deliberations of a committee its conclusions on the bill gradually emerge. They are embodied in a report which is made to the House and from which subsequent stages of the legislative process unfold.

(c) Reports of Committees

One of the primary tasks of a committee to which a bill has been referred is to appoint a rapporteur to make a personal study of the matter, to place it before members of the committee, and then to argue it before the House. This is an extremely important part of the procedure. It affects the future of the bill, whether it derives from the government or a private member, because in appointing the rapporteur the committee takes a certain attitude towards the bill. That attitude may foreshadow the conclusions the committee will ultimately reach and frequently the final decision of the House itself, because committees are as a rule constituted in accordance with a system of proportional representation of the various political parties.

This initial attitude is not revealed in Parliaments where committees do not appoint a special rapporteur for each particular matter. In countries following the British system such as Australia, Canada, Ceylon, Ghana, India, Ireland, Nigeria, New Zealand, and Sierra Leone the chairman of the committee himself acts as rapporteur; his function is first of all to direct the work of the committee and then report it to the House, though he is not also obliged as in the continental system to justify that report in debate. The chairman is responsible for making the report to the House in Israel, Japan, Laos and Spain.

In Finland and Sweden the written reports are the work of the whole committee and contain enough information to make the appointment of a rapporteur hardly necessary. This is also the position in the Netherlands where the report is usually drafted by the committee's staff. If explanations are requested in the plenary debate, they are usually given by the committee's chairman.

In some instances the appointment of a rapporteur has no relation to the views of the committee. In the Lebanon and Turkey every committee nominates a permanent general rapporteur whose func-

THE MAKING OF LAW

tion is to report on all matters coming before the committee. Conversely in the Federal Republic of Germany and Norway committees may appoint several rapporteurs for one and the same matter. In Switzerland there is always one German-speaking and one French-speaking rapporteur. In the Supreme Soviet of the U.S.S.R. a permanent committee designates a rapporteur for a bill only if the committee has itself originated the bill. When the committee makes a report on a bill from any other source, they appoint a co-rapporteur, the rapporteur being nominated by the source proposing the bill.

The main function of the rapporteur is to be the spokesman in the House of the political majority in the committee, especially where he has been elected by it, as he usually is. In these circumstances how can the rights of the minority to express its views be safeguarded? Any opposition which has emerged in the committee can of course put forward its views in the House when the matter comes up for debate. But this opportunity is inadequate and it comes too late. In a large number of countries the rights of the minority are safeguarded when the report is made. In practice when the rapporteur makes his report on the way in which the business has been conducted in committee, he is required to state the differences of opinion which have arisen. In addition, in some Parliaments publicity given to the work of the committee and in particular the distribution of reports of their proceedings may make up for any defects in the committee's report. In Great Britain, the United States and the Philippines, for example, the best way of finding out what was the minority opinion is to read the committee's proceedings.

Where publication of the proceedings of committees does not give enough information, there are other ways by which the minority can be given a fair hearing. In Belgium, the Federal Republic of Germany, Finland, India, Japan, Pakistan, Poland and Switzerland a statement of the minority's views is included as an annex to the report. In Libya the views of those who disagree are set out unless they wish otherwise. In Greece and Norway a committee may appoint two separate rapporteurs, one representing the majority, the other the minority. This is also the practice in the Federal Republic of Germany when differences of opinion are considerable. In the United States Congress the rapporteur of the committee is invariably the chairman of the sub-committee before which the public hearings took place. In the House of Representatives if some members of a committee whether or not from the majority party disagree with the committee's report, they may appoint a rapporteur to express their views. In the Senate this procedure can only be used if expressly authorised by that body if necessary on a majority of votes cast.

Another way is to make a separate minority report. This is what happens in the Argentine and Italy. In Austria if the minority on a committee consists of at least three members, it can make a written report.

In many Parliaments a rapporteur is not necessarily chosen on political grounds. If a bill is more technical than political in character, the special knowledge of a particular member may weigh more heavily than his belonging to a particular party or group.

When its deliberations are concluded, a committee agrees to a report, the drafting of which is entrusted either to the rapporteur, the chairman or the officers of the House. The report is printed and distributed to members of Parliament in the same way as the original bill or matter to which the report relates and before the topic in question comes up for debate in the House. The debate usually begins with an explanation of the report.

In an emergency a report may be made orally; but this is an exceptional procedure. In the Argentine, Chile and Switzerland it is used for important matters, in Luxembourg for the less important. In Czechoslovakia and Hungary a written report is only required if a bill has been amended.

Once the committee's report has been published, the important question for the powers of committees is whether the House will debate the bill as originally introduced or the bill as amended by the committee (if it is amended). This is the crux of the procedure on bills. The question is directly related to the influence exercised by committees in each Parliament and the action to be taken on their recommendations.

When the original bill is debated the committee which has considered it is placed on the same footing as members of Parliament: it can only put forward amendments. A report is made to the House, but it merely expresses an opinion on the bill as introduced, which may be favourable, unfavourable or suggesting modifications. This is the practice in Albania, Bulgaria, Hungary, Rumania, Czechoslovakia, and the U.S.S.R. where the work of committees which is done in close collaboration with the government enables amendments to be considered.

In Greece, Japan, Lebanon, the Netherlands and Somalia it is also the bill as introduced which is debated. France, followed by Cameroon and the Central African Republic, has also adopted this system for debating government bills. The abuses of the former system which allowed committees to alter bills radically to the detriment of the work of Parliament have been eliminated.

In some countries, including Denmark, Ethiopia, Libya and Luxembourg, the House itself decides at the beginning of the debate whether the original bill or the bill as amended in committee is to be debated.

The method most commonly found is for the debate to take place on the report of the committee. Obviously if no amendments have been proposed by the committee, the House will be debating the original text. In the United States, where in theory the original bill is debated, the amendments proposed by the committee are taken altogether. These amendments can represent virtually an alternative draft of the bill, and the procedure ensures priority for the work of the committee. In theory or practice this is the way in most Parliaments. It means that the committees are given considerable power unless, according to British practice, committees have to respect the principles of the bill as decided on its second reading in the House. At the other extreme committees can destroy a bill, a power which does not always enhance the clarity of their deliberations. But a committee's powers are frequently curtailed by a provision that the government may request the House at the beginning of the debate to consider its own original bill when it thinks the bill as amended by the committee is unacceptable.

2. CONSULTATION WITH OUTSIDE INTERESTS

As a general rule persons and bodies outside Parliament who are interested in the subject matter of a bill are consulted at some stage in order that it may be drafted with full knowledge. These consultations usually take place, as has been noted, at the committee stage through hearings or individual evidence. Falling as they do outside the purely internal work of a committee these consultations are not regarded as a separate stage in the legislative process—even in Sweden where organisations concerned are invited to give their views in writing on bills that are sent to them, or in the United States, where these consultations are seen as an essential part of the work of Parliament. In the Congress of the United States the first task of a committee considering a bill is to send a copy of the bill to every government department and interested organisation asking for their views. The individuals or groups consulted, whether they are professional organisations, trade unions or other bodies send back comments for or against the bill or they suggest alterations. They are then given an opportunity of developing their views at a public hearing which is often preceded by a detailed questionnaire. By virtue of these proceedings the general public is able to take part in the preparation of the bill to a greater extent than in any other classical democracy. Despite their interest these consultations remain part of the internal work of the committees. But in some countries they are regarded as a semi-official part of the drafting of the bill whose object is to test the bill against public opinion before it is debated in Parliament itself.

This type of consultation can take place before a bill is presented to Parliament. All governments have recourse to this procedure in varying degrees and generally in an empirical manner. Switzerland is one of the few countries where the process of preparing bills has been more or less codified. A bill is gone over carefully from the technical, legal and social angles before it is brought into the political arena. When the Federal Council prepares a bill, it usually appoints a committee consisting of members of both Houses, government officials and representatives of all the organisations concerned— associations of business men, industrialists, bankers, merchants, employees and workers—and places before this committee not only the main lines of the bill but also the full technical details. The committee endeavours to bring into line all the various trends of opinion. The bill that emerges is then sent to the chancellery where it is examined to ensure that it is compatible with existing legislation and also to the various interested ministerial departments which give their views. Only when this process of consultation has been completed is the bill presented to the Federal Council. The traditional procedure bears some relation to the techniques of direct democracy; in several instances these extra-parliamentary consultations are required by the federal constitution to be held.

A similar procedure is found in Sweden when a royal commission is asked to prepare a bill. Representatives of bodies concerned are invited to give their views to the minister reponsible for the bill.

In some countries the only consultations that have to take place before presentation concern the formal drafting of bills. This explains the part played by the Council of State (conseil d'état) in Belgium, France, the Lebanon and the United Arab Republic in preparing government bills. In the Netherlands its part extends also to bills introduced by individual members but only after they have passed both Chambers. It takes the form of an opinion on whether the Royal Assent should be given or withheld. The Council of State may not amend the bill when it has been passed: its function is cognate to that of other bodies which are responsible for ensuring the constitutional validity of laws. In Pakistan the consultative council on Islamic ideology gives opinions on whether a bill complies with the principle that must be respected.

THE MAKING OF LAW

Finally in some countries permanent bodies have been set up to tender advice on matters within their terms of reference. In Italy the national council on the economy and labour may be consulted either by the two Chambers or by the government. It is composed of experts and representatives of the productive industries. In certain circumstances it may initiate legislation. A similar part is played in France by the economic and social council in which social and professional categories are represented alongside the politicians. Matters may be referred to this council by the government only; any national plan or bill to implement an economic or social programme has to be referred to it. The council gives its opinion on the bills or matters submitted to it. One of its members may be appointed to express this opinion to Parliament.

Where extra-parliamentary consultations are held after a bill has been introduced in the House, they may at times represent a particular concept of the sovereignty of the people. In India and Pakistan a bill may be formally placed 'in circulation' in order to elicit further opinion on its merits. In India this procedure follows the adoption of a parliamentary motion. The secretariat of the House then send the bill to the government of the States and Territories which publish it and collect the views of particular or interested bodies. These views are sent to the secretariat of the House and are printed and distributed to members.

The most elaborate form of extra-parliamentary consultation, which derives from the principle of popular sovereignty as opposed to the strictly representative system, is the consultative referendum. This is provided for in the constitution of the United Arab Republic. The President of the Republic may consult the people on important matters touching the higher interests of the nation. In Yugoslavia the Federal Assembly can decide that a bill before being passed shall be submitted to the electorate in a referendum. In 1922 the Swedish constitution was amended to make provision for a consultative referendum. The King and the Riksdag acting together are empowered to seek the views of the people before a question is dealt with, whenever they think it necessary. The formal position is that the referendum is not binding for the future; it merely expresses public opinion at the moment. The Riksdag is not bound by the results of the vote, and it is free to decide what steps to take. It has, however, every reason for complying with the expressed desire of the majority. The referendum has only been used on three occasions since 1922. As a procedure it is in some ways difficult to apply; in particular it is slow and ponderous in a way that accords ill with the needs of modern legislation.

More effective and more realistic is the system of general public debate which operates in Yugoslavia and is a feature of the legislative procedure in the People's Democracies. In the U.S.S.R. bills are frequently referred for opinion to the supreme soviets and the councils of ministers of the Republics of the Union and also to the local soviets and to all interested organisations. Where the bill is of major importance, the whole people express their views on the alterations in the law. This procedure is used chiefly for the most important problems that arise from the political system and especially those dealt with in the first part of the constitution. But it may be used for other matters of public interest. For example the reform of education, of local councils and of the civil and penal codes have recently been submitted to a referendum in Hungary and the organisation and direction of agriculture in Poland.

When extra-parliamentary consultations have been completed, the ordinary procedure for the making of laws is taken up again in the assemblies. The contents of the bill are made known by all available means, and first and foremost the press, so that all sections of society are informed. Discussion follows within the basic organisations, industrial and agricultural undertakings, professional and trade organisations of all kinds, people's councils, social, scientific and economic institutions, and local and regional administrations. Opinions are gathered, and suggestions, amendments and perhaps counter-proposals are drawn up which are forwarded to Parliament and in particular to their appropriate committees. These committees examine them and may if necessary formally take them into consideration. Thus country-wide discussion takes place which introduces in some degree a new form of direct democracy made possible by the available media of communications. But the last word rests with the representatives of the people: it is for them to accept or reject the large number of suggestions addressed to them.

3. ORDER OF BUSINESS

The arrangement of the order of business is the keystone, so to speak, of the legislative process, between the preliminary consideration and the final passing of a bill. Once a bill has been introduced, distributed and considered in committee, it must be debated in the House. For that purpose it has to be placed on the order paper. To do so is more than a formality. Among all the many matters before Parliament a choice has to be made. The part played by the body which makes this choice and the provisions which govern it—whether deriving from the constitution, the rules of procedure or practice—are extremely important because they affect the control and therefore the efficiency of parliamentary business. The rights of the government and of individual members to introduce bills can only be effective to the extent that the rules governing the orders of business allow.

If the order of business is decided by the government, awkward topics can easily be disposed of, and the government may adopt a dictatorial attitude towards Parliament. Conversely the order of business may be settled by Parliament. This may seem equally improper if it is accepted that the work of legislation is valid only if it is directed by the government. The implication is that the government should be able to decide when Parliament shall consider the bills introduced by the government. Though the nature of modern legislation is an argument in its favour, such a prerogative is at variance with the old democratic principle that Parliament is master of its own order of business. The difficulty—and it is not simply a matter of procedure—is to find a compromise which will safeguard the independence of Parliament and at the same time provide the necessary powers to enable the government to be carried on. Few systems appear to meet both these conditions. Either the government enjoys an almost absolute priority, or the Parliament has the right to choose what matters it will deal with. Between these extremes some kind of *modus vivendi* has to be worked out, if serious crises in the relationship of the legislature and the executive are to be avoided.

In practice the order of business is settled either by the government, or by the President or Speaker of the House, or by the House itself, usually on the proposal of one of its official bodies. These three possibilities are worth considering in greater detail.

Here again there is a cleavage between the British system and the others. The British system is the outcome of a long evolution. Until after the Reform Bill of 1832 most of the legislation in the House of Commons was introduced by private members who had at their disposal all the time not expressly granted to the government. A reform in 1837 allowed the government two days a week to conduct its business. This tendency continued, and today the positions have been reversed: private members now have only a certain number of Fridays at their disposal in each session to introduce bills.

In both Houses the powers of the government are exercised through the leader of the House and the chief whip who are members of the government. It is they who arrange the order of business of the House after consultation with the leaders of the opposition and other members. This example has been followed by a number of countries. In Australia, Canada, Ceylon, India, Ireland, New Zealand, Nigeria and Pakistan the task of arranging the business of Parliament is given to the executive. In India and Pakistan the House is informed of the order of business by the minister for parliamentary affairs. In New Zealand it is settled by the clerk of the House on the instructions of the prime minister's office. In Ghana and Sierra Leone this duty is discharged by a special committee, the 'business committee', which has a majority of government members.

While it is generally the practice to consult the leaders of the opposition, the power of the executive over the programme of parliamentary business is absolute. The amount of time allowed for private members' business is proof of this. In the British House of Commons the government has also to set aside a given number of days on which the opposition has the right to choose the subject for debate. In total however this time amounts on average to only about one-fifth of the number of sittings in a session. In Australia private members are accorded scant opportunity for their business. It is accorded precedence in the Senate on Thursday after 8 p.m. and in the House of Representatives every other Thursday up to 12.45 p.m. During this time is has priority over business introduced by the government unless a decision is taken to the contrary, as frequently happens. On the other Thursday mornings, after financial matters have been taken, any member may address the House on any subject unless the House on the proposal of the government decides to adjourn further consideration of these matters. These sittings are known as 'grievance days'. In Canada the six Mondays and two Thursdays which follow the approval of an address in reply to the speech from the Throne are devoted to private members' business. But from 5 p.m. to 6 p.m. on Tuesdays and Wednesdays the House may take private members' bills. In India every Friday a period of two and a half hours before the adjournment is set aside for private members' business. In Ceylon the Wednesday sitting is set aside in this way. In Pakistan one day is reserved for private members' business for every five days set aside for government business. In Ireland government bills have priority at every sitting except between 6 p.m. and 7.30 p.m. on Tuesdays and Wednesdays in the period when ordinary financial business is not under consideration. The order in which private members' bills are taken is also significant. Whether it is decided by ballot or by the chronological order of presentation, the urgency or importance of the problems does not affect the issue.

This matter of organising parliamentary business is completely at variance with the continental concept of the parliamentary function, the essential feature of which is that a continuous part is played by members in the making of a bill as well as in the Houses' decision on that bill. The underlying principle is that the cabinet, which is primarily responsible for the conduct of affairs, should be given the leading role in the preparation of legislation. This principle conflicts with the theory of the separation of powers which was originally inspired by the working of British institutions. Since then the relationship between legislature and executive in Great Britain has altered profoundly. Today the main dividing line is not between legislature and executive but between the majority party which forms a government to implement its policy and to legislate and an opposition whose primary function is to criticise the action of the government and to develop an alternative policy. Theoretically a majority party in the House of Commons could if it so desired take over all the time set aside for debate. In practice the government party would be chary of being so imprudent (a quality which chimes ill with the British temperament), because intolerant actions of this nature would sooner or later rebound against it when through the normal democratic processes the elections went against the government and it then became the opposition. This kind of system gives the government considerable powers over the House. It also demonstrates the rights of the ordinary member acting as an individual. But the official opposition has gained especially in keeping a check on the government's activities.

In France the new methods of settling the order of business have the same results. The constitution of 1958 greatly altered the previous system which gave total power to Parliament. Now priority is given to government bills and other bills accepted by the government, and they are taken in the order that the government wishes. One sitting a week is set aside for members to put questions to ministers, though in so doing they may not trespass on the field of legislation. According to the rules of procedure the two Assemblies have the right to include in the order of business matters other than those accorded priority as government measures,if the Conference of Presidents recommends. This body consists of the President, the Vice-Presidents, the chairmen of committees and the chairmen of political parties or groups. A similar position is found in Cameroon. In Senegal, if requested by the President of the Republic, a government bill or a bill introduced by an individual member must be included in the order of business. In Monaco the procedure is more original: the National Council prepares the order of business which is sent to the minister of state at least three days in advance. But if the government so requests, at least one sitting of every two should be set aside to debate bills laid by the Prince.

In most other countries the government does not enjoy any priority. Parliament holds fast to its powers to make law and particularly settle the order of business. It would nevertheless be paradoxical to think of the government, which is responsible for the conduct of public affairs, being without any weapon it could use to put its own bills forward for debate. In practice it has various ways of achieving its purpose; in particular it can always appeal to its majority.

The powers of most Parliaments to settle the order of business are exercised in a variety of ways. First the arrangement of business may be entrusted to the President of the Chamber. In a few European countries such as Denmark, Greece and Spain, and also in Brazil, Japan, the Lebanon, Turkey and the United Arab Republic, he alone is responsible. In Norway the order of business is drawn up by the Presidents of the Storting and its two Chambers, the meetings of the Storting invariably having priority over those of either of the Chambers. The order of business of each of these three Assemblies is determined by its President within this framework. In Iceland the same system applies. In some countries the President may have occasion to consult certain bodies before taking his decision such as the Conference of Presidents in Iran, Somalia and Switzerland, the Bureau in Luxembourg and Laos and the Presidential Council in Finland. The system of giving the President the task of drawing up the order of business is flexible. Because the President has to discharge his duties impartially, the management of business is treated as a technical rather than a political operation. It is easier to take into account the requests of the government and to ensure a priority for them which is not given by any written rule. This is particularly the position in Denmark, Finland, Greece and Norway.

In the same way the two Houses of Congress do not themselves settle the order of their business. This is done in the House of Representatives by a conference of party leaders attended also by Mr Speaker, the majority floor leader and whip and some of the chairmen of committees. The Rules Committee exercises a discretionary power in this field: it asks for and obtains priority for bills which it has decided to support. If a bill has a majority of the members of this committee against it, it has little prospect of reaching the House unless the Speaker allows the presentation by a member of the permanent committee familiar with the details of a motion pressing its consideration. On the other hand the first and third Mondays of each month are given over to the consideration of bills which are likely to be unopposed. Members may request that their bills should be taken at this time. They are withdrawn even if only one member opposes them. Six official 'objectors'—three from the majority and three from the minority—look carefully at the list of bills to decide whether they should be opposed. In the Senate the order of business is fixed by the policy committee of the majority party. Because of the principle of separation of powers, any intervention by the executive in the work of Congress is excluded. Nevertheless it is the practice for leaders of the majority party to take into account the wishes of the President, even though he may not belong to the majority party.

The commonest procedure is for the House itself to determine its programme of work. Proposals may be put to it either by its President as in Albania, Hungary, Libya, the Netherlands and Yugoslavia or by one of its directing bodies such as the Bureau in the Belgian Senate, Czechoslovakia, Bulgaria and Rumania or the Presidium in Albania and Poland. In Poland the Presidium is helped by a Council of Elders, a body which in the U.S.S.R. alone discharges this duty. The Council of Elders is a special body set up for this purpose. It is found also in the Federal Republic of Germany where the Bundestag is in practice only consulted if the elders are seriously divided. The Government is represented as it is in Parliaments which rely on a Conference of Presidents on the French pattern. This conference usually consists of chairmen of committees and political groups. It considers requests made by the government or by committees and works out a programme of business which they submit to their Houses with a good chance that it will be accepted, because the political composition of these bodies reflects that of the Houses. Some such system is found in Austria, the Belgian House of Representatives, Italy and in the Argentine where the conference is known as the Committee on Parliamentary Business.

The practice of settling the order of business for a fairly long period ahead makes it possible to organise the work of Parliament methodically and gives a certain stability and continuity to the debates. Casual changes are hardly desirable. Besides confusing the conduct of business they may give rise to argument and snap votes which are hardly compatible with the dignity of Parliament. For this reason steps are frequently taken to prevent the order of business, once it has been settled, from being constantly re-opened.

These steps vary as the following examples show. In Italy a change proposed by a member in the order of business must be supported by a majority of three-quarters of the votes cast in the lower House and by two-thirds in the Senate. In Norway a simple majority is enough to agree to a proposal made by the President but two-thirds of the votes cast are required if it is put forward by a member. In the Federal Republic of Germany an item may always be withdrawn from the order of business if the Bundestag so decides but a new item may not be inserted if five members present oppose it.

The purpose of preparing an order of business, whether it gives the government the upper hand or confirms the traditional independence of Parliament, is to deal with one of the main obstacles to the working of Parliament today which is shortage of time. Modern Parliaments always have more work than they can do. The selection of bills for debate cannot be left to chance. If legislative business is to be effective, it must be properly organised. This need is seen in all aspects of parliamentary procedure.

4. DEBATE IN THE HOUSE

Debate in the House on bills before they are finally passed is the most spectacular phase of the legislative process because it takes place in public. It is also the most complex because of the rules that govern it and the most animated because of possibility of incidents and disorder. It is a contest, sometimes long and exciting, between those for and those against the proposed reform. The outcome is a bill that either satisfies one side or the other or represents a compromise between their views.

This open struggle tests the protagonists' oratorical qualities and strength of conviction. It is subject to general rules designed to ensure that the debates are seriously and fairly conducted and that they end within a reasonable time. In some instances debate is conducted according to a timetable or is otherwise restricted. In others it may be prolonged if the rights of members and especially their right of amendment is broadly construed or when the opponents of the measure exploit the available means of obstruction.

(a) General Features of Procedure

Parliament can be divided into two distinct categories according to whether they debate each bill only once or carry out a series of readings of the same bill. 'Reading' is used here in the Anglo-Saxon or Germanic sense to mean the successive debates held in one House before a decision on the bill is come to. In some bicameral Parliaments it can also be used to describe the successive debates in both

Houses when a bill is passed backwards and forwards between them in order to obtain agreement.

Many countries of Western Europe—for example Belgium, France, Italy, Luxembourg, the Netherlands and Switzerland—all the People's Democracies except Poland, several African states and such other countries as Brazil, Japan, Laos and the Lebanon, all have a single stage of debate in the House itself. This single debate usually has several phases in more or less continuous succession. They are the presentation of the committee's report which is preceded or followed by a statement by the government; a general debate which is open to all members; a debate on the clauses of the bill and amendments thereto; explanations of votes; and a vote on the bill as a whole.

As a general rule members cannot go back on any one of these phases once it has been completed, though an exception is often made if members of the government or the committee can give useful explanation to the House by doing so. After an interruption of this kind, the House resumes at the point at which it left off.

The list of phases set out above covers a series of procedures which differ greatly in detail, and it would be out of place to study them all here. The most that can be done is to point out some peculiarities which may affect the principle of the single reading.

There is first of all the procedure found in countries like Cameroon, France, Switzerland and the United Arab Republic of the 'second deliberation'. This is a re-opening of the debate on the bill as a whole or some parts of it before the vote is taken. The primary object is to alter a part of the bill which appears to be badly drafted or not in keeping with the rest of it, though another object may be to go back on a decision already taken. For this reason in France a second deliberation is mandatory when requested by the committee concerned or by the government; when requested by a member the National Assembly itself must decide unless the committee agrees. The bill is remitted, and the committee must present a new report. During the second deliberation the Assembly is required to make known its views only on the new proposals put forward by the committee or the government and on amendments relating thereto. In the United Arab Republic the same procedure is followed if requested by the government, the rapporteur or chairman of the committee, or twenty members. In the Second Chamber of the Netherlands provision is made for a second deliberation, confined strictly to drafting, where a bill has been heavily amended. In Belgium and Luxembourg a second deliberation is mandatory if a bill has been amended or some of its clauses negatived.

The feature of the single reading is that it takes place when the committees have made their report, so that in theory the debate in the House ought not to be interrupted by further stages elsewhere.

In Italy however there is a special type of procedure, the effect of which is to separate the public debates in the Chamber into two distinct parts. In some instances the Chamber may decide to debate a bill in a general way without touching on the individual clauses. In that event the final drafting is entrusted to the committee which made the original report. The bill as amended is then agreed to without debate by the Chamber after a kind of second reading debate in which explanation of votes are in order. This procedure is somewhat reminiscent of the British system which allows the House to define the essential principles of the bill before it is referred to a committee for the detailed work of considering the clauses.

The practice of having two readings, the first consisting of a debate on the general principles of the bill before it is committed and the second a detailed examination of the clauses of the bill and of amendments proposed by the committee, is optional in Austria; but it is normal usage in Poland. In the Polish Diet at the first reading the objects of the bill are explained by its proposer, its general principles are debated and the bill is either committed or rejected. At the second reading the report of the committee is presented, the clauses and amendments proposed are considered and a final vote is taken. The second reading may not take place for three days after the report has been circulated.

The system of two readings is also used in Greece, Iran and Turkey where the rules are somewhat different in that the report of the committee is a preliminary report. In Greece no bill may be passed which has not been debated and voted on by the House on two occasions at two different sittings which have to be separated by an interval of not less than two days. At the first reading the principles of the bill and the clauses are dealt with; at the second, the clauses and amendments thereto and the bill as a whole. If the bill has been amended the vote on the bill as a whole may not take place for twenty-four hours after the bill as amended has been distributed. In Iran the rules of procedure provide for two readings. The first reading consists of a general debate on the report of a committee. Amendments are referred without debate to the committee in order that they may be considered at the second reading after the committee has made another report on them. In Turkey there is an analogous system although here the two readings are separated by a period of not less than five days.

Most other Parliaments have a procedure of three readings. Here again a distinction must be made between the European continental countries and the countries influenced by British methods. Among the former reference has already been made to the special case of Finland in the study of legislative work in committee: the several readings are separated by the work of the special committee to which the bill has been committed and also of the grand committee which oversees all legislation. In Sweden there is also an unusual procedure: after presentation of the bill, there are three readings of the committee's report but debate is permitted only on the last reading. In Denmark, the Federal Republic of Germany, Iceland and Israel the procedure is somewhat closer to the classical type. There is a first reading or presentation of the bill when a debate on its general principles is held; the second reading is a debate on the committee's report, the clauses of the bill and any proposed amendments; and at the third reading the bill is passed in the form in which it emerged from the previous reading.

The British procedure is rather different, although it has the same number of readings. The first reading is a mere formality. It follows the presentation of the bill. The second reading is the essential stage, for the main principles of the bill are then determined before any committee work begins. Amendments are in order only if they propose the rejection of the bill as a whole—either by adjourning the second reading to a date after the session or by stating reasons for its rejection—or if they aim to dispose of the subject matter of the bill in some way other than by passing it. The committee stage follows. Next there is in the House on the bill as amended a detailed debate known as the consideration or report stage. This stage is to some extent a repetition of the committee stage, though the rules are stricter. Its main value is to enable ministers to make the changes they have agreed to in principle in committee. During the report stage the clauses are not voted on separately; the bill is considered as a whole. The third reading follows the report stage and as a rule takes place on the same day. It consists of a debate on the bill as it has emerged from the committee and report stages. Debate is confined on this occasion to what is in the bill; unlike what happens at the second reading no new proposals may be put forward. Only verbal amendments are in order at this stage.

With some differences, especially on the purpose of amendments and the time limits for submitting them, the Parliaments of Australia, Canada, Ceylon, Ghana, India, Ireland, New Zealand, Nigeria, Pakistan and Sierra Leone also give three readings to bills.

Under the rules of procedure of the United States House of Representatives there are three readings. The first reading is formal: it consists of registering the number, title and name of the proposer of the bill in the minutes of proceedings. The second reading is the important stage. It may take place either in the House or in committee of the whole House after the general discussion during which the time is fairly shared between the parties. The sponsor of an amendment has five minutes to defend it, and a member opposing it may also speak for five minutes. After the second reading the Speaker consults the House as to whether the bill should be taken into consideration and given a third reading. If the answer is affirmative, that stage usually amounts to reading out the title and voting on the bill as a whole. In the Philippines the procedure is essentially the same.

At these readings of bills debate, an essential feature of the democratic system, can take place. From this clash of ideas and exchange of views an Act of Parliament emerges. But if a bill is to be passed in reasonable time, debate must be conducted in accordance with the rules of order. This presupposes the existence of rules of procedure which protect the rights of the minority and secure the efficient working of the legislative process by eliminating systematic obstruction. To strike this balance is no easy task.

(b) Rules of Debate

Speeches are the lifeblood of Parliament. Restriction on them should be an exceptional measure. Experience shows that members' speeches do not lend themselves easily to self-discipline. In one or two Parliaments there is complete freedom in this respect, and it is not abused. In Finland and Sweden any member of Parliament or the government can speak for as long as he pleases and can have the floor as many times as he wishes. But this is quite exceptional. In most other Parliaments it has been found necessary to confine debates within reasonable limits.

Two chief methods are used to save Parliament's time. The first is to limit the number and duration of speeches by each member; the second, which is usually optional, is to fix a time-limit for a particular debate or to govern the way in which it is conducted.

(i) Limitations on the time for speaking. A time-limit on speeches especially in debate on bills is relatively common. But two categories of persons usually escape this rule. The first category is members of the government with right of access to Parliament: they have complete freedom to speak when they wish to do so. The second category is the spokesmen of committees, the chairman and rapporteurs, especially in Parliaments where committees have a specially important function. In general these speakers are not in any way limited, or they may have at any rate special privileges as compared with other members. In Iceland rapporteurs may speak on three different

occasions whereas an ordinary member has the right to speak only twice. In the U.S.S.R. a rapporteur may speak for an hour and a half to introduce a report and half an hour to explain his vote, whereas other members are allowed only twenty minutes for a first speech and five minutes for a second. In Brazil rapporteurs have twice the length of time allowed to other speakers. In Austria, Italy, Poland and the U.S.S.R. they are entitled to make the winding-up speech in the debate.

Other members of Parliament are usually less favoured: either the number of times or the length of time they may speak or both is limited in many Parliaments. According to British practice a member may speak more than once in a debate only with leave of the House. This rule is also observed in Laos and in the House of Representatives in the United States. Two speeches are allowed in Albania, Austria, Belgium, Chile, Iceland, the Lebanon, the Netherlands, Norway, Poland, the United Arab Republic, the U.S.S.R. and the Senate of the United States; and three in Libya.

The length of a speech is limited to fifteen minutes in Laos and the United Arab Republic, twenty minutes in Turkey, thirty minutes in the Argentine, Nigeria and Sierra Leone (though here proposers of bills or motions are allowed forty-five minutes), an hour in Luxembourg, the House of Representatives in the Philippines and two hours in the Senate. The length of time may vary with the subject under debate as in Denmark, Iran, Australia and New Zealand. In the last two countries there is a precise scale for the duration of speeches. When two speeches are permitted, the length of each may be specified: in Switzerland it is twenty minutes and ten minutes, in Poland fifty and ten minutes, in Norway one hour and twenty minutes, in Chile thirty minutes and ten minutes, in the U.S.S.R. twenty minutes and five minutes and in the Belgian House of Representatives thirty minutes and five minutes (one hour and ten minutes in the Senate).

Where a time-limit on speeches is not imposed by the rules, Parliament may decide to impose one for a particular debate. In Greece a limit may be proposed by the President or twenty members, in Yugoslavia by ten members.

In spite of the apparent strictness of all these rules, it must be borne in mind of course that in most Parliaments the President or Speaker is responsible for maintaining order during the debates, and he will ordinarily use a certain amount of discretion in exercising his authority. In the British House of Commons and those Parliaments which have followed its methods the powers of the Speaker are unusually wide in this direction. No member has any 'right' to speak; the Speaker alone is responsible for deciding when and in what order members are to speak. There are no formal rules on this head: it is for each member to request the Speaker to call him by 'catching his eye'. The House places full confidence in the Speaker's sense of what is right and trusts him to see to it that speeches are relevant and not repetitious and to ensure as far as possible that speakers from either side of the House are heard alternately.

The President has a good deal less authority in other Parliaments. He has invariably the power to recall speakers to the subject under debate, but as a rule he is required to follow the order in which their requests to speak have been put down on a list drawn up before or during the debate. In the French National Assembly members write their names in the register of speakers if they wish to speak, but it is for the President to decide the order in which they shall be called to speak. When he thinks that the Assembly has heard enough, he may invite a member to conclude his speech; and he may request a member to resume his seat if he is reading his speech. Reading speeches is forbidden at least in theory in several countries.

(ii) Limitation and organisation of debates. The second method of saving time is to shorten the total length of debate in the House by using some form of summary or abridged procedure.

A debate may be short because there is no fundamental disagreement on the bill. The procedure in the Italian Parliament which gives committees either complete legislative authority in certain matters or power to decide definitely the drafting of a bill has already been noticed. In France the procedure of voting without debate—which also applies in the Argentine and Cameroon—resembles the Italian procedure in that debate is restricted: only a representative of the government, the chairman or rapporteur of the committee concerned, the proposers of amendments and one representative of each political party or group may speak. No speech may be longer than five minutes.

Debate may also be curtailed because of the urgency of the decisions that Parliament has to take. In some Parliaments there are special rules under which bills can be passed quickly if they are declared to be urgent. This is true of Brazil, Ireland, Poland, Rumania, Spain and Yugoslavia. In Ireland in an emergency the Dail can decide to curtail the time normally taken on each stage of a bill. In the same way the President of the Spanish Cortes can shorten the time allowed under the ordinary procedure. In Brazil the forty-eight hour interval which must normally elapse between the first and second readings can be waived. In this country matters considered by Parliament are automatically grouped in three categories, namely, urgent, priority and ordinary.

A debate may also be limited if the House thinks that a measure should be passed by the given date. The best example is the procedure in the British House of Commons with the expressive title of the 'guillotine'. By passing a guillotine motion the House fixes a time-limit for the debate on the whole or specific parts of a bill or motion. A special committee known as the Business Committee on which the opposition is represented works out in detail how the bill or motion is to be divided. When the time-limit fixed for each part of the bill is reached, the Speaker automatically puts the question, and the House is obliged to vote forthwith.

Most Parliaments on the British model have adopted the guillotine system; but its drastic nature often makes it preferable when there is less urgency for the representatives of the government and the opposition to arrive at a voluntary agreement. This is a frequent practice in the United Kingdom, Ireland and Ceylon. A practice not unlike the guillotine is found in some Parliaments in the form of a decision that a debate shall not overrun an agreed time-limit. This practice is found in Hungary, Japan, the Netherlands, the Philippines, Poland and Rumania.

But the most far-reaching procedure is that known as the 'organisation of debates'. It is found in France, Cameroon and the Central African Republic. This duty falls to the Conference of Presidents which when dealing with bills consists of the President and Vice-Presidents of the Assembly, the chairmen of the political parties or groups, the chairmen and rapporteurs of the appropriate committees and a representative of the government. The conference decides on the number of sittings to be set aside for the debate. Having done that it allots the speaking time to the government, to committees and to the various political groups in accordance with their size. Each group may use the time allotted as it thinks best; but that time may not be exceeded. A similar system operates in the Netherlands. In the Federal Republic of Germany most debates are organised by the Council of Elders, in Israel by the House Committee, and in Japan by the House Management Committee. The Rules Committee of the United States House of Representatives exercises a discretionary power for the same purpose.

Time may be saved by these procedures. But their true efficiency should be judged by whether justice is done to minority opinion, because the right of the minority to express its opinion remains a basic principle of parliamentary government. Nevertheless various procedures are usually available for it to do so, whatever the attitude and conduct of the majority.

(c) *Procedural Motions and Obstruction*

Parliamentary procedure secures for every member the right to speak and submit amendments. It also offers a whole range of opportunities which though designed to ensure serious and honest debate can be distorted in ways that are tantamount to obstruction.

There are several procedural devices commonly used in Parliament to avoid or delay a decision. First there is the motion for the adjournment which is found in virtually all Parliaments. It consists of requesting the debate to be put off *sine die* or to a specific date. In the Finnish Parliament there is a special type of adjournment: at the request of one-third of the total number of members the final decision on a bill may be suspended after it has been debated on third reading until the first ordinary session following a general election.

Secondly there is the conditional motion (*motion préjudicielle*), which is a form of adjournment motion. Its object is to make further consideration of a bill dependent on one or several conditions, such as the collection of more information or a request for advice from other bodies. If the motion is adopted, the debate is postponed until these conditions have been met.

Thirdly reference back to a committee may be requested. This common device is used mainly in Parliaments which have a system of permanent committees and which give bills a single reading only. The argument used to justify this motion may be that some aspects of the bill have not been properly studied by the original committee or need to be submitted to other committees for their views.

Fourthly there is the less common device known as the 'previous question'. It may be proposed at the beginning of the debate and if it is agreed to, the debate does not take place. For practical purposes it is equivalent to the outright rejection of a bill. It is used in Parliaments of Western Europe and also in the House of Representatives of the United States.

Fifthly there is the proposal to change the order of business. It has the same effect as the previous question especially when it takes the form, as in the Federal Republic of Germany, Denmark and Iceland, of a motion to take up the next item or, in Italy, to pass on to the orders of the day.

Sixthly there is the request for a fresh deliberation, especially when as in Chile such proceedings cannot take place at once. In the same category is a motion 'to reconsider a decision' which is used in the Senate of the United States at the request of a senator who has voted with the majority or who did not take part in the vote. This procedure is also available to members of the Chilean Parliament but such a motion requires the support of two-thirds of the votes cast to be successful.

Finally there is the motion that a bill is inadmissible, on the grounds that its purposes conflict with provisions of the constitution. These motions are rare.

Other methods of prolonging debate are less orthodox. Where there is no rule to prevent it from doing so, a minority may have recourse to an endless series of amendments or may simply prolong its speeches beyond a reasonable length. The best known example is the 'filibuster' used in the American Senate where the concept of unrestricted debate is regarded as an essential attribute of a deliberative body. The rules do however provide that an obstructive speech may be closured on a motion proposed by sixteen senators and supported by a majority of two-thirds of the votes cast.

Other more technical opportunities are also available. There are requests for the sitting to be suspended; a call for a count of the House to see if a quorum is present before a vote is taken; the raising of a point of order which under the pretext of contesting the application of a rule delays debate on the main subject because a point of order always has priority; a request to make a personal statement or to correct an allegation; a request for a separate vote on each part of the bill or motion being debated; and a request for a public vote which wastes time when the sense of the House is clear and which is especially effective when a roll call has to be taken and the numbers checked before the result is announced.

Clearly the abuse of these various procedures is what constitutes obstruction, more especially when, as in the last instances cited, they are purely procedural devices and bear no relation to the substance of the matter under debate. Motions to adjourn or re-commit and the previous question are not necessarily obstructive so long as they are not systematically repeated and are not moved merely to indicate that a particular stand is being taken. In the U.S.S.R. and the People's Democracies this kind of motion is permitted, but it is never used for purposes of obstruction. In other Parliaments its use is hedged by specific conditions. In France only one point of order may be raised on each bill; and only one previous question and one motion to refer the bill to a committee may be moved. In the debate on each motion only the proposer, one speaker against, the government and the chairman or rapporteur of the committee concerned may speak. Nevertheless it is always open to the opposition so to use their rights as to set on foot dilatory manoeuvres. Certain precautions against this kind of activity are taken in the Bundestag of the Federal

Republic of Germany. A motion to pass to the next point on the agenda and the previous question may be proposed on second and third reading by any member before the final vote is taken on the bill. In this instance only one speaker may be heard for and one against the proposal. If such a motion is rejected, it may not be made again at the same reading; moreover it is out of order if the bill is a government bill or if it has come from the Bundesrat. Motions to adjourn debate on the bill must be supported by thirty members present; they must be distributed and included in the order of business. A bill may not be adjourned for more than four weeks. The period may only be extended with the agreement of the proposers of the bill. In Belgium according to rules of procedure of the House, if the President considers a motion for the adjournment or any other motion of the same kind has the effect of obstructing the work of the House he may immediately put it to the vote by sitting and standing, with or without debate.

Apart from provisions in the rules there are always ways of countering the stock methods of abusing the rules. First there are the disciplinary powers of the President who in some instances can terminate time-wasting speeches or has the right to refuse to accept motions at variance with the spirit if not the letter of the rules of procedure. Often the action of the majority is the best defence against obstructions: it can defeat motions as fast as they are submitted, although of course this does not help to shorten the debate. Stronger action can also be taken: in Canada, Luxembourg and the United States the majority can oppose debate of all procedural motions by resorting to a special kind of the previous question. In the Federal Republic of Germany the Bundestag can as a last resort decide, with the support of two-thirds of the members present, to suspend some of the rules of procedure allowing the moving of dilatory motions.

Dealing with obstruction is a more formidable proposition where the opposition makes use of such procedural tactics as calling a count of the House, moving to suspend the sitting, raising points of order or requesting roll calls. To avoid these abuses some Parliaments have taken the precaution of laying down strict rules governing the use of these devices. But the rules have not always been completely effective.

For this reason the quorum may only be checked at the request of the chairman of a party or group in the French National Assembly or by not less than five members in the Bundestag of the Federal Republic of Germany where the Bureau may reject the request if it is unanimous. In the Bundestag motions to take a vote by roll call must be backed by not less than fifty members in view of the time these votes take. In the Belgian House twelve members are enough. In

France a public vote is only automatic when requested in writing by the chairman of a party or group or a deputy whose name has previously been notified to the President. But the majority has one ultimate weapon at its command if it wishes to curtail the debate or to deal with any attempt at obstruction. This is the closure. Few Parliaments follow the example of Finland, Israel and Sweden in having to make no provision for this procedure because obstruction is unknown or at least rare. Closure is a means by which the majority can end a debate and pass directly to the next stage of a bill or if necessary to a vote on the whole or part of it. The effects of the closure are so drastic that its use is usually subjected to certain conditions to safeguard the rights of the minority. Sometimes short explanations of votes may be permitted. Again in many Parliaments a motion for closure may only be moved by the President or by a specified number of members. In the United Kingdom and in countries influenced by the British model the Speaker has the sole right to decide whether or not to accept the motion 'that the question be now put'. He refuses to accept if at that particular point of debate he thinks a closure would impair the rights of the minority. In the House of Commons a motion for closure must be supported by at least a hundred members.

In other Parliaments a motion for closure is not acceptable unless supported by a given number of members: the number is thirty in the Federal Republic of Germany, twenty in the Belgian House of Representatives, Ceylon and the Arab United Republic and ten in the Belgian Senate, Chile and Norway. In other countries sometimes any member may move the closure of the debate, but only after a given number of speakers against the motion have been heard: the numbers are one for and one against in Austria and France, two for and two against in Japan, three for and two against in the Philippines and three for and three against in Libya. In Iceland a debate may not be cut to less than three hours. In Ireland the closure may not be accepted unless the President is himself in the chair. In some instances the motion for closure requires the support of a specific majority: in the United States Senate and in the Swiss National Council two-thirds of the votes cast must be in favour.

Although there is provision for the closure in almost all Parliaments, it is not frequently used. Whatever justification is advanced and whatever precautions taken, it can very easily become a method of stifling the opposition. In Australia the closure is known as the gag. A majority tries to avoid being accused of using such tactics to achieve its ends because if it does so obstruction is likely to be regarded as a legitimate means of expression for the minority. Its main object is to make public opinion aware of what is going on, and the attitude of public opinion frequently determines the fate of the matter under debate. But the relative legitimacy of obstruction must not be used as an argument for incorporating it in the rules of procedure. In virtue of an equally democratic principle, ultimate power in Parliament must invariably rest with the majority.

(d) Amendments

The procedural motion is a tactic affecting the general course of a debate. Amendments on the other hand bear directly on the terms of the bill they are designed to modify. Each amendment is considered first in committee, if it is submitted early enough, and then in the House. In both places the procedure is roughly the same.

The right to submit amendments is universally recognised as one of the prerogatives of members of Parliament except in some upper Houses, such as the Second Chamber in Austria and in the First Chamber in the States-General of the Netherlands. It derives first and foremost from their right to introduce a bill. If a member is entitled to introduce a complete bill, he is *a fortiori* entitled to propose an amendment to a bill. The right to submit amendments can also be regarded as a concomitant of the right to speak. It is an essential feature of democratic practice. There are no restrictions on it in Albania, Czechoslovakia, Hungary, Rumania or the U.S.S.R. It has been shown how in these countries private individuals and organisations outside Parliament have the right to submit proposals relating to important bills that are being debated. This procedure helps to enhance the authority of the legislature and to create a respect for the bills when they are passed.

This method is comparable with the practice in other Parliaments where it is always possible for a person or body outside Parliament to suggest to a member of Parliament amendments which he can then move of his own accord. But unless public evidence is given to a committee or there are interventions of an official nature such as petitions, these covert methods can occasionally give rise to severe criticism.

As a general rule the government has the right to propose amendments to a bill either directly or through members of its own political persuasion; sometimes it has the formal right of amendment. In some Parliaments such as the Netherlands the term 'amendments' is kept for proposals by individual members, in contrast to 'government modifications' which differ from them in that they may arise in the course of debate. In most countries the government's right of amendment derives from its right to introduce bills. The right of members to move amendments is in many countries governed by rules designed to ensure that they are considered in a clear and orderly sequence and that amendments to bills with financial implications are restricted in scope. These rules require first of all the observance of certain formalities. In most Parliaments amendments must be submitted in writing. This is the position in Poland and Yugoslavia, though in the other People's Democracies and the U.S.S.R. as also in Ethiopia, Finland, Norway and Switzerland they may be moved in debate without being put in writing. Sometimes by analogy with the rules governing the right to introduce bills, amendments are only in order if they are supported by a specified number of members. In the Second Chamber of the Netherlands there must be at least five signatories of an amendment; in the Belgian Senate two (or five after the conclusion of the general debate), and in the House of Representatives (while the debate is still on) five; in the Austrian National Council eight, in the Spanish Cortes ten, in the Japanese House of Representatives twenty and in the House of Councillors ten, and in the Federal German Bundestag at the third reading fifteen. In Italy, if put forward within the hour of the opening of the sitting, an amendment must be supported by ten members. In Luxembourg however it may not be signed by more than five members.

As a rule amendments have to be distributed before they are considered. In most Parliaments it is enough to distribute them during the sitting at which they are to be taken, though if they are not circulated earlier the committee concerned or the government may request that they should be re-committed for further study. Notice of the terms of amendments is desirable because it makes for the orderly conduct of debate. But only rarely does an Assembly require them to be handed in before the sitting at which they are to be taken. Twenty-four hours' notice must be given in Denmark, Ghana, Iceland, Ireland, Israel, Italy and the United Arab Republic. In India amendments must be submitted before 3 p.m. on the last sitting day before the bill is considered. In Ireland amendments must be submitted two days beforehand, as in Pakistan where the rule is only applied by the Speaker if the member so requests. In the Argentine amendments have to be on the notice paper for twelve days before the sitting at which they are to be taken. Twelve days' notice is also obligatory for reports of committees that are to be debated. A similar procedure is found in France and Sweden. In the French National Assembly amendments may be submitted only during the four days following the distribution of the report of the committee concerned. In the Senate the period varies; it is settled by the Conference of

Presidents at the request of committees. In Sweden amendments must be laid not later than ten days after the introduction of the bill to which they relate. But the Assembly may extend this period to the first sitting that takes place within fifteen days of the introduction of the bill.

Apart from these rules governing form and notice, a good deal of latitude is generally left to proposers of amendments. They can either propose to leave out or amend a part, a clause, a paragraph, a sentence or particular words or to insert new provisions. But amendments must relate to the bill itself. The rules usually deal with 'counter proposals', that is to say, amendments which taken as a whole represent an alternative to the bill under discussion but an alternative embodying different principles. This type of amendment is obviously not permitted in those assemblies in which the general principles of a bill are defined before it is discussed in detail. The submission of a counter proposal is in practice the same as introducing a new bill, and it is hardly appropriate to the ordinary procedure for amending a bill. That is why as a general rule counter proposals and any other amendment which is outside the scope of the bill are held to be out of order.

Some Parliaments have other rules governing the subject matter of amendments. The main restrictions have to do with public money. Here practice varies very considerably. In Australia (House of Representatives), Ceylon and Ireland a member may not propose an amendment which would have the effect of increasing public expenditure or the incidence of taxation. In general among countries applying British procedure amendments of this kind are admissible only on the recommendation of the Crown or Head of State. In the House of Commons they must also be within the scope of a money resolution which is adopted before the bill is taken in committee, specifying the limits within which a change may be imposed if the bill is passed. In Japan amendments with financial implications must be supported by fifty members in the House of Representatives and by twenty members in the House of Councillors. In the Lebanon and Turkey amendments to increase expenditure or reduce revenue are only admissible during the debate on the budget. In Iran they are out of order if they have the effects of increasing the charge on the exchequer. The same principle is embodied in the constitutions of France, the Central African Republic and Senegal: bills and amendments thereto put forward by individual members are not admissible if they would have the consequence of diminishing the revenue or creating or increasing a charge. This provision in practice greatly reduces a member's right of amendment. In several countries, moreover, a government may claim that amendments which do not fall within the field of the law or which traverse powers delegated in a previous statute are out of order.

These are the main restrictions on the right to submit amendments. Some other procedures are worth special mention. In Ghana amendments to leave out a clause are inadmissible. In the United Arab Republic once an amendment has been agreed to, it can stand referred to the committee on legislation which ensures that it is properly drafted and is in harmony with the text of the bill. In Monaco an amendment has to be accepted by the government before it can be put to the vote. In Parliaments on the British model the rules governing the admissibility of amendments may vary with the stage of the bill: at the third and final reading, only verbal amendments are admissible.

It would be out of place here to go into the detailed methods of debating amendments. In general they are always considered before the part of the bill (the clause or paragraph) to which they refer is agreed to. They can themselves be modified by amendments to amendments provided that the main object of the original amendment is not traversed. Debate on an amendment is frequently limited by a five minute rule on the American pattern. In the French National Assembly only the proposer, the spokesman for the government, the chairman or rapporteur of the committee concerned and one speaker against may be heard.

An important problem which can have a decided effect on the final shape of the bill is the order in which competing amendments, that is, amendments relating to the same point in the bill but different in scope, are called. In countries which follow the British procedure, in Switzerland and in the U.S.S.R. and most of the People's Democracies, amendments are taken in the order in which they are handed in; and later amendments may fall if earlier amendments are agreed to. In Great Britain it is worth noting that an amendment to leave out words and insert other words takes precedence over other kinds of amendment. On the other hand in most countries of Western Europe, Cameroon, Japan, Lebanon, Turkey, the United Arab Republic and Yugoslavia priority is given to the amendment furthest away from the terms of the bill. In the United States amendments proposed by committees have precedence of others. In Norway and Poland the order is determined by the President.

The powers of the President of the House in the matter of amendments may also have a decided effect on the shape of a bill. As a general rule the President's powers are limited to assessing their admissibility or priority where there are precise rules on these matters. In the event of dispute the House has invariably the right to settle the issue in the last resort. In the British House of Commons the Speaker (and the Chairman of a Committee of the whole House or of a standing committee) has the unusual power to select from the amendments on the paper those which are to be debated. This wide power of selection has to be used with the greatest care. It presupposes great impartiality on the part of the Chair as well as a profound knowledge of the subject matter of the debate and an unusually acute political sense. This power of selection by the Speaker is not recognised in other Parliaments on the British model. Whatever the advantage to debate, the underlying principle is too controversial and its exercise too risky for it to be extended to other Parliaments.

Once the House has reached its decision on all the clauses in numerical order and on all the amendments relating to them, it has to vote on the bill as a whole. This vote is the last step in the process of enacting the law except for the agreement of the other House in bicameral Parliaments.

5. METHODS OF VOTING

In the course of its proceedings, and particularly when debate comes to an end, Parliament has to take various decisions. This is done by voting. From the vote a majority emerges on the matter under dispute, and the opinion of this majority according to the democratic rule overrides the opinion of the minority and becomes binding on all citizens. Naturally enough this crystallisation of the will of the people is surrounded by special ceremonial and is safeguarded by rules designed to eliminate any possibility of chance, error or fraud, and to ensure by publication that the electors have some control over the actions of members of Parliament.

(*a*) *Kinds of ballot*

Publication is not always desirable. It is generally avoided when the House functions as an electoral body, that is, when it makes its own appointments either within the House itself (President, Vice-Presidents and other members of the Bureau) or in the various bodies in which it is represented and for which it nominates members; or again where it exercises certain constitutional prerogatives such as the election of the Chancellor in the Federal Republic of Germany and the Head of State in Israel, Lebanon and Yugoslavia. The vote is secret,

THE MAKING OF LAW

which means that no one knows how any individual member has voted. The most that can be done is to check the members' names to ensure that they only vote once. For a secret vote ballot papers carrying the names of candidates are inserted in envelopes, and these are placed in a ballot box.

Secret voting is not always confined to appointments. In Rumania and Sweden it is the normal method of voting for checking credentials and for questions of immunity; in Yugoslavia it may be used, if the Chamber so decides, for checking credentials and for unseating a member. It is rare for secret ballot to be used in legislation. But it is the usual procedure in the Italian Chamber of Deputies and in the Rumanian Grand National Assembly for votes on bills considered as a whole. In these two instances voting papers are used for the ballot. In several Parliaments a secret ballot may be held if requested by a given number of members. Ten may do so in the Lebanon and the Central African Republic, twenty in the Italian Chamber of Deputies, twenty-five in the Austrian National Council and one-third of the members of the National Council of Monaco. In Albania and Rumania the Assembly may also decide to have a secret ballot on specified matters. In Turkey in that event the names of those requesting the ballot are noticed in the official report of the sitting.

Apart from appointments and these few other exceptions, decisions taken by Parliament are open and public. Most voting is public, in the sense that it takes place in the presence of people who have come to attend the sitting and can see what line a member is taking; but as a rule the term 'public voting' is confined to the type of vote in which the name of the member of Parliament and the way he has voted can be ascertained because it is published in the official report of debates. Some methods frequently used because they are time-saving make this impossible and give a measure of anonymity to the decisions taken.

First there is oral voting. The President calls upon members of the House to signify their views in turn by calling out 'Aye' or 'No'. The opinion which is expressed most loudly is regarded as being the opinion of the majority. At times it may be difficult to say what is the outcome of an oral vote. Proof of this is seen in the cautious wording used by the President or Speaker: 'I think that . . .', and in the frequency with which these votes are challenged. The margin of error inherent in the system limits its use for practical purposes to votes in which there is virtually no dissent. It comes close to a vote by tacit consent in that the question from the Chair whether there are 'any objections' usually leads to the adoption of a proposal. The vote by calling Aye and No is the usual method is Great Britain and several other countries such as Australia, Ghana, India, Liberia, Nigeria, New Zealand, Pakistan, the Philippines, Sierra Leone, Sweden and the United States (House of Representatives).

Secondly there is voting by show of hands. This method is more reliable than oral voting because it allows a rough count of those for and against a question. In Israel and Monaco every vote is taken by this method. It is normal practice in the U.S.S.R. and the People's Democracies and in many other countries such as Argentina, the Central African Republic, Chile, Ethiopia, the Federal Republic of Germany, France, Iceland, Italy, Laos, Lebanon, Luxembourg, Monaco, Somalia, Turkey and the United Arab Republic when no dispute arises and on matters for which a public ballot is not expressly required by the constitution or by the rules of procedure. In Ghana and Liberia voting by a show of hands is provided for when an oral vote does not give a certain result.

Thirdly there is voting by sitting and standing. This method resembles voting by show of hands but it is more accurate. It is often used to check a vote by show of hands or oral voting. The Speaker of the House of Commons may resort to this kind of vote in order to avoid taking a division if he thinks that a small minority of members is exploiting the time a division takes as a means of obstruction. Voting by sitting and standing is the classic method of voting in the Parliaments of Austria, Belgium, Ceylon, Denmark, Finland, Greece, Iran, the Netherlands, Norway, Spain, Sweden and Switzerland (National Council). When the result is difficult to decide, especially where the voting is close and the protagonists of each side of the question are scattered over the benches, the accuracy of a vote by sitting and standing can be improved by the President's asking members to gather together according to opinion on one side of the Chamber or the other in order to facilitate counting the votes. This is often done in the Italian Chamber of Deputies and in the United States House of Representatives where a teller for each side is appointed by the Speaker if one-fifth of the quorum, that is, forty-four members, request.

When these methods fail to give a result or when it is necessary to record the vote given by each member, a more precise form of open ballot is held. This is more time-consuming and can provide an opportunity for obstruction. But an open ballot makes it possible for the names of the voters and an indication of how they have voted to be recorded in the official report or the minutes of proceedings of the House.

Three main methods of voting achieve these objects. First, there is the division which along with oral voting is the method used in the

British House of Commons. Warning bells are rung throughout the building. After a few minutes the members wishing to take part in the voting are considered to have returned to the Chamber. The Speaker invites them to go into lobbies on either side of the Chamber, the Ayes through the lobby to the right of the Speaker's Chair, the Noes through the lobby to his left. As members pass through the lobbies their names are noted by the clerks. As they emerge from the lobbies numbers are counted by four tellers, two for the Ayes and two for the Noes. The two tellers for each lobby are drawn from among the members for and against the question on which the vote is being taken. Voting by division, with a few variations on the procedure just described, is also found in Australia, Ghana, India, Nigeria, New Zealand, Pakistan and the United States (House of Representatives). It is also used in the French Senate where it may take place without any formal checking or alternatively by open ballot. In that event each senator on leaving the hemicycle hands in a voting paper marked for or against. In the Bundestag of the Federal Republic of Germany a division takes place when members of the Bureau are not agreed on the result of a vote by show of hands or by sitting and standing. Members are invited by the President to leave the Chamber. The doors are then shut. Two secretaries are stationed at each of three doors marked 'Yes' 'No' or 'Abstention'. The doors are opened on the instructions of the President and members are counted as they pass through the door of their choice. When the process is completed, the President orders the doors to be closed. The secretaries at each door inform the President of the numbers of each category. The President and secretaries then vote, and the President announces the result.

The second kind of vote, the vote by roll call, is the most widely used. It can be found in most Western European countries and in Argentina, Canada, Ceylon, Chile, Ethiopia, Lebanon, Libya, the Philippines, Somalia, Turkey, the United Arab Republic and the United States. As his name is called out, each member replies 'Aye', 'No' or 'I abstain'. The replies are ticked off as they are made and the numbers in favour and against give the result.

The third method, by using voting papers, is quicker and where necessary it can be used for voting by proxy. Members are provided with voting papers marked with their names and differing in colour according to the way they wish to vote. They place these papers in urns that are passed round the benches. This is the basic method of voting in Cameroon, the Central African Republic and Laos and the subsidiary method in countries which use a system of electrical voting where there is a mechanical failure.

Finally there is mechanical voting, by some form of electric or electronic device, which has the advantages of speed and precision. It saves time and avoids disputes. Votes are cast by means of a series of buttons located on the desk of each member. The votes are registered instantaneously and computed. The results are shown immediately on a lighted board on the wall of the Chamber. Simultaneously all the particulars of the vote—the names of voters and the way in which they have voted—are photographed or printed so that the results can be published rapidly and completely. Electric or electronic voting is used in Argentina, Belgium, Finland, the French National Assembly, India and Sweden. It is being installed in Turkey.

The foregoing is a brief summary of the various kinds of voting used in Parliaments. Although they are varied, some general conclusions can be suggested.

First every Parliament has at least one method of each kind whether secret, anonymous or open. Ordinarily it uses anonymous voting, which is rapid and informal; if the result is in doubt it can resort to methods of open voting which are slower but more accurate. In some Parliaments these methods are compulsory for certain matters such as motions of censure and final votes on all bills or simply on money bills.

Secondly the British system is to rely on oral voting as the anonymous method and voting by division as the more public method, while on the European continent and in many other countries voting by show of hands or by sitting and standing is the anonymous and voting by roll call the more public method.

Finally most of the voting methods require members of Parliament to be present in person; voting by proxy is generally prohibited. Theoretically the proxy system is permissible in the House of Lords, but in practice the tradition is found only in Brazil and Luxembourg. The main objection to voting by proxy is that it encourages absenteeism; but it has the advantage of eliminating surprise votes, especially when the balance between majority and minority is a fine one. The system of 'pairing' lightens in some degree the burden of having to be present in order to vote. If a member of Parliament intends to be absent, he asks a member on the other side not to take part in votes called during his absence, so leaving the balance between majority and minority unaffected. This system, based on a gentleman's agreement, is practised mainly in Australia, Belgium, Great Britain and the United States. In France and the Central African Republic personal voting is tempered by a system of delegated voting: if a member is absent for specific reasons, he may appoint another member to vote on his behalf.

(b) Quorum and Equality of Votes

Whatever voting system is used, decisions are taken as a general rule by a majority of votes cast. As with rare exceptions voting by proxy is prohibited, the size of the majority is dependent on the number of persons present, and this has its drawbacks. It is possible for a bill to be passed in the name of an entire nation by an extremely small number of members of Parliament. As a safeguard, in most Parliaments the presence of a minimum number of members is required, if not for debate, at least for a vote. In some countries such as Finland, Israel and Sweden there is no obligation of this kind; in others such as France the quorum is formally noticed only if attention is called to it before a vote begins. But in many Parliaments a vote is not valid unless it says that a quorum is present. Usually the quorum is half the members of the House plus one as in the Argentine, Belgium, Lebanon, Monaco, the Netherlands and Somalia, and in the U.S.S.R. and most of the People's Democracies. In Australia, Austria, Greece and Poland it is one-third of the members. In Great Britain and Ireland the requirements are less stringent. In the House of Commons the minimum is forty, and in the House of Lords three; in the Dail twenty and in the Senate twelve. The main effect of the quorum is to ensure that in theory at least the number of votes in favour of any decision taken will be fairly substantial. In practice the question of a quorum rarely arises. It can only arise automatically when a form of voting that gives an exact count of heads is being used. It does not arise in anonymous votes which are the most common kind. In order to avoid possible obstruction, Parliaments often provide that the question of quorum may be raised only by a given number of members or by the leaders of parties or groups.

Given that ordinarily decisions are taken by a majority of the votes cast, what happens when there is no majority, when there is a tie in the voting? The answer usually given in most Parliaments is that the question put to the vote is not carried. This is logical because a majority consists of half the votes plus one. In the Netherlands the decision is postponed to a later meeting. Another vote is taken, and if it again results in a tie, the question is negatived. In a few instances the President or Speaker decides the matter by his own vote. In the Australian House of Representatives and in Japan the President also has a casting vote. In Finland and Sweden the decision is come to by drawing lots. The President places in a special box two voting papers identical in appearance, one marked 'Yes' and the other 'No', and enclosed in sealed envelopes. A member appointed by the President draws out one of the papers which decides the matter.

(c) Special Majorities

An exact count of the votes is always essential where a specific number of votes is necessary to pass a bill or agree to a motion; that is, a given proportion either of the votes cast or of the total number of members or of the two together. But this requirement is quite exceptional for ordinary legislation. Subject possibly to a rule governing the quorum, all decisions are normally taken by a simple majority of the votes cast. The practice in Cameroon hardly rates as an exception to the rule: if the prime minister of one of the federal states requests, a bill may not be passed unless the majority in favour of it contains a majority of members from each of the federated states.

In some countries 'organic bills', that is to say, bills which apply a principle laid down in the constitution, have to be passed by a special majority. The constitution of the United Arab Republic specifies a two-thirds majority of the members of the Assembly to pass these bills. The same is true of Austria. In France if agreement between the two Chambers is not forthcoming, an organic bill can only be passed by the National Assembly at its final reading if carried by an absolute majority of its members. According to the Greek constitution the appointment of a regent when the King is absent through illness must be formally approved by the Assembly in a resolution supported by a majority of three-quarters of the votes cast. In Sweden the extension of the lifetime of Parliament requires a majority of three-quarters of the votes cast in each House.

There are also examples of special majorities applying to bills of a financial character. In Finland a bill which imposes or increases a tax for a period exceeding one year must obtain two-thirds of the votes cast. In Switzerland expenditure over a certain sum must have the consent of a majority of the members. This rule acts as a brake on expenditure.

Other examples of special majorities in the field of legislation in different countries are a motion to declare a bill urgent as in Italy; a resolution to ratify a treaty which needs two-thirds of the votes cast in the Senate of the United States; and, also in the United States, a motion to end the process of sending a bill backwards and forwards between the two Houses and to override the President's veto or request for a second consideration. These proceedings are considered in a later Chapter.

Special majorities are used much more frequently to decide matters other than legislation. There are first matters relating to the internal organisation of Parliament and the status of members such as the election of the President and members of the Bureau or the adoption or suspension of rules of procedure, as in Australia, Austria, Denmark, Federal Republic of Germany, Italy and the House of Representatives of the United States; the closure as in the Senate of the United States; secret sittings as in the Federal Republic of Germany and Ireland; immunities as in Finland and the Netherlands; disqualification as in Japan, Lebanon and Libya; and the empowering of committees to make formal enquiries as in Lebanon.

Secondly there are matters touching the relations between Parliament and the executive such as the election, dismissal and impeachment of the Head of State and the prime minister, and votes of confidence or motions of censure.

Finally, there are constitutional matters. The constitution is generally considered more important than the ordinary law and in some countries proposals to amend it are treated differently.

6. CONSTITUTIONAL BILLS

In theory and practice the principle that the constitution overrides ordinary law is unchallenged today. In Great Britain however the manner in which power is distributed among various institutions can only be discovered by referring to a whole series of bills, customs and usage which in theory do not bind Parliament. But the respect in which the British people hold their institutions is a greater guarantee of stability than the provisions of a formal constitution. In the same way there is no written constitution in the strict sense in Israel. Certain laws have taken on the character of fundamental principles. They contain provisions which blur the formal distinction between constitutional and statute law. The law on the Knesset for instance may not be traversed by any regulations that may be adopted under urgent procedure; and some of its provisions may only be amended by a special majority. The position is the same in New Zealand. In theory the ordinary procedure for legislation applies to constitutional matters. But under an electoral law of 1956 some specified provisions may only be amended if carried by three quarters of the membership of the House of Representatives or as a result of a referendum.

In all the countries which have a written constitution, the actual supremacy of that constitution is reinforced by a formal supremacy: its essential feature is that all bills to revise the constitution are subject to extremely stringent rules. The methods devised by makers of constitutions to safeguard their work are many and varied: restrictions on the right to introduce a revising bill; time limits and special majorities; joint sittings of both Houses or the setting up of a constituent assembly; appeals to the country by general election or referendum; all these methods either singly or in combination make the path of the reformer thorny.

As a rule it is for the legislature to initiate a revision of the constitution. The procedure is normally the same as for the introduction of a bill. In some countries a proposal must be backed by a given number of members, for example, two-fifths in Albania, one-third in Tunisia and the United Arab Republic, a quarter in Brazil and Bulgaria, a fifth in Somalia, thirty members in Yugoslavia and ten in the Lebanon. In other countries the right of initiative may be extended to a specific portion of the people: 50,000 electors in Switzerland may request by petition either a complete or a partial revision or 10,000 electors in Somalia.

The procedure of popular consultation that precedes fundamental reforms in the U.S.S.R. and the People's Democracies has already been noticed. In federal states local legislatures may have the right of initiative. This is the position in the U.S.S.R. where it is exercised by the supreme soviets of the republics of the Union and in the United States by the state legislatures provided that two-thirds of them decide in the same way. In Brazil the state legislatures have the right of initiative if not less than half of them so decide by an absolute majority of the votes cast and within two years.

The procedure for revising the constitution varies with the form of the proposal. A motion of principle is usually moved, and it has to be decided before a bill is brought in and debated. Several countries have adopted this system with variations of greater or less complexity.

The simplest procedure is that of Tunisia. If the President of the Republic or one third of the members of the Assembly put forward a proposal to revise the constitution, it is debated and voted upon by the Assembly. An absolute majority of the votes cast is needed to carry the proposal. The object of the Assembly's resolution is to define the principle underlying the proposed revision which has already been considered in detail by the competent committee. Only when this resolution has been adopted can the reform go forward. It is then given two readings separated by an interval of not less than three months. At both readings a majority of two-thirds of the members is required to carry the reform.

In Yugoslavia proposals to revise the constitution may be presented by thirty members of the Federal Council, by the council of nationalities, by the President of the Republic or by the federal executive council. The Federal Council and the council of national-

THE MAKING OF LAW

ities first decide whether the proposal should be debated. If after two different debates they cannot agree on whether the proposal should go forward, no further action can be taken for one year. If they do agree, the proposal is submitted to the various Chambers of the Federal Assembly for their opinion. Then it is considered successively by the council of nationalities and the federal council who have to agree on the terms of a bill. If the Federal Council does not approve the bill drawn up by the council of nationalities, the matter must be adjourned for two months. At the end of this time the disputed provision may be debated twice in each Council. If agreement is still not reached, the two Councils may decide that a referendum on the bill should be held. If they cannot agree to do so, the Federal Council is dissolved. The bill may only be passed if supported by two-thirds of the members of these two Councils. It may be taken up again within fifteen days by not less than three other Councils. In that event it must be submitted to a referendum.

In the Lebanon the procedure is complicated for members; the government is entitled to submit directly to the Assembly a bill to amend the constitution. A member may proceed in the following way. Not less than ten members may propose that the constitution should be revised, making at the same time a specific statement of the articles they are seeking to amend. This proposal requires a majority of two-thirds of the membership of the Assembly; if successful it is sent to the government. If the government agrees, it must present a bill within four months. If it disagrees, the resolution is sent back to the Assembly with a request for a fresh deliberation. If the Assembly maintains its resolution by a majority of three-quarters of its membership, the President of the Republic has two possible courses open to him. He may accept the Assembly's proposal or he may dissolve Parliament. If he decides to dissolve, general elections must be held within three months. If the new Parliament persists with the proposal to reform the constitution, the government must introduce a bill within four months. The Chamber to which the bill is referred may only deliberate if two-thirds of its members are present, and decisions must be taken by a majority of two-thirds of the membership. In the period allowed for promulgation the President of the Republic may request a fresh deliberation during which the same majorities are required.

In Greece proposals to revise provisions of the constitution which are not fundamental require a majority of two-thirds of its membership of the Chamber. The resolution must specify the provisions it wishes to revise. Two votes separated by an interval of at least a month must be taken on the resolution. Once the principle of revision has been agreed to, debate on the substance of the amending proposals may only be begun by a Chamber which has been newly elected. The necessary majority is an absolute majority of the members.

In Argentina, Belgium and Luxembourg a special assembly is elected to consider proposals to revise the constitution. Elections are held in the Argentine, following a decision of Congress showing a favourable majority of two-thirds of its members; and in Belgium and Luxembourg following a declaration that the procedure for revising specific constitutional provisions may go forward. The dissolution of Parliament then takes place automatically. In Belgium the constituent chambers proceed independently with the proposals which to be approved require the support of two-thirds of the votes cast and the attendance of two-thirds of the membership. In Luxembourg the Chamber may only deliberate if three-quarters of its membership is present and decisions must be taken by two-thirds of the votes cast.

This last system comes close to that used in Finland, Iceland, the Netherlands and Sweden where the procedure is as follows: a bill is first debated and read the first time by Parliament. At this point Parliament is dissolved and general elections are held. The new Parliament takes up the bill to which its predecessors had given a first reading and votes on the bill as a whole, having no right to make amendments. A two-thirds majority in Finland and the Netherlands and a simple majority in Iceland and Sweden are necessary to carry the bill. In this way the people are playing an indirect part in the enactment of constitutional laws, with full knowledge of the issues at stake. In Finland there is a more expeditious procedure: if the House by a majority of five-sixths of the votes cast declares a revising bill to be urgent, it may proceed to the final decision by a two-thirds majority without a general election.

The procedure of a double consideration by the same Parliament is also found in Brazil, Italy, Somalia and, as was seen above, in Tunisia, though after a vote has been taken on a resolution determining the principle of the revision. In Brazil Parliament must decide the matter in two consecutive sessions by an absolute majority of the members of each House. The two considerations may take place during one session but in that case the majority becomes two-thirds of the membership. In Italy a bill to revise the constitution is passed by each House after two successive debates separated by an interval of at least three months. An absolute majority of members is required for the second vote. In Somalia the same minimum period of three months is required between the two debates; but the majority is an absolute majority in the first debate and a two-thirds majority at the second.

In most countries Parliament is the sole authority with power to amend the constitution; but it is customary to require a special majority to support an amendment in order to preserve the supremacy of the constitution. This majority may be an absolute majority of the total membership of each House provided that two-thirds of the members are present and voting, as in India where in some instances amendments are also required to be ratified by the legislatures of not less than one-half of the states; two-thirds of the votes cast, as in Ceylon, Nigeria, Norway (sitting as the Storting), Sierra Leone, as well as in Austria and Poland where the attendance of half the members is also required; and three-quarters of the members present, as in Libya.

In the Parliaments of Albania, Czechoslovakia, Bulgaria, Hungary, the Central African Republic, Rumania, Turkey and the U.S.S.R. the special majority is two-thirds of the membership of each assembly. The same majority is required in the Bundestag of the Federal Republic of Germany, while a majority of two-thirds of the votes cast is required in the Bundesrat. In Pakistan a proposal to revise the constitution requires a favourable vote of two-thirds of the membership, a majority which rises to three-quarters if the proposal is not approved by the Head of State. In the United States amendments to the constitution must be passed by each House of Congress by a majority of two-thirds of its members. Unlike ordinary laws, they do not go to the President for approval or veto; they are sent to the states and do not take effect unless ratified by three-quarters of the state legislatures or by conventions in three-fourths of the states.

In the Philippines the special majority is three-quarters of the members of Congress. In Cameroon a bill to revise the constitution may not be passed unless the majority which is supporting it comprises a majority of members for each of the federal states.

The last method of amending the constitution is to consult the people, as the original constituting authority, in a referendum. In Australia, Denmark, Ireland, Japan, Spain and Switzerland a bill to amend the constitution has first to be passed by Parliament and is then submitted to a referendum. In Australia the referendum may take place when a bill has only been adopted by one House if the second House after two debates separated by three months has declined to come to a decision on the bill or has rejected it. In Japan the preliminary vote on a revising bill must show a favourable majority of two-thirds of the members of each House. In Switzerland a constitutional reform must be approved not only by a majority of the people but also by a majority of cantons. In three countries the referendum is not obligatory. In Italy a bill to amend the constitution is only submitted if within three months of its publication a referendum is requested by one-fifth of the members of either House, by 50,000 electors or five regional councils.

In France a revising bill passed by both Chambers becomes definitive when approved by referendum. But the President of the Republic may decide that the bill should be considered by the two Chambers sitting as a congress instead of submitting it to a referendum. In that event the revising bill must be approved by a majority of three-fifths of the votes cast. A comparable procedure is found in Senegal although here of course Parliament comprises only one House.

These are the various procedures used today to safeguard the supremacy of constitutions and the stability of regimes. They must of course be flexible enough to allow institutions to evolve, as is sometimes essential. Modern experience shows that the procedure for reforming the constitution should not be so difficult that a recourse to violence is the only solution.

7. AGREEMENT BETWEEN THE TWO HOUSES

In bicameral constitutional systems legislation is the work of both Houses. The part played by each House may be equal to that of the other, or it may vary, according to a country's constitution. Whatever their relative strengths may be, agreement between the two Houses on a bill puts the final seal on the legislative process. It is therefore important to provide machinery for reaching agreement and to set some limit to exchanges of view if disagreement persists.

The problem scarcely arises in Parliaments where the lower House enjoys a distinct superiority over the upper House. Two examples are worthy of note. In Austria the National Council alone has legislative power. While the Federal Council has the right to challenge any bill by a resolution giving its reasons, the National Council can override it by reiterating its original decision, provided only that at least half its members are present. In the First Chamber of the Netherlands members may not introduce bills or propose amendments. But it has the power to throw out a bill passed by the Second Chamber; and if it does so its decision has to be accepted by the Second Chamber.

Conversely the principle of equality between the two Houses may at times greatly simplify the procedure for agreement. The method used in unicameral-bicameral systems such as in Iceland and Norway follows naturally from the artificial division into two Houses. All that need be done is to revert to their original form—Althing or Storting—and the disagreement disappears. Decisions must however be taken by a majority of two-thirds of the votes cast.

The procedure under which the two Houses meet together in a joint sitting is also used in India. If a bill is passed by one House and defeated in the other or if the amendments which each House wishes to make are not the same or if six months elapse without one of the Houses passing or rejecting a bill sent to it by the other, the President of the Union is empowered to convene a joint meeting. At this meeting decisions are taken by a majority of the members of the two Houses present and voting.

Everywhere else the relationship between the Houses is less cut and dried. Each House has a life of its own, and it is essential to establish a relationship which will enable agreement to be reached should the need arise.

The classical method is that each House in a series of readings examines the bill as passed by the other until the decisions on the whole bill are uniform. The bill is sent constantly from one House to the other, a process known in Western European Parliaments as '*la navette*'. It resembles the exchange of 'messages' used in the British Parliament and other Parliaments on the British model such as Australia, Canada, Ceylon, Ireland and Nigeria. The message sets out the differences in the views of the two Houses. When one House receives a message, it considers the points on which differences have arisen, and motions are introduced signifying agreement or disagreement with the other Houses or proposing new amendments to reach a compromise. The exchange of messages goes on until agreement is reached. If the two Houses do not agree, the bill cannot become law.

A different method, of which there are many examples, is to appoint a joint committee known under a variety of names such as 'mediation', 'conciliation' or 'conference' committees consisting of an equal number of members of each House. The function of these bodies is to come to an understanding and subsequently to submit a plan to each of the two Houses for their views.

These joint committees may be called upon to sit earlier in the legislative process, as they are sometimes in Great Britain. In Sweden every committee is a joint, permanent or special committee, and agreement is made easier by the fact that both Assemblies consider the bill at the same time. But in general joint committees are only used when differences have already become apparent in the two Houses after one or several debates.

This procedure is used in federal Parliaments to reconcile differences between the representatives of the people and those of the states. The most characteristic example of this procedure is found in the Federal Republic of Germany which has a permanent mediation committee consisting of eleven members of the Bundestag and eleven members of the Bundesrat with its own rules of procedure. In other federal states such as Australia, Brazil, the United States, the U.S.S.R. and Yugoslavia joint committees are not permanent; if there is disagreement, a special committee is set up. In the United States when a 'conference' is held, members of the House and of the Senate sit as separate groups. Decisions are taken by a majority of each group. Joint committees are also used in different ways and with varying frequency in France, Ireland, Japan, the Philippines and Turkey. In Libya and Switzerland joint committees consist of the appropriate permanent committee of each House sitting together.

What happens if agreement is not forthcoming? Settlement depends first and foremost on the particular brand of bicameral system; it differs according to whether or not the two Houses are on an equal footing in legislative matters. If they are, it is quite conceivable that no decision can be reached in the face of persistent intransigence on the part of one or other House. The legislative process cannot then be completed. This happens in Belgium and Italy when the process of sending the bill backwards and forwards does not result in complete agreement because the bill is laid aside if at any moment one of the Houses rejects it as a whole.

The bill may remain suspended despite the use of joint committees; they may be unable to evolve a compromise or to persuade their parent assemblies to adopt it. This can happen in the United States, Brazil and the Philippines. In Switzerland if the compromise worked out by the two permanent committees sitting together is not accepted by both Houses, the bill is regarded as rejected: the way out of the impasse is negative. In Libya in the same circumstances, the bill may not be taken up again for one month. The same result is achieved in Yugoslavia after a more complex procedure. First an attempt is made to resolve the differences by sending the bill backwards and forwards between the two Chambers concerned and if agreement is not forthcoming a joint committee is set up. If its work proves to be vain, the matters under dispute are considered afresh by the two Chambers. If disagreement persists, the bill is withdrawn from the order of business and may not be included again for at least six months. In Sweden if the disagreement persists, the matter is adjourned until a later session, with the exception of bills concerning the budget, the national bank or the public debt administration. A new vote is then taken in each House, and the grand totals of the 'Ayes' and 'Noes'

THE MAKING OF LAW

decide the issue. The lower Chamber has a considerable advantage because it has a larger membership. These are the only circumstances in which the principle of equality of the powers of the two Houses does not apply.

There is a more drastic solution, to dissolve Parliament. This can happen in a number of countries. In Australia the two Houses generally reach agreement after exchanging messages. Sometimes a 'conference' consisting of an equal number of members of each House is held. In the last resort the constitution contains 'deadlock provisions' for overcoming an impasse. If the House of Representatives sends a bill to the Senate on two separate occasions with an interval of three months between them and the Senate rejects or amends the bill on each occasion, the Governor-General may decree the simultaneous dissolution of both Houses. When the matter in dispute comes up again after the elections, a joint sitting may be held to settle it. In the same circumstances the U.S.S.R. also provides for an appeal to the country. If the Soviet of the Union and the Soviet of Nationalities disagree, the matter is brought before a conciliation committee formed by the two Houses on an equal footing. Should this committee fail to settle the dispute or should its decision fail to satisfy either of the two Houses, both Houses go into the matter again. Where the disagreement persists, the Presidium of the Supreme Soviet dissolves the Supreme Soviet and new elections are held.

Countries where the lower House has greater powers than the upper House do not need to go so far as this. Because of this difference, any disagreement can always be solved to the advantage of the popular House. This is the position in those countries where debate in the upper House is subjected to time limits of varying strictness. In Ceylon rejection or amendment of a bill by the Senate is effective only for one session. If the bill is taken up again by the lower House at the following session, the Senate is powerless to oppose it. In Ireland under the constitution the Senate has ninety days in which to consider bills sent up to it by the Dail. Within 180 days of the expiry of this ninety-day period, a bill passed only by the Dail is deemed to be passed by both Houses in the form in which the Dail approved it if the Dail so resolves. For money bills and bills declared to be urgent this period is much shorter. When the Senate, acting within its due rights, insists on its amendments to a bill, it may request the setting up of a 'conference' of members of the two Houses to reach an agreement.

In Great Britain the House of Lords no longer has more than a sort of suspensory veto. Should it reject a bill sent to it by the House of Commons or fail to agree with the House on the details of a bill, disagreement is effective only for two successive sessions, and for a total period of one year. At the end of that time the House of Commons can pass the bill again, and it can become law in spite of the opposition of the Lords.

Disagreements are also settled to the advantage of the lower House where it has the power to vote by a special majority, regardless of opposition in the other House, or where the procedure for conciliation allows the lower House the last word. This is the position in the Federal Republic of Germany for bills which do not require the formal consent of the Federal Council. If the mediation committee fails, if it approves the bill as passed by the Bundestag or if the Bundestag rejects its proposals, the Federal Council may protest. That protest may only be rejected by an absolute majority of the membership of the Bundestag. If the Federal Council has agreed to protest by a majority of two-thirds of the votes cast, the Bundestag may only reject it by a majority of two-thirds of the votes cast, representing more than half its membership. If the protest is rejected, the bill is deemed to be passed.

In Japan the use of a joint committee consisting of ten members of each House is a decisive stage in the legislative process. If this committee does not come to an agreement, the bill is rejected. But if a compromise is agreed to by a majority of two-thirds of the members of the committee, the bill as amended in committee becomes definitive and it is submitted as such to the two Houses, though priority is given to the House which has called for the setting up of a joint committee. If agreement is not forthcoming the House of Representatives may still take up the original bill and may pass it by a majority of two-thirds of the votes cast. In Turkey the use of joint committees is somewhat similar. The committee prepares a new bill different from but based on those passed by the Assembly and the Senate. All three bills are then submitted to the Assembly which must pass one of them without amendment. But where the Senate passes its own bill by an absolute majority of its members or a majority of two-thirds of the votes cast, the Assembly if it wishes to maintain its own bill must pass it by the same majority. In France the use of a joint committee comprising an equal number of members of each Chamber underlines the greater influence of the National Assembly over legislation. It is for the government to propose the setting up of a joint committee when a bill has not been passed after two readings by each Assembly or after one reading if the bill has been declared urgent. If the joint committee does not agree on a compromise bill or if the bill is not agreed to in the same form by both Chambers, the government may request the National Assembly to decide the matter finally after a new reading in each Chamber. The National Assembly may take up either the bill as amended by the joint committee or the bill as the Assembly had already passed it, modified if necessary by one or more amendments made by the Senate. In practice the French system may be distinguished from others in the same category by the constant power of the government to intervene and, by powerful methods like the block vote of which it disposes, to ensure the rapid passing of the bill in the form which it prefers.

15. The Promulgation of Laws

ROYAL ASSENT – PROMULGATION AND PUBLICATION – REQUEST FOR A NEW CONSIDERATION – THE VETO

The passing of a bill by both Houses is generally the final stage of the legislative process. The work done by the two Houses must then be promulgated. Promulgation authenticates a bill as a law and gives it binding force; it also entails its publication. Under a monarchy the act of promulgation takes the form of a 'royal assent'. In most countries it gives the executive a final opportunity to challenge the decisions of Parliament by using the procedure of veto or of the request for a fresh consideration. In some countries, as will be seen in the next chapter, it affords an opportunity for ensuring that the laws passed by Parliament do not conflict with the constitution.

1. ROYAL ASSENT

Royal Assent is the act with which the Sovereign consents to bills passed by the two Houses of Parliament. The implication is that the Sovereign shares the legislative powers with the two Houses; and in some countries this implication is still valid. In Ethiopia the Emperor may either slow down or prevent the carrying out of a law of which he does not approve. In Greece the King approves and publishes laws passed by Parliament. Any law not published within two months of the close of the session becomes null and void. In Libya the royal veto does not have an absolute character. The King must approve and promulgate laws within thirty days of receiving them; within this period he may refer them back to Parliament for a fresh consideration. If the two Houses on this occasion pass the bill by a majority of two-thirds of their membership, the King has to approve and promulgate it within thirty days. If the special majority is not attained, the bill may not be taken up again in the same session. In the next session it may be passed if it is carried by an absolute majority of the members of each House.

In most other monarchies, especially those in Western Europe, the right of the Sovereign to assent to bills is today a theoretical right. Its existence dates back to the time when the King was the sole legislator, and Parliament functioned merely as his advisory body. In Great Britain the Sovereign even today continues to hold this traditional prerogative because he is considered to form a part of Parliament. The Queen in Parliament has in theory the right to refuse her assent to a bill duly passed by both Houses. But it was last withheld in 1707, and it is most unlikely ever to be withheld again because its use is incompatible with the constitutional convention that the government and not the Sovereign is politically accountable. By analogy with the British system the royal assent is given in Australia, Ceylon, Nigeria and New Zealand, usually through the Governor-General who is the representative of the Crown.

The royal assent is also given to bills in Belgium, Denmark, Luxembourg, the Netherlands, Norway and Sweden. For the same reasons as in Great Britain the withholding of the royal assent would raise questions of leadership and responsibility. It would require the support of the government; so in practice it would only be withheld from a bill which had not been introduced by the government. A serious conflict could then arise which might entail the resignation of the cabinet or the dissolution of Parliament. It is interesting to note that in Norway, although withholding the royal assent is practically unknown, the constitution does enable Parliament to overcome such an action: a bill may come into force notwithstanding royal opposition if it is carried in the same form by the Storting in three different legislatures or in three ordinary sessions separated by two other sessions. In several countries such as Japan where the Emperor has thirty days in which to take action, the royal assent is normally signified at the same time as promulgation by the Sovereign's appending his signature at the end of the bill together with the counter-signature of the responsible minister.

2. PROMULGATION AND PUBLICATION

Promulgation is first and foremost a formality designed to make an Act of Parliament enforceable by giving official notice of it. This is essential both for the authorities which will have to apply the Act and for the public at large which will be subject to it.

An Act of Parliament may come into force either when it is promulgated or when it is published in the official journals and gazettes. Sometimes the constitution prescribes when Acts of Parliament which do not themselves contain a date of application shall come into force. The usual period is one day after publication in Austria, France and Monaco, three days later in Bulgaria, five days in Switzerland, eight days in Yugoslavia, ten days in Belgium, Greece and the U.S.S.R., fourteen days in the Federal Republic of Germany, fifteen days in Albania, Italy and Somalia, twenty days in Spain and Japan, twenty-one days in the Netherlands and twenty-eight days in Australia. In the Argentine and Brazil the period of grace before the act comes into force varies in different parts of the country according to their distance away. The same is true of Iran. An Act comes into force in the capital ten days after publication; in the provinces the period increases by one day for every 36 kilometres of distance from Teheran.

In several countries the executive takes no part in promulgating an Act; this is the duty of the legislature. The Act comes into force on being authenticated and published by the appropriate body within parliament. In Albania, Bulgaria, Hungary and the U.S.S.R. the President and Secretary of the Presidium are responsible for the publication of laws passed by Parliament. In the U.S.S.R. publication must take place within seven days of a law's being passed, and in each of the official languages of the republics of the Union. In Czechoslovakia the Presidential Bureau has fourteen days in which to ensure publication. In Poland this duty falls to the President and Secretary of the Council of State. In Rumania it is shared by the President of the Assembly and the President of the Council of State. In Yugoslavia laws are promulgated by the President of the Republic but the decree of promulgation has to be countersigned by the President of the Federal Assembly. In Switzerland the position is in practice somewhat similar as there is no machinery for promulgation in the Swiss constitution. The Presidents and Clerks of the two Houses sign the original copy of the Act and pass it on to the Federal Council for publication.

In most other countries responsibility for promulgation lies with the executive. Usually it is the task of the Head of State. Where he does not have full responsibility, the promulgating decrees must be countersigned by the members of the cabinet.

The real problem is whether promulgation is obligatory or optional for the executive power and whether at this point it can challenge the bill passed by Parliament. The logic of parliamentary government requires that the decision of Parliament should be final and that promulgation by the executive should be automatic. During the passage of a bill through Parliament the government has any number of opportunities for expounding its ideas and getting them accepted. If it is unable to do so, it ought to accept the bill which has been passed or resign. This is the position in Austria, Iceland and Israel where the executive has no means of preventing the law coming into force either temporarily or permanently.

The same principle is also observed in the Federal Republic of Germany and in Ireland, though here the question arises in a different form. In Germany apart from the question of their constitutional validity, laws must be signed by the Federal President, but the government is empowered to prevent their coming into force if they increase the expenditure above the level proposed by the government or directly or indirectly authorise new expenditure. In Ireland promulgation may be delayed if the President thinks that a bill is of such importance that it should be submitted to the people for approval. The decision of the President must however be founded on a petition addressed to him by a majority of the members of the Senate and at least one-third of the members of the Dail. After consulting the Council of State and if he thinks the petition is well-founded, the President will only sign the law if it is approved within eighteen months by a referendum or by a resolution agreed to by the Dail after a general election has been held.

3. REQUEST FOR A NEW CONSIDERATION

Where the executive power is required to promulgate laws, it may also be given the right to request Parliament to consider again a bill that has been passed. The object is to give Parliament an opportunity to look again at measures it may have taken without due consideration. The request for reconsideration, which must be made before the time limit fixed for promulgation, is simply an invitation to reflect on the matter. At the reconsideration Parliament is not bound to follow any particular procedure nor to pass the bill by a special majority. All it has to do is to debate and vote once more. Its final decision is then binding upon the executive.

This is the procedure followed in France, Italy, India and Turkey. According to the French constitution the President of the Republic must promulgate a bill as law within the fifteen days of its being sent to the government. But before the end of this period he may request Parliament to consider the bill or some of its provisions afresh. This request may not be refused. The same is true of Italy although here the President of the Republic has one month in which to exercise this power, and if he does so he has to send Parliament a message setting out the reasons for his action. A message must also be sent in India for all bills except finance bills. It is for the President to propose the amendments which he thinks necessary. A similar procedure is found in Turkey. The President of the Republic must use his powers within ten days but they do not apply to either finance or constitutional bills.

In the Lebanon, Senegal and Tunisia the Head of State enjoys a virtual right of veto although it is described as a request for a new deliberation. If Parliament in any of these countries decides to insist on a bill, it has to pass it by a special majority, a procedure which lends a political character to the power exercised by the President of the Republic. In the Lebanon he has one month from receiving the bill or five days if the bill is declared to be urgent in which to use this power. At the second deliberation a bill must be passed by an absolute majority of the members of the Assembly if it is to be promulgated. In Senegal and Tunisia the period allowed for promulgation is only fifteen days but the bill must be supported by a majority of two-thirds of the members of the Assembly in Tunisia and three-fifths in Senegal. In Senegal the bill is promulgated automatically when the periods laid down by the constitution have expired. If the bill is not promulgated by the Head of State the President of the National Assembly does so.

4. THE VETO

The right of veto is a different matter. Unlike a request for a new consideration, it implies a right to intervene decisively in the legislative process. It is a characteristic feature of the presidential system and especially of the constitution of the United States where it is the corollary to the principle of equal and separate powers. The President is independent of Congress and because he is elected by popular suffrage he too is entitled to participate in the process of legislation. He does this by vetoing bills passed by Congress if he sees fit to do so.

Every bill passed by Congress is sent to the President. If he does not approve of it, he must return it within ten days (Sundays excluded), stating his objections, to the House in which it was introduced. A bill left unsigned by the President ten days after it has been sent and not referred back to Congress enters into force provided that Congress is still sitting. The proviso enables the President to exercise a kind of tacit veto on bills presented to him less than ten days before the adjournment of Congress. This 'pocket veto'—so called because the President keeps the bill in his pocket and prevents it becoming law without openly expressing his opposition—has been used on many occasions. If the House passes by a two-thirds majority a bill returned by the President, it is sent with the President's objections to the second House. If that House also passes it by the same majority, the veto is overridden and the bill becomes law. The essential feature of the veto is that it is merely suspensory. Its original purpose was to safeguard the executive's rights in legislative matters. Gradually that purpose has been eroded, and the veto has become the method by which the President can test public opinion on any difference he may have with Congress. But he has to move carefully, because if Congress chooses to ignore his veto, this would be not only a parliamentary rebuff but also a public expression of dissatisfaction with his policy.

The procedure for the veto is similar in several other countries. In the Argentine and Brazil the period allowed to the President is also ten days; it is twenty sitting days in the Philippines and thirty days in Chile. A majority of two-thirds is required in all these countries to override the veto. In the Philippines a majority of three-quarters of the members of each House of Congress is required when a bill providing for a greater expenditure than ten per cent over the budget of the previous year or a bill which would have the effect of increasing the public debt is vetoed.

In Brazil, unlike in the United States, if the President withholds his agreement to a bill after the end of a session he must make public his decision. When Congress is informed of the Presidential veto it holds a joint meeting of both Houses. If it decides by a majority of two-thirds of those present to confirm the bill it is sent to the President for promulgation within forty-eight hours. At the end of this period the bill may be promulgated by the President of the Senate or at the end of another period of forty-eight hours by the Vice-President of the Senate. In Chile in the same circumstances, that is, in default of action by the President of the Republic, the bill is deemed to be promulgated after fifteen days.

The right of veto is also accorded to the Head of State in Liberia,

Pakistan, Somalia and the United Arab Republic. In the last three of these countries the time allowed to the President is thirty days. It is five days in Liberia. To override the veto a majority of two-thirds of the members is required in Pakistan and the United Arab Republic and two-thirds of the members present in Liberia and Somalia.

The powers of the President of the Finnish Republic bear some resemblance to the suspensory veto. When a bill has been passed by Parliament it is sent for approval to the President of the Republic. If the President does not give his approval within three months, the bill is regarded as dead, unless it is passed once more in the same form by a new Parliament after general elections have been held. The bill then becomes law without the President's approval. In Iceland if the President refuses to approve a bill passed by the Althing the disagreement is settled by a national referendum.

These examples show that the veto is not an insurmountable obstacle to the will of the legislators who have usually only to remarshal their forces or to bide their time in order to get their own way. But there are also examples in constitutional law of an absolute veto, as in Ghana or Spain, where if the Head of State refuses to approve a bill passed by Parliament, the bill is dead. This type of prerogative is linked directly with the royal assent in its original form.

With one or two exceptions promulgation provides the executive with a last opportunity to intervene in the legislative process. While it may be necessary for rounding off the process of legislation, the right to promulgate underlines the preponderant power of the executive in the legislative process, already seen in its right to introduce bills, to secure delegated powers and to dominate debate within Parliament. The principle that Parliament exercises exclusive legislative power no longer corresponds to reality in most countries today.

16. The Constitutional Validity of Laws

Control over the constitutional validity of laws is a classical theme of constitutional law. Both the principle of control and the practical difficulty inherent in it have given rise to controversy. As a form of control it flows logically from the principle that the constitution is supreme, at least in the many countries which have a 'rigid' constitution and a special procedure for its revision, thus showing that the constitution is above an ordinary law. The purpose of control over the constitutional validity of a law is to draw attention to a constitution which is binding on the whole country and so resist its infringement by the legislation. This is the overriding principle which the ordinary law must respect.

The first difficulty arises with the 'flexible' constitutions which can be altered by the passing of an ordinary Act of Parliament as in Great Britain. Here the status of the legislation as subordinate to the constitution is not formally laid down so that control over the constitutional validity of Acts of Parliament can have no meaning. It might be argued that control derives from the principles of jurisprudence in which all social organisation is rooted. But this justification takes no account of the practical difficulties of exercising the control. At best it is a matter for the conscience of the legislators who must themselves set limits to their own powers.

The notion of control presupposes a body which is independent of the institution to be controlled; otherwise judge and interested party become confused. This is the major difficulty. There are two objections to a controlling body outside Parliament. First it traverses the principle of the separation of powers, recognised in many countries, which precludes anybody other than the legislature itself from taking part in the law-making process. It cannot be argued that a court set up to verify that laws are valid is part of the legislative machinery because it has not been elected by the people. Secondly to submit the decisions of Parliament to an external body is to make that body superior to Parliament or at least to concede that Parliament must share the duty of interpreting the sovereign will of the people as expressed in the constitution.

It follows that where Parliament is considered to be the supreme authority in the state, there is no control over the constitutional validity of laws, even where there is a written constitution formally recognised as supreme by the provision of a special procedure for its amendment. This is the practice in Albania, Bulgaria, Czechoslovakia, Poland, Rumania and the U.S.S.R., where Parliament itself ensures that the constitution is respected. In Hungary the National Assembly may consult the procurator general and the president of the supreme court for this purpose.

This absence of control is also found in other countries. In Belgium Parliament is deemed to have decided a bill's constitutional validity by passing it. In the Netherlands the oath taken by members of

Parliament to abide scrupulously by the constitution is considered to make unnecessary any control over the constitutional validity of laws. Absence of control is also a feature of the systems in Iran, Israel, Laos, Lebanon, New Zealand and Spain.

Where this control is recognised, it can be exercised only by a body outside Parliament. But the difficulty of reconciling the powers of such a body with the powers of Parliament is precisely what has caused the failure of most attempts to exercise this control. In general two methods of control have been used, sometimes as in the Federal Republic of Germany and Turkey in combination or juxtaposition. The first is to keep a careful watch on legislative activity before it takes place and to nip in the bud any measure which appears to be unconstitutional; the second consists of an *a posteriori* scrutiny of laws already brought into force.

Prior control is exercised between the time when a bill is passed by Parliament and the time when it comes into force as law. It is entrusted as a rule to the political body responsible for promulgation, that is, to the Head of State who may either decide himself by refusing his assent or refer the bill to the body empowered to exercise this control.

In the Federal Republic of Germany before signing a bill the President has the right and the duty of making sure that it conforms to the constitution. However his only concern is the formal constitutional validity of the bill; he has to check that the correct procedure has been followed. In one instance of his refusal to approve a bill, the advice of the federal constitutional court was sought. Whether the President has himself the right to consider the substantive constitutional validity of a bill is a moot point. In Finland the President may refuse his assent to a bill that he considers unconstitutional. Before taking his decision he may seek an opinion from the supreme court of justice or the supreme administrative court or both these courts.

The President of Ireland has seven days after receiving a bill passed by Parliament to decide whether it should be referred to the Supreme Court. The court must give its decision within sixty days. If it deems any provision of the bill to be at variance with the constitution, the bill may not be promulgated.

In the Federal Republic of Germany and Ireland other ways of testing the validity of laws are available. France, Cameroon, the Central African Republic and Senegal on the other hand have the single procedure of prior control. In France before being promulgated organic bills must be submitted to the constitutional council which decides whether they conform to the constitution. Ordinary bills may be referred within the same period to the constitutional council by the President of the Republic, the prime minister, or the President of either Chamber. The council has one month in which to decide the matter or eight days at the request of the government if a bill is declared urgent. When a bill is referred to the constitutional council the period for promulgation is extended. If it is declared unconstitutional the bill may not be promulgated or put into force. The decisions of the council are final and they bind all public authorities and the administrative and judicial courts. A similar procedure is provided in the Central African Republic under which bills are referred to a constitutional council. Reference to the federal court of justice in Cameroon, and in Senegal to the Supreme Court, is reserved in this field to the Head of State alone.

The procedure of prior control is thus seen to be essentially political in character: it is applied before the bill becomes law and by authorities whose composition depends on the hazards of power. By contrast once a bill has been promulgated as law, the control appears to be a legal control, and it is natural for it to be exercised by the judiciary. The arguments in favour of this method of control are the independence, impartiality and professional training of a judge who is accustomed to settling legal disputes, and the advantage of court proceedings which furnish valuable safeguards for the contending parties. In practice where judicial control of constitutional validity is recognised two main procedures are followed; first control through a plea of constitutional invalidity and secondly control by direct action.

The first procedure presupposes that an action is brought in the ordinary courts, the courts being required to apply the disputed Act of Parliament. One of the parties may then ask the court not to apply the Act on the grounds that it is at variance with the constitution. One of two things may then happen: the court may decide the matter and the parties may if necessary appeal, through the usual hierarchy of courts; or the court of first instance must withhold decision and request the highest court to decide the matter.

The second of these proceedings is found in Ghana, Nigeria, the Philippines and Somalia where the Supreme Court alone has power to decide whether a bill conforms to the constitution. The first proceeding under which the ordinary courts are competent to judge the matter and the Supreme Court only intervenes if necessary in the last resort is more common. It has been written into several constitutions of which examples are the Argentine, Brazil, Canada, Chile, Japan and Liberia.

In Ireland the jurisdiction of the High Court extends also to the validity of Acts of Parliament, but a decision of the High Court may be appealed against before the Supreme Court whose ruling is final.

Control over constitutional validity is sometimes the result of case-law and precedent. The best-known example of this is the United States where since 1803 the judges of the Supreme Court have held that their constitutional function requires them to resolve conflicts between ordinary law and constitutional law in the same way as any other legal dispute. Precedent and case-law have also provided the ground for pleas that particular laws conflict with the constitution in such countries as Denmark, Greece, Iceland and Norway. In the United Arab Republic and in Sierra Leone the ordinary courts can take cognisance of these pleas.

When the control operates by way of a plea that a law is unconstitutional, the decision of the court at whatever level applies as a rule only to that particular case: if a law is held to be unconstitutional, it is simply laid aside as far as that case is concerned. It is not generally nullified, and it could if necessary be applied in other circumstances. That is the theory. In practice once a decision by the courts has been given in this sense, a law which has been judged unconstitutional is soon regarded as null and void.

Direct control can be distinguished from control by way of a plea in the courts by its results: if a law is held to conflict with the constitution, it is annulled absolutely and with universal application, not only for the parties in a suit. Control by direct action can also be distinguished by the way in which it comes into play. A special type of legal proceedings is initiated against the law in question either by private persons or by public authorities. Direct control can be exercised either before the highest judicial court or before a special judicial body set up for this purpose. In the first category there is the Supreme Court in Libya, the High Court in Australia and the Supreme Court in Ceylon where there is in the last resort an appeal to the Privy Council which sits in Great Britain. An action may be set on foot by any person who considers himself damaged, as in Monaco where the constitution stipulates that the Supreme Court shall decide any appeal to annul a law, to test its validity or to allow compensation where the liberties or fundamental rights of citizens may have been traversed. The Supreme Court has power to declare the law null and void. It may also take cognisance not only of substantive ordinances or decrees and regulatory measures taken by the executive powers as well as all decisions emanating from an administration but also of laws themselves; all become null and void from the day on which the court delivers an adverse judgment.

Control over the constitutional validity of laws may finally be exercised by a special body such as the constitutional court in Austria, Italy, the Federal Republic of Germany, Turkey and Yugoslavia. In the last three of these countries the powers of the court are broadly construed. In the Federal Republic of Germany a plea of unconstitutionality may come before an ordinary court in the first instance. The court must withhold its decision and request the federal constitutional court to decide the issue. Furthermore if differences of opinion or doubts arise whether a federal law is compatible with the fundamental law, the federal government, the government of a Land or one third of the members of the Bundestag may request the court to give a decision. Again if any person considers that a federal law impairs his fundamental rights as laid down in the fundamental law, he may challenge it before the constitutional court within one year of its entry into force.

In Turkey the constitutional court may also entertain pleas of unconstitutionality. A plea only lies in the ninety days following the publication of a law and it may only be entered by a specified number of persons or bodies, namely, the President of the Republic; a political party which has attained at least ten per cent of the valid votes in the previous general election, or its representatives in the National Assembly or its entire parliamentary party or group; one sixth of the membership of either Chamber; the higher council of the magistracy; the court of appeal; the council of state; the military court of appeal; and the universities.

In Yugoslavia the constitutional court decides the constitutional validity of a law if requested to do so by one of the Chambers of the Federal Assembly, the federal executive council (the government), the federal supreme court or the federal public prosecutor. The court is also empowered to consider questions of constitutional validity of its own volition. Workers' and citizens' organisations can move all these authorities to take action. If the constitutional council decides that a federal law conflicts with the constitution, the Assembly must amend the law within six months to make it conform. If the Assembly fails to do so, the provisions of the law that have been declared unconstitutional cease to have effect at the end of that period.

There has been a marked tendency in recent years to set up some system for controlling the constitutional validity of laws. The problem is to decide whether it serves any useful purpose. Is it a device for resisting arbitrary action by the legislature against human rights and public freedoms? Or is it one more device for diminishing the role of parliamentary assemblies?

PART FOUR

Powers of Parliament over Finance

Among the various items of parliamentary business, financial matters, and first and foremost the scrutiny of the national budget, are in a special category. This is mainly a matter of historical evolution. Nowadays, the law relating to public money is frequently regarded as a subsidiary aspect of constitutional law, and there is a tendency to lose sight of the fact that constitutional law in a sense derives from it. In the history of Parliament the powers to be won were powers over finance; they were the core around which modern constitutional systems gradually took shape. The legislative powers of Parliament which today are regarded as one of the bases of democracy were acquired after its powers over finance: the people demanded and won the right to consent to the levy of taxes before they began to bid for a share in law-making. It was the combination of this right with the right of petition that gave the House of Commons in England its power in the legislative sphere: by making the Crown accede to its wishes as a condition of its own consent to taxation, on the well-known principle that 'grievances precede supply', it gradually established its right first to suggest and then to impose legislation, and to see that effect was given to its will in all other fields of government as well as finance.

Parliament grew strong through the struggle to protect the country from extortion by the Monarch. But today the position is very different. Instead of keeping a tight hold on the purse-strings, Parliaments are often apt to be free with money. Their original functions of keeping expenditure within proper bounds has now been taken over by governments which are responsible for producing sound budgets and fight shy of any move which is likely to jeopardise them. This has become so much the rule that in many countries the powers of Parliament over finance have had to be restricted, though in some countries the principle of parliamentary sovereignty remains unqualified. Thus financial matters remain, as always, in a special category, though for different reasons.

17. Nature of the Budget

In a material sense the budget is an estimate of the total financial needs of the state and the total resources required to cover them. It is a sort of tabular conspectus of the estimated public expenditure and income over a given period, generally a year. The budget as a collection of financial data has several purposes. First, it enables total income to be compared with total expenditure; secondly, it allows expenditure to be classified and its relative importance and urgency to be assessed; thirdly, it enables its effect on the economic situation and on any national plan to be determined; and lastly, it facilitates parliamentary control.

These objects show that the budget is a representation in figures of the government's plan of action. But legal validity can only be given to it by Parliament. By approving the budget Parliament gives the executive authority to do two things. The first is to raise revenue. The principles of representative government require that the right to collect taxes should be formally approved each year by Parliament. In most countries the legislation under which taxes are imposed is permanent, but the authorisation to apply it is valid for only one year. By this means Parliament can exercise an important periodic check on the actions of the executive. In some states taxes can be gathered without the formal authorisation of Parliament. But Parliament can repeal or amend the relevant statutes at any time, so that in these countries Parliament's consent to a tax, though tacit, is still necessary.

Secondly, Parliament authorises the executive to spend money. Expenditure, like the levying of taxation, must be approved by Parliament. Originally, Parliament merely voted a specific sum of money which it handed over *in toto* to the Monarch to be used as he thought fit. The next stage was to insist on knowing how the sums granted were spent. Finally Parliament itself decided how they should be spent by allocating the money for specific, detailed purposes and forbidding the practice of 'virement', that is, of transferring unused sums from one type of expenditure to another. By these successive steps Parliament consolidated its financial authority. But this detailed control throws up its own problems. Modern expenditure is so complex that a thorough study of all its details is seldom practicable. The tendency today is to return to the old system of voting a lump sum to cover the expenses of a given sector of administration and of looking subsequently at the detailed heads and subheads of expenditure.

The budget may be regarded as a law passed by Parliament in that its approval by Parliament follows the ordinary rules of legislative procedure. In a more practical sense it is open to question whether a national budget can be appropriately assimilated to a statute. The law is a general and impersonal statement of rights and obligations. But an evaluation of revenue has generally no legal force, so that while in all countries the budget embraces all taxation, fiscal resources and all manner of public income, the resulting obligations as they affect the man in the street do not derive from the budget itself but from permanent statutes establishing the system of taxation in force and having an existence of their own that is distinct from that system. In the same way the estimates of expenditure given in the budget have no legal force in most countries. The authorisation granted to the government to spend money does not by itself create subjective rights or obligations; they are the outcome of financial legislation which is separate from the budget, and the figures in the budget merely represent its application for one year. Only to this extent can it be said that the budget is binding on the departments of state.

On this reasoning several countries hold that the budget as such does not partake of the nature of legislation: it is regarded as a purely administrative measure. According to the constitution of the United Arab Republic, the draft national budget must be submitted to the National Assembly for examination and approval. How that approval is to be given or how the rights of Parliament are safeguarded is not specified. Similarly, in Switzerland the budget is not embodied in a bill but in a government decree which sets out an approximate estimate of the revenue and expenditure for the year ahead. Both income and expenditure are founded on provisions other than those in the budget. Approval by Parliament is a separate act which does not affect the nature of the document to which it gives approval.

In Iceland, Norway and Finland where the same distinction is made, it is emphasised by a procedure that departs substantially from the traditional legislative pattern. In Iceland and Norway the budget is considered by a joint meeting of both Chambers—that is, sitting as the Althing in Iceland and the Storting in Norway. The budget may not include anything but the estimates of revenue and expenditure and the joint meeting may not alter existing legislation. If the contents of the budget should call for the amendment of the existing law, separate bills must be introduced. The same applies in Finland where in addition the budget is given a single reading instead of the three readings needed for passing an ordinary bill.

In the same way, the British system does not regard the budget as a bill dealing with public revenue and expenditure. It is simply a financial programme put forward by the government to justify the amounts sought in the appropriation bills. It is introduced in a formal statement by the chancellor of the exchequer, the minister primarily responsible for public finance. It consists of a number of proposals whose object is to adjust revenue to expenditure. Budget resolutions concerned chiefly with the incidence of taxation embody these proposals and eventually provide the foundation for the finance bill. The budget itself is not a piece of legislation; provisions to apply its proposals have to be brought forward in the form of bills. This procedure which is the outcome of a pragmatic concept of a budget means that bills dealing with expenditure and finance bills dealing with taxation and revenue are debated and passed separately. This concept and the consequential procedure is also found with variations of detail in Australia, Canada, Ceylon, Ghana, India, Ireland, Nigeria and Pakistan.

In the United States the budget is adopted by Congress in much the same way. Every year in January some days after sending Congress his message on the state of the union, the President sends a message on the budget setting out in a single document the complete financial provision for one year. But this budget is not more than a basis for discussion because Congress is then called upon to pass a whole series of appropriation bills, and, if necessary, a revenue bill. This distinction between what is strictly speaking the budget and the bills which give effect to it is also found in Japan. The budget goes through the ordinary procedure of a bill, but it is not promulgated and does not carry full legal authority. No public body may legally recover revenue or contract for expenditure which has not been specifically authorised by a bill or a regulation made under a bill.

In most other countries Parliament formally approves the substance of the budget in the form of a bill. This bill which makes due provision for revenue and expenditure goes through the same stages as any other bill, including promulgation, and is then regarded as carrying the same authority as any other statute. The example of France is especially significant. Even the term budget has been abandoned in favour of the term financial bill, which comprises the total revenue and expenditure. Under the heading of revenue are found taxes and fines, payments for services, rents, dues and royalties, funds from investments, gifts and legacies, revenue from public property and public investments in nationalised industries, repayment of loans and advances and other miscellaneous revenues. The expenditure of the state comprises ordinary expenditure on such matters as servicing the public debt, grants for public authorities, the cost of staff and supplies for the public services and of state intervention in economic, social and cultural expenditure, capital investment, comprising straightforward investment, subsidies and war damage payments, and loans and advances approved by the state. The unity of the budget is preserved by passing a single bill which has effect for one year. Broadly, the same system applies in most of the countries of Western Europe and in the U.S.S.R. and the People's Democracies. The budget is also presented in the form of a bill in Cameroon, the Central African Republic, Ethiopia, Iran, Laos, Libya, Senegal and Somalia. Even where the estimate of revenue and expenditure is annexed to the finance bill as in Israel, it constitutes an essential part of the bill and is passed along with the bill.

The practice of treating the budget as a single annual financial bill is sometimes exploited in order to pass through Parliament provisions which, strictly speaking, have nothing to do with public revenue and expenditure. Tacking provisions on to this financial bill is usually forbidden though sometimes it is a convenient way of disposing of a matter which if raised by itself would not have the same chance of being approved.

In some countries, especially Belgium, Italy and the Netherlands, the use of the ordinary procedure of legislation has been taken to extremes: there are as many separate financial bills as there are ministries, and each is debated and passed separately. This method may have the dangerous consequence that if one or more of the bills is rejected, amended or retarded without regard to the effect on the others, the unity of the government's budgetary proposals may be seriously disturbed.

18. Preparation and Presentation of the Budget

The primacy of the executive right from the start of the procedure on the budget is absolutely clear. There is an unusual measure of agreement that the government alone has the right to draw up and present a budget. This exclusive right stems from the realities of the situation. The budget is first and foremost an instrument of policy. It can bring about a radical redistribution of the national income and influence profoundly the economic and social structure of the country. It spells out with detailed facts and figures the government's programme of action. It is only proper that the executive should have a completely free hand to work out all the implications of this programme. These arguments are especially cogent for countries in which the budget is worked within the ambit of a long-term national plan.

The second reason for the executive's powers in budgetary matters is a technical one. The government is the only authority that has an accurate picture of the needs of the various services and of the amount of revenue likely to be available. Ministers alone are in a position to assess accurately the cost of running the public services; and only the finance departments are equipped to make a synthesis of all this expenditure and to strike a balance between it and the total revenue.

The complexity of a modern budget is such that only a small group of persons who are both fully informed and highly skilled can undertake its preparation. It must first and foremost be homogeneous, a characteristic which is hard to reconcile with a large deliberative assembly's having a hand in it. In this context the experience of the United States before the reforms of 1921 is revealing. Until that date, because of the strict observance of the principle of the separation of powers, the task of preparing a draft budget fell to Congress itself. Each service prepared its own estimates of expenditure and submitted them to Congress through the medium of the secretary to the treasury. The function of the treasury was limited to this transmission and to computing the total receipts. The budget did not represent a preconceived total but simply the sum total of separately formulated demands. Most often they were directly considered by sub-committees working without any co-ordination within Congress. This procedure reflected the original distrust in which the states held the President. But it frequently happened that contradictory decisions were made, and it was almost impossible to detect waste or to make any adequate appreciation of the total budgetary expenditure which could alone provide some remedy for the continual deficits. Only with the greatest reluctance did Congress recognise the need for executive responsibility in this field despite its desire to see a national budget established. An attempted reform in 1909 foundered on the traditional fear that the executive would become too powerful. In 1921 Congress passed the budget and accounting Act which entrusted the President with the duty of preparing and presenting to Congress the federal budget. It also set up a budget office within the treasury with important powers. For eighteen years this office carried out its duties in a strictly financial sense, laying special emphasis on economies in expenditure and limits on taxation. Yet events proved the need to give the President himself adequate powers to carry out his constitutional function; and in 1939 the budget office was brought directly under him. Since that date he has had full authority to control, alter and co-ordinate the estimates of government departments before submitting them to Congress as a single document.

This experience illustrates perfectly the need to entrust the preparation of the budget to the executive power. But this arrangement need not exclude consultations at this early stage with members of Parliament; and in many countries members with special knowledge are consulted. Only in Czechoslovakia have these consultations been formally recognised: here the estimates of government departments have to be submitted to the committees of Parliament before the budget as a whole is presented and their conclusions are considered by the government. This is an exceptional provision. As a general rule Parliament does not have the right of initiative in budgetary matters. Its only power is to amend bills introduced by the government subject to certain conditions which will be considered later. The only initiative Parliament can be said to enjoy is indirect, to the extent that the bills of individual members frequently have financial implications which find their way into subsequent budgets.

As it is for the government to present the budget, so it must be for the government to prepare the budget. Preparation is an administrative matter which is carried out in most countries along similar lines. The most prominent part is played by the ministry of finance, the department to which the task of estimating the revenue and suggesting any changes in taxation naturally falls. The responsibility of the chancellor of the exchequer in Great Britain, who must keep his budget proposals secret even from his cabinet colleagues until budget day, is well known. Without the same aura of mystery the same duties devolve upon the holder of the portfolio in all other countries. But what reveals most clearly the superior status enjoyed by the minister of finance in relation to his cabinet colleagues is the procedure for preparing and estimating expenditure. Estimates of expenditure are first worked out by the competent divisions of each of the departments; then they are gathered together under the direction of the department's minister and then sent to the minister of finance. The

PREPARATION AND PRESENTATION OF THE BUDGET

question then arises what powers the minister of finance can exercise over these estimates. In some instances he can do no more than take note and include them *en bloc* in the draft budget, leaving the cabinet as the only body which can make an alteration before they are submitted to Parliament. In most countries, however, the minister of finance can, on his own initiative, invite the ministers concerned to make changes in their estimates. If agreement cannot be reached, the matter in dispute is referred to the head of the government or, in the last resort, to the cabinet as a whole. Constitutionally the minister of finance has no greater powers than his colleagues but he makes his influence felt effectively in this way. This system works empirically in most countries in which the minister of finance is solely responsible for preparing the budget. In Finland, the budget estimates are drawn up by the minister of finance; they are considered first by the government's finance committee and then by the government as a whole.

In the United Arab Republic treasury control does not extend to the provisions relating to salaries and allowances; they have to be referred for approval to the central organ of organisation and administration before being sent to the ministry of finance. In Japan treasury control operates in two ways: first the estimates forwarded by each ministry are scrutinised and a provisional allocation of expenditure made which has to be approved by the cabinet. Then a detailed statement of the expenditure of each ministry is prepared. This makes for a more detailed control; and proposals can be put to the cabinet for reductions in expenditure that appear necessary. Should these reductions concern independent bodies such as the two Houses of Parliament, the supreme court or the audit office, they must be specified in the final budget together with explanations for them. In the Federal Republic of Germany there is an express provision in the budget code for the settlement of disputes between the minister of finance and the rest of the cabinet. All differences of opinion are brought first before the federal government. If the finance minister's view is overruled, he may enter a protest; in that event the item of expenditure in dispute may not be included in the budget unless a majority of all the federal ministers so decides, and unless the federal chancellor votes with the majority. In the same spirit the pre-eminence of the minister of finance is officially recognised in India where his rights over all expenditure and especially new expenditure are absolute and in Ireland where all expenditure must be expressly sanctioned by the minister of finance. In Norway disputes are considered by a 'budget conference' of the ministers concerned; but if they fail to agree the minister of finance settles the matter on his own responsibility.

The special status enjoyed by the minister of finance in both theory and practice sometimes gives rise to criticism. Since the budget is the most vital act of government policy, it is a legitimate question whether the responsibility for preparing it should not rest with the head of the government himself. This is in fact what happens in countries organised on the presidential system. In the United States, as was shown above, the duty of preparing the budget has been passed successively from Congress to the Department of the Treasury and finally to the President himself. Today three bodies, the committee of economic counsellors, the budget bureau and the secretariat of the treasury, co-operate in the work of preparing the budget. But the President alone settles disputes and takes decisions.

To sum up, with the exception of Czechoslovakia, any intervention by Parliament at the preparatory phase of the budget is virtually ruled out. It remains to consider the extent of Parliament's powers to debate and approve the work which the government has prepared.

19. The Budget and Public Corporations

On the principle that the national budget should be comprehensive, every source of income and every object of expenditure has to be shown. According to a theory favoured by liberal economists this rule should apply only to expenditure incurred by the administrative services which are public by their very nature and to revenue designed to cover that expenditure; expenditure for broader economic purposes ought to be met in some other way. Today however in the People's Democracies the state embraces all economic activities; and its tendency to play an increasing part is apparent in most countries, even including the United States where private enterprise is the basic economic credo. Here it is true that the state's intervention has been generally limited to questions of national defence or public welfare such as atomic energy, flood control or afforestation. In some circumstances however Congress has created autonomous public enterprises such as the Panama Canal Company, the celebrated Tennessee Valley Authority or the Atomic Energy Commission. In setting up these organisations Congress usually lays down the principles governing their scope of action. Moreover it has provided that reports on their activities should be made by these enterprises at periodic intervals. It is also the practice for their budgets to be laid before Congress for approval to see whether public funds ought or ought not to be put at their disposal.

Though still limited in number and scope in the United States most other countries have industrial or commercial undertakings owned wholly or partly by the state or subsidised by it. What should be their relationship to the national budget? Too strict an application of the principle that the national accounts should be comprehensive would make serious difficulties for the managers of these undertakings because the activities of these bodies are akin to those of similar establishments in the private sector. They frequently enjoy a measure of financial autonomy, that is the power to manage their businesses without being subjected to the accounting disciplines of a government department. In the U.S.S.R. and most socialist states where the national economy is wholly dependent on public corporations these bodies combine central direction with freedom of management. The capital programme of each corporation is authorised by the state on a rolling basis but its statement of revenue and expenditure and its account at the state bank are separate. Expenditure is covered by earnings from production. Surpluses are partly ploughed back into the enterprise to increase production in pursuance of social and cultural objects and are partly paid into the national budget as a deduction from profits. Losses are met by the profits from other corporations, by the council of the national economy (Sovnarkhoz) or by the state budget.

In countries where there is a large measure of private enterprise the relationship of public corporations to the national budget varies. It is usually determined by the law under which these bodies are set up. Several kinds of corporation can be distinguished, First there are those which are in some way assimilated to the ordinary administrative sources. Their earnings are paid directly into the exchequer and their expenditure appears as an item in the budget. They are not markedly commercial in character nor so monopolistic that it is impossible for private firms to do business of the same kind.

Secondly there are corporations which do not have separate legal status but do produce goods or provide a service as a commercial undertaking. Their accounts though separate from the national budget may take the form of an appendix to it and in this way are submitted to Parliament for approval.

The third and most common type of public corporation combines financial autonomy with a legal status distinct from that of government departments. While corporations in the first two categories are wholly subject to parliamentary control, those in the third category are free from the ordinary rules of public accountability and are not subject to the ordinary budgetary procedures. They come within the purview of the Parliament only in so far as they have to be granted subsidies, advances, loans or guarantees to enable them to cover their deficits or make new investments. In Great Britain for example these corporations only appear in the budget 'below the line', that is, in the part dealing with capital expenditure. Reference to them in debates on the budget tends to be sporadic and partial.

Parliamentary control over public corporations is exercised in various ways. Parliament's right to be kept informed of what is happening in these bodies is frequently recognised. Control may also be applied by the appointment of members of Parliament to the directing boards; by special supervisory bodies; by periodic scrutiny of the accounts carried out by committees or sub-committees; by holding inquiries; or through reports by the responsible minister, the audit office or the comptroller and auditor general.

In France the government is required to lay before Parliament every year a statement of the accounts of nationalised industries and mixed corporations. As an example of the different kind of scrutiny applied by Parliament to all these bodies, it may be interesting to cite the example of India where they fall into three categories.

The first category comprises industries like the railways and the post office which are state-owned yet function on commercial principles. The receipts and expenditure of each of these bodies are included in the national budget and are debated in Parliament in exactly the same way as the budget of a government department.

In the second category are public bodies set up by law. Only the ordinary loans and investment sums granted to them appear in the budget. The exercise of control by Parliament is thus limited and these corporations enjoy complete independence of management within the ambit of certain broad principles.

In the third category are private enterprises in which the government holds more than fifty per cent of the shares. The accounts of these bodies have to be audited by the comptroller and auditor general who makes a report on them to Parliament or to the public accounts committee.

In the Federal Republic of Germany the budgetary code makes detailed provision for Parliament's scrutiny of certain commercial enterprises whose actions pertain in whole or in part to the Federation. Estimates of the following sums are set out in the general

THE BUDGET AND PUBLIC CORPORATIONS

budget: receipts and profits resulting from federal participation in these enterprises; receipts from the sale of shares; receipts resulting from the winding up of enterprises; expenditure necessary to set up a new enterprise or to buy shares; and subsidies and loans granted to ensure their smooth running.

Moreover, if the shares of these bodies have a particular value or significance, the government must obtain parliamentary authority to sell or mortgage them or before a merger with other societies in which the federation does not hold a majority of shares takes place. Parliament also has the right to audit the accounts of these bodies.

The powers of Parliament to take action are not always so strictly guaranteed. In most instances however Parliament is able to ensure that its general powers of political control over government departments extends to public bodies which come under their authority.

20. The Budget and Bicameral Parliaments

In the first Part of this book it was shown that it is rare for the two Houses in bicameral Parliaments to enjoy equal powers. This inequality is as a rule most marked in financial and budgetary matters: here the powers of the upper House are either restricted or abolished. The effect is to alter profoundly the ordinary procedure by which agreement is reached between the two Houses. In some instances it ceases to apply.

In states built up on federal lines such as Switzerland and the U.S.S.R. the two Houses are as a rule on an equal footing; and they remain so even when they are dealing with financial matters. This is also true of the Federal Council and the Councils of Working Communities in Yugoslavia. The same principle applies to Italy, a non-federal state, where the two Chambers have exactly the same powers in financial matters. The concern to preserve equality is pursued to such a point that half the budget proposals are submitted to each House; the half submitted first to the Chamber of Deputies in one year is submitted to the Senate in the following year and *vice versa*. The same system is in operation in Belgium with a variation which is mentioned later.

In several other countries where the two Houses have generally speaking the same legislative powers the scales are weighted to some extent in favour of the lower House when financial bills are considered, usually by giving some degree of priority to the lower House. This practice derives from British budgetary procedure before the reforms of 1911 which placed the two Houses on a different footing in all matters. It is applied in the United States, at least for the granting of supply. In practice the budget is sent to Congress by the President and is referred by the Speaker of the House of Representatives and the President of the Senate to the committee on appropriations of each House. After many hearings by sub-committees which are empowered to examine the estimates of expenditure of each department, separate bills authorising grants of supply are prepared and presented to the House of Representatives. Custom alone imposes this priority; no constitutional provision prevents a bill's being first introduced in the Senate. But the constitution does reserve the initiative in financial bills for the House of Representatives while the Senate has the right of amendment. Priority is also enjoyed by the lower House in Argentina, Brazil and the Philippines. In Belgium the priority enjoyed by the House of Representatives in considering measures proposed by the ways and means committee is simply a matter of tradition because the constitutional law establishing it was repealed in 1921. In Norway and Iceland the question of priority cannot arise because the budget is debated by the two Houses meeting jointly as the Storting and the Althing. The only inequality stems from the disparity in the number of members of each House. A similar position arises in Sweden. Here the budget is first considered by joint committees and then debated in each House simultaneously. If the two Houses continue to disagree, a separate vote is taken in each House and the results are added together, giving an advantage to the larger body.

In all these countries the degree of inequality between the two Houses in financial matters is only slight; but its effect is more noticeable when it is merely one element of an inequality that applies more generally. There are few countries where the upper House does not find its already inferior powers still further curtailed when the time comes to examine the budget. In the Netherlands however the position of the upper House is not appreciably more subordinate in budgetary matters. As with other kinds of legislation, it has no right to initiate or to amend; but it does have the right to adopt or to reject *en bloc*.

In other bicameral Parliaments the fundamental lack of equality between the two Houses is greater still where budgetary matters are concerned. This difference appears to derive from the old monarchical system under which the consent of the people to new taxes had to be obtained. Historically the popular House was set up precisely to give this consent, and frequently they make a point of emphasising their privilege in the face of the upper House which is often handicapped by being aristocratic in origin.

In France the Senate has less power over bills than the National Assembly. This inferiority is reflected in proceedings on the budget. It must be laid first before the National Assembly; and although the National Assembly has forty days in which to read the budget for the first time, the Senate is given only the following fifteen days in which to do so. It has already been noted that where the two Houses disagree the last word rests with the National Assembly.

In Japan the House of Representatives not only debates the budget first but also has power to override decisions of the House of Councillors. If agreement cannot be reached through the medium of a joint committee or if the House of Councillors does not succeed in passing a measure within thirty days of its receipt, the decision of the House of Representatives is deemed to be the decision of the Diet. This procedure is distinctly harder on the upper House than the ordinary legislative procedure. In Turkey the annual financial bill has to be considered by a joint committee consisting of thirty-five members and fifteen senators. It is first introduced in the Senate and if the Senate makes an amendment the bill is sent to the joint committee. The National Assembly considers it last but its decisions are final.

In Australia the House of Representatives examines financial bills first. The Senate may reject them like any other bill but its right to amend them is limited in certain ways. It may not amend a bill creating taxes or granting supply for the ordinary annual services of the Government nor any other bill if the result of an amendment would be to increase any proposed charge or burden on the people. Nor may the Senate amend a taxation measure so as to cause an increase or decrease in the incidence of a tax. The Senate is able however to make requests for amendment in all instances in which its power of amendment is limited by the constitution. On the same principle the Canadian Senate may move to reduce taxation and expenditure but it may not propose their increase.

The superior status of the popular House is still more marked in some other bicameral Parliaments on the British model. In Great Britain itself the role of the House of Lords in this field has been virtually extinguished since the reforms of 1911 and 1949. Money bills are sent to the House of Lords after they have been passed by the

House of Commons, but they can receive the royal assent after one month whether or not they have been approved by the Lords. It is for the Speaker of the Commons to decide what constitutes a money bill. In Ceylon the procedure on these bills is the same: one month after a bill has been sent to the Senate it may be taken again by the House with or without amendments made by the Senate, and with the approval of the Governor-General it comes into force. In India the primacy of the lower House is equally clear. The upper House (Rajya Sabha) is in practice restricted to a general debate on the budget; and it does not vote on estimates of expenditure. Money bills and finance bills are sent to the upper House after being passed by the House of the People (Lok Sabha), but only to obtain its recommendations. These must be formulated within fourteen days. If they are approved by the lower House, the bill is deemed to be passed by both Houses with amendments proposed by the upper House and accepted by the lower House. If they are not accepted or if the bill is not sent back within fourteen days, the bill is deemed to be passed by both Houses in the form approved by the lower House.

Similarly in Ireland, the Senate has a mere twenty-one days to present its recommendations to the Dail which is empowered to decide the matter. This relegation of the upper House in financial and budgetary matters is not only confined to Parliaments of the British type. It is found on the European Continent as well. In Austria, the Federal Council may not oppose the budget as approved by the National Council. In the Federal Republic of Germany the annual financial bill has to be considered by the Federal Council but it is one of those bills that does not require the consent of the Federal Council in order to be passed. The Federal Council's only course if it disapproves of the budget bill wholly or in part is to appeal to the mediation committee or if necessary to submit a protest; but the Diet may reject the protest if the conditions laid down in the rules governing the majority of members who must vote for rejection are fulfilled.

Generally speaking where the powers of the upper House in financial matters continue to be roughly identical to those of the lower House the procedure for reaching agreement between the Houses is the same as that ordinarily used for legislation. In Belgium and Italy the financial bills are sent backwards and forwards between the two Houses so that they can reach agreement. In Brazil, France, Philippines, Switzerland, the United States, the U.S.S.R. and Yugoslavia conciliation, mediation or conference committees are used to find common ground between the two Houses. In Chile the annual financial bill is considered by such a committee as soon as it is laid before Parliament. In the Federal Republic of Germany and Japan the part played by these committees is less important because of the greater powers of the lower House. In Ethiopia and Libya disagreements on the budget are settled at a joint meeting of the two Houses sitting in congress by majority vote.

21. Rights of Members of Parliament

The primacy of the executive in preparing and presenting the budget is generally accepted. To what extent do members have the right to alter it once it is presented to Parliament?

The rights enjoyed by members depend upon the weight given to each of two contradictory propositions. The first is a practical point: the crucial importance of the budget, affecting as it does the whole national life, ought logically to lead democratic countries to grant Parliament powers of the most absolute kind, or in concrete terms the authority to increase or reduce as it thinks fit both revenue and expenditure, even to the point of overturning the budget as balanced by the government. The second proposition is more technical: the need to balance the budget and hard economic facts must place practical limits on the powers that may be exercised by Parliament to make changes in a budget on which the economic and social development of an entire country depends. This is technically an imperative need that no state can afford to ignore.

Thus if Parliament is determined to preserve its prerogatives intact it must voluntarily restrict its own powers to alter the budget, merely keeping a close watch on its execution or if necessary calling the government to account for a budget which is by definition its major instrument of policy. Where the self-discipline of Parliament does not appear to be equal to the task, the solution is to set constitutional limits to its powers in budgetary matters. This tendency is seen in many of the constitutional experiments of recent times. In a number of countries however members of Parliament have been able to keep the same rights over the budget as over other legislation. Doubtless the inference to be drawn is that in those countries freedom draws its own boundary-lines. Most of them are in Europe where the historic tradition that constitutional law arises out of financial law is still alive. Members of the Folketing in Denmark, the Althing in Iceland and the Storting in Norway are free to move amendments to the budget without any restriction of substance or form. In Finland a member may move a motion on financial matters and even propose that new items of expenditure should be included in the budget provided that he does so within seven days of the budget's being presented to Parliament. This apparent restriction is no more than the application of the ordinary legislative practice to budgetary matters. Members of the Riksdag in Sweden have similar powers. Motions relating to revenue and expenditure are in order whatever their purport provided they are presented in due time. Proposals entailing expenditure do not have to be accompanied by proposals for finding the money to cover it.

The Nordic countries are not the only countries in Europe where the rights of members in budgetary matters are unrestricted. In Luxembourg and the Netherlands every member has an unrestricted right to put forward amendments. In Belgium in spite of the rule of the House of Representatives that reports on bills entailing expenditure not provided for in the budget must show how the necessary funds are to be raised, the position is in practice the same. The rule soon became a mere formality and no longer restricts the rights of members.

In Austria and Switzerland, the annual financial bill is given the same treatment as any other government bill: amendments put down by individual members are in order whatever their implications.

In Albania, Bulgaria, Czechoslovakia, Rumania, the U.S.S.R. and Yugoslavia members can also move amendments to reduce or increase revenue and expenditure. Parliament being the sovereign body, it is for its members to decide within the ambit of the national plan the level of revenue and expenditure.

Outside Europe few Parliaments allow their members unrestricted rights over the budget. In Israel the budget is subject to the ordinary rules governing the debating of bills: a member of the Knesset may propose amendments to increase or reduce the sums earmarked for various purposes. This is also the governing principle in Libya and Somalia. In the United States the rights of Congress derive from the separation of powers under which the two Houses monopolise the legislative function. Nevertheless an amendment to a bill authorising a general grant of expenditure must relate to expenditure of the department concerned. Nor may it have the effect of altering a law already in force. In the Argentine the rights of members are not restricted in any particular way while in Brazil procedure on the budget follows special rules which among other things provide for a period of eight days in which amendments may be put down.

In many Parliaments however the need to use public funds to the best advantage has led to a marked reduction in Parliament's powers. To obviate the danger likely to result from ill-advised moves by individuals specific rules have been made restricting Parliament's powers over public finance. For example for more than two hundred years the British House of Commons in a series of standing orders the oldest of which goes back to 1707 has virtually handed over to the executive its rights to introduce bills dealing with finance. In 1713 it decided that 'this House will receive no petition for any sum relating to the public service or proceed upon any motion for a grant or charge upon the public revenue, whether payable out of the consolidated fund or out of money to be provided by Parliament, unless recommended from the Crown'. The effect of these rules is that the figures produced by the government have to be regarded as ceilings which amendments put down by unofficial members must remain below.

The unique feature of the British system lies in the fact that it forbids not merely increases in expenditure but also more surprisingly increases in revenue. Any private member may propose the reduction or abolition of a tax or duty but he may not propose that new taxes should be devised or that the rates of the old taxes should be increased beyond the limits laid down in the Queen's recommendation as expressed in the statement of the chancellor of the exchequer. The explanation of this provision can be traced to the early days of the House of Commons to the time when it met to consider demands for subsidies made by the Crown. Its task was to decide whether to comply with the demand and, if so, within what limits and by what means. This explains the prohibition on proposals to increase expenditure and consequently on proposals to increase taxation. The British Parliament still respects this long-standing custom and practice; as a result it may not vote sums in excess of the government's estimates. So the only amendments that are in order are those which aim to reduce the sums requested. In fact the real purpose of motions to reduce the estimate is to enable members of Parliament to raise grievances on specific points and force the government to furnish explanations before the sums in question are approved. These motions seldom result in major amendments to the estimates since more often than not they merely propose token cuts. They are commonly used in most of the countries influenced by the British Parliament, and something like them is also known to continental Assemblies.

POWERS OF PARLIAMENT OVER FINANCE

Another restriction on the powers of members of Parliaments on the British model is that certain payments from a 'consolidated fund' do not have to be approved annually. In Great Britain the consolidated fund is an account opened by the government at the Bank of England into which all public revenue is paid and out of which all public payments are made. Some of the charges on the consolidated fund are authorised for an indefinite period by particular Acts of Parliament and do not have to be subjected to the rigours of yearly debates. They include payments relating to the National Debt, and the civil list of the Crown for which security of payment is essential and the salaries of certain public officials such as the Speaker, the Comptroller and Auditor General and the judges, who are independent of the executive and should not therefore have to depend on the Government's favour to have their salaries included in the annual estimates.

Historically the object of the restrictions on British members, which reflect a long-standing custom reinforced by standing order, was to protect the citizen from the Crown. Today the same restrictions serve to protect the finances of the country from irresponsible electioneering. The logic of the British system based on two parties which succeed one another in holding office in any event discourages members from any move that might damage the financial stability of the country. The majority party support the general policy of the government and the opposition while seeking to defeat the government must be mindful of making commitments which they will themselves be faced with in the event of victory at the polls. By and large all that is involved is a voluntary renunciation of rights which have no practical effect rather than restrictions imposed by formal rules.

This position has only been secured in other countries by specific provisions in the constitution. This has happened for instance in Australia (House of Representatives), Canada, Ceylon, Ireland, New Zealand and Pakistan which have followed the British example in withdrawing from members the right to propose increases in expenditure or revenue without the recommendation of the Crown, the President or the government. In India, Nigeria, and Sierra Leone the prohibition applies only to expenditure; proposals to increase public revenue are in order. In other countries special rules apply to the consideration of the budget. In Ghana members do not have the right of amendment. In Ethiopia and Iran they may not propose an increase in expenditure. In the United Arab Republic and Lebanon the constitution provides that the National Assembly may not alter the budget without the approval of the government. In Monaco the National Council does not formally exercise, without the preliminary agreement of the minister of state representing the Prince, the right to increase the estimates of expenditure or to reduce or eliminate them. In Spain and Turkey Parliament is formally forbidden from proposing increases in expenditure or decreases in revenue. It has already been shown that in France proposals and amendments are not in order if their effect would be to diminish the revenue or create or aggravate a charge on the public. This rule is markedly stronger when applied to the budget: no new clause or amendment to the finance bill may be presented if even by implication it eliminates or reduces an expenditure or creates or increases revenue or touches the control of public expenditure. Similar provision is made in the Central African Republic, Cameroon and Senegal; but in Cameroon and Senegal members may move to create or increase a public charge or to reduce revenue if they indicate how the resulting deficit is to be met.

Several recent constitutions have tackled the problem from the angle of a balanced budget. The Italian Constitution provides that the bill to approve the budget may not be amended to provide for new expenditure or new taxation and that any other bill entailing new or increased expenditure must include provisions to pay for it. In the Federal Republic of Germany any proposal for new expenditure, whether put forward in the debate on the budget or at any other time, must show how the revenue to pay for it is to be raised. The task of considering the ways and means of covering expenditure is left to the budget committee. If the committee finds that the proposed expenditure cannot be made up, the proposal is deemed to have been rejected. In Poland the rules of procedure of the committees that consider the budget and the plan expressly provide that any proposal for additional expenditure must indicate the means by which it is to be paid for.

These examples show the nature of the present trend very clearly: it is to avoid in the interests of sound public finance an ill-considered action by Parliament which might disturb the basic assumptions on which the budget has been carefully drawn up.

The budget is regarded more as an overall plan in which all the parts are closely linked together. As a unity it represents the chief expression of the power of the executive; as such it should be assessed by Parliament. The role of the House is not to challenge every detail from a technical angle but to make a broad judgment of its value as an instrument of policy.

22. Timing of the Budget

Budgets are as a general rule presented annually. The only exception is Spain where budgets are biennial. An annual budget means that public expenditure and revenue are settled for one year at a time. It also means that the budget has to be approved by Parliament once a year. The practice of approving the budget is closely bound up with the growth of the parliamentary system. It originated as a means of bolstering the authority of Parliament against the power of the executive. Today it helps to secure proper parliamentary control of all governmental activity.

For a long time the principle of an annual budget went unchallenged, perhaps because it dealt only with expenditure on necessary administrative services. But the issue has recently been raised in the context of the steady encroachment by the state upon economic and social life. The expression in budgetary terms of long-range investment programmes cannot always be made to fit the narrow framework of a single year. With the general trend towards economic planning proposals have been made that the rhythm of national budgets should be adapted to suit national, long-term plans.

Nevertheless all countries including those which have an entirely planned economy such as the U.S.S.R. and the People's Democracies have remained faithful to the principle of annual budgets. Doubtless the reason is in part a respect for Parliament which can in this way make its sovereign will felt more frequently. But annual budgets also have certain inherent financial advantages. For one thing an annual budget makes it possible to make an accurate assessment of the financial position; for another surer forecasts can be made over this relatively short space of time. The system of annual budgets has been applied for centuries in private enterprise; it was transferred from there to public affairs. Everywhere it has become standard practice and has finally come to be regarded as a natural process, especially where the financial year coincides with the calendar year.

In most countries the financial year begins on 1 January and ends on 31 December. For reasons of convenience however and particularly in order to extend the period of drawing up and debating the budget over a longer period, it has sometimes been found preferable to defer the beginning of the financial year. The date on which the financial year begins in various countries is as follows:

TIMING OF THE BUDGET

1 March	Turkey
21 March	Iran
1 April	Canada, Denmark, Great Britain, India, Ireland, Israel, Japan, Libya, New Zealand, Nigeria, Sierra Leone
1 July	Australia, Cameroon, Italy, Laos, Pakistan, the Philippines, Sweden, the United Arab Republic, the United States
8 July	Ethiopia
1 October	Ceylon, Ghana
1 November	Argentina

Whatever date is chosen the essential significance of an annual budget is that each year the budget can only be put into effect with the approval of Parliament. Without the agreement of the representatives of the people, the government cannot spend any money or collect any revenue for the year in question, an impotence which would lead to a total paralysis of public life. So it is important for the budget to be passed in good time, that is, before the beginning of the twelve-month period to which it relates. Several countries including Great Britain and other countries which have followed its example have modified this principle in practice. But where its observance is regarded as essential, it raises two problems: first the problem of placing before Parliament the budgetary papers on which it must express its views before the beginning of the new financial year; and secondly the problem of the measures to be taken if the budget for one reason or another cannot be passed in due time.

As a general rule the constitution or the law provides that the government must submit its budget within a given length of time before the beginning of the financial year so as to give Parliament reasonable time to study, debate and pass it. The time given to Parliament varies according to the country, but it is seldom less than two months. Often it is longer. In Austria the period is ten weeks; in Belgium, the Federal Republic of Germany, the Netherlands and Turkey three months; in Chile four or five months; and in Italy five months. In the Argentine the budget is presented before 15 July for the financial year beginning 1 November. Where the financial year begins on 1 January the budget is usually presented to Parliament at the beginning of the ordinary session before that date. This is done in Brazil, the Central African Republic, France, Lebanon, Luxembourg, Monaco, the Netherlands, Switzerland and Senegal. It often happens that the government sends to the parliamentary committees concerned copies of the relevant papers in advance of their formal presentation to Parliament.

In most countries the time allowed to Parliament runs to the day before the first day of the new financial year. But some countries take steps to ensure that Parliament has completed its business before that late stage in order to avoid upsetting the annual pattern and resorting to emergency measures which are open to public criticism. In Sweden the budget must be approved by Parliament by 31 May, though the financial year begins on 1 July. In Cameroon and Ethiopia it must be approved a month before the beginning of each financial year. In Senegal the National Assembly has sixty days in which to pass the annual financial bill. In France if the National Assembly has not given the bill a first reading within forty days from its introduction the government must refer it to the Senate which has to take the first reading within the next fifteen days.

These measures may seem stringent; but it is not always easy to ensure that the budget is passed in good time because political life is subject to fluctuations which are invariably unforeseeable and can upset the ordinary time-table. In those circumstances the problem is to bridge the budgetary gap which would otherwise exist between the end of one financial year and the passing of the budget for the following year. Various methods are used to prevent the machinery of government or even the economic life of the nation from being arrested.

In some countries such as Laos and Turkey no provision is made for this eventuality. In Sweden and Ceylon the only remedy is the dissolution of Parliament before the budget is approved; in Sweden if that happens, the existing budget remains valid until the Riksdag approves a new one after the general election. In Ceylon the Governor General may incur expenditure until a new House of Representatives is elected and if necessary for the following three months.

Most constitutions however do make special provision. The most important step is to authorise expenditure. Revenue more often than not has an existence independent of the budget, and a mere authorisation is enough to enable it to be levied. The question is therefore to assess the importance of the part played by Parliament in determining the amount of expenditure to be appropriated provisionally.

First it is conceivable that if Parliament fails to complete its work, there will simply be a provisional reversion to the level of expenditure approved in the budget for the previous year. Several countries adopt this course. In Brazil if the annual financial bill has not been sent to the President for signature by 30 November the current budget is automatically continued into the next financial year. In Ethiopia and the United Arab Republic if the budget has not been approved before the beginning of the financial year the budget for the preceding year remains in force until the new budget is passed. In Cameroon the

President of the Republic re-enacts the previous budget in monthly instalments until the adoption of the new one. In the Netherlands it is traditionally assumed that the budget will not be adopted before 1 January. The government is automatically allotted four-twelfths of the expenditure authorised in the previous year's estimates to cover the first four months of the year.

In Austria if the National Council has not approved the annual financial bill in good time and does not take any other steps, the constitution provides for certain measures to have effect for the first two months of the financial year in question. Imposts and taxes remain at existing levels and expenditure is authorised within the ceiling contemplated in the financial bill to the extent of one-twelfth of the total sum for each month. After two months a provisional bill has to be passed in accordance with the ordinary procedures.

Instead of a time-limit after which existing levels of expenditure are provisionally relied upon, a limitation on expenditure by categories is sometimes imposed. This is what happens in the Federal Republic of Germany where under the fundamental law the federal government may spend any sums needed to maintain the departments of state, take the steps laid down by law to meet the federal state's legal obligations or carry out public works and other productive activities. The only condition is that funds have already been appropriated for the same purposes in previous budgets. The fundamental law also provides that if revenue is not enough to cover all this expenditure the government may use treasury funds amounting to one quarter of the revenue of the preceding year.

Closely akin to the procedure for extending the previous budget is that in which direct steps are taken by the executive. Both procedures can be used without reference to Parliament. In the second the government on its own authority disburses the moneys needed to carry on the business of state. This executive action may ultimately have to be ratified by Parliament; it may be effective only for limited time; or it may be absolute and final. In the last instance Parliament can play no further part if the delay in passing the budget is its own fault. This has been the procedure in France since the reforms of 1958. It has already been seen that the National Assembly has forty days and the Senate fifteen days to complete the first reading of the annual financial bill. In any event it must be passed within seventy days. If it is not passed its provisions may be brought into force directly by decree, that is, by the direct action of the executive. Another procedure is provided for the contingency that the delay is the responsibility not of Parliament but of the government. When the government has failed to present its bill in good time, that is, at least seventy days before the beginning of the financial year, the government can request Parliament to consider urgently authorising taxation and can decree expenditure relating solely to 'voted services', namely, the expenditure of the previous financial year altered where necessary to take account of measures approved by Parliament or decided by the government within the limits of their respective powers. In Monaco this restriction to voted services also applies when the budget has not been passed before 31 December.

Something like the French procedure is also found in the Central African Republic and Senegal. In the Central African Republic the budget is considered during the session which opens in the second fortnight of October. If the National Assembly has not passed it before the end of this session, the government may bring it into force by decree, modified to take account of amendments made by the Assembly and accepted by the government. In Senegal the annual financial bill is introduced not later than the opening day of the first ordinary session and the Assembly has then sixty days in which to pass it. If the bill has not been introduced in good time for the Assembly to dispose of it in the sixty days before the session ends, an extraordinary session has to be held. It continues for long enough to make up for the time lost in the previous session. If the bill has not been finally passed after sixty sitting days, it may be brought into force by decree modified to take account of amendments passed by the Assembly and accepted by the President of the Republic. If in spite of all these precautions the financial bill has not come into force before the beginning of the financial year, the President of the Republic is authorised to give effect by decree to the 'voted services'.

The same kind of procedure is found in Chile. The budget must be introduced four months before the beginning of the financial year to which it relates. If it cannot be passed before that date, it is brought into force in the form in which it has been presented by the President of the Republic. In Pakistan in the same circumstances the President may authorise ordinary expenditure contemplated in the annual budget statement presented to the National Assembly. In the Lebanon the procedure is more elaborate but is essentially similar. The ordinary session which begins on the first Tuesday after 15 October and lasts until the end of the year is primarily devoted to debate on the budget. If the Chamber has not finally passed the budget before the end of the session, the President of the Republic convenes an extraordinary session until the end of January. If the budget has still not been passed the President of the Republic may by decree made on the advice of the council of ministers bring the budget into force in the form in which it was presented to the Chamber. But he may only use this power if the bill has been presented to the Chamber not less than fifteen days before the beginning of the session in October. During the extraordinary session in January at which the budget is further debated taxes can still be imposed at the previous level and expenditure is authorised to the extent of one-twelfth of the total expenditure of the previous year. In Libya provisional monthly sums are authorised by royal decree. They too are calculated on the basis of one-twelfth of the total expenditure of the previous year.

This absence of any parliamentary influence on the content of the provisional budget is in some measure a feature of the procedure followed by some of the Parliaments influenced by the British model. In Nigeria the ministry of finance is empowered to continue acting on existing powers for four months if the budget has not been approved in good time. In Sierra Leone they may only be exercised for three months without the express authorisation of the House. In New Zealand the Public Revenues Act of 1953 authorised the government to spend money during April, May and June to the level of one-quarter of the amount voted by Parliament in the previous year. After 30 June and until November, the period in which the budget has finally to be adopted, provisional supply must be granted by legislation.

In most of the People's Democracies the budget does not have to be approved before the financial year begins. Except in Poland and Yugoslavia the government takes the necessary steps: the council of ministers allocates funds to departments. In Rumania this allocation is made by decree of the Council of State. In Albania and Hungary the council of ministers may not use this procedure for longer than six months.

The final procedure used to offset the delay in passing the budget is the grant of provisional sums by Parliament itself. Provisional funds are agreed to by Parliament as votes on account, more often than not under urgent procedure, and are subsequently included in the budget. The commonest formula is the 'provisional twelfths'. Month by month Parliament is called upon to vote on account without approving any future commitment a sum corresponding to one twelfth of the total sums in the last budget, so as to make it possible to carry on current business. In some countries the proportion may be larger than a twelfth. It may even be large enough to warrant the description 'provisional budget' rather than 'provisional twelfths'. But the essential principle is that Parliament takes a hand, even where it does not do so every month. This is the procedure followed in Argentina, Belgium, Denmark, Finland, Greece, Iceland, Iran, Israel, Italy, Japan, Liberia, Luxembourg, Norway, Poland, Somalia, Switzerland

and Yugoslavia. In the United States it is used regularly because the bills to authorise supply to the departments of state are passed between August and November while the financial year begins on 1 July. In Somalia and Yugoslavia provisional sums may not be granted to the government after the third month or in Italy after the fourth. In Japan a special procedure is provided for the contingency that the House of Representatives may be dissolved during the debate on the budget. If the budget cannot be approved before the beginning of the financial year the cabinet convenes the House of Councillors in emergency session and lays before it a provisional budget for one or two months. The measures taken under the procedure must subsequently be ratified by the new House of Representatives within ten days of the opening of the session.

The principle followed by Parliaments on the British model is entirely different. Contrary to the usual practice the rule in these Parliaments is only to approve the budget after the beginning of the financial year. Strictly speaking moreover it is not the budget itself which is approved but a series of 'budget resolutions' and a finance bill which is needed to give them the full force of law. Votes on account so far from being exceptional are normal practice.

In Great Britain the financial system works broadly in the following way. It has already been noted that certain payments are made regularly from the consolidated fund, and Parliament is relieved of the need to review this expenditure year after year. Of the estimates that are subject to annual review, Parliament determines the amount in a series of stages. The first stage consists of a vote on account by which the funds needed by the various government departments to meet their expenses from the beginning of the financial year until the passing of the Appropriation Act are made available. For this reason the vote on account must be agreed to before 1 April. In the ordinary way it covers five-twelfths of the total amount provided in the estimates, divided up among the various departments. The provisions in the vote on account are first examined by the whole House sitting as the Committee of Supply. The committee agrees to a resolution which is reported to the House. Next the House sits as the Committee of Ways and Means to vote the sum required to cover the grants so far agreed to. The procedure ends with the passing of the Consolidated Fund Bill authorising the spending of the necessary public funds. This whole series of operations normally takes place in four sittings where, as is usual in matters relating to the estimates, the opposition plays the main part because it has the right to choose the votes for debate and usually moves that the chosen vote be reduced by a token amount.

TIMING OF THE BUDGET

The items arising out of the vote on account may be regarded as advances on the main grant which is only finally approved towards the end of July at the close of the whole budgetary process when both the Appropriation Bill authorising expenditure and the Finance Bill authorising the raising of the corresponding revenue are given the royal assent and become law. The broad lines of this system are reproduced in Australia, Ghana, India and Ireland. In Ireland votes on account are calculated on a period of four months and in Ghana on a quarter of the sums necessary for each department; in India the period covered by the vote on account is limited to one month because Parliament has to come to its decision on the budget within seventy-five days of its presentation which is in practice only a short time after the beginning of the financial year.

All these procedures, different though they are, have one object in common; it is to ensure that whatever happens the machinery of government will continue to function. Many of them have another common factor: the wide scope of devices such as falling back on the previous budget, the charges on the consolidated fund which do not have to be voted, the automatic reapplication of the existing budget and disbursement by decree—all these procedures give the executive plenty of scope for manoeuvre and hold off serious debate of the budget in Parliament which is often a sore trial for the Government.

23. Procedure for Considering the Budget

COMMITTEES AND THE BUDGET – DEBATE ON THE BUDGET

The procedure for considering the budget in Parliament differs as a rule from the ordinary procedure on bills in two important respects. The first is the part played by committees, the second debate on the floor of the House.

1. COMMITTEES AND THE BUDGET

The difference between the British conception of the part played by committees and the continental or American conception is strongly marked in the legislative field generally but is especially clear in financial matters. There are two reasons. First in Parliaments where permanent committees exist the committee dealing with financial matters is exceptionally important. The reports that it makes on the financial papers laid before it greatly influence debate in the House. Secondly in the British system the principle holds good that the financial powers of Parliament are the exclusive province of the House itself and the effect of this is to rule out entirely the use of smaller working bodies. In practice this means that the budget resolutions and the finance bill are not referred to a standing committee or a select committee. The budget is dealt with by the Committee of the whole House which resolves itself into Committee of Supply in order to approve expenditure contained first of all in the vote on account, and then in the estimates proper; and it resolves itself into a committee of ways and means to vote the funds for covering this expenditure and to debate the question of revenue.

A similar system obtains in Ceylon, Ireland, Nigeria, Sierra Leone and in the Canadian House of Commons though a distinction is not always made between these two committees of the whole House. The system embodies the classic procedure of debating bills in several stages because the bills and resolutions considered in committee of the whole House have to be reported to the House itself and to be agreed to by the House.

Some of the countries which have followed the example of the procedure found in the British House of Commons have seen fit to reduce the number of these stages, some of which are purely procedural. In Ghana, India and Pakistan the estimates are considered by the House sitting as a House and not as a committee. A reasonable time is set between the presentation of the budget and the debate to enable members to study its contents. In India for example the debate proceeds as follows. There is first a general debate which lasts four to five days during which members may raise questions on the budget as a whole and on matters of principle. After the general debate the estimates for each ministry are considered separately. Members may move motions known as 'cut motions' to reduce these estimates. The Speaker may declare them out of order if he thinks they are abusive in tone or obstructive in purpose. When the estimates have been agreed to along with a bill authorising payment, the House takes up the finance bill. On this occasion members may raise matters of

PROCEDURE FOR CONSIDERING THE BUDGET

general administration or particular grievances or call the government to account for its monetary and financial policy. At no point in this procedure do committees come into the picture.

In most of the other countries the debate on the budget follows the ordinary rules of procedure on bills, so that before the budget is examined in the House it is first referred to a committee.

The usual method is for the budget to be referred to one particular committee which has powers to deal with all financial matters. In view of the political importance of the budget this committee acquires immense prestige, and frequently there is the likelihood that it may virtually take control of the debate in the House. For this reason the part played by finance committees is frequently regarded as an essential feature of the continental and American parliamentary system.

Yet the British procedure has left a decided mark on the United States Congress. The division of powers established in the House of Commons between expenditure and revenue is also found in the House of Representatives where there are two committees whose task it is to examine the budget; the Committee of Ways and Means deals with revenue and the Committee on Appropriation deals with expenditure. Bills dealing with taxation or the grant of supply may also be debated in the Committee of the whole House. But the real work is done by the permanent committees, especially the Committee on Appropriation. This committee appoints several sub-committees; each one corresponds to a different administrative service and, proceeding by means of 'hearings', makes a thorough inquiry into all requests for public funds.

Sub-committees are also appointed by the finance committees of several other Parliaments, including those of Albania, Bulgaria and the U.S.S.R.; as many as fifteen are sometimes appointed. In Brazil the committee on the budget is divided into three parts. As there are no rigid rules, these small bodies can carry out thorough and rapid inquiries.

Finance committees are not always the only committees to pass judgment on the budget. In view of the repercussions of the budget on all branches of public life it is sometimes found desirable to consult other committees affected by the grant and distribution of funds. But whether the finance committee alone has the right to report on the substance of the budget or whether it has the final word on the budget as a whole, the committee enjoys an exceptionally high status. Indeed it is often regarded as the guarantor of a sound financial system.

In some countries such as Cameroon, France, Monaco and Norway the specialised committees have the right to put before the

House their views on problems within their terms of reference in the form of separate reports. In other countries their views are submitted to the finance committee which takes them into account in making its own report to the House. This is the procedure applied in Israel and the Federal Republic of Germany. In Poland a similar procedure is followed. The programme for considering the budget is drawn up in accordance with special rules by the finance committee. A general rapporteur is appointed. The budget is then submitted to several committees which study the various parts in which they are interested, either separately or in joint meetings. Again rapporteurs are appointed. The study of the budget as a whole is then taken up again by the finance committee which accepts or rejects the amendments proposed by the various committees. Finally the general rapporteur reports to the Diet on the proceedings as a whole.

Although some of the details vary, this is broadly the procedure that applies in Hungary, Rumania and Czechoslovakia. In the Argentine the finance and economic committee may not introduce into the annual financial bill any provision which falls within the terms of reference of another committee without its agreement.

When the budget is referred to the finance committee alone, other committees interested in particular heads of the budget may make known their views by sending representatives to the finance committee. This happens in the Central African Republic, Lebanon, Libya, Somalia and the United Arab Republic.

In some countries the role of the finance committee is less obtrusive. In Italy the finance committee has the prior right to put forward its views on the budget as a whole. The other committees then examine separately the proposals relating to their particular fields and make written reports to the House on matters of substance. In Belgium again the power to consider and report on the substance of the budget is divided: there are as many committees as there are ministerial departments, and each committee is required to examine the proposals relating to its own department. Only strictly financial proposals (ways and means, pensions, national debt) are reserved for the finance committee. In the second Chamber of the Netherlands the budget is considered in the same way. In Sweden four committees normally consider the budget: the committee of ways and means considers revenue; the bank committee matters relating to the bank of Sweden and the national office of the public debt; the committee of agriculture matters relating to agriculture, forestry and fisheries; and the budget committee, which is the vital one, all other matters. In Turkey the annual financial bill is considered by a joint committee of thirty-five members and fifteen senators.

2. DEBATE ON THE BUDGET

It has been shown how the special nature of Parliament's consideration of the budget has led to some restriction of the right of members to amend the government's proposals and to some re-adjustment of the powers of the two Houses in bicameral legislatures.

With these reservations the consideration of the budget on the floor of the House generally follows the same procedure that has already been described as applying to bills.

Exceptions to this general statement are Norway and Iceland where the two Houses are required to hold joint sittings to consider financial matters. In the Norwegian Storting the budget debate follows a special pattern: there is first a 'financial debate' on the report of the finance committee. Secondly the reports of the other permanent committees are considered, and a number of resolutions are agreed to provisionally. These resolutions must then be approved by the Storting after considering further reports made by the finance committee, one of which is specifically concerned with the balance of the budget. In Finland too financial procedure departs considerably from the rules of procedure governing legislation. The annual financial bill is debated only at a single reading instead of the usual three readings. But if amendments to the bill as reported by the finance committee are agreed to by the Diet, the bill is referred back to the committee and the bill as further considered by the committee is once again reported to the House for a resumed debate on the single reading.

Whatever departures are made from the ordinary rules for considering legislation, the two essential stages are always held in public: first the general debate on the budget as a whole and secondly a clause by clause consideration. It has already been shown that there is a tendency to group together a number of items in the budget in order to reduce the number of votes which an Assembly has to take. In France for example only one vote is taken on the provision for revenue in the general budget and only one vote on the various categories of special accounts annexed to the budget. For expenditure a single vote is taken on 'voted services'; a single vote on each head of expenditure (public debt, public authorities, services, investments, subsidies); and within each head a single vote on new expenditure by each ministry. Moreover expenditure which it is not proposed to modify may only be considered in a shortened debate. The Central African Republic follows a similar procedure.

How much importance is attached to the general debate and how much to the clause by clause consideration? The answer varies according to the concept of Parliament's function in working on the budget proposals and particularly to the limitations on Parliament's powers to amend them. Obviously if the power to alter the budget is seriously restricted, the clause by clause examination of the budget will become secondary to the general debate. Every member has the opportunity to make broad criticisms in the general debate and the less likelihood there is of specific action being taken to give effect to that criticism, the more widely that right will be used. For this reason most countries stress the ample opportunities for members to put their own case and air their grievances in the general debate rather than during the consideration of details. But it has to be remembered that pressure on Parliament's time is just as heavy when it is dealing with the budget as with other matters; and special steps may have to be taken to speed up debate and prevent it exceeding reasonable limits. The length of speeches is limited in Belgium, Denmark, Israel, the Netherlands, Norway, Turkey and the United Arab Republic. In the United States House of Representatives, under the 'closed rule' when necessary only amendments put forward by the committee concerned are called. In Libya and the United Arab Republic financial bills are automatically treated as urgent. In the British system some precise limits are laid down. For instance the maximum number of days allotted for the discussion of supply in the House of Commons is twenty-six. In Ceylon the number is twenty days. Similar limits are to be found in India where the general debate on the budget lasts four to five days.

The peculiar features of the British procedure on the budget arise out of the meaning given to the word 'budget'. In Britain the budget is not a tabular conspectus of all revenue and all expenditure which Parliament has to authorise. It comprises rather a series of proposals for adjusting public revenue to the expenditure likely to be incurred, the annual rate of income tax being one of the most important sources of income. A distinction has to be made between the total amount of expenditure proposed in the estimates and the method of meeting it out of public funds.

Against this background the way in which the budget is debated in Great Britain can be traced. The debate opens with the 'budget statement' made by the Chancellor of the Exchequer to the House sitting as the Committee of Ways and Means. The Chancellor reviews the expenditure and revenue, and in a general way the economic state of the nation, and in the course of this review, he makes a number of proposals on taxation. The statement is followed by a general debate, at the end of which budget resolutions are passed giving effect to the Chancellor's proposals. When the House has agreed to them, a finance bill founded on those resolutions is then introduced, and it

PROCEDURE FOR CONSIDERING THE BUDGET

goes through the same stages as an ordinary bill. As the financial year has already begun the resolutions passed by the Committee of Ways and Means have legal force for four months, provided that they are agreed to by the House within ten sitting days and that the finance bill which is founded on them is read a second time within twenty sitting days of that agreement and receives the royal assent within four months of the resolutions' being agreed to by the committee.

The estimates of expenditure are considered in the Committee of Supply before the end of March for the vote on account and before the end of July for the expenditure as a whole. A series of resolutions are passed by the Committee of Supply during the twenty-six days of debate. Next the Committee of Ways and Means has to authorise payments out of the consolidated fund to meet the expenditure so determined. Once the resolutions of these two committees have been reported to the House and approved by it, a bill is brought in to appropriate the necessary sums. This bill receives the royal assent as the 'appropriation act'. In practice some twenty days are devoted to debate on the most important estimates. It is seldom possible to go into the detail of a modern budget with the result that the debates in the Committee of Supply have undergone a change of character. The earlier practice of minutely examining each item has given way to debates on the government's policy as revealed by the action of one or several of its departments. Amendments may be, and often are, moved by members to reduce the salary of this or that minister. This procedure enables the House to take a vote on the policy of the government.

This procedure cuts out a feature that is characteristic of most continental countries, namely, the thorough scrutiny of all the items of the budget and related estimates. But the result is that debate is keen; all problems become problems of general policy. The budget is first and foremost a matter of confidence. The majority hands over to the government the responsibility for ensuring the proper functioning of the state in the financial field, and thus for crystallising their political views in the form of a programme of expenditure and income. The opposition attacks government policy on a broad front without necessarily challenging every single item in the budget. From one angle this procedure can be said to show Parliament exercising its powers to scrutinise government policy rather than taking part in the business of making laws. But it does avoid a danger experienced by many Parliaments that debates on the budget may be too long and too specialised. This danger is usually manifested in an apathetic attitude on the part of public opinion towards an act of policy which after all is crucially important for the entire nation.

PART FIVE

Control of the Executive by Parliament

The control that Parliament exercises over the executive stems from one basic principle; Parliament embodies the will of the people and it must therefore be able to supervise the way in which public policy is carried out so as to ensure that it remains consonant with the aspirations of the nation as a whole.

This principle is difficult to apply in practice because it raises the whole problem of the relationship between Parliament and the executive. Public policy finds its chief expression in legislation and financial control. The part played by Parliament in legislation and in financial matters has been discussed in previous chapters. But these specialised tasks do not give a complete picture of the power of Parliament. The strength of a Parliament lies in its ability to scrutinise the whole of the political and administrative action of the executive, even to the point of arresting it when it no longer corresponds to the movement of public opinion. A variety of procedures are available to enable Parliament to discharge this duty and to resolve any conflict with the executive. In a strictly parliamentary regime the efficacy of those procedures is the key to the power of Parliament. By definition this is not true of regimes founded on the separation of powers, commonly referred to as presidential systems, where each arm is self-contained and functions independently. But in the nature of things there is always some measure of control by Parliament even though it may not rest, as in a strictly parliamentary regime, on the ultimate sanction that a government failing to apply a policy in tune with the views of Parliament can be defeated and turned out of office.

24. Appointment of the Executive

THE HEAD OF STATE – THE HEAD OF GOVERNMENT AND MINISTERS – HIGH OFFICIALS

Parliament exercises a measure of control over the executive in several ways. The first is through its part in appointing the various persons and bodies that constitute the executive power. The structure of the executive is outside the scope of this book, but some reference must be made to it in order to indicate the various opportunities open to Parliament. In the countries whose constitutional practice is studied in this book, three chief forms of executive power can be distinguished. In the first form there is in parallel with Parliament a single power responsible for executive functions, more often than not in the person of a President whose powers are vested in him by universal suffrage. He is surrounded by persons who help him to govern. But their essential purpose is merely to prepare and to administer; they play no part in the decisions that are taken: they are in theory at least public servants, they do not govern. This is the characteristic feature of the presidential system.

In the second form the executive power comprises two separate persons and bodies. This form is the outcome of a long history. It is bound up with the development of parliamentary government in Great Britain as a result of a gradual weakening of the power of the Crown and the corresponding growth of the powers of ministers who were originally nothing more than the assistants of the Monarch. This has resulted in the emergence of a Head of State who embodies and represents the whole nation and a cabinet of ministers whose task is directly to manage public affairs. This two-fold form of executive is found in most contemporary states, whether or not they use the term 'cabinet government'. It gains strength where one of the members of the cabinet stands by law or in practice above the rest: side by side with the Head of State there is then a head of government, president of the council or prime minister.

The system in force in the U.S.S.R. and in the People's Democracies with the exception of Czechoslovakia and Yugoslavia differs considerably from the first two forms. The functions of Head of State are fulfilled between sessions by a collegiate body known as the Presidium, or the Council of State in Poland and Rumania. This body is not considered to be part of the executive, which consists solely of the council of ministers. Emanating directly from Parliament, the Presidium or Council of State is the supreme power in the state.

1. THE HEAD OF STATE

In hereditary monarchies Parliament has evidently little to do with designating the occupant of the throne. The order of dynastic succession generally follows specific rules laid down in the constitution or hallowed by ancient custom. Parliament has no occasion to intervene except where necessary to ensure that the rules are observed.

The association of the monarchy with a parliamentary form of government is found in many states especially in Western Europe: Belgium, Denmark, Great Britain, Greece, Luxembourg, Monaco, the Netherlands, Norway and Sweden are examples. Outside Europe hereditary monarchies among the countries included in the present study are Ethiopia, Iran, Japan, Laos and Libya. Special mention has been made of members of the Commonwealth such as Australia, Canada, Ceylon, New Zealand and Sierra Leone whose sovereign is the occupant of the throne of Great Britain and is represented by a Governor-General appointed on the recommendation of the prime minister of the country concerned. This formula allows each Parliament a measure of influence over this appointment because the head of government is accountable to it.

In all hereditary monarchies the time does come when Parliament is called upon to take a hand in designating the Sovereign. In Great Britain the two Houses no longer have to approve the accession of the Monarch to the throne. But they retain their power to settle the question of succession of the reigning Sovereign though he would have to give his assent. They could for example decide to change the order of succession for religious reasons. They have also to approve the abdication and the change in the succession which an abdication entails. In Norway the constitution stipulates that if there is no Prince to succeed to the throne, the King may propose to the Storting the name of an heir, and the Storting may itself elect a successor if the King's proposal is not agreed to. In Sweden the Riksdag alone has the power to designate a new royal line if the Bernadotte dynasty should die out. It is also empowered to elect one, three or five regents if the King should die. In the Netherlands there is a provision for Parliament to take action if the House of Orange should die out. The procedure is very unusual: the new King would be designated by an electoral college consisting of all the sitting members of the two Chambers and an equal number of persons elected by the people for this purpose. A similar procedure is applied in Greece. If the throne is vacant, the chamber elects a provisional regent; within three months a number of persons equal to the total number of members of Parliament are elected by the people; and at a joint meeting with the members they elect the new King who has to obtain a majority of two-thirds of the total number of persons entitled to attend the joint meeting. The Chamber may also intervene to ensure that a regency is set up where the heir to the throne has not come of age. In Belgium Parliament is called on to play a part in various circumstances specified in the constitution. If the King has no male descendant, he may appoint his successor with the agreement of the two Houses which must declare themselves by a majority of two-thirds of the votes cast. Not less than two-thirds of the membership of each House have to be present. If the heir is a minor (under 18 years of age) or in the event of the King's incapacity, the two Houses hold a joint meeting and arrange for guardianship or a regency. If the throne should fall vacant, the two Houses act in the same way; but the arrangement they make lasts only until a new Parliament has been elected during the next two months and has filled the vacancy permanently.

The constitution of the kingdom of Libya also provides for the throne's being vacant. The Senate and House of Representatives immediately hold a joint meeting and must designate a successor within ten days of the vacancy's occurring. Their joint resolution requires a majority of two-thirds of the votes cast comprising not less than three-quarters of the membership. If a successor has not been appointed within this time the two Houses meet together on the eleventh day and may then designate a successor by absolute majority provided that a majority of the members of each House are present. If the House of Representatives has been dissolved, it must meet immediately and remain in session until the King has been designated. Parliament also has to confirm the government's choice of a regent or council of regency if the heir is a minor.

It is clear from these few examples that Parliament plays a small part in designating a hereditary Monarch. Its part is still smaller in certain republics where the Head of State is elected directly by the people. The object of this election is to build up side by side with the legislative power an executive power which will have at least as much authority because it too derives its authority from the people.

This equality of status between the powers is a characteristic feature of the classic type of presidential system especially where the

CONTROL OF THE EXECUTIVE BY PARLIAMENT

Head of State is also the head of the government. It is found in the United States, Argentina, Brazil and the Philippines. It is true that in the United States the people do not designate the President himself but only the presidential electoral college. But this procedure is a pure formality because each member of the electoral college is bound to follow the choice of the votes in his State. The result of this is that the presidential election, that is, the vote recorded by the electoral college has become a mere legal formality of which the man in the street is hardly aware. It is only at this stage that Congress comes into the picture because the votes have to be counted in Congress. Its task ends there, except in the improbable contingency that none of the candidates obtains an absolute majority of the electoral votes. If this should happen, the House of Representatives have to elect the President and the Senate the Vice-President.

The election of the Head of State by universal suffrage and the combination of that office with the office of head of the government have figured in several recent constitutions. Cameroon, the Central African Republic, Senegal, Tunisia and the United Arab Republic are examples. In the Central African Republic the Head of State is elected at the same time as the members. His name is at the head of the single national list. In the United Arab Republic the National Assembly chooses the candidate for the Presidency of the Republic by an absolute majority of its members. The candidate proposed then faces the electorate and becomes President of the Republic provided he obtains an absolute majority of the votes cast. Otherwise the Assembly puts up a new candidate and the same procedure is repeated.

The election of the Head of State by universal suffrage is not exclusively a feature of the presidential system. It is also found in states in which executive authority is shared, thus preserving important aspects of a strictly parliamentary regime such as the accountability of the government to one or both Houses. Among these states are Austria, Finland, France and Ireland where the Head of State has an undoubted authority and prestige that are independent of the powers devolved upon him. In Finland election is by universal suffrage: the President is elected by an electoral college of three hundred persons elected for this purpose. In France and Ireland members of Parliament play a part in choosing candidates. In France each candidate must be sponsored by at least 100 persons who must be members of Parliament, members of the economic and social council, general councillors or elected mayors. In Ireland a candidate other than a former President or the outgoing President must be sponsored either by twenty members of either House of Parliament or by the

APPOINTMENT OF THE EXECUTIVE

Councils of four administrative counties. In Iceland the part played by Parliament is somewhat peculiar. The Althing does not elect the President of the Republic, but it has the authority to divest him of his powers by an adverse vote of two-thirds of its membership, though this motion has to be confirmed within two months by a popular vote.

The republican tradition has not always looked with favour on a Head of State elected by universal suffrage inasmuch as it may promote personal power. That is why in many constitutions the function of Head of State is regarded as one of moral leadership. The need for this quality is clear; but it is also important to prevent any autocratic leanings. One method is to make Parliament responsible for his appointment. Election by Parliament reassures Parliament about its own sovereignty and has the advantage of being simple. So the primary manifestation of parliamentary control over the executive is the appointment by Parliament of the Head of State.

In states with a fairly marked federal structure, participation by Parliament may be robbed of some of its significance where it is shared with representatives of the various regions. This is what happens in the Federal Republic of Germany. The federal President is elected by the federal convention which consists of the members of the Bundestag and an equal number of other persons elected by the Parliaments of the Länder according to a system of proportional representation. This concern to take account of the will of the electoral body at the moment of the election as well as the views of members of Parliament elected earlier is not unlike the procedure in the Netherlands and Greece for choosing a new Sovereign.

In India the President is elected by an electoral college comprising the members of the two Houses of Parliament and those of the legislative assemblies of the states. In Italy the President of the Republic is elected by members of the two Houses and three delegates elected by each regional council.

In other countries such as Czechoslovakia, Israel, Lebanon and Somalia Parliament alone has the authority to choose the Head of State. In Parliaments with two or more Houses election normally takes place with the Houses sitting jointly as a Congress. This is true of Turkey and Yugoslavia. A similar procedure is used in Switzerland, but with an unusual constitutional twist. The executive power as a whole is in the hands of a federal council elected for four years by both Houses. One of the members of the council is elected in the same manner, but for one year only, as President of the confederation. He acts as Head of State, but he has no authority over the other members of the council; he is merely *primus inter pares*. The federal council wields governmental authority and embodies the unity of the executive power.

Ghana also requires separate classification. Parliament, the supreme legislative body, consists of the President and the National Assembly. The term of office of the President and members of Parliament is the same; both are ended by the dissolution which the President announces at least every five years. As a result the election of the President takes place at the same time as the general election. The method of his appointment ensures that he will usually be the head of the victorious party. The constitution provides that the result of an election for the presidency brought about by the dissolution of the National Assembly shall depend upon the choice made before the general election by persons already elected members of Parliament or, if none of the candidates for the presidency obtained more than half the votes cast, by members of the new Parliament in a secret ballot. In the event of the death or resignation of the President, Parliament appoints a new President by secret ballot. If the Assembly has not made an appointment after five votes have been taken, it is deemed to be dissolved.

The practice in the U.S.S.R., Albania, Bulgaria, Hungary, Poland and Rumania is to place the functions of Chief of State in the hands of a collective body known as the Presidium, or in Poland and Rumania the Council of State. It consists of a President, vice-presidents, secretaries and ordinary members who are elected by Parliament from among its own membership. This institution bears no resemblance to anything existing in the Western countries; and it is hard to classify it constitutionally because it cannot be regarded as part of the executive. It is the supreme public authority in the state. Its powers are of two kinds. First there are those normally enjoyed by a Head of State in a parliamentary regime. Secondly there are more important powers deriving from its status as the directing body of Parliament. It exercises the powers of Parliament when Parliament is not sitting, as for instance over the accountability, appointment and dismissal of the council of ministers. Because its authority proceeds directly from Parliament, it is at all times responsible to Parliament for its actions.

2. THE HEAD OF GOVERNMENT AND MINISTERS

In regimes of the presidential type the functions of Head of State and head of the government are fused in one and the same person who is elected by universal suffrage. Parliament has no part in this process. Moreover ministers do not constitute a coherent, collective entity: they simply help the Head of State who appoints and dismisses them as he wishes. Again Parliament is not concerned. This is the position in the United States, Argentina, Brazil, Chile and the Philippines, and in several African States such as Cameroon, the Central African Republic, Senegal and Tunisia. In the United States the President's cabinet, consisting of the departmental heads, has no statutory existence. It is not mentioned in the constitution and it can wield no legal authority. It is merely customary to have a cabinet, though its membership and functions vary at the discretion of the President. But the appointment of members of his cabinet is not at the President's discretion; appointments must be made on the advice and with the consent of the Senate. This provision, which is one of the classical 'checks and balances' of the constitution of the United States and is unusual in view of the separation of powers, makes sense if appointments are regarded as an administrative rather than a political action. This is how they should be regarded, for it has to be remembered that secretaries of state are in principle civil servants. Congress has laid down special qualifications for some posts, and has provided that some posts may not be held at the same time as others. In practice when a nomination is submitted to the Senate by the President, it is referred to the permanent commission which deals with the department concerned. The committee at public hearings and private meetings considers the candidate's qualifications. In practice the Senate exercises only the power to approve or disapprove and not the power to propose an alternative candidate. In the Philippines too the appointment of the members of the cabinet must also be approved by a parliamentary body, namely, the commission on appointments, consisting of twelve members of the House of Representatives and twelve senators with the President of the Senate as chairman.

In Pakistan where there is also a presidential type of regime, the sole obligation laid on the President who is elected by an indirect form of universal suffrage is to choose his ministers from persons who are eligible for membership of the National Assembly. The original character of the institutions of Ghana has already been noted; here the President has to choose ministers from among members of Parliament. In Ethiopia and the United Arab Republic ministers are appointed at the discretion of the Head of State but they are individually responsible to Parliament.

In all other countries where the government is separated from the Head of State, Parliament plays a part either direct or indirect in the procedure for designating the head of the government and the cabinet and so exerts authority to a greater or less degree over the government.

The method of direct election ensures the closest dependence of the government on Parliament. Government by delegation from Parliament is a feature of the Soviet constitution. At the first session of each legislature the Supreme Soviet in a joint sitting of both Chambers appoints the president of the council of ministers of the U.S.S.R. by an absolute majority of the votes in each Chamber. The members of the government are then proposed by the president of the council of ministers and approved by the Supreme Soviet according to the same procedure. Side by side with the power of appointment are equally broad powers of individual or collective dismissal. This machinery throws light on the procedure of the downward delegation of powers found in the Soviet system. The highest authority is the Supreme Soviet. When it is not sitting it delegates its powers to the Presidium which exercises them, particularly over the council of ministers which is the executive and administrative organ of power though the personality of the president of the council frequently helps to raise its prestige as an institution. In Albania, Bulgaria, Hungary, Poland and Rumania the procedure for appointing the government closely resembles that followed in the U.S.S.R. In Rumania candidates for the post of president of the council must be proposed either by the Council of State or by the Bureau of the Grand National Assembly.

In Czechoslovakia and Yugoslavia proceedings differ from those in other People's Democracies in that the President of the Republic resembles in many respects the Head of State of the classical type of parliamentary regime. In Yugoslavia however the President of the Republic merely proposes to the Federal Assembly a candidate for the office of president of the federal executive council. When he has been appointed he submits a list of ministers who have to be chosen from members of the Assembly. The committee on elections and appointments gives its views on these candidates which have then to be confirmed by the Assembly.

In Czechoslovakia the method of appointing the government resembles more closely the procedure that applies in systems of cabinet government. The President of the Republic appoints the head and the other members of the government before any action is taken by Parliament. When the government has taken office it must appear before Parliament, outline its programme and obtain a vote of confidence.

This procedure brings out one of the main features of the parliamentary system of government, namely, the joint action of the Head of State and of Parliament in appointing the government. The problem is to decide when and how the approval of Parliament as the necessary authority for the investiture of the government, is to be given: should it come before or after the formal act of appointment by the Head of State? Should it be explicit or simply a matter of tacit consent? The replies given to these questions exemplify two related but differing concepts of the role of Parliament: one is academic and might almost be called radical; the other empirical and traditional.

According to the first concept there is a clear intention that the cabinet should be appointed by election; the part played by the Head of State is purely formal. In Ireland the Head of State appoints the prime minister only after a resolution has been agreed to by the Dail. Similarly he appoints the other members of the government on the recommendation of the prime minister, when the prime minister has taken office, but after the approval of the Dail has been signified by resolution.

In Japan too Parliament expresses its views before the formal act of nomination takes place. The Diet appoints the prime minister from among its own members and the Emperor has to approve this appointment. Motions to appoint the prime minister are moved in both Houses; but if the House of Representatives and House of Councillors cannot agree on the person to be appointed or if the House of Councillors does not give its views within ten days of the resolution being agreed to in the House of Representatives, the views of the House of Representatives are deemed to be those of the Diet. The prime minister himself appoints the ministers of state who form the cabinet. According to the constitution a majority of them must be members of the Diet.

In Israel the Head of State has more important duties. He consults with representatives of the various parties and then entrusts a member of the Knesset with forming a government. Once it is formed, that member comes before the Knesset, outlines his programme and asks for a vote of confidence which must be obtained before the Cabinet may legally take office. After a general political debate the President of the Knesset puts the motion of confidence to the vote. If it is passed, the new ministers take the oath. Only at that moment is the new ministry constituted. This procedure and the form of the oath ('I pledge myself . . . to abide by the decisions of the Knesset') underline the dependence of the government on the Knesset.

In the Federal Republic of Germany the procedure is more complex, but it belongs to the same category. The chancellor is elected without debate by an absolute majority of the membership of the

Bundestag on the proposal of the Federal President. The Bundestag is not bound to agree to this proposal. It can set aside the proposed candidate and elect another during the fourteen days after the first vote, also by an absolute majority. If the Bundestag does not succeed in electing a chancellor in this way, another vote is taken immediately, and the candidate obtaining the largest number of votes is elected. If this number is more than a majority of the members of the Bundestag, the federal president has to appoint this candidate within seven days of the election. If the candidate obtained a simple majority only the federal president then has two courses open to him: he can either appoint the person elected within seven days or dissolve the Bundestag. The federal chancellor chooses his cabinet after talks with the parliamentary groups and submits them to the President for formal appointment. Members of the government then take the oath before the Bundestag.

Another way of ensuring that Parliament has a preponderant influence is to require the government, once appointed by the Head of State, to submit itself to Parliament in order to obtain a vote of confidence. This is the rule in Greece, Italy and Turkey, and it is the custom in Belgium and the Lebanon.

In Turkey the President of the Council must appear before the National Assembly within one week of his appointment by the President of the Republic. In Greece the government must as soon as it is constituted seek a vote of confidence from the Chamber. If parliamentary business has been interrupted because of the formation of the government, the Chamber must be convened within fifteen days in order to express its views on the new government. In Italy also the government is appointed before there is any vote by Parliament, but the constitution provides that the government must obtain the confidence of both Houses within ten days. It is interesting to note that the cabinet must be acceptable not only to the lower House but also to the upper House. This is also true of Belgium. The King names a person to form a cabinet, and then appoints as ministers the persons whose names are submitted to him by the prime minister. As soon as the government is in office, the prime minister outlines his programme to each House. If the programme does not obtain the approval of a majority of each House, the prime minister hands in his government's resignation to the King.

In the Lebanon the Constitution provides only that the President of the Republic is to appoint and dismiss ministers and select one of them as president of the council of ministers. In practice when the government is formed after the various shades of political opinion have been consulted the president of the council of ministers appears

APPOINTMENT OF THE EXECUTIVE

as soon as possible before the assembly to obtain a vote of confidence. If he does not obtain it, the government must resign.

In these last examples the decision of the Head of State is by itself enough to appoint the government. The agreement of the two Houses flows from a general belief that Parliament ought to take some part in the appointment. This is the only respect in which there is some resemblance to the method of appointing the government in countries which have followed the British model. In Great Britain, the principle is simple. Members of the government are appointed by the Crown. In theory the prime minister can remain at the head of the government against the express wishes of both Houses. But he could only do so for a limited period because he has to seek each year the necessary supply to carry on the government and he must obtain the agreement of both Houses to continue in force the Army Act which gives the executive the right to maintain a standing army in time of peace. In practice the prime minister receives the tacit support of the House of Commons as soon as he assumes office until an adverse vote by the House on a matter held to be important by the government entails its resignation. Parliament plays no formal part in the matter. In practice the Monarch chooses the prime minister from the party which has a majority.

The absence of a formal investiture of the government before Parliament is a feature of this system. It is found in countries influenced by British institutions such as Australia, Canada, Ceylon, India, New Zealand, Nigeria and Sierra Leone; in parliamentary monarchies such as Denmark, Libya, Luxembourg, the Netherlands, Norway and Sweden; and in some republics such as Austria, Finland, France and Iceland where the Head of State has a position of importance by virtue of his election by universal suffrage. In some of these countries however the method of appointing the head of the government differs from the British system because of the multiplicity of parties and of the Head of State's right to choose a prime minister from outside Parliament.

The feature common to all these procedures, as to those providing direct election by Parliament, is that every government must have the confidence of Parliament if it is to be able to govern. This is one of the principles of parliamentary government. This particular aspect of parliamentary control leads into the more general problem of ministerial accountability which is at the heart of parliamentary life.

3. HIGH OFFICIALS

Administration is the province of the executive; and the appointment of civil servants is usually a matter for the executive alone. Paradoxically the few exceptions to this general rule that exist are to be found in countries which otherwise follow most faithfully the principle of the separation of powers.

In the United States the appointment of ambassadors, consuls and many federal officials are made by the President only upon the advice and consent of the Senate. Judges of the supreme court are appointed in the same way. In practice the permanent committees of the Senate, each in its own field, exercise this authority by holding inquiries, sometimes in public, before which the candidates proposed by the President appear. This departure from the separation of powers needs some explanation. It is that the Senate was originally conceived by the founding fathers of the American Constitution not only as a legislative body but also as a kind of council set up alongside the President to help him in his task as chief executive. This idea was soon outmoded by constitutional developments. But some of the prerogatives that flowed from it have survived, in particular the unusual sharing with the executive of the power of appointment.

On the analogy of the procedure in the United States, the constitutions of Argentina and Brazil give this right to the federal Senate. In the Argentine the nomination of judges of the federal supreme court, ambassadors and diplomatic agents, and other high officials have to be approved and in Brazil diplomatic missions, the prefect of the federal district, members of the national economic council and directors of public corporations with a certain degree of autonomy. In the Philippines the appointments of higher civil servants have to be approved by a joint committee of the two Houses.

Apart from these countries there are no important exceptions to this rule except Japan, where the appointment of a number of high civil servants has to be approved by the two Houses, and Yugoslavia (see below).

In other countries the exclusive nature of the executive's powers to appoint officials is to some extent shown by the fact that as a rule Parliament is concerned only with posts for which independence of the executive is desirable, that is, with high judicial officers or officers responsible for the control of public finance rather than with ordinary civil servants.

Examples are numerous. Parliament elects the judges of the supreme court and the public prosecutor in Albania, Czechoslovakia, Hungary, Rumania and the U.S.S.R. In Czechoslovakia it also elects

APPOINTMENT OF THE EXECUTIVE

members of the central committee of control and statistics and in Poland members of the supreme chamber of control which is responsible for overseeing the economic and financial administration of certain public authorities and local branches of public departments. In Yugoslavia apart from members of the constitutional court the Federal Assembly appoints judges of the federal courts and the federal prosecutor. In Somalia the Assembly elects two members of the constitutional court and six members of the court of justice. In the financial sphere the Irish and Norwegian Parliaments choose the auditors of public accounts. In the Netherlands Parliament submits candidates for the court of accounts. In Belgium the House of Representatives appoints the councillors of the court of accounts and the Senate fills vacancies that arise in the court of appeal. Both Chambers take part in turn in making appointments to the council of state. In Austria the President and Vice-President of the court of accounts are elected by the National Council. In Israel the controller general is appointed by the Head of State but on the recommendation of the Knesset committee.

In the Federal Republic of Germany Parliament elects not only the judges of the federal constitutional court but also takes part in the appointment of judges of all the supreme federal courts through its committee on the election of judges which consists of nine members of the Bundestag. In addition the fundamental law provides that the federal Diet shall nominate a defence commissioner of the Diet to protect the fundamental rights of citizens and to help the Diet in its duties of parliamentary control.

A comparable institution is the Ombudsman which is found in Sweden, Finland, Denmark, New Zealand and Norway. In Sweden the Riksdag elects two commissioners, one for civil affairs and the other for military affairs for four years. These commissioners are elected by an electoral college consisting of twenty-four members of each Chamber. The Riksdag also elects six commissioners of the Bank of Sweden and seven commissioners of the National Debt Office.

25. Accountability of the Government to Parliament

THE MEANING OF MINISTERIAL ACCOUNTABILITY – FORMS OF MINISTERIAL ACCOUNTABILITY – MINISTERIAL ACCOUNTABILITY AND DISSOLUTION

Parliament and government are linked as partners in the conduct of public affairs by a whole network of relationships; but the partnership is seldom an equal one, even when the draftsmen of a constitution have intended that it should be so. An analysis of these relationships makes it possible to assess accurately the influence exerted by the one on the other.

It has already been shown how in some countries the executive has the upper hand in legislative and financial matters. At the same time a general tendency for Parliament to exercise its powers increasingly in the form of influencing or controlling government action has been noted. The primacy of Parliament can begin to make itself felt, as has been shown, in the procedure for appointing the members of the government and it can make itself felt even more decisively in the procedure for their dismissal. This poses the problem of ministerial accountability which has many facets; as constitutional practice shows, it is often closely related, though it is also in a sense contradictory, to the procedure for dissolution.

1. THE MEANING OF MINISTERIAL ACCOUNTABILITY

Theoretically there are three types of ministerial accountability. There is first personal financial accountability which is the obligation on ministers to make good financially any harm caused through their fault to the interests of the tax-payer. This question is not pursued here, because it has nothing to do with the relationship between the executive and Parliament and because it is largely an academic problem.

Secondly there is penal accountability which is the obligation upon ministers to answer for criminal acts such as treason, misappropriation or extortion, corrupt practices and encroachment upon the

ACCOUNTABILITY OF THE GOVERNMENT TO PARLIAMENT

freedom of the individual. This question, though at the root of political responsibility, raises the broader issue of political trials and is considered later in this book to the extent that it leads to Parliament's taking action. It is of importance in states where political accountability has ceased to apply.

Lastly there is political accountability which is founded not on criminal or civil offences determined objectively but on essentially subjective factors to be assessed by Parliament. Its scope is infinitely vast. It may apply to any act performed by a minister in the exercise of his duties or to his policy, his actions or failure to act, or even his intentions. His conduct is regarded in the light not of its legality but simply of its political wisdom in the face of the views expressed by Parliament. Because ministers are accountable politically, the will of Parliament can make itself felt.

In systems where the separation of powers is the rule, the ministers are politically answerable only to the Head of State, and he alone can dismiss them when he disapproves of something they have done. Elsewhere political accountability implies for practical purposes the obligation on the part of the government to act constantly in accordance with the views of the majority in Parliament. What gives this obligation political force is the threat of loss of office by the minister or by the whole cabinet if what is being done is not approved by the representatives of the nation.

This type of accountability and the penalties that go with it were not directly the brain-children of theorists on constitutional law. They are the fruits of a long evolution characteristic of the British institutions, originating in the procedure known as 'impeachment'. This penal procedure made its first appearance as early as the sixteenth century. A minister could be arraigned by the House of Commons and subsequently tried by the House of Lords. In this form it was used to attack those ministers whose proximity to the Sovereign was considered undesirable and who could not be proceeded against for a crime or misdemeanour under the ordinary law. As the power of Parliament grew, ministers learnt to pay attention to a hostile expression of opinion. This is what happened in 1742 when a prime minister for the first time resigned after being defeated in the House of Commons. The weapon of impeachment became obsolete. Political accountability to Parliament was born.

This concept has had a prodigious influence, for it established the power of modern Parliaments. Once the principle is accepted that a ministry can only continue in power so long as it complies with the will of Parliament, there is nothing to stop Parliament from laying down conditions governing the confidence they place in it. In so acting Parliament is embodying the sovereignty of the people.

This explains why in many bicameral Parliaments only the lower House, elected by direct universal suffrage has the power to call ministers to account. This is the position in Australia, Austria, Canada, Ceylon, France, the Federal Republic of Germany, Great Britain, India, Ireland, Japan, Laos, Libya and Turkey. Where the upper House is on the same footing electorally as the lower House, it enjoys the same powers over the government as in Belgium, Iceland, Italy, Norway, Sweden and the U.S.S.R. In Iran and the Netherlands the two Houses also have equal powers in this respect though in the Netherlands in practice the government is answerable primarily to the lower House (Second Chamber).

Political accountability of government to Parliament as the sole embodiment of national representation is the best reflection of the principles that should underlie a genuine democracy. It is different where the executive itself comes to power through universal suffrage and so has the same authority as the legislature. It is characteristic of presidential regimes to resist any procedure to call to account ministers whose proper status and function is to assist the Head of State. This is what has happened in the United States, Argentina, Brazil, Chile, Liberia and the Philippines as well as in Cameroon, the Central African Republic, Senegal and Tunisia. It is interesting to note that in Pakistan the constitution of 1962 preserved certain procedures which belong to the parliamentary regime such as questions to ministers and motions for the adjournment; but it also provides that if the government is defeated on this kind of occasion it does not have to resign. In the United Arab Republic although the regime is distinctly presidential in character, ministers are responsible to the National Assembly. The position in Switzerland is proof enough that the principle of ministerial accountability as it is known in cabinet regimes is not an essential ingredient of democracy. Here the federal council is elected for four years and cannot be brought down by Parliament. The result of a serious disagreement with Parliament is not a ministerial crisis but a modification of government policy. In practice the federal council is not so much a government as an agent for carrying out the decisions taken by Parliament. Although not answerable to the federal Parliament, the federal council is subordinate to it. In every session the federal council has to make a report to Parliament on its administration and on the state of the confederation. At the end of the debate on that report resolutions are agreed to laying down the directives with which the council must comply.

But in most countries in which the government is autonomous in that it is separate from both the Head of State and Parliament, ministerial accountability is regarded as the only way of ensuring effective parliamentary control. Parliamentary control can take two forms. It may be individual or collective, according to whether a single minister or the entire cabinet is implicated. As hardly an action performed by a minister is not linked to general policy, ministerial accountability is usually a collective matter. Several constitutions refer to it exclusively in this form, as do those of France, the Federal Republic of Germany, Israel, Japan and Somalia. This is also the practice in regimes with cabinet governments on the British model. If Parliament expresses a lack of confidence in one of the ministers, the prime minister has to decide whether the entire government should resign on the principle of ministerial solidarity or whether the resignation of the minister in question is enough. Though seldom put to the test the individual responsibility of members is a feature common to most of the Parliaments of continental Europe and to Iran, Lebanon, Libya and Turkey.

Individual accountability is also the general rule in countries where ministers are the direct instruments for the execution of the policy laid down by Parliament. Each one may be asked to give an account of the way in which he is carrying out that policy within his own department. This is the sense of the procedure of dismissal, especially in the People's Democracies which may extend to the government as a whole.

2. FORMS OF MINISTERIAL ACCOUNTABILITY

Dismissal, an act of authority which leaves no room for interpretation on the part of its victims, is the sanction that gives force to the accountability of ministers in the parliamentary type of government. The power of dismissal is self-contained. It need not necessarily be linked to a specific procedure of parliamentary control because Parliament is kept constantly informed of the activity of the government through the reports regularly submitted to it. Dismissal is an autonomous decision which can be directed at the government as a whole or at an individual minister. So Parliament is in a position at any moment to pass judgment on the government's actions and decide whether it should remain in office.

The power to dismiss ministers, like the power to appoint them, is vested in the Parliaments of Albania, Bulgaria, Hungary, Poland, Rumania and the U.S.S.R. In all these countries the intention is to ensure that the will of Parliament is done at all times. In view of the length of the periods between sessions, control of the executive when the Parliament is not sitting is assured by their Presidium, or Council of State in Poland and Rumania, who appoint and dismiss ministers and take any other necessary action subject only to subsequent approval by Parliament itself (which is not the case in Rumania). In Hungary the president, vice-president and members of the council of ministers cannot be members of the Presidium of the people's republic. In Bulgaria according to a new provision of the rules of procedure of the National Assembly the Assembly must express its views on the report of its activities which the government has to lay before it every year. In Yugoslavia and Czechoslovakia the existence of a President of the Republic alters the perspective of this problem. In Yugoslavia it falls to him to propose the dismissal of members of the federal executive council. Twenty members of the Federal Assembly may also make this proposal. In Czechoslovakia dismissal like nomination is the prerogative of the President of the Republic, if necessary on the proposal of the National Assembly. When a vacancy occurs and the duties of the President of the Republic are assumed by the government, the Presidential Bureau of the National Assembly may appoint and dismiss ministers. In most of the People's Democracies the principle of responsibility to Parliament is widely applied; its power of dismissal extends to some of the higher judicial authorities such as the supreme court and the public prosecutor and even to some special bodies such as the supreme chamber of control in Poland or the central committee of control and statistics in Czechoslovakia.

The power wielded by Parliament through the political accountability of the government is less drastic in those countries which have drawn directly on the British tradition. The cabinet nominated on the responsibility of the prime minister in practice enjoys an existence in its own right, and its members are not regarded as mere agents for carrying out the will of Parliament. If there is a disagreement with Parliament, ministers are not dismissed. It is for the cabinet as a body to resign the moment it loses the confidence of Parliament and can no longer govern effectively and legitimately. The margin of choice left to ministers may be extremely narrow because the ministry may no longer have the necessary legislative and financial authority to continue governing the country.

Generally the procedure by which ministerial accountability is raised is not in any way cut and dried. The form in which disagreements between Parliament and government are expressed is unimportant. It is possible for Parliament to pass an explicit motion

ACCOUNTABILITY OF THE GOVERNMENT TO PARLIAMENT

of censure which brings the disagreement out into the open in unequivocal terms. Provision is made for this procedure in the House of Commons where the motion is usually put down by the leader of the opposition and in practice the government usually agrees to debate it immediately. If the motion is carried, the government must resign or ask the Queen to dissolve Parliament. In practice the two-party structure, which is a fundamental feature of the British system, means that there is little likelihood of a government's being defeated because it is sure of the support of its majority. It is equally possible for the government to ask for a vote of confidence which will enable it to demonstrate the fact that it has a strong majority in Parliament. This kind of motion is more or less complementary to a motion of censure and it follows the same rules.

Ministerial accountability can arise indirectly at any moment out of any subject whatever on which the views of Parliament differ from those of the government, such as the adoption of a motion, the passing of a bill, the imposition of a tax or the granting of funds. The practice today in Great Britain and generally speaking in all the countries influenced by Great Britain is to regard any vote hostile to the government's policy or administration as a matter of confidence. This is the position, for example, of the vote on motions for the adjournment. In accordance with a special procedure, the House of Commons can take up 'definite' matters of 'urgent public importance' and discuss them forthwith. It is left to the Speaker to decide whether the questions raised at the beginning of the sitting are definite and urgent. With his agreement and if enough members consider the matter to be of public importance, the debate takes place in the evening between 7 and 10 p.m. and all other business is deferred. Technically all that the motion calls for is the adjournment of the House. But a defeat of the government could well force the government or the minister primarily responsible to resign. This procedure resembles the continental procedure of 'interpellation'; but in practice it is seldom successfully claimed by members. It is also used in Ceylon and Australia. In Australia there are normally two forms of motion of censure; it is either a substantive motion setting out the reasons for the censure, or it may be an amendment for example to the budget put down during the second reading of the annual finance bill.

In many other countries such as Denmark, Finland, Iceland, Israel, Luxembourg, Norway and Turkey there are as many ways of calling ministers to account as in Great Britain. As a general rule they extend beyond explicit motions of confidence or no-confidence and interpellations to all parliamentary activity; frequently the passing of the budget is the most important test of parliamentary confidence in the government. In Sweden the absence of a specific procedure for calling ministers to account is seen in its most striking form. Motions of censure and matters of confidence are unknown, and all attempts to introduce them have failed. The government is accountable to the Riksdag first when bills or proposals come up for debate and secondly in a debate initiated by the opposition on a report by the committee on the constitution which has the duty of examining minutes of proceedings of the council of ministers. It is interesting to note that the original object of this last procedure was to indict ministers who had failed in their duty. It resembles the British procedure of impeachment and it has developed in the same way. This quasijudicial procedure has given place to a form of parliamentary control which the constitution never contemplated.

In theory there is a grave danger if there are no formal rules governing ministerial accountability, because any vote implying the lack of confidence would mean the fall of the ministry at any time or on any occasion during the debate, however small the majority in favour of the motion and the number of members present in the House. This constant subordination of the government to Parliament is hardly compatible with a system of collaboration between the various powers in the state which postulates a certain measure of independence for the executive. But in many instances the subordination is largely offset by the support given to government policy by a coherent majority party. This ensures that the ministry remains stable and strong.

In countries where the political situation cannot be reduced to such simple terms and where a large number of parties militate against the emergence of a solid majority, government stability becomes a matter of concern. Unhappy experiences in this respect have led some countries to lay down more or less strict rules governing ministerial accountability in order to avoid hasty or thoughtless votes of censure by Parliament. This is an instance of what has been called the 'rationalisation' of the parliamentary system.

The underlying intention may be merely practical. In Belgium several principles have been gradually evolved on which the circumstances for invoking ministerial accountability have been more precisely defined. Before the government can be forced to resign, its difference of opinion with Parliament must be on a matter of importance; it must be on a matter of general policy and not on an isolated administrative matter; and it must be raised categorically as a matter of confidence. The government may take the initiative itself, or the members of Parliament may do so, by making use of the procedure of

ACCOUNTABILITY OF THE GOVERNMENT TO PARLIAMENT

interpellation which invariably ends in a vote of confidence or censure.

In several countries provision is made in the constitution to prevent ministerial responsibility from being invoked on any and every occasion. The simplest provisions are that the government is not obliged to resign unless a motion of censure or no confidence has been passed. This is the position in Somalia as well as in Japan where the cabinet may however dissolve the House of Representatives within ten days.

In Austria the National Council must also express its want of confidence in an explicit resolution agreed to in the presence of at least half of its members.

In the United Arab Republic a motion of censure on a particular minister may only be passed as a result of an interpellation, and if it is tabled by ten members of the Assembly. In addition, no vote may be taken for three days after the motion has been tabled and a vote of no confidence requires a majority of the membership of the Assembly. In Lebanon a period of five days for reflection may be requested by the government before the Chamber takes a vote on a question of confidence or a motion of censure.

In Libya the procedure is more complicated. A vote of censure entails the resignation of the government only if it is supported by a majority of the members of the House. A proposal to proceed with such a vote may not be taken into consideration unless it is put forward by at least fifteen members. It cannot be debated for eight days and the vote may not be taken for two days after the end of this debate.

The Italian constitution explicitly provides for ways of calling ministers to account. Here again the intention is to obviate constant ministerial crises, a precaution made all the more necessary because the cabinet is subject to a vote of no-confidence in either House. A distinction is made between any vote against the government and an explicit vote of no confidence. Only an explicit vote of no-confidence automatically entails the resignation of the government. Moreover the relevant rules of procedure eliminate any possibility of a snap vote. Motions of no confidence must be signed by at least one-tenth of the members of the House and must give reasons. The motion cannot be debated for three days after it has been put down. Voting has to be by roll call.

In Greece although the government may request a vote of confidence at any time the opportunities for private members are more limited. A motion of censure must be signed by at least twenty members and must set out clearly the matter to which the censure applies. The motion may not be tabled for two months after the rejection of a similar motion unless it is signed by at least half the total number of members. Debate on the motion may not be opened for at least two days after it has been tabled nor last longer than five days. A vote on a question of confidence or a motion of censure may be adjourned for forty-eight hours if twenty members so request. A motion is not agreed if the majority comprises fewer than two-fifths of the members.

All these rules designed to bolster ministerial stability are likely to be ineffective if the government has the option of resigning in circumstances other than those specifically dealt with in the constitution. If it lacks the support of Parliament, even if the lack of confidence is not expressed in so many words, the government is rendered impotent and has to resign. However ingeniously the rules are drafted, they cannot by themselves solve the problem of government stability which is dictated rather by the hard facts of political life.

It was for this purpose that in France a new procedure for calling the government to account was introduced. The initiative may be taken either by the National Assembly or by the government by way of motion of censure. This motion is only admissible if signed by at least one-tenth of the members. There are also rules governing the notice which must be given and the majority which must be obtained. The debate may only open forty-eight hours after the motion has been tabled and the motion is only adopted if it has the support of an absolute majority of the members of the Assembly. The essential innovation is that only the votes in favour of the motion of censure are taken into account and that there is no risk of the government's being put out of office by a relative majority. When a motion of censure has been rejected, the signatories may not table another motion in the same session except in the circumstances referred to in the next paragraph.

The government may seek a vote of confidence in two ways. First it may request a vote on its programme or on a statement of general policy. In that event no special rules apply. If the government is defeated it has to resign. Secondly it may state that a particular bill is the subject of confidence. This bill is considered to be passed unless a motion of censure tabled in the following twenty-four hours is passed under the procedure already described. The effect of this original provision is to allow a bill to be passed by the National Assembly without any vote on the text as a whole.

Although they may not measure up to the highest canons of procedural orthodoxy, these various provisions taken together with the right of dissolution which vests in the Head of State do contribute to the stability of government without extinguishing the opportunities of the opposition.

The rules in the Federal Republic of Germany ought to be judged from the same standpoint. The Bundestag has the power to overthrow the government; it does so by a vote of no-confidence. But that vote does not of itself entail the fall of the cabinet. The Assembly must first elect a new chancellor by a majority of its membership. Only then can the federal President relieve the defeated chancellor of his office. By making the effectiveness of a vote of no-confidence conditional upon the appointment of a successor to the chancellor in office, the fundamental law has endeavoured to cope with the danger of repeated and insoluble crises of the kind that took place during the Weimar Republic. Its aim is to make any majority which may form in opposition to the government to present a coherent and constructive purpose. In practice it is extremely difficult to overthrow a federal chancellor.

Furthermore the concern to ensure the stability of the government is seen in the fact that here more than anywhere else ministerial accountability is linked with the dissolution of Parliament, if the question of accountability and resignation has been raised by the government itself. In other words if a motion tabled by the federal chancellor in order to obtain a vote of confidence is not agreed to by a majority of the members of the Bundestag, the federal President on the advice of the chancellor may dissolve the Bundestag within twenty-one days. Meanwhile however the Bundestag may appoint a new federal chancellor, again by a majority of its members, and prevent the dissolution from taking place.

This example illustrates the link between ministerial accountability and dissolution of Parliament, a link which some consider to be the cornerstone of the classic parliamentary system based on balance between the powers.

3. MINISTERIAL ACCOUNTABILITY AND DISSOLUTION

According to the principles underlying parliamentary regimes, the power to dissolve Parliament is for the government what the invoking of ministerial accountability is for Parliament. It gives a cabinet which finds itself without a majority in Parliament the right to have its difference of opinion with Parliament settled by the electors.

Dissolution is not always a means of settling disagreements between the government and Parliament. In some rare instances Parliament has power to dissolve itself; if it did so, it would not necessarily be challenging the executive. More frequently dissolution can be a factor in the relationship between the two Houses of a Parliament. In Australia, the U.S.S.R. and Yugoslavia, for instance, it is the ultimate sanction when the two Houses are unable to agree upon the contents of a bill.

In the context of the relationship between Parliament and the executive there are many facets to a dissolution because it has meaning only in relation to the politics of the country where the question arises. Like most other constitutional weapons, the power of dissolution has no value in itself. Political scientists are divided on its merits. Yet the dissolution of Parliament is no more a creature of political thought than is ministerial accountability of which it is a corollary. At first it was used pragmatically by the Monarch to get rid of a House after he had got from it what he wanted. It became the counterpart of ministerial accountability only from the time when national representation was established on a permanent footing and the authority of the cabinet replaced that of the Crown. This established the balance between the executive and Parliament, in England first of all. If the government were dismissed by the House, the government could reply by dismissing Parliament. This system enabled the cabinet to avoid total subjugation to Parliament, and as two more or less equal forces were being opposed to each other it made collaboration between them possible.

For these reasons side by side with accountability, the power to dissolve Parliament has become one of the essential cogs in the parliamentary machine. Following the British model it was built into most constitutional monarchies during the nineteenth century, being regarded first and foremost as a royal prerogative. Looked at from another angle as a basic principle of the parliamentary system, it was adopted by many republican constitutions. But it has often been resisted as undemocratic, especially by the U.S.S.R. and the People's Democracies, on the grounds that it subordinates Parliament to the executive and traverses the sovereignty of representative assemblies. The advocates of the power to dissolve Parliament argue that it is not a question of subjecting Parliament to the wishes of the government but to the wishes of the people themselves, and on these grounds they consider this procedure admirably democratic.

In its classic form the power to dissolve Parliament is strictly speaking one of the prerogatives of the Head of State, the Monarch or President of the Republic, who is called upon to arbitrate on a dispute between the executive and legislature. This is the spirit of the provision made for this power in Italy and more recently in France where dissolution is the exclusive prerogative of the Head of State. No special conditions are laid upon its exercise unless it is to consult first the prime minister or the presidents of the two Chambers or to abstain from its exercise at certain times; in Italy during the last six months of the President's term of office or in France in the year after elections set off by a dissolution.

The role of the Head of State as an arbitrator disappears when the government takes the initiative on finding that Parliament has no confidence in it. This is what happens in Australia, Belgium, Ceylon, Denmark, Finland, Iceland, India, Japan, Luxembourg, the Netherlands and Sweden. In Great Britain where the system originated dissolution today has lost much of its character as a means of arbitration between the cabinet and the House of Commons because the dominance of the majority party has so strengthened the links between executive and legislature that the defeat of the government in the House of Commons is now rare. The power of dissolution remains; but it is dissociated from the problem of political accountability. Nowadays Parliament is most frequently dissolved in order to cut short its life when approaching the end of its legal term; or when the government hopes to strengthen its own position by a new general election. More rarely it has recommended dissolution when it thought a particular problem had arisen on which the electorate should be consulted , as on tariff reform in 1923.

In none of these hypotheses is the government appealing to the electors to settle a difference with Parliament: the classic notion of dissolution has been totally transformed. The purpose of dissolution is no longer to regulate the relationships between the government and Parliament. Its only object is to strengthen the links between the party in power and public opinion, albeit with a risk of rejection at the polls. Viewed from this angle, the power to dissolve Parliament no longer appears as a threat to democratic institutions.

In the Federal Republic of Germany too the power of dissolution is not a weapon for use against Parliament. It is more a force compelling the parties to form a homogeneous majority in the Bundestag in the face of which dissolution becomes an impossibility. It can only take place in two circumstances. The first is where the Bundestag does not succeed in electing a chancellor. In that event the federal President can either appoint as chancellor the person who has received most votes or dissolve Parliament. This is not a matter of settling an issue between the executive and Parliament because there is no executive. Moreover, dissolution is to some extent dependent on the Bundestag itself. All it has to do is to elect a chancellor by an absolute majority, and the exercise of the power to dissolve is ruled out. The second contingency arises where the Bundestag has disagreed to a motion of confidence put forward by the chancellor. In that event the chancellor may ask the federal President for a dissolution. The Bundestag may force the chancellor to resign by electing a successor; only if it votes the chancellor down without being able to designate a successor may the power of dissolution be used, which is the first contingency described above. The power to dissolve would seem therefore to be not so much a weapon in the hands of the executive as a procedure for strengthening the authority of the Bundestag by compelling it to constitute a solid majority.

These few examples show how the principle of dissolution common to all these countries may vary in practice depending on the context in which it is applied. Although this is not its sole purport, the dissolution of Parliament, with the fall of a government, is the most dramatic expression of the control exercised by Parliament over the executive.

Parliamentary control is manifested in other less drastic ways. All of them are designed to keep members of Parliament aware of the policy of the government by giving them right of access to information and the right to explanations in affairs of concern to them.

26. Machinery of Parliamentary Control

GENERAL DEBATE AND INTERPELLATIONS – QUESTIONS TO MINISTERS – COMMITTEES OF INVESTIGATION – THE OMBUDSMAN AND OTHER FORMS OF CONTROL

If Parliament is to scrutinise the government's actions and either accord or withdraw its confidence as the practical situation requires, it must be kept fully supplied with information. In every country Parliament has a variety of means of investigation at its disposal in fields other than those of legislation and finance, so forming a network of links with the executive. The increasing scope of government activity has made information at once essential for Parliament if it is to discharge its representative function and difficult to obtain in all its diversity. The first problem is to adapt the machinery of control to fit its purpose, because the activities of the government do not always lend themselves to the type of supervision which large non-specialist bodies can exercise. Yet Parliaments are constitutionally provided with a variety of ways and means of accomplishing this task. The second and more important problem is how to use these devices judiciously, as each of them has been conceived with a particular task in mind—control of policy, supervision of the administration, protection of the individual, or bringing to light and eliminating abuses and injustice.

1. GENERAL DEBATE AND INTERPELLATIONS

In some countries the provisions of the constitution require the executive to give Parliament periodic accounts of its stewardship, thus providing an opportunity for it to exercise regular control. This provision is primarily characteristic of constitutions founded on separation of powers; it helps to make up for the fact that the executive is not directly accountable to Parliament for its actions. In the United States the President each year reports to Congress on the state of the Union, and all the points in his speech are the object of minute scrutiny on the part of the members. In addition he makes more than thirty reports a year, some at three-monthly, others at six-monthly intervals. The heads of each department also make reports on their activities during the past year, and in one way or another Congress receives several hundred reports from the executive during a year.

Another illustration of this regulatory procedure in the absence of direct ministerial accountability is Switzerland. Here the presentation of the annual report of the federal council to both Houses is followed by a debate. This report is published and distributed by the chancellery. It is examined by a committee of each House, and then debated in the House itself. It is a detailed statement, describing not only the policy pursued by the federal council but also with supporting figures the activities engaged in over the previous year by each of the seven ministerial departments and their subsidiary bodies by the two federal courts and by the federal chancellery. The debate on the report lasts on an average three days in the National Council and two days in the Council of States.

In countries where the government is accountable for its actions, an annual report of this kind is not so essential, as Parliament usually has other means of putting pressure on the executive. It should be noted however that in Finland this method does much to help Parliament maintain control over public administration. Each year a report on the measures taken by the government is submitted to the Diet. The same result is obtained in parliamentary monarchies such as Great Britain, Luxembourg, the Netherlands and Sweden through the speech from the throne which gives rise to a debate on the government's broad policy.

Something similar is found in the U.S.S.R. and the People's Democracies in the system of progress reports frequently made to both Houses by the ministers in the course of the session. Except in Bulgaria where the government has to make a report once a year and the Assembly takes formal note of it, these reports are not mandatory, and they are not required to be made at any particular intervals. But they are traditionally made during a session. They may be asked for by both Houses or volunteered by the ministers themselves. They are usually debated, and the debate may conclude with the passing of resolutions relating to the particular field of government.

In most countries matters of general policy are not automatically subject to periodic examination. Most often they would come up for debate if specifically raised by a member. Alternatively the government might itself decide at an appropriate moment to make a 'communication' or 'statement' to Parliament over and above its critical statement of policy in seeking the Assembly's confidence. Making a statement should be classed as a procedure for giving information rather than as a method of control, especially in such countries as France where it is given priority over the business to be taken on that day and may not give rise to debate.

In order to ensure that the executive and the legislature regularly exchange views, most countries provide an opportunity for members to raise particular subjects in the form of an 'interpellation'. This is the stock procedure for obtaining information and exercising control in the classical parliamentary system. An interpellation is addressed by a member of Parliament either to a minister to explain something his department has done or to the head of the government on a matter of general policy. An interpellation has two essential features: first it gives rise to a general debate; and secondly it carries a political sanction because the debate culminates in a vote on a motion expressing either the satisfaction or the dissatisfaction of the House with the explanations furnished by the government.

An interpellation is a most effective proceeding because ministers are called directly to account. It is not simply a device for obtaining information, but a direct form of control; indeed it is bound up with the history of the parliamentary system. In France it goes back a long way; as early as 1791 the constitution specified that 'ministers should be heard when they are required to give explanations'. Interpellations became a regular practice under the monarchy of 1830 and were used increasingly in the third and fourth republics. But the disorders to which this procedure sometimes gave rise had led to its condemnation even before the reforms of 1958. Today ministers can be brought to account on matters of confidence only under the carefully regulated procedure of the vote of censure.

Even in classical parliamentary regimes the procedure of interpellation can only retain its value if it is used sparingly and to debate matters of enough importance to justify applying a political sanction to the government. In several countries especially in Western Europe it retains its prestige because these conditions are fulfilled. In Belgium it is regarded as the best means at the disposal of a member for raising matters of confidence. The President of the Chamber must be informed in writing of the matter that a member wishes to raise or the facts about which he desires an explanation. This request may be made by one member only. The interpellation is then included in the order of business for the next Tuesday though it may be treated as urgent if not less than fifty members so request. In the debate the initiator of the interpellation may not speak for more than half an hour. After the minister has replied, not more than four speakers may be heard for up to ten minutes each. The debate concludes with a vote which allows the Chamber to express its views. If a motion expressing or implying a lack of confidence in the government is carried, the government or the minister concerned has to resign.

The procedure of interpellation is often closely regulated in order to prevent its abuse. In Turkey a short debate is on held every request for an interpellation made by members or political groups: only representatives of groups, the government and the proposer of the request may speak. If the request is accepted a day for the debate on the substance of the matter is immediately fixed. The interpellation may be taken not sooner than two days nor later than one week from the day of the short debate. In the debate on the interpellation any member may speak. A vote of confidence may only be taken one clear day after the debate has ended.

In the Lebanon an interpellation takes the same form as a written question. The government must reply to it within ten days of its being tabled. If it does not do so, the interpellation has to be included in the order of business for the next sitting at which questions and interpellations are to be taken. Notice of the interpellation is given to members at least two days before this sitting. A general debate takes place during which the proposer and the government each have a prior right to speak on two occasions. The debate concludes with a vote on a reasoned motion either to pass from the interpellation or to accept that the substance of the motion is well founded. In the second event a vote on the motion has to be taken forthwith.

In Libya the day for the debate on an interpellation is fixed by the Chamber for the first convenient sitting, after the responsible minister has been heard. The debate on the substance of the interpellation may not take place for eight days after the interpellation has been tabled unless the matter is agreed with the government to be urgent. If the proposer or any other member wishes, the debate may close with a vote of confidence. In the United Arab Republic a period of not less than seven days must elapse between the tabling of an interpellation and its debate. That time may also be shortened if the matter is urgent and if the minister agrees.

In Finland interpellations serve the same purpose of challenging the government. They must be supported by twenty members of Parliament. A reply must be furnished by the minister concerned within fifteen days, or if the government does not intend to reply it must notify Parliament within the same period explaining why it does not intend to do so.

In the Federal Republic of Germany the procedure corresponding to an interpellation is known as the 'major question'. It must be submitted by at least thirty members. The President of the Bundestag sends it to the government with the request for a statement whether it proposes to reply and when. The government is not obliged to reply though it has to take full responsibility if it decides not to do so. The text is distributed to all the members of the Bundestag and the debate is put down on the order paper for a day chosen to suit the government. The initiator first makes his case, and a debate follows if thirty members present ask for one. If the government refuses to reply or is not prepared to do so within the period of fifteen days the Bundestag may place the debate on the order paper provided that thirty members present call for it. Moreover a representative of the government must attend the debate if a motion to that effect is passed.

In Sweden interpellations and questions are not essentially different. An interpellation requires the permission of the Chamber and it produces a written reply from the government before any debate takes place in public. The day for the debate is left to ministers. In general the simplest question obtains the most rapid answer. Although an interpellation in Switzerland has to be supported by ten members of the National Council and three of the Council of States members do make use of it in order to obtain the most publicity for specific charges and criticisms. By this means they exert an effective political control.

In the U.S.S.R. and some of the People's Democracies it is also difficult to make a sharp distinction between the interpellations and questions. Both procedures follow similar rules; for instance ministerial answers to both have to be given within three days in Rumania and the U.S.S.R., the duration of the session in Bulgaria, and thirty days in Czechoslovakia. In Albania interpellations take the form of a general debate followed by a vote expressing the Assembly's satisfaction or a request that the minister concerned should amplify his answer. In Poland the minister to whom the interpellation is directed has to answer within seven days either in writing or orally. If the answer is not satisfactory the proposer may request the Presidium to include the interpellation in the order of business for a plenary sitting. The Diet is then called upon to debate and if necessary vote upon a resolution requesting the minister to amplify his reply. In Hungary a request for an interpellation is communicated to the Assembly at the beginning of each sitting. The Assembly fixes a day for its debate. An answer must be given during the same session; if the Assembly declares the matter urgent it must be given at that sitting or the following sitting. In exceptional cases and for precise reasons an answer may be given in writing only and within thirty days. But the proposer of the interpellation has the right to appeal to the Assembly if he thinks the answer is unsatisfactory. The matter may then be taken up in debate.

In the British system the procedure of interpellation is unknown, though the 'adjournment motion' is not unlike it. The adjournment motion moved immediately before the beginning of a recess gives an opportunity for raising a series of matters with the government, but no vote is taken. On the other hand the adjournment motion on a 'definite' question of 'urgent public importance' may end in a vote in the same way as the continental style of interpellation. But this kind of adjournment is often linked, though it need not be linked, to the essential machinery for parliamentary control which is questions to ministers.

2. QUESTIONS TO MINISTERS

Questions to ministers is a procedure for information and control used in the Parliaments of all countries in which the government is politically accountable. As it carries no direct sanction, it is also used in such countries as the Central African Republic, Pakistan, Senegal, and Spain where the executive is not accountable to Parliament.

Questions may be either oral or written: the member asking the question may request the appropriate minister to answer orally in the Chamber or in writing. Questions are more often than not tabled in writing so that members of Parliament and the ministers concerned are informed of their contents.

Like so many other parliamentary practices, the procedure of questions originated in Great Britain. As the control of the time of the House passed to the government questions to ministers took the place of many of the older methods by which grievances had been ventilated or government policy examined. Questions became a distinct procedure in 1849 when a special part of the sitting known as 'question time' was, and still is, given over to answering them. In 1902 the practice of asking questions for written answers was introduced, and written answers to oral questions which for lack of time could not be given oral answers were also permitted. Today several thousand questions are asked every year.

A question is a request by a member of the House to a minister for explanation of a specific matter. It has no immediate political sanction, and so is clearly distinguishable from other procedures of parliamentary control such as motions of censure or interpellations which also seek explanations from the government but which do have a sanction in that they conclude with a vote of confidence in the government.

But although it seems less important in political terms, the procedure of questions is in great demand as a means of protecting individual rights and liberties. Its purpose is to elicit concrete information from the administration, to request its intervention and where necessary to expose abuses and seek redress. It is also used to obtain detailed facts which will help members to understand the complicated subject matter of bills and statutory instruments laid before Parliament. Many questions are of a routine character; but the procedure provides the opposition with a means of discovering the government's weak points and because of the publicity given to them they have a salutary effect on the administration.

In the House of Commons questions have to comply with rules of order. The Speaker decides finally whether a question is admissible.

A member wishing to ask a question must first of all put it in writing and hand it in to the clerks at the Table. If he wishes for an oral answer, he marks it with a star; at least two clear days' notice of starred questions must be given. If he wants the answer sooner, he may make a special request by which he can gain a day. For more urgent matters a special procedure is provided. A member wishing to take advantage of it must give notice of his question to the minister concerned and to the Speaker before noon of the day on which he proposes to put the question. This type of question is not published, as its name 'private notice question' implies. It has to comply with the rules applicable to ordinary questions and must also be of an urgent character. The Speaker is the final judge especially of the urgency. In any event the private notice question may not be accepted if another question has already been put down on the same subject. Answers in the House are given to private notice questions on the same day after the time allowed for ordinary questions. No member may put more than two questions for oral answer in a single day.

Ministers invariably reply to oral questions on the day fixed, but they have more latitude for written questions. Answers to written questions are sent directly to Hansard for publication. If answers are not forthcoming within a reasonable time, the member may make the question one for oral answer. Members frequently use the written question to deal with individual cases or administrative details.

Oral questions are taken for one hour at the beginning of the sitting on Mondays, Tuesdays, Wednesdays and Thursdays. A rota of ministers answering questions at each sitting is published in advance. The order on this rota varies each week and is decided after consultation between the parties. Thus every minister in due course comes to the head of the list to answer questions about his department. Questions are grouped together by ministries and within each group appear in the order in which notice of them has been given. Unless a member postpones his oral question to which for lack of time an oral answer cannot be given, a written answer is printed in Hansard along with the answers to written questions.

The exchanges between minister and member follow a ritual which the Speaker ensures is strictly observed. When his name is called, the member indicates the number of his question. The minister answers by reading the reply prepared by his department. The member then has the right to put a 'supplementary question' to which the minister again replies. The exchange of question and answer may go on for some minutes, with other members taking part also, until the Speaker decides that it is time to pass on to the next question. The brevity and speed of these exchanges can be gauged from the number of questions disposed of in the course of an hour, which is often about fifty. The procedure for oral questions is very popular. An important reason for this popularity is that the supplementary question can easily embarrass a minister because he may have to answer it without the help of a brief prepared beforehand.

The spontaneity born of supplementary exchanges is one of the marks of question time in the House of Commons. Other countries have sought to reproduce it, and their success has varied. Question time in substantially the British form can be found in Australia, Canada, Ceylon, Ghana, India, Ireland, Nigeria, New Zealand, Pakistan and Sierra Leone. In several instances questions have to relate to the control of administration rather than to matters of general policy.

The technique of parliamentary questions has also been applied beyond the sphere of British influence. The variety of practice justifies the citation of some examples.

In Italy with the exception of questions for written answers, questions are placed on the order paper for the next sitting but one after they are handed in. In the Chamber the first forty minutes, and in the Senate the first hour, of each sitting is taken up with oral questions. If a question remains on the paper for two months without receiving an answer, it is deemed to be dead and is removed from the paper. For written questions the ministers have ten days in which to reply.

In the Federal Republic of Germany question time on the English model has recently been introduced in the Bundestag. Every sitting begins with one hour of questions. Their purpose is to obtain quickly information on local or regional matters and statements of general interest on federal, internal or foreign policy. Questions are grouped according to departments. The President of the Assembly decides the order in which they are to be called. The list of questions is printed and distributed to members. The member asking a question, or any other member, may put two supplementary questions to the minister. Questions not answered during question time receive written answers which are printed in the official report of debates in the place which they would have occupied had they been answered orally.

In addition to oral questions the rules of procedure also provide for written questions or minor questions to obtain information of a more specialised kind on detailed points. This form of question is in contrast to major questions which are kept for problems of general policy and which amount to interpellations.

In Belgium three kinds of question are known in the House of Representatives. First there are written questions which may not be signed by more than three members. Answers must be given within fifteen days and are published in a paper known as the 'bulletin of questions and answers' which appears once a week. If no answer is forthcoming in that time, the question is published again in the bulletin with an indication that the minister has failed to answer. Secondly there are oral questions. The President, or if necessary the Conference of Presidents, decides whether they are in order. Unless the House requires otherwise, not more than half an hour at the beginning of every Thursday's sitting is given over to questions. They are taken in the order in which they were handed in. This procedure is broadly comparable with question time in the British House of Commons, but supplementary questions cannot be put after the minister's reply. Thirdly there are urgent questions. If the President and the minister concerned agree, a member may put a question at some time other than question time. The questioner may speak for not more than five minutes. A similar procedure is found in the Belgian Senate where there is no question time.

In the Netherlands written questions must be answered within thirty days and oral questions within three days. A feature of the Dutch procedure is the broad powers given to the Presidents of the two Chambers. They decide not only whether the question is in order but also whether it should be put. They can for instance refuse a question if its subject matter is to be debated in Parliament in the near future.

In Finland questions must be answered, either verbally or in writing at the choice of the minister concerned, within thirty days. In Israel the appropriate minister is required to answer orally at the tribune of the Knesset within twenty-one days. The questioner then has the right to ask orally one supplementary question. In Japan the time allowed for answering a written question is only one week. Oral questions are kept for urgent matters subject to the consent of the House.

The two Houses of the Libyan Parliament also use the procedure of oral questions. A question has to be handed in in writing by one member only at least forty-eight hours before the sitting at which it is taken. Questions are sent to ministers who may delay their answers for one week if the Assembly agrees. An answer must be given to written questions within one month. When a member is not satisfied with the attitude of a minister, he may change his question into an interpellation; but this change cannot be made at the same sitting. In the Lebanon a question may be changed into an interpellation at the same sitting. Oral questions are taken each week at a sitting specially devoted to questions and interpellations. The minister concerned may reply immediately or at the next convenient sitting or he may request that the question should be put in writing. Replies to written questions must be given within ten days.

The procedure of questions has long been a feature of the rules of procedure of French assemblies. It has taken on a special importance since the constitutional reforms of 1958 which suppressed the right of interpellation. Oral questions are now the only business that a private member can initiate which are certain to be included in the Assembly's order of business, because the constitution provides that one sitting a week is to be reserved for questions by members and replies by the government. Among oral questions a distinction is made between questions without debate and questions with debate. In the first category only the minister concerned followed by the questioner may speak; they are allowed five minutes each. In the second category when the question has been explained by the member and the minister has replied a general debate may take place. Although it is forbidden to take a vote, this last procedure is closer to an interpellation than to a question. The Conference of Presidents is empowered to select the oral questions which shall be taken at the weekly sitting for questions. The French Parliament now makes extensive use of this procedure for questions and also of written answers to questions which have normally to be given within one month. If an answer is not forthcoming, a written question may be changed into an oral question.

Questions are undoubtedly one of the most widely used parliamentary procedures. Apart from the countries mentioned above, they are found with variations of practice in Albania, Bulgaria, Cameroon, the Central African Republic, Czechoslovakia, Denmark, Ethiopia, Greece, Iceland, Indonesia, Iran, Luxembourg, Norway, Rumania, Senegal, Somalia, Turkey, the United Arab Republic and the U.S.S.R. Emphasis is often placed on the time allowed the government to furnish its reply. It is three days in Rumania and the U.S.S.R., five days in Albania and the whole session in Bulgaria. It rises to ten days in the Central African Republic, twenty days in Somalia and thirty in Czechoslovakia. The fact that time limits exist in most countries means that the government is obliged to furnish the information asked for, and this obligation, whether based on the constitution, the law, standing orders or established practice, is what gives the procedure of questions its real strength. In most Parliaments it is open to ministers to invoke reasons of public interest in order to defer giving an answer or to refuse one altogether.

The popularity of this procedure can be attributed to the fact that in making use of his right to ask questions the member of Parliament is a completely free agent. The only limits on his freedom of action are the rules governing the admissibility of questions which are concerned with matters of form and not with the merits of the subject.

3. COMMITTEES OF INVESTIGATION

The contribution made to the control of the executive by the interpellation in the continental tradition and by questions to ministers in the British tradition is made in the United States by the parliamentary investigation. Inquiries on behalf of Congress can be conducted either by permanent committees or by committees specially set up for the purpose known as investigating committees.

It was shown above that in some countries committees on bills have, or may request, powers to make investigations. In the United States, in addition to the general committee function of overseeing the execution of the laws reported by them, all the committees of the Senate and three committees of the House are given this power; the others need a special authorisation. Although the rule is that committees may only undertake investigations vital to the legislative business referred to them, they are in the habit of carrying out research which often has only a very remote relation to their remit. Conversely in countries such as France, Italy, the Netherlands and Sweden committees on bills may not carry out inquiries calling for powers of a judicial character. The same principle applies in the Federal Republic of Germany: of the permanent committees, only the committee on defence and the committee appointed under article 45 of the fundamental law to safeguard the rights of the Bundestag have these powers and may use them to make inquiries normally reserved for special committees of investigation.

But whereas committees on bills are rarely given powers to make inquiries, committees of investigation are widely used to study specific issues. For this purpose Parliament instructs a number of its members to collect such information as it needs to enable it to exercise proper control, and to make a report on which the House will, if it thinks fit, hold a debate and come to a decision. The right to institute an inquiry is a natural corollary of the principle that Parliament must be fully informed of any matter on which the executive takes action. While in some countries such as Finland, Norway and Sweden Parliament has been refused the right to set up committees of inquiry vested with special powers, this principle finds its fullest expression in the United States where committees of inquiry lie at the heart of the Congressional system.

These committees have extremely wide powers which they do not hestitate to use. They can call before them any person whom they think should be heard, and they have the right not only to punish persons who fail to appear but also to oblige them to do so by issuing subpoenas. The scope of their action is unlimited, though in practice their activities are wholly directed towards the administration. Frequently it is the political head or director who is the target of an attack on a service or department. When this is the position, the supervision exercised by the investigating committee is somewhat akin to the classic form of parliamentary control. The parallel is even closer where the Secretary of State of his own accord asks to be heard by a committee: the implication is that he is anxious to obtain its assistance or the power to pursue his policy.

In countries where the executive is politically accountable to Parliament, committees of inquiry have less significance, even when the means of investigation open to Parliament are as ample as they are in the United States. The prerogatives of the Belgian Parliament for example are unusually wide: under both the constitution and the law both Houses are at liberty to hold an inquiry with the same powers as are given to an examining magistrate by the code of criminal procedure. Yet unlike the American Congress, the Belgian Parliament only exercises its right in quite exceptional instances. Similarly in the Federal Republic of Germany the Bundestag rarely makes use of its right to appoint committees of inquiry. A motion to appoint one has to be signed by a quarter of the members. In France an 'organic' decree made in pursuance of the constitution of 1958 considerably restricted the use of committees of inquiry. They may not in any circumstance sit for longer than four months and they are forbidden to take into consideration any matter which has been the subject of a judicial prosecution. Members of these committees are under a pledge of secrecy and, unlike the legislative committees which are constituted by proportional representation, they are appointed by majority vote.

In some countries it is difficult for committees of inquiry to make an effective inquiry. Often they have no power to compel persons to attend except by ordinary process in the courts. This entails the intervention of governmental authorities, slows down the committee's proceedings and mutes the effect of its inquiry. Practical difficulties of this kind make rare the use of this procedure for exercising control over the executive. Yet the best way of making a parliamentary inquiry effective is by taking evidence on oath. The machinery of taking the oath is provided for if not always used in most Parliaments which make inquiries, and especially those influenced by the British tradition. The practice of taking evidence on oath is unknown in the U.S.S.R. and the People's Democracies; but a witness who gives false testimony is criminally liable. In Denmark, Iceland and Switzerland, committees of inquiry are not entitled to ask witnesses to take the oath.

Evidence given by civil servants to committees of inquiry raises a special problem because they are subordinate to the minister in charge of their particular department. How far can the government order them not to reply to questions put to them by parliamentary committees? The question has seldom been decided. Only in Japan has it been the subject of legislation. The effect is that if an official refuses to reply to questions put to him by a committee, the reason for his refusal must be explained to Parliament by the department employing him. Parliament may then, if necessary, ask the cabinet to confirm that for the official to speak would prejudice the vital interests of the nation. If the cabinet makes no reply within ten days the witness is deemed to be free from the obligations of professional secrecy and has to give his evidence. In the Federal Republic of Germany, the consent of the department concerned is always required; but it may not be withheld unless to furnish the information required would be 'prejudicial to public security or liable to jeopardise or make difficult the carrying on of the public service'. This is in practice the position in most countries, even where there are no written regulations governing the matter.

Authorisation or refusal by the minister raises a problem of political accountability which is a pragmatic issue rather than one based on legal principles. It is true that the British House of Commons has the power to have a civil servant who refuses to reply imprisoned for contempt. But apart from the fact that the House would generally be reluctant to go so far, it is extremely likely that if a civil servant obeying instructions refused to give evidence, the question raised would not be his own liability but the political responsibility of the minister concerned, indeed that of the cabinet as a whole. In other words, the effect of the refusal would be to raise the problem of the political relationship between Parliament and government and would be decided as a matter of confidence by the government.

It should be noted that whatever the system, the committee set up to conduct an inquiry is nothing more than an investigating and fact-finding body whose sole function is to make a report to the House which has set it up. It is always a matter for the House itself to draw the necessary conclusions from the inquiry and data elicited by it. A committee of inquiry can never of itself take a decision on the matter it is asked to investigate.

Both the working and the results of the procedure of inquiry suggest that its efficacy is extremely variable. Where inquiries are of a technical nature, and particularly where they constitute a sort of inspection by Parliament of the administrative services designed to secure improvements, the results are frequently excellent. The value of an inquiry is more debatable where, on the pretext of throwing light on a particular issue, it is used for political ends or attempts to replace the normal judicial processes.

4. THE OMBUDSMAN AND OTHER FORMS OF CONTROL

Since the beginning of the eighteenth century the Swedish Parliament has had a special instrument of control over the government: it is known as the 'Ombudsman' or parliamentary commissioner.

This office originated in a royal decree of the year 1713. It was designed to ensure that the government and the ministry of justice observed the law in force at the time and that the public service in general was run properly. The constitution of 1809 took over and reinforced a tradition which was already firmly established. By 1915 the work had become so great that it was decided to divide the office and to appoint one commissioner for civil affairs and another for military affairs. These two officials are appointed by Parliament in accordance with a special procedure. They must be persons eminent in the law and of recognised integrity. Each Chamber appoints from among its members twenty-two electors who meet within ten days and choose the commissioners. A commissioner's term of office is four years, but there is provision for dismissal on a recommendation of the committee of Parliament that is responsible for supervising the activities of the commissioners.

The commissioners are primarily parliamentary officials. But as far as public opinion is concerned, they are regarded mainly as 'tribunes of the people' who keep a permanent watch for the abuses and shortcomings of the administration. The most striking of the functions of the commissioners is to defend the ordinary citizen against the powers that be. But the commissioners may also act on their own initiative, even where no move is made by a private individual to safeguard his rights, and it is here that their activities, backed by the delegated authority of Parliament, are seen to be an effective means of control by Parliament over the whole field of government activity. In practice this control takes the form of an annual report which is made to Parliament and published. No doubt the office goes distinctly beyond the traditions of the classic type of parliamentary system, and in the countries where it is used it is flexible and works quickly.

These virtues have led Finland, Denmark and other countries, most recently Norway and New Zealand, to set up an ombudsman. In Finland there is one commissioner who is elected for a term of four years. Each year he reports to the Diet on the way in which the laws have been applied by the courts and all public authorities. In Denmark, the commissioner supervises the civil and military administration of the state in the name of the Folketing. He too makes an annual report to the Folketing. In New Zealand the first ombudsman was chosen in 1962. His principal task was to inquire into complaints against administrative decisions. Appointed by the Governor-General on the recommendation of the House of Representatives, he draws up a report each year on Parliament's behalf.

Two other institutions may be cited as akin to this institution. In the Federal Republic of Germany there is a defence commissioner elected by the Bundestag whose duty is to safeguard the rights of soldiers, sailors and airmen and to assist the Bundestag in controlling the armed forces. Secondly there is the commissioner-general in the U.S.S.R., Albania, Bulgaria, Hungary and Rumania. This official is elected by Parliament to ensure respect for the law and the decisions of the courts. His powers of control cover the whole of the public administration. The commissioner-general in these countries is at the head of a large hierarchy of officials.

A more unusual institution is the supreme chamber of control in Poland. This is a permanent body nominated by and solely accountable to the Diet itself. Under the terms of the constitution the supreme chamber is responsible for ensuring the legality, efficiency and expediency of the economic, financial and administrative work of the central and local departments of state. It is empowered to supervise the government itself together with the services, institutions and undertakings for which the government is responsible. It acts either on a recommendation by the Diet or at the instance of a parliamentary committee. The supreme chamber is also required to report to Parliament each year on how effect has been given to the budget and the economic plan and to comment on financial statements made by the government. It has to supply parliamentary committees, should they so request, with all relevant information on the work of any minister, institution or establishment.

The exercise of control over the government and the administration by the representatives of the people is regarded as vital by all the countries under review. The various procedures described above are as important for Parliaments that have lost ground in legislative and budgetary matters as for those which in their relationship with the executive come up against the abstract bar of the separation of powers. But over and above the relations between the powers, the real meaning of parliamentary control is to be sought in the safeguard it ensures for liberty, individual and collective alike.

27. Accounting to Parliament for Public Expenditure

Control over the way in which effect is given to the financial provision made by Parliament is an important and distinct aspect of the general powers of control exercised by Parliament over the executive. It is important because of the wide impact of the national budget; and it is distinct because of the special features of the procedure by which it is exercised.

Parliament's right and obligations do not end when the budget and the related estimates are agreed to. It has still to make sure that effect is given to the measures which it has authorised. Only then can Parliament be satisfied that the executive has duly carried out its injunctions. For this reason Parliament takes a hand at the end as well as at the beginning of the financial cycle.

Parliaments agree on the scope of this control. But they are not unanimous on the form that it should take. In practice it is difficult to separate this kind of control from the checks and controls applied by other administrative or judicial authorities. Nevertheless whether Parliament acts directly or through instructions given to special bodies, whether its action coincides with the budget or happens later, some form of parliamentary initiative in this field is invariably found.

Of the forms of parliamentary control the first derives from the general powers of supervision normally enjoyed by Parliament, and is exercised through such procedures as interpellations, questions or inquiries. These are essentially procedures for calling the government to account in the political arena. This makes them less suitable for a specialised, accounting type of scrutiny.

Another form of control is one that belongs to financial procedure proper. In practice the estimates are rarely agreed to absolutely, in the sense that they cannot be subsequently varied. During the financial year the picture changes; and whenever the government comes to Parliament with a request for some modification of the estimates, Parliament can see how its original grant was used. In most countries supplementary estimates sought by the government follow the same procedure as the original estimates. Parliament has an opportunity not only to obtain information as to how expenditure has been handled, but also to put pressure on the government, if the out-turn has not been in keeping with the original decisions. Once again however this method of control tends more often than not to become identified with approval or disapproval on political grounds.

It is essential that this particular form of scrutiny should be conducted impartially. It must also bear upon the detailed and specialised information on which the budget and related estimates have been founded. So it is important for Parliament to be furnished with information of much greater detail than that needed to exercise its political controls. The simplest method is for the government to make periodic reports to Parliament giving this information. Parliament can then draw its own conclusions.

The practice in several countries especially in the U.S.S.R. and the People's Democracies is for general reports to be made by the government or the administration. In addition Parliament and its committees in these countries can at any time ask for an oral report on the way in which the budget or the plan is being implemented. In Poland it is the duty of the council of ministers to make an annual report to the Diet on the use of the funds which have been granted. Attached to this report is a commentary by the supreme chamber of control proposing that, subject to any observations it may have made, the expenditure should be finally discharged. The committee on economic planning, budget and finance considers these documents together with other committees so far as they are concerned. In so doing they are assisted by representatives of the supreme chamber of control. Finally a report is made to the Diet by the finance committee.

In Finland Parliament can exercise a measure of control over the handling of public finance on the occasion of the annual review of the government's report on the state of the exchequer. In Chile a similar report is made every six months. The Japanese constitution stipulates that at regular intervals, not less than once a year, the cabinet is to report to the Diet and to the people on the state of the national finances. Finance laws further stipulate that the cabinet must report to the Diet and to the nation at least once a quarter on the use made of public funds and on the general financial situation. In the Federal Republic the ministry of finance has to lay before the committee on the budget every three months a statement showing how actual expenditure has exceeded estimated expenditure and commenting on any unusual spending.

These general reports are extremely useful. But they are not full enough to give an effective picture of day-to-day financial management where any irregularities would tend to be found. For this reason these methods for providing general information are supplemented by fact-finding machinery entrusted directly to certain parliamentary bodies or to special supervisory bodies functioning under the authority of Parliament.

In Parliaments with a system of permanent committees the part played by finance committees is particularly important. Apart from eliciting general information, these committees can obtain more specialised information through sub-committees set up to deal with specific matters or through their rapporteur. In France the members of Parliament who make a report on a departmental budget on behalf of the committee concerned are empowered to keep under constant review the expenditure of that department. They may send for papers and carry out inquiries on the spot. Under these powers all relevant information has to be placed before them. In Switzerland in the same way the out-turn of the departmental budgets is supervised by a small body consisting of six members of the finance committee of each House. In the Federal Republic of Germany the Bundestag's committee on the budget has to approve particular expenditures subject to conditions laid down by law. It also chooses from among its own members a sub-committee to examine all accounts laid before the Bundestag by the government as well as the statements on them made by the audit office; subsequently a report is made to the Bundestag. In Sweden the committee on the budget also constantly reviews expenditure. It may issue statements or directives affecting the way in which the financial programme is carried out. Similarly in the U.S.S.R. and the People's Democracies the task of carrying out a systematic control over the way in which the administration has applied financial decisions falls to the finance committees.

In many other countries finance committees make an important contribution, especially in the United States Congress. But it should be noted that in Anglo-Saxon procedure, the accounts are scrutinised in the first instance by a body outside Parliament, usually a controller general of public accounts. In Great Britain this high officer is known as the Comptroller and Auditor General. He is appointed by the Crown and he can only be removed by an address agreed to by both Houses. He is completely independent of the executive; and his task is to check the regularity of all expenditure, both from the consolidated fund and from funds voted by Parliament. He makes periodic reports to the House of Commons on the findings of his investigations. These reports are considered by the Public Accounts Committee, a special committee which in this respect has a somewhat similar function to that of the permanent committees on finance in other Parliaments. The Public Accounts Committee has fifteen members. The chairman is by tradition a member of the opposition which enhances its status as a controlling body. The Financial Secretary to the Treasury is a member *ex officio*, although he seldom attends its meetings. In practice the committee's essential function is to scrutinise matters drawn to its attention by the reports of the Comptroller and Auditor General. Where it appears that some irregularity has been committed, the committee investigates the matter and decides whether the incident should be brought before the House. Within a fairly short time it issues a report on the accounts of government spending and there may be a debate in the House if the opposition so requests.

The main features of this system based on regular scrutiny by officials outside Parliament, but under the auspices of a select committee, have been taken over by a number of countries influenced by the British model such as Australia, Canada, Ceylon, Ghana, India, Ireland, Nigeria, Pakistan and Sierra Leone. In Australia and India the public accounts committee is a joint committee of both Houses, consisting of seven members of the House and three members of the Senate in Australia, and fifteen members of the lower House and seven members of the upper House in India.

In the United States the main controlling body is the General Accounting Office, the head of which, the Comptroller General, is appointed by the President for fifteen years. The appointment has to be approved by the Senate. He can only be removed by a resolution of both Houses of Congress, and only in the circumstances prescribed by law. His office is extremely important because he exercises control over all expenditure. Throughout the year he sees the papers that touch expenditure, and he can stop payment and call the officials concerned to account. He issues periodic reports on the financial administration of the various departments and makes a report to Congress on the financial position at the end of the financial year. Nevertheless the supervision exercised by the committees on appropriations is greatly simplified by the work of the Comptroller General. One particularly useful function he fulfils is to advise Congress on the desirability of including certain items in the following year's budget.

A more important role is played by Parliament where the auditing of the accounts is in the hands of a body chosen by and dependent upon itself, as in Denmark, Finland, Iceland, Norway and Sweden. In these countries the controlling authority is a collegiate body which allows the various political trends to be represented. The Finnish Parliament each year appoints five commissioners of accounts, the Danish Folketing four and the Althing in Iceland three elected by proportional representation; and in Norway five auditors are appointed by the Storting. In the Netherlands the three members of the court of accounts are appointed by the Crown, but on the nomination of the Second Chamber of the States-General. In Sweden the main financial control is in the hands of twelve auditors, six being elected from each House by proportional representation. By this means the opposition is automatically represented and takes its turn in providing the chairman of the auditors. This fact does not prevent them from carrying out their duties efficiently and in a non-party manner. The auditors have to make a printed report by not later than 15 December each year. The report is sent first to all the government departments which have come in for criticism, and their observations are annexed to it. The report is then laid before the Riksdag; it is referred to the committee on the budget which itself produces a report embodying recommendations for the Riksdag to consider and if it thinks right to approve. In the next session the government has to inform Parliament of the measures it has taken to comply with those recommendations.

In Israel public accounts fall within the purview of the Controller General who is elected by the Knesset. His powers are defined in a special law. He makes a report to the finance committee who, after hearing explanations from departments, themselves make a report which is debated.

The last method of control is that by which Parliament formally approves the accounts for each financial year. This system has the virtues of symmetry: it completes the cycle which began with the presentation of the budget. Theoretically it offers Parliament considerable safeguards. In practice it is effective only if Parliament takes up the accounts reasonably soon so that the problems thrown up are still of current concern and members are interested enough to bring ministers to book for shortcomings.

Public accounts have to be formally approved in many countries. Approval is signified in various ways such as a formal discharging of the accounts in Poland or a resolution in Denmark and Iceland. In Japan when the accounts have been examined by the controller's office, they are approved by each House separately. Their decisions

ACCOUNTING TO PARLIAMENT FOR PUBLIC EXPENDITURE

are not necessarily the same; in other words the procedure differs from that for approving the budget.

Most often approval is given in the form of legislation. The government presents a bill to approve the public accounts which follows the ordinary procedure on bills. Here its value as a means of control depends on how soon the bill is introduced. In Bulgaria, Hungary and Rumania the accounts for the previous financial year are considered by Parliament along with the budget for the current year. In Lebanon the accounts are settled before the budget for the financial year after next is introduced.

In many countries including Austria, France, Greece, Iran, Italy, Somalia and Turkey the bill to approve the public accounts is taken only after an initial audit has been carried out by a body with the status of a high administrative tribunal known as the court of accounts. In Poland this duty falls to the supreme chamber of control. In Belgium the court of accounts has two special features. First the court's control is not only *a posteriori*; it has to make a prior check on all expenditure. Secondly its members are appointed by the House of Representatives which means that it is in practice a parliamentary body.

As a rule the court of accounts is made up of officials with the status of irremovable judicial officers. The idea underlying the court is that auditing the public accounts should be in the hands of an independent and impartial body free from any political influence. In this way any action it may take is a guarantee of regularity which is essential to the handling of public money. At the same time it does introduce an element of delay, sometimes a considerable one, which subtracts from the general interest in the bill to approve the public accounts. In practice it means waiting until spending by the government and other public authorities for the year of account is complete and until the bodies responsible for control and the court of accounts have completed their audit. Only at this point can the effective expenditure and income be summarised in a document for Parliament to approve. The result is that more often than not approval is a mere formality, members having lost all interest in the subject matter. But Parliament's acceptance of this state of affairs must not be taken as a relinquishment of its sovereignty; it is rather a tribute to the effectiveness of the network of controls exerted by other bodies, administrative or judicial, who are better equipped for this kind of work and whose impartiality cannot be questioned.

Furthermore, a close examination of the procedures of control makes it clear that the interest shown by Parliament in the effect given to financial decisions varies in inverse proportion to the part played by Parliament in the examination of the budget and the related estimates. This shows that in most Parliaments there is in practice if not in explicit constitutional terms a balance between their financial function and their controlling function that enables them to maintain the essential powers to discharge adequately their duty of representing the nation.

28. Parliament and Foreign Policy

For a long time foreign policy was not considered to be the concern of Parliament. Diplomacy was 'the province of Princes, not of commoners'. Contemporary history has demonstrated the folly if not the danger of that view. But although the world-wide problems of war and peace have been brought home to every person, Parliament itself has not in every country been able to insist on methods of scrutiny and control commensurate with the importance of these problems. This deficiency may reflect the thinking of early writers on constitutional law who, accepting ideas handed down to them, ruled out any participation by the people in the conduct of international affairs. Moreover it is only recently that the man in the street has become aware of these matters: they have forced themselves on his attention without any particular effort by politically enlightened persons to awaken this interest.

It can be argued that international politics is a specialised subject and is too complex to be debated publicly. But there is hardly any problem, political, economic or social, which does not have its technicalities and does not need to be clarified and understood. Nor is there any problem more closely bound up with the needs of the community than the problems of international peace and security. Obviously there can be no question of entrusting the conduct of foreign relations to the whole body of representatives of the people, particularly as they are quite likely to have divergent or even antagonistic views. But the same thing is no less true of domestic affairs, and there is no more reason why the one type should be entrusted solely to the government than the other. Yet the constitutional practices of most countries suggest that the executive enjoys an independence in this field which greatly limits the possible scope of action by Parliament, whether it takes the form of prior consultation, of subsequent scrutiny or of authorisation for ratifying treaties.

It would not be practicable for Parliament to take a hand in decisions on international issues if only because the need for them occurs so often and so suddenly and because some types of negotiation have to be conducted in secret. But it is much more doubtful whether Parliament should be kept in ignorance of the general policy on which the diplomatic activities of the state are based. Yet few constitutions formally provide for Parliament to play any part at this stage. Even when they do, it may require only that the general principles should be outlined to Parliament, a concession which leaves the government free to interpret them as it thinks best.

In the U.S.S.R. and in the People's Democracies, Parliament lays down the principles of foreign policy to which the government has to conform. In most of the other countries no formal provision is made for entrusting this role to Parliament. In practice however the position is not appreciably different because the gap between the two systems is largely filled by the pragmatic workings of Parliament which for this purpose relies on the political accountability of the executive. It can be argued that there is no need to make explicit rules defining the part played by Parliament where these arise in practice out of its ordinary prerogatives, particularly its right to apply various procedures such as general debates, interpellations and motions in order to bring problems of interest into the limelight and to make known its views. Moreover in several countries the investiture of the head of the government gives Parliament an opportunity to approve the programme outlined in his speech, and this programme invariably refers to the way in which the state's foreign policy is to be conducted.

Whatever the system, the part played by Parliament would appear to be generally slight. The balance between the general advice given by Parliament and the wide range of governmental activity makes it impossible to regard the part played by Parliament in framing foreign policy as an effective one. While at best it may be able to insist on a particular orientation of policy, Parliament is denied a real hand in policy-making. That makes it all the more important that its powers of control should be well safeguarded.

All Parliament's usual methods of control can be applied to the government policy. It can take action through general debates and debates on particular aspects of foreign policy; or it can appoint committees to seek information or make thorough investigations; or its members can act individually by questioning ministers.

The budget debate is an indirect means of control. Theoretically it is confined to the financial implications of the government's foreign policy but it can be used to challenge the basic assumptions of that policy. Motions to reduce a grant, whether token or otherwise, are as effective as general debate in obliging the foreign minister to give explanations on specific points.

Debates in the House on foreign policy can take a variety of forms in different countries. There are the statements made by the government and the summaries and reports which the statutes may require to be laid from time to time. This is the position in most of the eastern European countries. In Switzerland these reports are concerned only with the economic measures arising out of agreements concluded with foreign states. The government may also find time for a debate, as it sometimes does in Great Britain, to allow it to test parliamentary opinion.

Control through debate in the House may also be initiated by Parliament; and it can be particularly effective in the form of a debate followed by a vote. This is what happens with interpellations or motions of censure which culminate in a decision to approve or disapprove the policy of the government. The views of Parliament may also be expressed in the form of motions moved by members though if carried they do not bind the government.

The procedure of questions to the foreign minister can be extremely valuable provided that it is flexible enough to keep pace with the movement of international events. It is an interesting fact that this procedure was introduced in France specifically to facilitate the supervision of foreign policy. It was felt that the public character of debate and the extempore nature of many statements made in debate were dangerous, whereas the procedure of questions gave a minister time to reflect. In practice the extremely small number of questions asked on foreign affairs suggests that the evolution of this procedure owes little to the considerations which led to its introduction.

The sober and dispassionate nature of the work of parliamentary committees would appear to be particularly suited to this type of problem. Indeed the appointment of a permanent, specialised committee has evidently been found technically attractive because most Parliaments have set up a committee of this kind. Its appointment has even been advocated in Great Britain despite the inherent restrictions imposed by the British system of committees.

A separate committee for foreign affairs makes for a type of control which, *mutatis mutandis*, can be compared with the control exercised in its own sphere by the finance committee. It is as a rule kept informed through the personal testimony of the minister about the changing international situation. Moreover, as its views reflect fairly accurately those of the House, it may be valuable to the government to know what those views are before embarking on a particular policy it regards as opportune. But the committees are in practice rarely consulted in this way. The difference between the two functions which a committee can fulfil is particularly clear in the Netherlands where the Foreign Affairs Committee of the First Chamber is merely empowered to receive information whereas the Second Chamber's committee can be consulted by the government.

Prior advice is sometimes sought by the government from special bodies. In the Federal Republic of Germany the Bundestag has an advisory council for agreements on commercial policy. It consists of nine members of the committee on external trade and four members of the Bundesrat. It ensures close co-operation between the Bundestag and the government when trade agreements are being drawn up; and it gives its views on whether a particular agreement requires the consent of Parliament or not. Sweden has an advisory council on foreign affairs. This is a committee of the executive of which the King takes the chair; but it includes a number of members of the foreign affairs committee of the Riksdag sitting with representatives of the government. The council does not take decisions or give advice as a body; all it does is put forward the views of each member. In New Zealand a committee comprising the prime minister, the leader of the opposition and other members is kept constantly informed about foreign relations.

These various types of control are hardly calculated to hamper the freedom of action of the government. In practice it is completely independent except for the limits imposed by its ordinary, political accountability. In some countries once this type of control has been exercised, the task of Parliament is finished; in others it continues when international relations crystallise in the form of treaties.

In general it is not possible either legally or practically for Parliament to take part in the negotiations leading up to the conclusions of treaties; nor can they, except on rare occasions, force the government to embark on negotiations. But it would seem to be a more simple matter, and consonant with the principles of parliamentary government, for Parliament to exercise *ex post facto* control over treaties after they have been signed though before they are ratified by the Head of the State. Yet this is far from being the general position. In some countries Parliament has no powers over treaties. In Ghana, India, Israel and Pakistan, for example, no provision is made for Parliament to take part in ratifying treaties.

In most countries Parliament has to authorise specific categories of treaties enumerated in the constitution or by law before they are ratified. The length of the list is the measure of the power of Parliament. In Great Britain, Ceylon and Ireland the approval of Parliament is necessary only if the proposed treaty entails changes in domestic legislation or has financial implications. In Great Britain parliamentary control in practice goes further: treaties of any kind may be debated if the opposition or a large enough number of members so request. But when debates do take place, they seldom end in a vote.

In some countries the kind of treaties requiring the approval of Parliament before they are ratified may be specified. In France the list comprises peace treaties, trade agreements, treaties or agreements relating to international organisation, treaties involving public funds, treaties modifying the law or touching the status of persons and treaties for the cession, exchange or acquisition of territory. A similar list is found in Belgium, the Central African Republic, Senegal and the United Arab Republic. In some instances emphasis is laid on particular aspects of treaties such as integrity of territorial waters in Iceland; but in general the consent of Parliament is required before any treaty can come into force if it entails legislation or the grant of funds.

It would be a mistake to assume that such provisions place any real curb on the independence of the executive, since even the apparently full lists often leave out major political treaties and treaties of alliance which are incontestably the ones that exert most influence over the destiny of a nation. Some constitutions have repaired this omission. In the Federal Republic of Germany treaties requiring the agreement of Parliament expressly include those which regulate the 'political relations' of the federation. The same is true in Austria of 'political treaties' and in Yugoslavia of treaties concerning 'political or military co-operation'. The same would appear to be true of important treaties of the same kind in Bulgaria, Canada, Italy, Somalia, Sweden and the U.S.S.R.

All treaties require parliamentary authorisation before they can be ratified in Czechoslovakia, Denmark, Japan, Laos, Luxembourg, the Netherlands, Norway and Switzerland. But there are some special points to be noted. In Japan the constituion provides that when the government concludes treaties the approval of the Diet may be given before or after according to the circumstances. In the Netherlands the approval of the States-General may be either explicit or tacit. Under the explicit procedure a bill to approve a treaty is introduced, debated and passed in accordance with the ordinary legislative procedure. Under the tacit procedure the government lays the text of the treaty before both Houses together with a letter asking for their agreement. Approval is assumed to have been given if within a period of thirty days no request has been made for approval to be given under the explicit procedure in the form of a bill. Such a request must be sponsored by at least one fifth of the members of either House. Although somewhat more cut and dried, this system is not unlike the procedure followed in the British House of Commons. It has been adopted in Australia since 1961. The government now lays all treaties before both Houses, whether or not they specifically require parliamentary approval. Members have twenty-one days in which to make their views known, and if necessary to hold a debate, before the treaty is signed and ratified. In Switzerland on the other hand if a treaty is to last indefinitely or more than fifteen years, it must have the prior approval not only of the federal Parliament but also of the nation by way of referendum.

In countries where the ratification of treaties is reserved for the Presidium or Council of State the ambivalent nature of this body makes it possible to regard its action as emanating not only from the Head of State but also from Parliament.

The most famous example of the powers of Parliament over treaties is found in the Constitution of the United States. The freedom of action of the President of the United States is markedly curtailed by the provision that before any treaty can be ratified it must have the assent of the Senate. That assent must be signified by not less than two thirds of the members present. This might appear to be an excessive power when compared with the arrangements made in other countries. But it is understandable as part of the Senate's function which is not to represent the will of the people but to protect the independence of the states comprising the union. All the same the powers of the Senate make it incumbent upon the President, if he wishes to avoid a rebuff, to canvass senators whose influence carries weight in foreign affairs. Thus it is paradoxically a system of separation of powers that gives the most effective example of parliamentary control. The same kind of control is found in Argentina, Brazil, Chile and the Philippines.

Whatever the procedure followed, the part played by Parliament in the ratification of treaties must not be exaggerated. Its freedom of action is usually qualified in two ways. The first qualification is procedural: it is not the text of the treaty that is the subject of debate but simply the authorisation to ratify the treaty. Even where this authorisation is requested in the form of legislation as in Belgium, France, the Federal Republic of Germany and the Netherlands Parliament has no power to amend the treaty: it can only be accepted or rejected as it stands. The second qualification is political: to refuse to ratify a treaty is an act of the utmost gravity. It is not easy publicly to disavow the government of one's country and to go back on pledges it has given to other states. Parliament is faced with a *fait accompli* to which it was not a party yet for which in the last analysis it will have to take the responsibility.

Two other points must be borne in mind. The procedure of parliamentary approval does not extend to all treaties. Moreover treaties as such represent only a small proportion of the diplomatic measures (of which declarations, agreements, arrangements and, in the United States, 'executive agreements' are some others) at the disposal of the executive. Most of these do not come within the control afforded by parliamentary authorisation.

In foreign policy the role of Parliament is to approve and confirm rather than to direct the action of the Government. The importance of progress in this field is in proportion to the extent to which diplomacy is thought to be the concern of the people.

29. Judicial Function of Parliament

Parliament is often called upon to act in a judicial capacity. Usually its purpose in so doing is to take steps against politicians who in carrying out their duties have in some way traversed the public interest. A few Parliaments, especially those influenced by the British tradition, can move against private individuals for 'breaches of privilege'. But more generally Parliament's powers are directed against members of the executive.

The way in which the political responsibility of ministers developed from their penal liability has already been noted. That liability is still alive in a number of contemporary constitutions; but its utility is challenged on two main counts. From a theoretical angle it raises the more general problem of political justice which is outside the scope of this study; and in practice it has been entirely supplanted by political accountability at least as far as members of the government are concerned. It is true that penal liability still constitutes a weapon for use not against ministers but against the Head of State unless he is a monarch who is not politically accountable; and in a constitution that embodied the separation of powers, where the Head of State is not politically accountable to Parliament, it is a most important feature of parliamentary authority.

If it is allowed that the Head of State and ministers should be liable to penalties when they abuse their trust, the question arises as to the part that Parliament should play in the procedure by which they can be arraigned and brought to justice. Three main procedures have been developed.

In the first the trial of the accused persons is entrusted to the ordinary courts, usually the supreme judicial court of the country. The case is brought before the court by Parliament. This system is followed in Belgium. The constitution lays down that the House of Representatives has the right to bring charges against ministers and to arraign them before the court of appeal, which sitting in joint session has the sole right to judge them. Similarly in the Netherlands the Second Chamber has the power to bring ministers before the supreme court on the charge of violating the law. In Iceland charges brought against ministers are a matter for the Althing, and they are tried by the court of arraignment. Only with the agreement of the Althing may the President have the charges against the ministers withdrawn or the penalties imposed on them remitted. The President of the Republic and ministers of Somalia may be arraigned by the Chamber before the supreme court. In the United Arab Republic a proposal to arraign the President of the Republic must be tabled by one third of the members of the National Assembly and the resolution of arraignment must be approved by a majority of its members. For ministers the requisite figures are respectively one fifth and two thirds of the members. In Finland Parliament may decide by a majority of three quarters of the votes cast to bring the President of the Republic before the supreme court of justice for treason or high treason; these are the only crimes of which he can be accused.

In Austria members of the government may be arraigned by the National Council and they are tried by the constitutional court. In Italy too the constitutional court is the competent body when a matter is referred to them by the two Houses of Parliament at a joint sitting. In the Federal Republic of Germany the motion of arraignment must be proposed by at least a quarter of the members of the Bundestag or a quarter of the votes cast in the Bundesrat. The motion itself is only agreed to if it obtains a majority of two thirds of the members of the Bundestag and two thirds of the votes cast in the Bundesrat. In Turkey the arraignment of the President of the Republic for high treason has to be proposed by two thirds of the members of the National Assembly and decided by the two Houses at a joint sitting where a majority of two thirds of the total membership is required.

Under the second main procedure the trial of the accused is in the hands of a special court, usually known as the high court. Parliament or one of its Houses has the exclusive right to arraign them. In addition it may take a more or less important part in the arrangements for appointing the members of the high court.

In Greece the special court sits under the president of the court of appeal. It comprises twelve judges whom the president chooses by lot in public from the presidents and members of the various courts of appeal who were in office before the charge against the ministers was brought. In Denmark part of the membership of the high court of the realm consists of a certain number of judges elected by the Folketing from persons other than its members. In Norway the same body comprises both members of the Lagting and professional judges who are members of the supreme court. In Finland the high court consists of *ex officio* members and judicial officers designated by the parliamentary 'electors'. Its function is to try members of the government brought before it by Parliament on a resolution agreed to by a simple majority. It should be remembered that the President of the Republic must be brought to justice before the supreme court and that a charge against him requires a resolution agreed to by three quarters of the votes cast.

In the Lebanon Parliament appoints seven members to sit on the high court along with the eight senior judges in the country. The high court is empowered to try the President of the Republic and ministers arraigned before it by the Chamber on a resolution supported by a majority of two thirds of its members. The President of the Republic can be arraigned for violating the constitution or for high treason and ministers for high treason or serious failure to discharge their duties.

The high court of justice may be composed exclusively of members of Parliament. This is the position in France. Twenty-four titular judges and twelve substitutes are elected by the National Assembly and by the Senate from among their members. The high court can try the President of the Republic for high treason after he has been arraigned by the two Assemblies on a vote by open ballot showing an absolute majority of the members composing each Assembly. The high court can also try ministers accused of crimes or misdemeanours and their accomplices in any plot against the security of the state.

The French institution of a high court composed of members of Parliament comes close to the third main procedure under which Parliament deals with the matter itself without the help of any other body. The lower House initiates the charge, the upper House is the judge. This is the procedure known as impeachment which in

England goes back to the fourteenth century. The House of Lords has preserved the judicial character which it has had from the very beginning of its history, for to this day it remains the final court of appeal in Great Britain. But the procedure of impeachment has not been used since 1805. Parliament may also proceed by passing a bill of attainder. This is a legislative measure passed in exactly the same way as any other piece of legislation. There is no judgment; the bill sets out the various charges and the punishment imposed. This procedure in which the powers of the legislature and the judiciary are closely entwined is now obsolete.

Impeachment has fared better outside Great Britain. It has been faithfully reproduced by the constitution of the United States where it is applicable not only to ministers but to the President, Vice-President and all the federal officials. The initiative lies with the House of Representatives which sets up an investigating committee. On its report the House can decide to bring an action for impeachment before the Senate. The Senate sits as a court, and the trial takes place in private. The penalty is dismissal from office. It must be agreed to by two thirds of the senators. Only one President has ever been impeached: a charge was brought against President Johnson in 1868, and he was acquitted. In Argentina, Brazil, Chile, Liberia and Pakistan impeachment on the model of the United States is also available as part of the presidential system.

Among the various systems under which Parliament may sit in judgment on the executive or some of its members, mention may be made of the particular type of procedure practised in Norway and Sweden, comprising features both of political control proper and penal control. The Norwegian Storting has the right of access to the proceedings of the council of ministers, and it exercises this right through the protocol committee of the Odelsting. In its report to the House, this committee may recommend a political penalty, but it can also recommend the impeachment of a minister. If the Odelsting upholds the charge of impeachment, the minister is brought before the high court of the realm comprising members of the Lagting and of the supreme court. In Sweden a similar dual form of control is exercised by the constitutional committee. Neither country has ever had occasion to use this procedure.

It has been the fate of all systems designed to apply judicial penalties to members of the executive to fall rapidly into disuse. Most countries have regarded them as superfluous and have abandoned them in favour of political accountability on the one hand and due legal process on the other. By these means recourse to exceptional forms of proceeding can be avoided.

INDEX

A.S.G.P. (Association of Secretaries-General of Parliaments): 87
Abuses, eliminating: 289, 294. *See also* Grievances
Accountability, ministerial: collective (the unanimity rule), 279; individual, 279; penal, 276–7, 277, 316; personal (financial), 276; political, 214, 277, 301, 313, 316, 319. *See also next below.*
Accountability of government (executive) to Parliament: 266, 276–88, 304–11; meaning of, 276–9; forms of, 276–7, 279–85 (*see also* Interpellations)
 Sanctions: 279–80, 291, 294; dismissal and resignation, 279–80, 281; censure (*or* no confidence) motions, 280–5
 circumstances in which raised, 280–5; rules for, 282–5; and dissolution *q.v.*, 285, 285–8; for estimates and expenditure, 304–10; and foreign policy *q.v.*, 310–16. *See also next above.*
Accounting Office, General (USA): 307
Accounting to Parliament for public expenditure: 304–10
Accounts (public): approval and auditing of, 308–9; Court of, 308–9
Acts Interpretation Act: 154
Acts of Parliament: individual, *indexed under titles*; promulgation and publication of, 213–19 (*see also* Laws)
Adjournment, motion for the: 188, 189, 190, 278, 281, 293
Administration of Parliament: 77–88. *See also* Administrative services *and* Directing authority
Administration (government), supervision of: 289
Administrative services of Parliament: 84–8; Secretary-General, 85; secretariat, 86–8; ancillary, 87–8
'Affirmative' (*and* 'negative') procedures: 154
Agenda: *see* Order of Business

Ages for voting (minima): 16 & *n*
Agreement (*and* disagreement) between the two Houses (of bicameral legislatures): 202, 208–13
Aim of this study: xi
Albania (*See also* People's Democracies): *Structure of Parliament:* unicameral system in, 12–13 *passim*; elections and electorate, 14–23 *passim*; 49–52 *passim*; ballots, 23–40 *passim*; Members of Parliament, 40–55 *passim*, 59–77 *passim*
 Organisation of Parliament: administration of, 77–88 *passim*; independence of, 88–97 *passim*; parties and groups, 97–102 *passim*; committees of, 102–22 *passim*; sittings of, 122–30 *passim*
 Legislative function of Parliament: limitations on, 133–40 *passim*; introduction of bills, 140–51 *passim*; delegated legislation, 151–9 *passim*; making of law, 159–213 *passim*; promulgation of laws, 213–19 *passim*; constitutional validity of laws, 219–24 *passim*
 Financial powers of Parliament: the budget, 227–41 *passim*, 246–59 *passim*; rights of Members, 241–5 *passim*
 Control of Executive by Parliament: appointment of executive officers, 263–75 *passim*; accountability of government, 276–88 *passim*, 304–10 *passim*; machinery of control, 288–304 *passim*; in foreign policy, 310–16 *passim*; judicial function of Parliament, 316–19 *passim*
Amendments to bills: 170–1, 183, 184, 188, 192–6; proposed for obstruction, 189; right to submit, 192–3, 195; procedure for, 193–6; subject matter of, 194; and the budget, 242–5
Answers to questions: *see* Questions

PARLIAMENTS

Appointment of the Executive: 263–75:
  Head of State: 264–8; in hereditary monarchies, 264–6; by universal suffrage, 266–7; in republican and federal states, 265, 267; in other states, 267–8; by Parliament, 267, 268
  Head of government and ministers: 268–73; in presidential states, 268–9; by Parliament, 270–3; in USSR and People's Democracies, 270; jointly by Head of State and Parliament, 270–1; in Great Britain, 273; by Head of State (alone), 273; confidence of Parliament essential in, 273
  High Officials: 274–5
Appropriation Bills and Acts: 252, 253, 259
Argentina: *Structure of Parliament:* bicameral system in, 3–7 *passim*; elections and electorate, 14–23 *passim*, 49–52 *passim*; ballots, 23–40 *passim*; Members of Parliament, 40–55 *passim*, 59–77 *passim*
  Organisation of Parliament: administration of, 77–88 *passim*; independence of, 88–97 *passim*; parties and groups, 97–102 *passim*; committees of, 102–22 *passim*; sittings of, 122–30 *passim*
  Legislative function of Parliament: limitations on, 133–40 *passim*; introduction of bills, 140–51 *passim*; delegated legislation, 151–9 *passim*; making of law, 159–213 *passim*; promulgation of laws, 213–19 *passim*; constitutional validity of laws, 219–24 *passim*
  Financial powers of Parliament: the budget, 227–41 *passim*, 246–59 *passim*; rights of Members, 241–5 *passim*
  Control of Executive by Parliament: appointment of executive officers, 263–75 *passim*; accountability of government, 276–88 *passim*, 304–10 *passim*; machinery of control, 288–304 *passim*; in foreign policy, 310–16 *passim*; judicial function of Parliament, 316–19 *passim*
Army (Annual) Act (UK): 273
Assemblies, number of: 3–13; depends on history and tradition, 12, 13; constituent assemblies, 204
Attainder, Bill of: 319
Auditors of public accounts: 308–9

Australia: *Structure of Parliament:* bicameral system in, 3–7 *passim*; elections and electorate, 14–23 *passim*, 49–52 *passim*; ballots, 23–40 *passim*; Members of Parliament, 40–55 *passim*, 59–77 *passim*
  Organisation of Parliament: administration of, 77–88 *passim*; independence of, 88–97 *passim*; parties and groups, 97–102 *passim*; committees of, 102–22 *passim*; sittings of, 122–30 *passim*
  Legislative function of Parliament: limitations on, 133–40 *passim*; introduction of bills, 140–51 *passim*; delegated legislation, 151–9 *passim*; making of law, 159–213 *passim*; promulgation of laws, 213–19 *passim*; constitutional validity of laws, 219–24 *passim*
  Financial power of Parliament: the budget, 227–41 *passim*, 246–59 *passim*; rights of Members, 241–45 *passim*
  Control of Executive by Parliament: appointment of executive officers, 263–75 *passim*; accountability of government, 276–88 *passim*, 304–10 *passim*; machinery of control, 288–304 *passim*; in foreign policy, 310–16 *passim*; judicial function of Parliament, 316–19 *passim*
Austria: *Structure of Parliament:* bicameral system in, 3–7 *passim*; elections and electoratek, 14–23 *passim*, 49–52 *passim*; ballots, 23–40 *passim*; Members of Parliament, 40–55 *passim*, 59–77 *passim*
  Organisation of Parliament: administration of, 77–88 *passim*; independence of, 88–97 *passim*; parties and groups, 97–102 *passim*; committees of, 102–22 *passim*; sittings of, 122–30 *passim*
  Legislative function of Parliament: limitations on, 133–40 *passim*; introduction of bills, 140–51 *passim*; delegated legislation, 151–9 *passim*; making of law, 159–213 *passim*; promulgation of laws, 213–19 *passim*; constitutional validity of laws, 219–24 *passim*
  Financial powers of Parliament: the budget, 227–41 *passim*, 246–59, *passim*; rights of Members, 241–5 *passim*

INDEX

Control of Executive by Parliament: appointment of executive officers, 263–75 *passim*; accountability of government, 276–88 *passim*, 304–10 *passim*; machinery of control, 288–304 *passim*; in foreign policy, 310–16 *passim*; judicial function of Parliament, 316–19 *passim*

'Automatic return' of bills: 160

Balance between Executive and Legislature: 8, 285, 286. *See also* Separation.

Ballot, the: 23; methods of voting, 28–33
 Characteristics of the vote: compulsory voting, 28–30; voting by proxy and by post, 30–2; secrecy of the vote, 32–3
 Organisation of the ballot: voting papers, 33–5; counting the votes, 35–7; fraud at elections, 37–8; contested elections, 38–40. *See also* Polling *and* Voting at elections

Belgium: *Structure of Parliament:* unicameral-bicameral system in, 7–12 *passim*, 208–9 *passim*; elections and electorate, 14–23 *passim*, 49–52 *passim*; ballots, 23–40 *passim*; Members of Parliament, 40–55 *passim*, 59–77 *passim*
 Organisation of Parliament: administration of, 77–88 *passim*; independence of, 88–97 *passim*; parties and groups, 97–102 *passim*; committees of, 102–22 *passim*; sittings of, 122–30 *passim*
 Legislative function of Parliament: limitations on, 133–40 *passim*; introduction of bills, 140–51 *passim*; delegated legislation, 151–9 *passim*; making of law, 159–213 *passim*; promulgation of laws, 213–19 *passim*; constitutional validity of laws, 219–24 *passim*
 Financial power of Parliament: the budget, 227–41 *passim*, 246–59 *passim*; rights of Members, 241–5 *passim*
 Control of Executive by Parliament: appointment of executive officers, 263–75 *passim*; accountability of government, 276–88 *passim*, 304–10 *passim*; machinery of control, 288–304 *passim*; in foreign policy, 310–16 *passim*; judicial function of Parliament, 316–19 *passim*

'Below the line' items (in budget of UK): 236

Bicameral (two-chamber) systems (*general*): origins (historical), 3–4, 7–8; theory of, and arguments for, 8–9; classification of, and relative powers of Chambers, 9–12; reasons for choice of, 13; initiation of legislation in (rights), 142–3
 in federal states, 3–7, 13, 208–13
 in non-federal (unitary) states, 7–12, 13, 208–13

Bills, parliamentary: government, 105, 106, 113, 190; private members', 105, 106, 113, 116, 118, 175, 176; 'hybrid', 106, 113; with financial effects, 146, 147–8, 149, 202, 217, 218, 258–9, 281; constitutional, 203–8, 217; organic, 202, 221; Finance, 258–9, 281 (*see also* Budget)
 Introduction of: 140–51; by individuals or groups, 144–5, 148, 232; by committees, 148–9; by opposition members, 150; methods of presentation, 145–8; time limits on, 148
 Stages of procedure: first and second readings, 161–3, 171, 180–4; committee stage, 161–71; third reading, 182–7

Brazil: *Structure of Parliament:* bicameral system in, 3–7 *passim*; elections and electorate, 14–23 *passim*, 49–52 *passim*; ballots, 23–40 *passim*; Members of Parliament, 40–55 *passim*, 59–77 *passim*
 Organisation of Parliament: administration of, 77–88 *passim*; independence of, 88–97 *passim*; parties and groups, 97–102 *passim*; committees of, 102–22 *passim*; sittings of, 122–30 *passim*
 Legislative function of Parliament: limitations on, 133–40 *passim*; introduction of bills, 140–51 *passim*; delegated legislation, 151–9 *passim*; making of law, 159–213 *passim*; promulgation of laws, 213–19 *passim*; constitutional validity of laws, 219–24 *passim*
 Financial power of Parliament: the budget, 227–41 *passim*, 246–59 *passim*; rights of Members, 241–5 *passim*

323

Control of Executive by Parliament: appointment of executive officers, 263–75 *passim*; accountability of government, 276–88 *passim*, 304–10 *passim*; machinery of control, 288–304 *passim*; in foreign policy, 310–16 *passim*; judicial function of Parliament, 316–19 *passim*

Budget, the: nature of, 227–30; purpose of, 227; revenue and expenditure in, 227–30; and legislation, 228–9; and appropriation, finance and revenue bills, 229; 'tacking on' non-financial matter to, 230; preparation and presentation of, 230–4; primacy of the Executive, 230–2; secrecy of, 232; and public corporations, 234–7; and bicameral parliaments, 237–40; in Chambers on equal footing, 237; in Chambers on unequal footing, 238–40; rights of Members of Parliament over, 241–5; control of (by Parliament), 241–5

Timing the budget: 246–53; annual budgets (advantages and significance of), 246, 247; financial years (various dates of), 246–7; periods allowed for consideration, 247–8, 250; measures to avoid a 'gap', 248–53; 'provisional budgets', 251–2; in Great Britain (and countries conforming), 252–3

Consideration of the budget (procedure): 253–9; in committees, 254–6 (sub-committees, 255); debates on, 257–9, 312; speeding up, 258; in British House of Commons, 258–9

as a test of confidence, 281–2

Budget and Accounting Act (USA): 232

Bulgaria (*See also* People's Democracies): *Structure of Parliament:* unicameral system in, 12–13 *passim*; elections and electorate, 14–23 *passim*, 49–52 *passim*; ballots, 23–40 *passim*; Members of Parliament, 40–55 *passim*, 59–77 *passim*

Organisation of Parliament: administration of, 77–88 *passim*; independence of, 88–97 *passim*; parties and groups, 97–102 *passim*; committees of, 102–22 *passim*; sittings of 122–30 *passim*

Legislative function of Parliament: limitations on, 133–40 *passim*; introduction of bills, 140–51 *passim*; delegated legislation, 151–9 *passim*; making of law, 159–213 *passim*; promulgation of laws, 213–19 *passim*; constitutional validity of laws, 219–24 *passim*

Financial power of Parliament: the budget, 227–41 *passim*, 246–59 *passim*; rights of Members, 241–5 *passim*

Control of Executive by Parliament: appointment of executive officers, 263–75 *passim*; accountability of government, 276–88 *passim*; 304–10 *passim*; machinery of control, 288–304 *passim*; in foreign policy, 310–16 *passim*; judicial function of Parliament, 316–19 *passim*

Bulletin of Questions and Answers (Belgium): 297

Bureaux, parliamentary (Speakers' or Presidents' Colleges): 81–2, 83–4, 89; composition of, 81–2, 83–4; role of, 81; powers of, 82; and rules of procedure, 96 *bis*; and parties, 101; and committees, 113, 114, 115; and order of business, 178, 179; and obstruction, 190; and promulgation of laws, 215; and appointment and dismissal of ministers, 280

Business, Order of: *see* Order

By-elections: 27–8. See *also* Election campaigns *and* Elections

Cabinet, the: 269, 271, 272; its role in legislation, 177; accountability (responsibility) of, 279, 280; and Parliament (differences of opinion), 285, 287; authority of, 286; and evidence by departmental civil servants, 301; and national finances, 305

Cameroon: *Structure of Parliament:* unicameral system in, 6, 7, 12–13 *passim*; elections and electorate, 14–23 *passim*, 49–52 *passim*; ballots, 23–40 *passim*; Members of Parliament, 40–55 *passim*, 59–77 *passim*

Organisation of Parliament: administration of, 77–88 *passim*; independence of, 88–97 *passim*; parties and groups, 97–102 *passim*; committees of, 102–22 *passim*; sittings of, 122–30 *passim*

Legislative function of Parliament:

INDEX

limitations on, 133–40 *passim*; introduction of bills, 140–51 *passim*; delegated legislation, 151–9 *passim*; making of law, 159–213 *passim*; promulgation of laws, 213–19 *passim*; constitutional validity of laws, 219–24 *passim*

Financial power of Parliament: the budget, 227–41 *passim*, 246–59 *passim*; rights of Members, 241–5 *passim*

Control of Executive by Parliament: appointment of executive officers, 263–75 *passim*; accountability of government, 276–88 *passim*, 304–10 *passim*; machinery of control, 288–304 *passim*; in foreign policy, 310–16 *passim*; judicial function of Parliament, 316–19 *passim*

Canada: *Structure of Parliament:* bicameral system in, 3–7 *passim*; elections and electorate, 14–23 *passim*, 49–52 *passim*; ballots, 23–40 *passim*; Members of Parliament, 40–55 *passim*, 59–77 *passim*

Organisation of Parliament: administration of, 77–88 *passim*; independence of, 88–97 *passim*; parties and groups, 97–102 *passim*; committees of, 102–22 *passim*; sittings of, 122–30 *passim*

Legislative function of Parliament: limitations on, 133–40 *passim*; introduction of bills, 140–51 *passim*; delegated legislation, 151–9 *passim*; making of law 159–213 *passim*; promulgation of laws, 213–19 *passim*; constitutional validity of laws, 219–24 *passim*

Financial power of Parliament: the budget, 227–41 *passim*, 246–59 *passim*; rights of Members, 241–5 *passim*

Control of Executive by Parliament: appointment of executive officers, 263–75 *passim*; accountability of government, 276–88 *passim*, 304–10 *passim*; machinery of control, 288–304 *passim*; in foreign policy, 310–16 *passim*; judicial function of Parliament, 316–19 *passim*

Candidates at parliamentary elections: *see* Election campaigns

Cards, electoral: 16

Censure: motions of, 203, 281, 294, 312; votes of, 281–5, 291

Central African Republic: *Structure of Parliament:* unicameral system in, 12–13 *passim*; elections and electorate, 14–23 *passim*, 49–52 *passim*; ballots, 23–40 *passim*; Members of Parliament, 40–55 *passim*, 59–77 *passim*

Organisation of Parliament: administration of, 77–88 *passim*; independence of, 88–97 *passim*; parties and groups, 97–102 *passim*; committees of, 102–22 *passim*; sittings of, 122–30 *passim*

Legislative function of Parliament: limitations on, 133–40 *passim*; introduction of bills, 140–51 *passim*; delegated legislation, 151–9 *passim*; making of law, 159–213 *passim*; promulgation of laws, 213–19 *passim*; constitutional validity of laws, 219–24 *passim*

Financial power of Parliament: the budget, 227–41 *passim*, 246–59 *passim*; rights of Members, 241–5 *passim*

Control of Executive by Parliament: appointment of executive officers, 263–75 *passim*; accountability of government, 276–88 *passim*, 304–10 *passim*; machinery of control, 288–304 *passim*; in foreign policy, 310–16 *passim*; judicial function of Parliament, 316–19 *passim*

Ceylon: *Structure of Parliament:* bicameral system in 7–12 *passim*; elections and electorate, 14–23 *passim*, 49–52 *passim*; ballots, 23–40 *passim*; Members of Parliament, 40–55 *passim*, 59–77 *passim*

Organisation of Parliament: administration of, 77–88 *passim*; independence of, 88–97 *passim*; parties and groups, 97–102 *passim*; committees of, 102–22 *passim*; sittings of, 122–30 *passim*

Legislative function of Parliament: limitations on, 133–40 *passim*; introduction of bills, 140–51 *passim*; delegated legislation, 151–9 *passim*; making of law, 159–213 *passim*; promulgation of laws, 213–19 *passim*; constitutional validity of laws, 219–24 *passim*

Financial power of Parliament: the budget, 227–41 *passim*, 246–59 *passim*; rights of Members, 241–5 *passim*

Control of Executive by Parliament: appointment of executive officers, 263–75 *passim*; accountability of government, 276–88 *passim*, 304–10 *passim*; machinery of control,

PARLIAMENTS

288–304 *passim*; in foreign policy, 310–16 *passim*; judicial function of Parliament, 316–19 *passim*

Chairman (and Deputy Chairman) of Ways and Means: 79

Chambers, debating: shape of, 122, 123, 124; seating arrangements in, 122–5

Chambers (Houses), legislative: numbers of, 3–13; in federal parliaments, 4

First (lower): 8; duration of, 53; ministerial accountability to, 278 (*see also* Accountability)

Second (upper): functions of, 8; in unitary states, 8–9; general powers and recruitment of, 8–12; duration of, 53; powers in financial and budgetary matters, 237; ministerial accountability to, 278 (*see also* Accountability)

Chancellor of the Exchequer (UK): 229, 232, 243. *See also* Finance, Minister of

Changes, constitutional (in states): ix, x

Checks and balances, constitutional and procedural: 60, 104, 269, 304

Chile: *Structure of Parliament:* unicameral-bicameral system in, 7–12 *passim*, 208–9 *passim*; elections and electorate, 14–23 *passim*, 49–52 *passim*; ballots, 23–40 *passim*; Members of Parliament, 40–55 *passim*, 59–77 *passim*

Organisation of Parliament: administration of, 77–88 *passim*; independence of, 88–97 *passim*; parties and groups, 97–102 *passim*; committees of, 102–22 *passim*; sittings of, 122–30 *passim*

Legislative function of Parliament: limitations on 133–40 *passim*; introduction of bills, 140–51 *passim*; delegated legislation, 151–9 *passim*; making of law, 159–213 *passim*; promulgation of laws, 213–19 *passim*; constitutional validity of laws, 219–24 *passim*

Financial power of Parliament: the budget, 227–41 *passim*, 246–59 *passim*; rights of Members, 241–5 *passim*

Control of Executive by Parliament: appointment of executive officers, 263–75 *passim*; accountability of government, 276–88 *passim*, 304–10 *passim*; machinery of control, 288–304 *passim*; in foreign policy, 310–16 *passim*; judicial function of Parliament, 316–19 *passim*

Church, the: its right to initiate legislation, 144

Civil List: 244

Civil servants: 269, 274, 275; appointment of, 269, 274, 275; evidence given by (in committees of inquiry), 301

Clerk: of the House of Commons, 85–6, 95; of the Parliaments, 85–6, 95

Clerks of Parliament: ix, 85–6, 95

Closure, motion for the: 191, 203

College, Speaker's (parliamentary secretariat): *see* Bureaux

Colleges, electoral: *see* Electoral

Commissioners: defence, 303; -General, 303; parliamentary (Ombudsman), 45, 275, 302–3

Committees, parliamentary (*general*): ad hoc, 103, 105, 106, 108, 110; on bills, 148–9, 254–6, 299 (*see also* Law, making of); and the budget, 254–6; business, 187; characteristics of the system, 121–2; of conciliation, 209; of conference, 209, 210, 211, 240; 'extraordinary', 107; and initiation of legislation, 164; and introduction of bills, 148–9 (*see also* on bills); joint, 110–12, 209–10, 212–13, 238; with legislative powers, 108, 111, 163–8, 170; mediation, 209, 212, 240; numbers of, 107; on parliamentary business, 179; permanent, 105–8, 110–12, 118, 162, 165, 167, 209–10, 255, 274, 299, 312; procedure in, 120–1; proceedings of (published), 169; on public accounts, 307; purposes of, 102–4; 'reference back' to, 188; reports by, 120–1; role of (in legislation), 102–4; 'select', 105, 106, 109, 113, 116, 154, 307; 'special', 109, 118, 164, 166, 187, 209, 210; specialised, 106–9, 162, 165; standing, 103, 105–6, 108, 113, 116, 117, 166, 167; steering, 114; temporary, 105, 108, 109;

Composition and organisation of: 112–22; appointment of, 113–15; chairmen (directing authorities) of, 115, 117–20 (*ex officio*, 118); obligation of Members of Parliament to serve on, 113; public and private meetings of, 115–16; replacement of members, 115; seniority of members, 115;

326

INDEX

'strangers' in, 116–17; 'substitution' and 'titular' members, 114–15

Legislative work in: 160–7; initiation of legislation, 164; introduction of bills, 148–9, 299; powers of, 108–11, 163–8, 170; reference to, 161–3, 188, 254–6; reports by, 120–1, 168–71; role of (in legislation), 102–4

Committees, parliamentary (*named*): on Accounts, 307; on Appropriations, 255, 307; of both Houses (joint), 105, 110–12; Chancellery, 82, 86, 94; of Control, 109; on delegated powers, 158; on Elections, 114; on financial matters, 118; Finance, 255–6, 306; on Foreign Affairs, 115, 312–13; 'Grand', 107, 183; House and House Management, 187; of Inquiry or Investigation, 108–9, 203, 299–302; of Privileges, 64; of Public Accounts, 93, 119; on Rules, 114, 178, 187; Scottish standing, 105; of Selection, 105, 113–14, 115, 118; on Standing Orders, 118; on Statutory Instruments, 154; of Supply, 103, 252, 254, 259; of Ways and Means, 103, 112, 149, 238, 252, 258, 259; of the whole House, 79, 102–6, 116–18, 146, 149, 163, 166–7, 196, 254–5

'Communication' by Executive to Legislature: 290

Communist Party in U.S.A.: 48

Comptroller and Auditor-General: 93, 306–7, 307

Comptroller-General (USA): 307

Confidence (or non-confidence), votes of: 203, 281–5, 291, 294

Congress, The (USA): 4; and President's veto, 217–18; and election of President, 266; inquiries on behalf of, 299–300. *See also* United States.

Consideration, fresh (of bills passed): 213, 214, 216–17. *See also* Deliberation

Consolidated Fund: 244, 259; Bill and Act, 252

Constituencies, electoral: 20–3; advantages of, 20–1; single-member and multi-member, 20–1; nation-wide, 20–1; sizes of, 21, 22; boundaries of, 21–2; independent territories, 23; national minorities in, 24

Constituent assemblies: 204

Constitution, The: amendment or revision of (procedure), 203–8; and ordinary law, 203; and legislation, 213, 215, 220; supremacy of, 220; and appointment of Head of State, 264, 265

Constitutions, 'flexible' and 'rigid': 220

Consultation (legislative) outside Parliament: 166, 167, 171–4; public debate, 174; referendum, 173, 174

Contempt: of Parliament, 65; to an M.P., 65

Control, parliamentary: over Executive, *see* Executive; machinery of, *see* Machinery

Control, supreme chamber of (financial): 303, 305, 309

Controller-general (of accounts): 308

Corporations, public: 234–7; and state intervention, 234–5; kinds of, 235–6; parliamentary control over, 236–7

Council of State: 80, 91, 151, 152, 215, 251, 263–4, 268, 280

Council, Presidential (of Chambers): 82

'Counter-proposals' (amendments fundamentally altering bills): 194

Countries studied in this book: x

Courts: constitutional, 219–24 *passim*; of accounts, 308, 309; Supreme (of Justice), 221–4 *passim*

Czechoslovakia (*See also* People's Democracies): *Structure of Parliament:* unicameral system in, 12–13 *passim*; elections and electorate, 14–23 *passim*, 49–52 *passim*; ballots, 23–40 *passim*; Members of Parliament, 40–55 *passim*, 59–77 *passim*

Organisation of Parliament: administration of, 77–88 *passim*; independence of, 88–97 *passim*; parties and groups, 97–102 *passim*; committees of, 102–22 *passim*; sittings of, 122–30 *passim*

Legislative function of Parliament: limitations on, 133–40 *passim*; introduction of bills, 140–51 *passim*; delegated legislation, 151–9 *passim*; making of law, 159–213 *passim*; promulgation of laws, 213–19 *passim*; constitutional validity of laws, 219–24 *passim*

Financial power of Parliament: the budget, 227–41 *passim*, 246–59 *passim*; rights of Members, 241–5 *passim*

Control of Executive by Parliament:

PARLIAMENTS

appointment of executive officers, 263–75 *passim*; accountability of government, 276–88 *passim*, 304–10 *passim*; machinery of control, 288–304 *passim*; in foreign policy, 310–16 *passim*; judicial function of Parliament, 316–19 *passim*

Deadlock, provisions in case of (in bicameral constitutions): 211
Debates: 180–96; amendments in, 170–1, 183, 184, 188, 192–6; on bills reported on, 170–1; on budget and estimates, *see* Budget *and* Estimates; on foreign policy, 312; general (and interpellations *q.v.*), 289–93, 311; limitations on (rules), 184–7; procedural motions and obstruction, 188–92; rules for (limitations), 184–7; 'short', 165
Deliberation, fresh: motion for, 188, 205; request for (by Head of State), 217. *See also* Second deliberation.
Democracies: 'basic', 7; bicameral system in, 8–9; unicameral system in, 13; People's, *see* People's Democracies
Democracy: as legitimate basis of power, xi; 'direct', 174; and Executive's power of dissolution, 286
Denmark: *Structure of Parliament*: unicameral system in, 12–13 *passim*; elections and electorate, 14–23 *passim*, 49–52 *passim*; ballots, 23–40 *passim*; Members of Parliament, 40–55 *passim*, 59–77 *passim*
Organisation of Parliament: administration of, 77–88 *passim*; independence of, 88–97 *passim*; parties and groups, 97–102 *passim*; committees of, 102–22 *passim*; sittings of, 122–30 *passim*
Legislative function of Parliament: limitations on, 133–40 *passim*; introduction of bills, 140–51 *passim*; delegated legislation, 151–9 *passim*; making of law, 159–213 *passim*; promulgation of laws, 213–19 *passim*; constitutional validity of laws, 219–24 *passim*
Financial power of Parliament: the budget, 227–41 *passim*, 246–59 *passim*; rights of Members, 241–5 *passim*
Control of Executive by Parliament: appointment of executive officers, 263–75 *passim*; accountability of government, 276–88 *passim*, 304–10 *passim*; machinery of control, 288–304 *passim*; in foreign policy, 310–16 *passim*; judicial function of Parliament, 316–19 *passim*
Differences between Houses: *see* Agreement
Directing authority of Parliament (President or Speaker): 77–84; historical details, 77–8; Speakers *or* Presidents of Chambers, 78–84; selection and appointment of, 78–9, 80–1; duties of, 79–81, 82–3, 84; and committees, 79–80; his 'dossier', 88; and staff grievances, 91; and estimates and expenditure, 92, 93; and Rules of procedure *q.v.*, 96; and appointments to committees, 113, 115. *See also* Independence.
Director-General (of Parliament): 85–6
Dissolution of Parliament: 285, 285–8; uses of, 285–6; history of, 286; in Great Britain, 287; present purpose of, 287–8
Division of power: 152. *See also* Equality *and* Separation.

Eire: *see* Ireland
Election campaigns: 49–52; equality of opportunity in, 49–50; limitations on spending in, 50; corruption in, 51; propaganda, 51; financial assistance, 51; radio and television, 51; disputes in, 52
Elections, parliamentary: 14, 23–40; by-elections, 27–8; general elections, 204, 216, 219; fraud at, 37–8; penalties, 38; contested elections, 38–40. *See also* Constituencies, Franchise, Polling, Registers *and* Voting.
Electoral colleges: 4, 10, 20–1, 264, 266 *bis*, 275
Electoral systems: 24–7. *See also* Polling *and* Voting
Electorate, the: 14–23; qualifications of, 14–18. *See also* Constituencies, Franchise, Registers *and* Voting.
Equality of the powers: 217, 265–6. *See also* Division *and* Separation.
Estimates: 232–3, 238, 254, 305, 309, 310. *See also* Finance *and* Financial matters.
Ethiopia: *Structure of Parliament:* bicameral system in, 7–12 *passim*; elections and electorate, 14–23 *passim*, 49–52 *passim*; ballots,

328

INDEX

23–40 *passim*; Members of Parliament, 40–55 *passim*, 59–77 *passim*
Organisation of Parliament: administration of, 77–88 *passim*; independence of, 88–97 *passim*; parties and groups, 97–102 *passim*; committees of, 102–22 *passim*; sittings of, 122–30 *passim*
Legislative function of Parliament: limitations on, 133–40 *passim*; introduction of bills, 140–51 *passim*; delegated legislation, 151–9 *passim*; making of law, 159–213 *passim*; promulgation of laws, 213–19 *passim*; constitutional validity of laws, 219–24 *passim*
Financial power of Parliament: the budget, 227–41 *passim*, 246–59 *passim*; rights of Members, 241–5 *passim*
Control of Executive by Parliament: appointment of executive officers, 263–75 *passim*; accountability of government, 276–88 *passim*, 304–10 *passim*; machinery of control, 288–304 *passim*; in foreign policy, 310–16 *passim*; judicial function of Parliament, 316–19 *passim*

Evidence on oath given before committees: 300–1

Executive, the: appointment of, *see* Appointment; and elections, 38; and dissolution of Parliament, 53, 285–8; and M.P.s, 43–4, 61; and Legislature, 8, 69–70, 71, 95, 126–9, 133, 134, 142, 150, 151, 155, 177, 285–8; and Secretary-General of Parliament, 85; and Parliament's own expenditure, 91–4; and committees, 107, 108, 166; and sessions of Parliament, 126–9 *passim*; powers of (in an emergency), 136–40; and initiation of legislation, 141–2, 147, 150; as legislative body, 158–9 (*see also* Legislation, delegated); and order of business, 175–6; and promulgation of laws, 215–19; and financial bills, 230–1, 243
Parliamentary control over: 136–40, 142, 151, 155, 158, 227, 246, 259, 261–319; basic principles of, 262; forms of, 263–4. *See also* Accountability, Accounting Appointment, Foreign policy, Judicial functions *and* Machinery.

Expenditure, public: details of, 230; accounting for, 304–10
Expert witnesses: 167

Federal Parliaments: 3–7; bicameral, 3–7; unicameral, 6, 7, 12–13; stock type of, 4
Federations: bicameral system in, 3–6; unicameral system in, 6–7
Filibustering: 189
Finance Acts and Bills: 229, 253. *See also* Budget.
Finance, Minister (and Ministry) of: 232–4, 243. *See also* Chancellor of the Exchequer.
Finance, powers of Parliament over: 225–59. *See also* Budget, Financial matters *and* Money bills.
Financial matters: amendments involving, 194; initiation of bills on, 143; parliamentary powers and procedure in, *see* Budget; public expenditure, accounting for, 304–10; rights of M.P.s in, 241–5. *See also* Budget *and* Money bills.
Financial Secretary to the Treasury (UK): 307
Financial years, dates of: 246, 247 (*table*)
Finland: *Structure of Parliament:* unicameral system in, 12–13 *passim*; elections and electorate, 14–23 *passim*, 49–52 *passim*; ballots, 23–40 *passim*; Members of Parliament, 40–55 *passim*, 59–77 *passim*
Organisation of Parliament: administration of, 77–88 *passim*; independence of, 88–97 *passim*; parties and groups, 97–102 *passim*; committees of, 102–22 *passim*; sittings of, 122–30 *passim*
Legislative function of Parliament: limitations on, 133–40 *passim*; introduction of bills, 140–51 *passim*; delegated legislation, 151–9 *passim*; making of law, 159–213 *passim*; promulgation of laws, 213–19 *passim*; constitutional validity of laws, 219–24 *passim*
Financial power of Parliament: the budget, 227–41 *passim*, 246–59 *passim*; rights of Members, 241–5 *passim*
Control of Executive by Parliament: appointment of executive officers, 263–75 *passim*; accountability of government, 276–88 *passim*, 304–10 *passim*; machinery of control, 288–304 *passim*; in foreign policy, 310–16 *passim*; judicial function of Parliament, 316–19 *passim*

Foreign policy, parliamentary control

PARLIAMENTS

over: 310–16; principles involved, 310–11; in practice, 311–16; debates on, 312; treaties, 313–16
France: *Structure of Parliament:* bicameral system in, 7–12 *passim*; elections and electorate, 14–23 *passim*, 49–52 *passim*; ballots, 23–40 *passim*; Members of Parliament, 40–55 *passim*, 59–77 *passim*
Organisation of Parliament: administration of, 77–88 *passim*; independence of, 88–97 *passim*; parties and groups, 97–102 *passim*; committees of, 102–22 *passim*; sittings of, 122–30 *passim*
Legislative function of Parliament: limitations on, 133–40 *passim*; introduction of bills, 140–51 *passim*; delegated legislation, 151–9 *passim*; making of law, 159–213 *passim*; promulgation of laws, 213–19 *passim*; constitutional validity of laws, 219–24 *passim*
Financial power of Parliament: the budget, 227–41 *passim*, 246–59 *passim*; rights of Members, 241–5 *passim*
Control of Executive by Parliament: appointment of executive officers, 263–75 *passim*; accountability of government, 276–88 *passim*, 304–10 *passim*; machinery of control, 288–304 *passim*; in foreign policy, 310–16 *passim*; judicial function of Parliament, 316–19 *passim*
Franchise, the: 14–18:
Qualifications and disqualifications for: sex, 14–15, 18; nationality, 15; residence, 15–16; age, 16 & *n*, 18; mental and physical condition, 16; education, moral conduct and business integrity, 17; penury, 17
Deprivation of: seldom permanent, 18; restriction of, 18. *See also* Polling *and* Voting.

'Gag, the' (closure in Australia): 191
Germany, Federal Republic of:
Structure of Parliament: bicameral system in, 3–7 *passim*; elections and electorate, 14–23 *passim*, 49–52 *passim*; ballots, 23–40 *passim*; Members of Parliament, 40–55 *passim*, 59–77 *passim*
Organisation of Parliament: administration of, 77–88 *passim*; independence of, 88–97 *passim*; parties and groups, 97–102 *passim*; committees of, 102–22 *passim*; sittings of, 122–30 *passim*
Legislative function of Parliament: limitations on, 133–40 *passim*; introduction of bills, 140–51 *passim*; delegated legislation, 151–9 *passim*; making of law, 159–213 *passim*; promulgation of laws, 213–19 *passim*; constitutional validity of laws, 219–24 *passim*
Financial power of Parliament: the budget, 227–41 *passim*, 246–59 *passim*; rights of Members, 241–5 *passim*
Control of Executive by Parliament: appointment of executive officers, 263–75 *passim*; accountability of government, 276–88 *passim*, 304–10 *passim*; machinery of control, 288–304 *passim*; in foreign policy, 310–16 *passim*; judicial function of Parliament, 316–19 *passim*
Ghana: *Structure of Parliament:* unicameral system in, 12–13 *passim*; elections and electorate, 14–23 *passim*, 49–52 *passim*; ballots, 23–40 *passim*; Members of Parliament, 40–55 *passim*, 59–77 *passim*
Organisation of Parliament: administration of, 77–88 *passim*; independence of, 88–97 *passim*; parties and groups, 97–102 *passim*; committees of, 102–22 *passim*; sittings of, 122–30 *passim*
Legislative function of Parliament: limitations on, 133–40 *passim*; introduction of bills, 140–51 *passim*; delegated legislation, 151–9 *passim*; making of law, 159–213 *passim*; promulgation of laws, 213–19 *passim*; constitutional validity of laws, 219–24 *passim*
Financial power of Parliament: the budget, 227–41 *passim*, 246–59 *passim*; rights of Members, 241–5 *passim*
Control of Executive by Parliament: appointment of executive officers, 263–75 *passim*; accountability of government, 276–88 *passim*, 304–10 *passim*; machinery of control, 288–304 *passim*; in foreign policy, 310–16 *passim*; judicial function of Parliament, 316–19 *passim*
Government and Opposition: 99, 177
Government's right to submit amendments to bills: 192–3
Great Britain (United Kingdom): *Structure of Parliament:* bicameral

INDEX

system in, 7–12 *passim*; elections and electorate, 14–23 *passim*, 49–52 *passim*; ballots, 23–40 *passim*; Members of Parliament, 40–55 *passim*, 59–77 *passim*
Organisation of Parliament: administration of, 77–88 *passim*; independence of, 88–97 *passim*; parties and groups, 97–102 *passim*; committees of, 102–22 *passim*; sittings of, 122–30 *passim*
Legislative function of Parliament: limitations on, 133–40 *passim*; introduction of bills, 140–51 *passim*; delegated legislation, 151–9 *passim*; making of law, 159–213 *passim*; promulgation of laws, 213–19 *passim*; constitutional validity of laws, 219–24 *passim*
Financial power of Parliament: the budget, 227–41 *passim*, 246–59 *passim*; rights of Members, 241–5 *passim*
Control of Executive by Parliament: appointment of executive officers, 263–75 *passim*; accountability of government, 276–88 *passim*, 304–10 *passim*; machinery of control, 288–304 *passim*; in foreign policy, 310–16 *passim*; judicial function of Parliament, 316–19 *passim*

Greece: *Structure of Parliament:* unicameral system in, 12–13 *passim*; elections and electorate, 14–23 *passim*, 49–52 *passim*; ballots, 23–40 *passim*; Members of Parliament, 40–55 *passim*, 59–77 *passim*
Organisation of Parliament: administration of, 77–88 *passim*; independence of, 88–97 *passim*; parties and groups, 97–102 *passim*; committees of, 102–22 *passim*; sittings of, 122–30 *passim*
Legislative function of Parliament: limitations on, 133–40 *passim*; introduction of bills, 140–51 *passim*; delegated legislation, 151–9 *passim*; making of law, 159–213 *passim*; promulgation of laws, 213–19 *passim*; constitutional validity of laws, 219–24 *passim*
Financial power of Parliament: the budget, 227–41 *passim*, 246–59 *passim*; rights of Members, 241–5 *passim*
Control of Executive by Parliament: appointment of executive officers, 263–75 *passim*; accountability of government, 276–88 *passim*, 304–10 *passim*; machinery of control, 288–304 *passim*; in foreign policy, 310–16 *passim*; judicial function of Parliament, 316–19 *passim*

Greffier (of Parliament): 85–6, 95
'Grievance days': 176
Grievances, ventilation and redress of: by motions to reduce estimates, 243; by petition, 226; precede Supply, 226; older methods of, 294; by questions to ministers *q.v.*, 294
Groups, political: *see* Parties
Guillotine, the (in Parliament): 187

'Hansard' (Reports of proceedings in Parliament): 295
Head of Government and Cabinet (*See also* Prime Minister): 263, 264; and budget, 234; election of, 266
Head of State: status of, 263; powers of (in an emergency), 136–40; and initiation of legislation, 141; and financial amendments, 194; election, appointment, dismissal and impeachment of, 4, 203; absence of, 80, 83, 202; and amendment of Constitution, 205, 207, 208; and promulgation of bills passed, 213–14, 215–16; his veto on bills passed, 202, 207, 217–19; absolute veto of, 219; and constitutional validity of bills, 221, 222, 224; and ministers, 268–73, 277; and power of dissolution, 286–7; his accountability (to Parliament), 317
'High Court' (judicial) for trial of Heads of State and of Governments: 137
House of Commons (UK): 8, 9, 78; Speaker and Deputy Speaker of, 77–84; administration of, 79; officers of, 79; party system in, 99, 100; and committees, 102–3, 105, 106, 113–14, 116, 118–21; debating chamber of, 123, 124, 125; sessions of, 127; and Messages from the Crown, 142; introducing bills in (procedure), 146, 149; and statutory instruments, 154; and order of business, 175, 176; Government and Opposition in, 177; legislation in (stages of passing bills through), 183; and 'right to speak' in, 185; 'guillotine' in, 187; the closure (motion for), 191; and amendments, 194, 196; voting in, 198,

331

PARLIAMENTS

199, 200; quorum in, 201; and disagreement with House of Lords, 211–12; and the budget *q.v.*, 243–4; its power over legislation (origins of), 226, 243; and money bills, 239–40; and the budget, *q.v.*, 254, 255; and appointment of Head of Government, 273; and impeachment, 277; and motion of censure, 281; and accountability of government or ministers, 281; and Cabinet, 287; and dissolution, 287; and evidence given by civil servants, 301

House of Lords (UK): 8, 9, 78; powers of, 8, 9, 143; and committees, 114; and money bills, 143, 238, 239–40; and order of business, 175; voting in, 200; quorum in, 201; its suspensory veto, 211–12; and impeachment, 277, 319; judicial functions of, 319

Houses, Upper and Lower: *see* Chambers

Hungary: *Structure of Parliament:* unicameral system in, 12–13 *passim*; elections and electorate, 14–23 *passim*, 49–52 *passim*; ballots, 23–40 *passim*; Members of Parliament, 40–55 *passim*, 59–77 *passim*
Organisation of Parliament: administration of, 77–88 *passim*; independence of, 88–97 *passim*; parties and groups, 97–102 *passim*; committees of, 102–22 *passim*; sittings of, 122–30 *passim*
Legislative function of Parliament: limitations on, 133–40 *passim*; introduction of bills, 140–51 passim; delegated legislation 151–9 *passim*; making of law, 159–213 *passim*; promulgation of laws, 213–19 *passim*; constitutional validity of laws, 219–24 *passim*
Financial power of Parliament: the budget, 227–41 *passim*, 246–59 *passim*; rights of Members 241–5 *passim*
Control of Executive by Parliament: appointment of executive officers, 263–75 *passim*; accountability of government, 276–88 *passim*, 304–10 *passim*; machinery of control, 288–304 *passim*; in foreign policy, 310–16 *passim*; judicial function of Parliament, 316–19 *passim*

Iceland: *Structure of Parliament:* unicameral-bicameral system in, 7–12 *passim*, 208–9 *passim*; elections and electorate, 14–23 *passim*, 49–52 *passim*; ballots, 23–40 *passim*; Members of Parliament, 40–55 *passim*, 59–77 *passim*
Organisation of Parliament: administration of, 77–88 *passim*; independence of, 88–97 *passim*; parties and groups, 97–102 *passim*; committees of, 102–22 *passim*; sittings of, 122–30 *passim*
Legislative function of Parliament: limitations on, 133–40 *passim*; introduction of bills, 140–51 *passim*; delegated legislation, 151–9 *passim*; making of law, 159–213 *passim*; promulgation of laws, 213–19 *passim*; constitutional validity of laws, 219–24 *passim*
Financial power of Parliament: the budget, 227–41 *passim*, 246–59 *passim*; rights of Members 241–5 *passim*
Control of Executive by Parliament: appointment of executive officers, 263–75 *passim*; accountability of government, 276–88 *passim*, 304–10 *passim*; machinery of control, 288–304 *passim*; in foreign policy, 310–16 *passim*; judicial function of Parliament, 316–19 *passim*
Immunities of Members of Parliament: 59–64, 203
Impeachment: 4, 137, 277, 282
Inadmissibility of bills, motions for: 189
Independence of Parliament: 59, 88–97; administrative, 89–91; financial, 91–4; procedural, 94–7
India: *Structure of Parliament:* bicameral system in, 3–7 *passim*; elections and electorate, 14–23 *passim*, 49–52 *passim*; ballots, 23–40 *passim*; Members of Parliament, 40–55 *passim*, 59–77 *passim*
Organisation of Parliament: administration of, 77–88 *passim*; independence of, 88–97 *passim*; parties and groups, 97–102 *passim*; committees of, 102–22 *passim*; sittings of, 122–30 *passim*
Legislative function of Parliament: limitations on, 133–40 *passim*; introduction of bills, 140–51 *passim*; delegated legislation, 151–9 *passim*; making of law, 159–213 *passim*; promulgation of laws,

INDEX

213–19 *passim*; constitutional validity of laws, 219–24 *passim*

Financial power of Parliament: the budget, 227–41 *passim*, 246–59 *passim*; rights of Members, 241–5 *passim*

Control of Executive by Parliament: appointment of executive officers, 263–75 *passim*; accountability of government, 276–88 *passim*; 304–10 *passim*; machinery of control, 288–304 *passim*; in foreign policy, 310–16 *passim*; judicial function of Parliament, 316–19 *passim*

Individual citizens, protection of: 289, 294. *See also* Ombudsman.

Information, obtaining: 288–303; by debates and interpellations, 289–93; by questions to ministers, 294–9; by committees of investigation, 299–302; by other means, 302–3

Injustice, eliminating: 289. *See also* Ombudsman.

Inquiries, parliamentary: 108–9, 203, 299–302, 304

International Centre for Parliamentary Documentation: ix, x; Governing Board of (*names*), x–xi

Inter-Parliamentary Union: ix–xii *passim*

Interpellations: 167, 281, 282, 290–3, 294, 298, 299, 304; history of, 291; procedure for, 291–3; questions to ministers, 296, 297; and foreign policy, 311, 312

Interpreters and translators: 87

Investigation, committees of: 108–9, 203, 299–302, 304, 311

Iran (*formerly*) Persia: *Structure of Parliament:* bicameral system in, 7–12 *passim*; elections and electorate, 14–23 *passim*, 49–52 *passim*; ballots, 23–40 *passim*; Members of Parliament, 40–55 *passim*, 59–77 *passim*

Organisation of Parliament: administration of, 77–88 *passim*; independence of, 88–97 *passim*; parties and groups, 97–102 *passim*; committees of, 102–22 *passim*; sittings of, 122–30 *passim*

Legislative function of Parliament: limitations on, 133–40 *passim*; introduction of bills, 140–51 *passim*; delegated legislation, 151–9 *passim*; making of law, 159–213 *passim*; promulgation of laws,

213–19 *passim*; constitutional validity of laws, 219–24 *passim*

Financial power of Parliament: the budget, 227–41 *passim*, 246–59 *passim*; rights of Members, 241–5 *passim*

Control of Executive by Parliament: appointment of executive officers, 263–75 *passim*; accountability of government, 276–88 *passim*, 304–10 *passim*; machinery of control, 288–304 *passim*; in foreign policy, 310–16 *passim*; judicial function of Parliament, 316–19 *passim*

Ireland (Eire): *Structure of Parliament:* bicameral system in, 7–12 *passim*; elections and electorate, 14–23 *passim*, 49–52 *passim*; ballots, 23–40 *passim*; Members of Parliament, 40–55 *passim*, 59–77 *passim*

Organisation of Parliament: administration of, 77–88 *passim*; independence of, 88–97 *passim*; parties and groups, 97–102 *passim*; committees of, 102–22 *passim*; sittings of, 122–30 *passim*

Legislative function of Parliament: limitations on, 133–40 *passim*; introduction of bills, 140–51 *passim*; delegated legislation, 151–9 *passim*; making of law, 159–213 *passim*; promulgation of laws, 213–19 *passim*; constitutional validity of laws, 219–24 *passim*

Financial power of Parliament: the budget, 227–41 *passim*, 246–59 *passim*; rights of Members, 241–5 *passim*

Control of Executive by Parliament: appointment of executive officers, 263–75 *passim*; accountability of government, 276–88 *passim*, 304–10 *passim*; machinery of control, 288–304 *passim*; in foreign policy, 310–16 *passim*; judicial function of Parliament, 316–19 *passim*

Israel: *Structure of Parliament:* unicameral system in, 12–13 *passim*; elections and electorate, 14–23 *passim*, 49–52 *passim*; ballots, 23–40 *passim*; Members of Parliament, 40–55 *passim*, 59–77 *passim*

Organisation of Parliament: administration of, 77–88 *passim*; independence of, 88–97 *passim*; parties and groups, 97–102 *passim*; committees of, 102–22 *passim*; sittings of, 122–30 *passim*

Legislative function of Parliament:

PARLIAMENTS

limitations on, 133–40 *passim*; introduction of bills, 140–51 *passim*; delegated legislation, 151–9 *passim*; making of law, 159–213 *passim*; promulgation of laws, 213–19 *passim*; constitutional validity of laws, 219–24 *passim*
Financial power of Parliament: the budget, 227–41 *passim*, 246–59 *passim*; rights of Members, 241–5 *passim*
Control of Executive by Parliament: appointment of executive officers, 263–75 *passim*; accountability of government, 276–88 *passim*, 304–10 *passim*; machinery of control, 288–304 *passim*; in foreign policy, 310–16 *passim*; judicial function of Parliament, 316–19 *passim*

Italy: *Structure of Parliament:* unicameral-bicameral system in, 7–12 *passim*, 208–9 *passim*; elections and electorate, 14–23 *passim*, 49–52 *passim*; ballots, 23–40 *passim*; Members of Parliament, 40–55 *passim*, 59–77 *passim*
Organisation of Parliament: administration of, 77–88 *passim*; independence of, 88–97 *passim*; parties and groups, 97–102 *passim*; committees of, 102–22 *passim*; sittings of, 122–30 *passim*
Legislative function of Parliament: limitations on, 133–40 *passim*; introduction of bills, 140–51 *passim*; delegated legislation, 151–9 *passim*; making of law, 159–213 *passim*; promulgation of laws, 213–19 *passim*; constitutional validity of laws, 219–24 *passim*
Financial power of Parliament: the budget, 227–41 *passim*, 246–59 *passim*; rights of Members, 241–5 *passim*
Control of Executive by Parliament: appointment of executive officers, 263–75 *passim*; accountability of government, 276–88 *passim*, 304–10 *passim*; machinery of control, 288–304 *passim*; in foreign policy, 310–16 *passim*; judicial function of Parliament, 316–19 *passim*

Japan: *Structure of Parliament:* unicameral-bicameral system in, 7–12 *passim*, 208–9 *passim*; elections and electorate, 14–23 *passim*, 49–52 *passim*; ballots, 23–40 *passim*; Members of Parliament, 40–55 *passim*, 59–77 *passim*
Organisation of Parliament: administration of, 77–88 *passim*; independence of, 88–97 *passim*; parties and groups, 97–102 *passim*; committees of, 102–22 *passim*; sittings of, 122–30 *passim*
Legislative function of Parliament: limitations on, 133–40 *passim*; introduction of bills, 140–51 *passim*; delegated legislation 151–9 *passim*; making of law, 159–213 *passim*; promulgation of laws, 213–19 *passim*; constitutional validity of laws, 219–24 *passim*
Financial power of Parliament: the budget, 227–41 *passim*, 246–59 *passim*; rights of Members, 241–5 *passim*
Control of Executive by Parliament: appointment of executive officers, 263–75 *passim*; accountability of government, 276–88 *passim*, 304–10 *passim*; machinery of control, 288–304 *passim*; in foreign policy, 310–16 *passim*; judicial function of Parliament, 316–19 *passim*
Journal of the House: 141
Judicial functions of Parliament: 316–19; *vis à vis* Head of State and ministers, 317–19; impeachment *q.v.*, 318–19
Procedures: in ordinary court, 317; in special court, 318; by impeachment, 318–19
Judiciary, the: independence of, 61, 133; and constitutional validity of laws, 222–3

Languages, official and permitted: 87–8, 215
Laos: *Structure of Parliament:* bicameral system in, 7–12 *passim*; elections and electorate, 14–23 *passim*, 49–52 *passim*; ballots, 23–40 *passim*; Members of Parliament, 40–55 *passim*, 59–77 *passim*
Organisation of Parliament: administration of, 77–88 *passim*; independence of, 88–97 *passim*; parties and groups, 97–102 *passim*; committees of, 102–22 *passim*; sittings of, 122–30 *passim*
Legislative function of Parliament: limitations on, 133–40 *passim*; introduction of bills, 140–51 *passim*; delegated legislation, 151–9 *passim*; making of law, 159–213

passim; promulgation of laws, 213–19 *passim*; constitutional validity of laws, 219–24 *passim*

Financial power of Parliament: the budget, 227–41 *passim*, 246–59 *passim*; rights of Members, 241–5 *passim*

Control of Executive by Parliament: appointment of executive officers, 263–75 *passim*; accountability of government, 276–88 *passim*, 304–10 *passim*; machinery of control, 288–304 *passim*; in foreign policy, 310–16 *passim*; judicial function of Parliament, 316–19 *passim*

Law (*general*): constitutional, 164, 203. 242; and public money, 226; ordinary, *see* Law, making of; statute, 203

Law, making of: 132, 159–213; preliminaries etc., 159–61

Committees (*q.v.*), *role of:* 161–74; reference to, 161–3; powers and functions of, 163–8, 170, 171; reports by, 168–71

Consultation with outside bodies: 166, 167, 171–4; referendum, 173, 174; public debate, 174

Order of Business: 174–80; changes in, 179–80; settled by Parliament, 178–9

Debate in the House: 170–1, 180–96; procedure (readings), general, 170–1, 180–4; rules of, *q.v.*, 184–7; procedural motions and obstruction, 188–92; amendments, 170–1, 183, 184, 188, 192–6

Voting in Parliament: methods of, 196–203; kinds of ballot, 196–200; quorum and equality of votes, 201; special majorities, 202–3

Constitutional bills: 203–8

Agreement between the Houses: 202, 208–13

Laws, promulgation of: 213–19; Royal Assent, 213–14; and publication, 215–16; request for new (fresh) consideration, 216–17; the veto *q.v.*, 217–19

Laws, validity (constitutional) of: 134, 172, 216, 219–24; difficulties, 220, 221; absence of control, 220–1; prior control over, 221–2; legal control (after promulgation), 222–3; control by constitutional court, 224; conclusions, 224

Lebanon, the: *Structure of Parliament:* unicameral system in, 12–13 *passim*; elections and electorate, 14–23 *passim*, 49–52 *passim*; ballots, 23–40 *passim*; Members of Parliament, 40–55 *passim*, 59–77 *passim*

Organisation of Parliament: administration of, 77–88 *passim*; independence of, 88–97 *passim*; parties and groups, 97–102 *passim*; committees of, 102–22 *passim*; sittings of, 122–30 *passim*

Legislative function of Parliament: limitations on, 133–40 *passim*; introduction of bills, 140–51 *passim*; delegated legislation, 151–9 *passim*; making of law, 159–213 *passim*; promulgation of laws, 213–19 *passim*; constitutional validity of laws, 219–24 *passim*

Financial power of Parliament: the budget, 227–41 *passim*, 246–59 *passim*; rights of Members, 241–5 *passim*

Control of Executive by Parliament: appointment of executive officers, 263–75 *passim*; accountability of government, 276–88 *passim*, 304–10 *passim*; machinery of control, 288–304 *passim*; in foreign policy, 310–16 *passim*; judicial function of Parliament, 316–19 *passim*

'Left' and 'right' (in politics): 124, 125

Legislation, delegated: 151–9; basic ingredients of, 151; other delegated authority, 151–2; 'laws' and 'regulations', 152–5 *passim*; the dilemma, 152–3; the hazard, 153; in Great Britain, 153–4; and statutory instruments, 154; control of (by Parliament), 154–5, 157; and rigid constitutions, 155–6; regularised, 157–8

Legislation, initiation of: 140–51; the right of, 141–4; in bicameral parliaments, 142–3; by petition, 144; by individual members (private bills), 149–51; by committees, 164; by national council (Italy), 173

Legislative function and power of Parliament: 132–224:

Limitations on: 133–40; sphere of 'law' and of 'regulations', 133–5, 152; the referendum, 135–6, 173; state of emergency, 136–40

Origins of, 226; no longer exclusive, 219

Laws: introduction of bills, 140–51; making of law, 159–213; promulgation of laws, 213–19; validity of

laws, 219–24; delegated legislation, 151–9. *See also* Law *and* Laws.
'Legislative necessity': 140
Legislature and Executive: 8, 69–70, 71, 95, 126–9 *passim* 133, 134, 142, 150, 151, 155, 177, 285–8
Liberia: *Structure of Parliament:* bicameral system in, 7–12 *passim*; elections and electorate, 14–23 *passim*, 49–52 *passim*; ballots, 23–40 *passim*; Members of Parliament, 40–55 *passim*, 59–77 *passim*
Organisation of Parliament: administration of, 77–88 *passim*; independence of, 88–97 *passim*; parties and groups, 97–102 *passim*; committees of, 102–22 *passim*; sittings of, 122–30 *passim*
Legislative functions of Parliament: limitations on, 133–40 *passim*; introduction of bills, 140–51 *passim*; delegated legislation, 151–9 *passim*; making of law, 159–213 *passim*; promulgation of laws, 213–19 *passim*; constitutional validity of laws, 219–24 *passim*
Financial power of Parliament: the budget, 227–41 *passim*, 246–59 *passim*; rights of Members, 241–5 *passim*
Control of Executive by Parliament: appointment of executive officers, 263–75 *passim*; accountability of government, 276–88 *passim*, 304–10 *passim*; machinery of control, 228–304 *passim*; in foreign policy, 310–16 *passim*; judicial function of Parliament, 316–19 *passim*
Libya: *Structure of Parliament:* bicameral system in, 7–12 *passim*; elections and electorate, 14–23 *passim*, 49–52 *passim*; ballots, 23–40 *passim*; Members of Parliament, 40–55 *passim*, 59–77 *passim*
Organisation of Parliament: administration of, 77–88 *passim*; independence of, 88–97 *passim*; parties and groups, 97–102 *passim*; committees of, 102–22 *passim*; sittings of, 122–30 *passim*
Legislative function of Parliament: limitations on, 133–40 *passim*; introduction of bills, 140–51 *passim*; delegated legislation, 151–9 *passim*; making of law, 159–213 *passim*; promulgation of laws, 213–19 *passim*; constitutional validity of laws, 219–24 *passim*

Financial power of Parliament: the budget, 227–41 *passim*, 246–59 *passim*; rights of Members, 241–5 *passim*
Control of Executive by Parliament: appointment of executive officers, 263–75 *passim*; accountability of government, 276–88 *passim*, 304–10 *passim*; machinery of control, 288–304 *passim*; in foreign policy, 310–16 *passim*; judicial function of Parliament, 316–19 *passim*
Life Peerage Act (1958): 8
Life Peers: 8
Lord Chancellor (UK): 78
Lords Spiritual and Temporal: 8
Luxembourg: *Structure of Parliament:* unicameral system in, 12–13 *passim*; elections and electorate, 14–23 *passim*, 49–52 *passim*; ballots, 23–40 *passim*; Members of Parliament, 40–55 *passim*, 59–77 *passim*
Organisation of Parliament: administration of, 77–88 *passim*; independence of, 88–97 *passim*; parties and groups, 97–102 *passim*; committees of, 102–22 *passim*; sittings of, 122–30 *passim*
Legislative function of Parliaments: limitations on, 133–40 *passim*; introduction of bills, 140–51 *passim*; delegated legislation, 151–9 *passim*; making of law, 159–213 *passim*; promulgation of laws, 213–19 *passim*; constitutional validity of laws, 219–24 *passim*
Financial power of Parliament: the budget, 227–41 *passim*, 246–59 *passim*; rights of Members, 241–5 *passim*
Control of Executive by Parliament: appointment of executive officers, 263–75 *passim*; accountability of government, 276–88 *passim*, 304–10 *passim*; machinery of control, 288–304 *passim*; in foreign policy, 310–16 *passim*; judicial function of Parliament, 316–19 *passim*

Machinery of Parliamentary control: 288–304; general debates and interpellations, 289–93; reports (periodical) by Executive, 289–90; questions to ministers *q.v.*, 294–9; committees of investigation, 299–302; Ombudsman, 45, 275, 302–3; other forms and institutions, 303–4

'Major' question, the: 292. *See also* Interpellations.
Majorities: 201–3; absolute, 202, 206, 207, 217, 265, 266, 272, 284; five-sixths, 206; simple, 201, 202, 206, 318; special, 202–3, 203, 203–4, 205, 212, 217; three-fifths, 208; three-quarters, 202, 203, 205, 218; two-thirds, 202, 205, 206, 207, 212, 217, 218, 219, 265, 267
Mandates, parliamentary: 52–3
Members of Parliament: and the budget, 241–5; and committees (service on), 112–13, 115 (*see also* Committees); and constituents (contact with), 53; *de jure* and *ex officio*, 10–11; expulsion of, 54–5; immunities of, 59–64, 203; independence of, 59–64; inviolability of (protection from legal processes), 60–4; legal position of, 60–4; non-accountability of, 59–60 (exceptions, 60); and private bills (time allowed for), 175, 176; privilege of (protection from offences against Parliament), 64–6
Remuneration of: 71–7; expense allowances, 73–6; justification for, 71–2; official facilities, secretaries etc., 73, 76; rates of, 72–6; pensions on retirement, 75–6; other benefits, 76–7
Rights of: to speak in debates, 185, 188, 192; to submit amendments, 192; over the budget, 241–5
Status of: 59–77. *See also* Membership of Parliament.
Membership of Parliament: absenteeism, 55; candidates and political parties, 46–9, 49–52 (*see also* Elections); civil servants, 67–8; and the 'mandate', 52–3; ministers and public officials, 69–70; substitutes, 70
Qualifications for: 40–3; age, 41; moral rectitude, 42; nationality, 41–2; others, 42–3
Disqualifications for: 203; ineligibilities, 43–5, 54, 66, 68; incompatibilities, 43–5, 66–71, 72, 75 (exceptions, 67)
Termination of membership: expulsion, 54–5; recall or resignation, 53–5, 66, 69. *See also* Members of Parliament.
Messages between Houses: 209, 211
Messages from Head of State: initiating legislation, 141–2; proposing amendments to laws before promulgation, 217; on finance, 229
Ministerial accountability: *see* Accountability
Ministers appearing before committees on bills: 165–6
Minorities, rights of: in committees, 169–70; in debates, 187
Monaco: *Structure of Parliament:* unicameral system in, 12–13 *passim*; elections and electorate, 14–23 *passim*, 49–52 *passim*; ballots, 23–40 *passim*; Members of Parliament, 40–55 *passim*, 59–77 *passim*
Organisation of Parliament: administration of, 77–88 *passim*; independence of, 88–97 *passim*; parties and groups, 97–102 *passim*; committees of, 102–22 *passim*; sittings of, 122–30 *passim*
Legislative function of Parliament: limitations on 133–40 *passim*; introduction of bills, 140–51 *passim*; delegated legislation, 151–9 *passim*; making of law, 159–213 *passim*; promulgation of laws, 213–19 *passim*; constitutional validity of laws, 219–24 *passim*
Financial power of Parliament: the budget, 227–41 *passim*, 246–59 *passim*; rights of Members, 241–5 *passim*
Control of Executive by Parliament: appointment of executive officers, 263–75 *passim*; accountability of government, 276–88 *passim*, 304–10 *passim*; machinery of control, 288–304 *passim*; in foreign policy, 310–16 *passim*; judicial function of Parliament, 316–19 *passim*
Money bills: 211. *See also* Finance and Financial matters.

Navette, la (process): 209
Netherlands, the: *Structure of Parliament:* bicameral system in, 7–12 *passim*; elections and electorate, 14–23 *passim*, 49–52 *passim*; ballots, 23–40 *passim*; Members of Parliament, 40–55 *passim*, 59–77 *passim*
Organisation of Parliament: administration of, 77–88 *passim*; independence of, 88–97 *passim*; parties and groups, 97–102 *passim*; committees of, 102–22 *passim*; sittings of, 122–30 *passim*
Legislative function of Parliament:

PARLIAMENTS

limitations on, 133–40 *passim*; introduction of bills, 140–51 *passim*; delegated legislation, 151–9 *passim*; making of law, 159–213 *passim*; promulgation of laws, 213–19 *passim*; constitutional validity of laws, 219–24 *passim*
Financial power of Parliament: the budget, 227–41 *passim*, 246–59 *passim*; rights of Members, 241–5 *passim*
Control of Executive by Parliament: appointment of executive officers, 263–75 *passim*; accountability of government, 276–88 *passim*, 304–10 *passim*; machinery of control, 288–304 *passim*; in foreign policy, 310–16 *passim*; judicial function of Parliament, 316–19 *passim*
New Zealand: *Structure of Parliament:* unicameral system in, 12–13 *passim*; elections and electorate, 14–23 *passim*, 49–52 *passim*; ballots, 23–40 *passim*; Members of Parliament, 40–55 *passim*, 59–77 *passim*
Organisation of Parliament: administration of, 77–88 *passim*; independence of, 88–97 *passim*; parties and groups, 97–102 *passim*; committees of, 102–22 *passim*; sittings of, 122–30 *passim*
Legislative function of Parliament: limitations on, 133–40 *passim*; introduction of bills, 140–51 *passim*; delegated legislation, 151–9 *passim*; making of law, 159–213 *passim*; promulgation of laws, 213–19 *passim*; constitutional validity of laws, 219–24 *passim*
Financial power of Parliament: the budget, 227–41 *passim*, 246–59 *passim*; rights of Members, 241–5 *passim*
Control of Executive by Parliament: appointment of executive officers, 263–75 *passim*; accountability of government, 276–88 *passim*, 304–10 *passim*; machinery of control, 288–304 *passim*; in foreign policy, 310–16 *passim*; judicial function of Parliament, 316–19 *passim*
Nigeria: *Structure of Parliament:* bicameral system in 3–7 *passim*; elections and electorate, 14–23 *passim*, 49–52 *passim*; ballots, 23–40 *passim*; Members of Parliament, 40–55 *passim*, 59–77 *passim*
Organisation of Parliament: administration of, 77–88 *passim*; independence of, 88–97 *passim*; parties and groups, 97–102 *passim*; committees of, 102–22 *passim*; sittings of, 122–30 *passim*
Legislative function of Parliament: limitations on, 133–40 *passim*; introduction of bills, 140–51 *passim*; delegated legislation, 151–9 *passim*; making of law, 159–213 *passim*; promulgation of laws, 213–19 *passim*; constitutional validity of laws, 219–24 *passim*
Financial power of Parliament: the budget, 227–41 *passim*, 246–59 *passim*; rights of Members, 241–5 *passim*
Control of Executive by Parliament: appointment of executive officers, 263–75 *passim*; accountability of government, 276–88 *passim*; 304–10 *passim*; machinery of control, 288–304 *passim*; in foreign policy, 310–16 *passim*; judicial function of Parliament, 316–19 *passim*

'No debate' procedure: 165, 180, 184–7 *passim*

Norway: *Structure of Parliament:* unicameral-bicameral system in, 7–12 *passim*, 208–9 *passim*; elections and electorate, 14–23 *passim*, 49–52 *passim*; ballots, 23–40 *passim*; Members of Parliament, 40–55 *passim*, 59–77 *passim*
Organisation of Parliament: administration of, 77–88 *passim*; independence of, 88–97 *passim*; parties and groups, 97–102 *passim*; committees of, 102–22 *passim*; sittings of, 122–30 *passim*
Legislative function of Parliament: limitations on, 133–40 *passim*; introduction of bills, 140–51 *passim*; delegated legislation, 151–9 *passim*; making of law, 159–213 *passim*; promulgation of laws, 213–19 *passim*; constitutional validity of laws, 219–24 *passim*
Financial power of Parliament: the budget, 227–41 *passim*, 246–59 *passim*; rights of Members, 241–5 *passim*
Control of Executive by Parliament: appointment of executive officers, 263–75 *passim*; accountability of government, 276–88 *passim*, 304–10 *passim*; machinery of control, 288–304 *passim*; in foreign policy,

INDEX

310–16 *passim*; judicial function of Parliament, 316–19 *passim*

Obstruction in parliamentary debates: 188–92

Offences against Parliament: 64–6

Officers of Parliament: *see* Administrative services *and* Directing authority

Ombudsman: 45, 275, 302–3

Opposition, parliamentary: 99, 177; and committees (chairmen and members of), 119–20; and votes of account, 252; and the budget, 259; Leader of the, 99, 100, 281

Order of Business (Agenda): 174–80; settled by government, 178–9; changes in, 179–80, 188; interpellations in, 291, 292, 293; and questions to ministers, 298

Order Paper: 174, 292

Order, points of: 189

'Organisation of debates' procedure: 187

Organisation of Parliament: 59–130. *See also* Administration, Chambers, Committees, Independence, Members, Membership, Parties, political, Sittings *and* Timetable.

Pakistan: *Structure of Parliament:* unicameral system in, 6, 7, 12–13 *passim*; elections and electorate, 14–23 *passim*, 49–52 *passim*; ballots, 23–40 *passim*; Members of Parliament, 40–55 *passim*, 59–77 *passim*

Organisation of Parliament: administration of, 77–88 *passim*; independence of, 88–97 *passim*; parties and groups, 97–102 *passim*; committees of, 102–22 *passim*; sittings of, 122–30 *passim*

Legislative function of Parliament: limitations on, 133–40 *passim*; introduction of bills, 140–51 *passim*; delegated legislation, 151–9 *passim*; making of law, 159–213 *passim*; promulgation of laws, 213–19 *passim*; constitutional validity of laws, 219–24 *passim*

Financial power of Parliament: the budget, 227–41 *passim*, 246–59 *passim*; rights of Members, 241–5 *passim*

Control of Executive by Parliament: appointment of executive officers, 263–75 *passim*; accountability of government, 276–88 *passim*, 304–10 *passim*; machinery of control, 288–304 *passim*; in foreign policy, 310–16 *passim*; judicial function of Parliament, 316–19 *passim*

Parliament, special aspects of: duration of (long and short), 53; and Executive, *see* Executive; recall of, 128–9; role of, ix; and sovereignty of the people, 277–8.

See also: Administrative services; Directing authority; Independence; Judicial functions; Law, making of; Laws, promulgation of; Legislative functions; Organisation; Privilege; Sittings; Structure; Timetable, etc.

Parliament Acts: *1911*, 95, 143; *1949*, 95

Parties, political (and groups): 46–9, 97–102; and candidates for election, 46–9; in Parliament, 97–102, 105; official recognition of, 46–9, 98, 99, 101–2; their value, 98; in one-party states, 98, 99; regional groups, 99; fragmentation of, 99–100, 119; role and power of, 100; secretariats of, 101; functions of, 101; and individual members, 102; represented on committees, 105, 113–16, 119; and appointment to committees, 113–15; and chairmanship of committees, 119; and seating in legislative chambers, 123–5; and constitutional validity of laws, 224

Payment of Members: 71–7. *See also* Members

People's Democracies (Albania *q.v.*, Bulgaria *q.v.*, Czechoslovakia *q.v.*, Poland *q.v.*, Rumania *q.v.*, *and* Yugoslavia *q.v. See also* U.S.S.R.): legislatures of, 5, 7, 13; franchise in, 15, 16, 17; electoral registers in, 19–20; elections in, 25, 38; voting in, 30; qualifications for M.P.s in, 43; political parties in, 48–9; the 'mandate' (parliamentary), 52; dissolution of Parliament in, 53, 286; immunities of M.P.s in, 62, 63; offences against Parliament, 65; incompatibilities in, 66; remuneration of M.P.s, 71, 75; parliamentary staff in, 89; parliamentary estimates in, 92; committees in, 107, 110, 114, 117, 121, 165, 166; chairmanship of committees, 119; initiation of legislation, 143–6 *passim*; delegated legislative powers in, 151,

339

PARLIAMENTS

153, 158; law making in, 163, 165, 166, 174; public debate (on bills), 174; debates (parliamentary), 181, 189; amendments, 195; voting parliamentary) in, 198; quorum in, 201; reforms in procedure (fundamental), 204 (*see also* 174); budget and finance bills, 230, 246, 251; economic activities and the state in, 234; Executive (form of), 263–4; Head of Government (appointment of), 270; ministerial accountability in, 279, 280; and progress reports, 290; interpellations and questions to ministers, 293; accounting for public expenditure, 305; finance committees in, 306; foreign policy in, 311

'Permanent assembly' system: 126, 129

Persia: *see* Iran

Petition(s): 192; right of, 226

Philadelphia Convention (1787): 3

Philippines, the: *Structure of Parliament:* unicameral-bicameral system in, 7–12 *passim*, 208–9 *passim*; elections and electorate, 14–23 *passim*, 49–52 *passim*; ballots, 23–40 *passim*; Members of Parliament, 40–55 *passim*, 59–77 *passim*
Organisation of Parliament: administration of, 77–88 *passim*; independence of, 88–97 *passim*; parties and groups, 97–102 *passim*; committees of, 102–22 *passim*; sittings of, 122–30 *passim*
Legislative function of Parliament: limitations on, 133–40 *passim*; introduction of bills, 140–51 *passim*; delegated legislation, 151–9 *passim*; making of law, 159–213 *passim*; promulgation of laws, 213–19 *passim*; constitutional validity of laws, 219–24 *passim*
Financial power of Parliament: the budget, 227–41 *passim*, 246–59 *passim*; rights of Members, 241–5 *passim*
Control of Executive by Parliament: appointment of executive officers, 263–75 *passim*; accountability of government, 276–88 *passim*, 304–10 *passim*; machinery of control, 288–304 *passim*; in foreign policy, 310–16 *passim*; judicial function of Parliament, 316–19 *passim*

Poland (*See also* People's Democracies): *Structure of Parliament:* unicameral system in, 12–13 *passim*; elections and electorate, 14–23 *passim*, 49–52 *passim*; ballots, 23–40 *passim*; Members of Parliament, 40–55 *passim*, 59–77 *passim*
Organisation of Parliament: administration of, 77–88 *passim*; independence of, 88–97 *passim*; parties and groups, 97–102 *passim*; committees of, 102–22 *passim*; sittings of, 122–30 *passim*
Legislative function of Parliament: limitations on, 133–40 *passim*; introduction of bills, 140–51 *passim*; delegated legislation, 151–9 *passim*; making of law, 159–213 *passim*; promulgation of laws, 213–19 *passim*; constitutional validity of laws, 219–24 *passim*
Financial power of Parliament: the budget, 227–41 *passim*, 246–59 *passim*; rights of Members, 241–5 *passim*
Control of Executive by Parliament: appointment of executive officers, 263–75 *passim*; accountability of government, 276–88 *passim*, 304–10 *passim*; machinery of control, 288–304 *passim*; in foreign policy, 310–16 *passim*; judicial function of Parliament, 316–19 *passim*

Policy, control of (by Parliament): 289. *See also* Executive, parliamentary control over

Polling: *see* Elections, Franchise, Registers *and* Voting

Powers, relative (of Chambers): 5. *See also* Chambers.

Precedents: 95

President and Vice-President of Chambers: 78–84; and who shall speak, 186; and obstruction, 190; and closure, 191; and amendments, 195–6; casting vote (in ties), 201; and promulgation of laws, 215; and questions to ministers, 296–7. *See also* Directing authority.

President of the Council: 263

Presidential system: 262, 263; right of veto in, 217; budget in, 234; equality of status in, 265–6; ministerial accountability in, 278; impeachment in, 319

Presidents' Colleges: 81–2, 83–4. *See also* Bureaux.

Presidium (in U.S.S.R. and People's Democracies): 144, 151, 163; 179, 211, 215, 263–4, 268, 280, 293; status and powers of, 268, 270

Pressure groups: 167

INDEX

'Previous question', the: 188, 189, 190 *bis*
Prime Minister: 166, 203, 263, 271, 272, 273, 279, 280, 287, 313. *See also* Head of Government.
Privilege, parliamentary: 64–6; breach of, 90
Procedure, parliamentary, ix *and throughout*
Proportional representation: 24, 25–7, 98, 267; in committees, 114, 119
Provisional twelfths: 251
Public debate on bills: 174
Public Revenues Act (N.Z., 1953): 251
Public voting in Parliament: *see* Voting in Parliament

Qualifications and disqualifications: for the franchise, *see* Franchise, for membership of Parliament, *see* Membership
Questeurs: 81, 84, 92 *bis*
Question time: 294–9; in British House of Commons, 294–6, 297; elsewhere, 296–9
Questions to ministers: 167, 278, 293, 294–9, 299, 304; examples of (beyond British sphere), 296–9; on foreign policy, 311, 312; strength and popularity of, 298–9
Kinds of: oral, 295–8, private notice, 295; supplementary, 295–8; written, 295–8
Quorum (of Chamber): 189, 190, 198, 201

Rapporteurs: 104, 117, 120, 165, 168–9, 170, 181, 184–5, 187, 189, 195, 256, 306
Rationalisation of parliamentary system: 282–5
'Readings' of bills: 180–4, 257
Reconsideration of bills: before passing, 188; passed, 213, 214, 216–17
Referendum: 135–6, 173, 174, 216, 219, 315; for amending the Constitution, 204, 205, 207–8
Reform Bills (1832 & 1837): 175
Regents, appointment of: 202, 264, 265
Registers, electoral: 16, 18–20; and cards, 16; purposes of, 18, 20; compilation and exhibition of, 19–20; revision of, 20; appeals, 20
'Regulations' (statutory instruments): 152–7
Reports: of proceedings (official), 87; Hansard, 295; on financial position (general and periodical), 305–6
Representatives, House of (USA): 4
Returning officers: *see* Elections
Revenue (in detail): 229–30
'Right' and 'left' (in politics): 124, 125
Right to speak in Parliament, M.P's: 185, 188, 192
Royal Assent to legislation: 172, 213–14, 219, 253. *See also* Veto
Rules of procedure: 94–7, 184; making and amending, 95–7; their force, 97; and parties and groups, 98, 101; and committees, 102, 111, 112, 117; and making of law, 147, 175; on 'voting without debate', 165; and order of business, 175, 177; and obstruction, 190; adoption or suspension of, 202–3; and reports by government, 280; and questions to ministers, 296. *See also* Standing Orders.
Rumania (*See also* People's Democracies): *Structure of Parliament:* unicameral system in, 12–13 *passim*; elections and electorate, 14–23 *passim*, 49–52 *passim*; ballots, 23–40 *passim*; Members of Parliament, 40–55 *passim*, 59–77 *passim*
Organisation of Parliament: administration of, 77–88 *passim*; independence of, 88–97 *passim*; parties and groups, 97–102 *passim*; committees of, 102–22 *passim*; sittings of, 122–30 *passim*
Legislative function of Parliament: limitations on, 133–40 *passim*; introduction of bills, 140–51 *passim*; delegated legislation, 151– *passim*; making of law, 159–213 *passim*; promulgation of laws, 213–19 *passim*; constitutional validity of laws, 219–24 *passim*
Financial power of Parliament: the budget, 227–41 *passim*, 246–59 *passim*; rights of Members, 241–5 *passim*
Control of Executive by Parliament: appointment of executive officers, 263–75 *passim*; accountability of government, 276–88 *passim*, 304–10 *passim*; machinery of control, 288–304 *passim*; in foreign policy, 310–16 *passim*; judicial function of Parliament, 316–19 *passim*

Scandinavia: tendency to unicameralism in, 12–13

'Second deliberation' on bills: 181, 188, 202
Secretariat of Parliament: 86–8; independence of, 89–91. *See also* Bureaux
Secretaries-General of Parliaments, Association of: 87
Secretary-General of Parliament: 85–6, 95
Section system (in Parliament): 105
Senate, the (USA): powers and rights of, 4; and Cabinet, 269; and ratification of treaties, 315
Senegal: *Structure of Parliament:* unicameral system in, 12–13 *passim*; elections and electorate, 14–23 *passim*, 49–52 *passim*; ballots, 23–40 *passim*; Members of Parliament, 40–55 *passim*, 59–77 *passim*
  Organisation of Parliament: administration of, 77–88 *passim*; independence of, 88–97 *passim*; parties and groups, 97–102 *passim*; committees of, 102–22 *passim*; sittings of, 122–30 *passim*
  Legislative function of Parliament: limitations on, 133–40 *passim*; introduction of bills, 140–51 *passim*; delegated legislation, 151–9 *passim*; making of law, 159–213 *passim*; promulgation of laws, 213–19 *passim*; constitutional validity of laws, 219–24 *passim*
  Financial power of Parliament: the budget, 227–41 *passim*, 246–59 *passim*; rights of Members, 241–5 *passim*
  Control of Executive by Parliament: appointment of executive officers, 263–75 *passim*; accountability of government, 276–88 *passim*, 304–10 *passim*; machinery of control, 288–304 *passim*; in foreign policy, 310–16 *passim*; judicial function of Parliament, 316–19 *passim*
Separation of functions: 70. *See also* next below.
Separation of powers: 70, 88, 133, 141, 142, 156, 167, 177, 179, 217, 220, 242, 262, 269, 274, 277, 304, 315. *See also* Division, Equality *and* next above.
Serjeant-at-Arms: 85
Sessions of Parliament: 125–30; definition of, 125; principles involved, 125, 217–18; frequency and length of, 125–30; 'permanent assembly' system, 126, 129; annual, 126, 128; fixed by Executive, 127; 'ordinary', 128; vacations, 128; 'extraordinary' (emergency), 128–9
Sierra Leone: *Structure of Parliament:* unicameral system in, 12–13 *passim*; elections and electorate, 14–23 *passim*, 49–52 *passim*; ballots, 23–40 *passim*; Members of Parliament, 40–55 *passim*, 59–77 *passim*
  Organisation of Parliament: administration of, 77–88 *passim*; independence of, 88–97 *passim*; parties and groups, 97–102 *passim*; committees of, 102–22 *passim*; sittings of, 122–30 *passim*
  Legislative function of Parliament: limitations on, 133–40 *passim*; introduction of bills, 140–51 *passim*; delegated legislation, 151–9 *passim*; making of law, 159–213 *passim*; promulgation of laws, 213–19 *passim*; constitutional validity of laws, 219–24 *passim*
  Financial power of Parliament: the budget, 227–41 *passim*, 246–59 *passim*; rights of Members, 241–5 *passim*
  Control of Executive by Parliament: appointment of executive officers, 263–75 *passim*; accountability of government, 276–88 *passim*, 304–10 *passim*; machinery of control, 288–304 *passim*; in foreign policy, 310–16 *passim*; judicial function of Parliament, 316–19 *passim*
Sittings of Parliament: 88, 122–30; definition of, 125; and of Committee of the whole House, 103; secret, 203; joint (of both Houses), 204, 209, 211, 228, 238, 256, 265, 267. *See also* Chambers *and* Sessions.
Somalia: *Structure of Parliament:* unicameral system in, 12–13 *passim*; elections and electorate, 14–23 *passim*, 49–52 *passim*; ballots, 23–40 *passim*; Members of Parliament, 40–55 *passim*, 59–77 *passim*
  Organisation of Parliament: administration of, 77–88 *passim*; independence of, 88–97 *passim*; parties and groups, 97–102 *passim*; committees of, 102–22 *passim*; sittings of, 122–30 *passim*
  Legislative function of Parliament: limitations on, 133–40 *passim*;

INDEX

introduction of bills, 140–51 *passim*; delegated legislation, 151–9 *passim*; making of law, 159–213 *passim*; promulgation of laws, 213–19 *passim*; constitutional validity of laws, 219–24 *passim*
Financial power of Parliament: the budget, 227–41 *passim*, 246–59 *passim*; rights of Members, 241–5 *passim*
Control of Executive by Parliament: appointment of executive officers, 263–75 *passim*; accountability of government, 276–88 *passim*, 304–10 *passim*; machinery of control, 288–304 *passim*; in foreign policy, 310–16 *passim*; judicial function of Parliament, 316–19 *passim*
'Sovereign', the: *see* Head of State *and* Royal Assent
Sovereignty of the people embodied in Parliament: 277–8
Soviet Union: *see* U.S.S.R.
Spain: *Structure of Parliament:* unicameral system in, 12–13 *passim*; elections and electorate, 14–23 *passim*, 49–52 *passim*; ballots, 23–40 *passim*; Members of Parliament, 40–55 *passim*, 59–77 *passim*
Organisation of Parliament: administration of, 77–88 *passim*; independence of, 88–97 *passim*; parties and groups, 97–102 *passim*; committees of, 102–22 *passim*; sittings of, 122–30 *passim*
Legislative function of Parliament: limitations on, 133–40 *passim*; introduction of bills, 140–51 *passim*; delegated legislation, 151–9 *passim*; making of law, 159–213 *passim*; promulgation of laws, 213–19 *passim*; constitutional validity of laws, 219–24 *passim*
Financial power of Parliament: the budget, 227–41 *passim*, 246–59 *passim*; rights of Members, 241–5 *passim*
Control of Executive by Parliament: appointment of executive officers, 263–75 *passim*; accountability of government, 276–88 *passim*, 304–10 *passim*; machinery of control, 288–304 *passim*; in foreign policy, 310–16 *passim*; judicial function of Parliament, 316–19 *passim*
Speaker and Deputy Speaker (of Chambers): 77–84, 90, 178; *not present* in Committee of the whole House, 103; and nomination of chairmen of committees, 118; and who is to speak, 186–7; and 'guillotine', 187; and obstruction, 190; and closure, 191; and amendments, 196; his casting vote (in ties), 201; and money bills, 240; and motions for the adjournment, 281; and questions to ministers, 294–5. *See also* Directing authority.
Speakers' Colleges: 81–2, 83–4. *See also* Bureaux.
Special majorities: 202–3, 203, 203–4. *See also* Majorities.
Specialisation in Parliament: 104, 106, 107. *See also* Committees.
Speech from the Throne: 142, 290
Standing Orders: 94–7, 114, 159. *See also* Independence, procedural *and* Rules of procedure.
Stability and instability of governments: 282–5; in France and Germany, 284–5
Staff, parliamentary: 89–91. *See also* Secretariat.
State enterprise (public corporations): 234–7
'State of the Union' Message to Congress (USA): 229, 289
'Statement' (of policy) by Executive to Legislature: 290
Statutory Instruments: 154; Act (1946), 153
Statutory Orders (Special Procedure) Act (1945): 95
Structure of Parliament: *see* Assemblies, Bicameral system, Unicameral system, Ballot, Constituencies, Elections, Electorate, Mandate, Members, Membership, Polling, Registers *and* Voting
Suffrage: 14, 27, 88; direct, *see* universal; indirect, 7; universal (direct), 6–12, 14–19, 30, 55, 143, 266, 267, 269, 278
Sweden: *Structure of Parliament:* bicameral system in, 7–12 *passim*; elections and electorate, 14–23 *passim*, 49–52 *passim*; ballots, 23–40 *passim*; Members of Parliament, 40–55 *passim*, 59–77 *passim*
Organisation of Parliament: administration of, 77–88 *passim*; independence of, 88–97 *passim*; parties and groups, 97–102 *passim*; committees of, 102–22 *passim*; sittings of, 122–30 *passim*
Legislative function of Parliament:

limitations on, 133–40 *passim*; introduction of bills, 140–51 *passim*; delegated legislation, 151–9 *passim*; making of law, 159–213 *passim*; promulgation of laws, 213–19 *passim*; constitutional validity of laws, 219–24 *passim*

Financial power of Parliament: the budget, 227–41 *passim*, 246–59 *passim*; rights of Members, 241–5 *passim*

Control of Executive by Parliament: appointment of executive officers, 263–75 *passim*; accountability of government, 276–88 *passim*, 304–10 *passim*; machinery of control, 288–304 *passim*; in foreign policy, 310–16 *passim*; judicial function of Parliament, 316–19 *passim*

Switzerland: *Structure of Parliament:* bicameral system in, 3–7 *passim*; elections and electorate, 14–23 *passim*, 49–52 *passim*; ballots, 23–40 *passim*; Members of Parliament, 40–55 *passim*, 59–77 *passim*

Organisation of Parliament: administration of, 77–88 *passim*; independence of, 88–97 *passim*; parties and groups, 97–102 *passim*; committees of, 102–22 *passim*; sittings of, 122–30 *passim*

Legislative function of Parliament: limitations on, 133–40 *passim*; introduction of bills, 140–51 *passim*; delegated legislation, 151–9 *passim*; making of law, 159–213 *passim*; promulgation of laws, 213–19 *passim*; constitutional validity of laws, 219–24 *passim*

Financial power of Parliament: the budget, 227–41 *passim*, 246–59 *passim*; rights of Members, 241–5 *passim*

Control of Executive by Parliament: appointment of executive officers, 263–75 *passim*; accountability of government, 276–88 *passim*, 304–10 *passim*; machinery of control, 288–304 *passim*; in foreign policy, 310–16 *passim*; judicial function of Parliament, 316–19 *passim*

Symposium, international: ix

Taxation: *see* Budget, Finance *and* Financial matters

'Ten minute rule': 146

Timetable, parliamentary: *see* Debates *and* Order of business

Tradition, parliamentary: its effect on number of Chambers, 3–4, 7–8, 12, 13; and electoral systems, 24; and procedure, 95; democratic, 133; of constitutional and financial law, 242

Translators and interpreters: 87

Treasury control over expenditure: 233

Treaties, international: *see* Foreign policy

Treaties, ratification of (by Parliament): 313–16; in USA, 315. *See also* Foreign policy.

Tunisia: *Structure of Parliament:* unicameral system in, 12–13 *passim*; elections and electorate, 14–23 *passim*, 49–52 *passim*; ballots, 23–40 *passim*; Members of Parliament, 40–55 *passim*, 59–77 *passim*

Organisation of Parliament: administration of, 77–88 *passim*; independence of, 88–97 *passim*; parties and groups, 97–102 *passim*; committees of, 102–22 *passim*; sittings of, 122–30 *passim*

Legislative function of Parliament: limitations of, 133–40 *passim*; introduction of bills, 140–51 *passim*; delegated legislation, 151–9 *passim*; making of law, 159–213 *passim*; promulgation of laws, 213–19 *passim*; constitutional validity of laws, 219–24 *passim*

Financial power of Parliament: the budget, 227–41 *passim*, 246–59 *passim*; rights of Members, 241–5 *passim*

Control of Executive by Parliament: appointment of executive officers, 263–75 *passim*; accountability of government, 276–88 *passim*; 304–10 *passim*; machinery of control, 288–304 *passim*; in foreign policy, 310–16 *passim*; judicial function of Parliament, 316–19 *passim*

Turkey: *Structure of Parliament:* bicameral system in, 7–12 *passim*; elections and electorate, 14–23 *passim*, 49–52 *passim*; ballots, 23–40 *passim*; Members of Parliament, 40–55 *passim*, 59–77 *passim*

Organisation of Parliament: administration of, 77–88 *passim*; independence of, 88–97 *passim*; parties and groups, 97–102 *passim*; committees of, 102–22 *passim*; sittings of, 122–30 *passim*

Legislative function of Parliament: limitations on, 133–40 *passim*;

INDEX

introduction of bills, 140–51 *passim*; delegated legislation, 151–9 *passim*; making of law, 159–213 *passim*; promulgation of laws, 213–19 *passim*; constitutional validity of laws, 219–24 *passim*

Financial power of Parliament: the budget, 227–41 *passim*, 246–59 *passim*; rights of Members, 241–5 *passim*

Control of Executive by Parliament: appointment of executive officers, 263–75 *passim*; accountability of government, 276–88 *passim*, 304–10 *passim*; machinery of control, 288–304 *passim*; in foreign policy, 310–16 *passim*; judicial function of Parliament, 316–19 *passim*

U.A.R.: *see* United Arab Republic
U.K. (United Kingdom): *see* Great Britain
U.S.A.: *see* United States of America
U.S.S.R. (Union of Soviet Socialist Republics *or* Soviet Union): *Structure of Parliament:* bicameral system in, 3–7 *passim*; elections and electorate, 14–23 *passim*, 49–52 *passim*; ballots, 23–40 *passim*; Members of Parliament, 40–55 *passim*, 59–77 *passim*

Organisation of Parliament: administration of, 77–88 *passim*; independence of, 88–97 *passim*; parties and groups, 97–102 *passim*; committees of, 102–22 *passim*; sittings of, 122–30 *passim*

Legislative function of Parliament: limitations on, 133–40 *passim*; introduction of bills, 140–51 *passim*; delegated legislation, 151–9 *passim*; making of law, 159–213 *passim*; promulgation of laws, 213–19 *passim*; constitutional validity of laws, 219–24 *passim*

Financial power of Parliament: the budget, 227–41 *passim*, 246–59 *passim*; rights of Members, 241–5 *passim*

Control of Executive by Parliament: appointment of executive officers, 263–75 *passim*; accountability of government, 276–88 *passim*, 304–10 *passim*; machinery of control, 288–304 *passim*; in foreign policy, 310–16 *passim*; judicial function of Parliament, 316–19 *passim*

Unicameral system (*general*): 9, 12–13, 14; where suitable, 12–13; in Scandinavia, 12–13; reasons for choice of, 13

Unicameral system in federal states: 6–7; Cameroon, 6, 7; Pakistan, 6, 7; Yugoslavia, 6–7, 13

Unicameral system in non-federal states: 12–13

Unicameral-bicameral systems: 11, 208–9

Union of Soviet Socialist Republics: *see* U.S.S.R.

United Arab Republic: *Structure of Parliament:* unicameral system in, 12–13 *passim*; elections and electorate, 14–23 *passim*, 49–52 *passim*; ballots, 23–40 *passim*; Members of Parliament, 40–55 *passim*, 59–77 *passim*

Organisation of Parliament: administration of, 77–88 *passim*; independence of, 88–97 *passim*; parties and groups, 97–102 *passim*; committees of, 102–22 *passim*; sittings of, 122–30 *passim*

Legislative function of Parliament: limitations on, 133–40 *passim*; introduction of bills, 140–51 *passim*; delegated legislation, 151–9 *passim*; making of law, 159–213 *passim*; promulgation of laws, 213–19 *passim*; constitutional validity of laws, 219–24 *passim*

Financial power of Parliament: the budget, 227–41 *passim*, 246–59 *passim*; rights of Members, 241–5 *passim*

Control of Executive by Parliament: appointment of executive officers, 263–75 *passim*; accountability of government, 276–88 *passim*, 304–10 *passim*; machinery of control, 288–304 *passim*; in foreign policy, 310–16 *passim*; judicial function of Parliament, 316–19 *passim*

United Kingdom of Great Britain and Northern Ireland: *see* Great Britain

United States of America: *Structure of Parliament:* bicameral system in, 3–7 *passim*; elections and electorate, 14–23 *passim*, 49–52 *passim*; ballots, 23–40 *passim*; Members of Parliament, 40–55 *passim*, 59–77 *passim*

Organisation of Parliament: administration of, 77–88 *passim*; independence of, 88–97 *passim*; parties and groups, 97–102 *passim*; com-

mittees of, 102–22 *passim*; sittings of, 122–30 *passim*
Legislative function of Parliament: limitations on, 133–40 *passim*; introduction of bills, 140–51 *passim*; delegated legislation, 151–9 *passim*; making of law, 159–213 *passim*; promulgation of laws, 213–19 *passim*; constitutional validity of laws, 219–24 *passim*
Financial power of Parliament: the budget, 227–41 *passim*, 246–59 *passim*; rights of Members, 241–5 *passim*
Control of Executive by Parliament: appointment of executive officers, 263–75 *passim*; accountability of government, 276–88 *passim*, 304–10 *passim*; machinery of control, 288–304 *passim*; in foreign policy, 310–16 *passim*; judicial function of Parliament, 316–19 *passim*

Value of this study: xi
Veto, the: 217–19; right of, 213; absolute, 219; Head of State's, 202, 207, 217, 217–19; 'pocket', 218
'Virement': 227
Vote, the: *see* Franchise *and* Suffrage
'Voted services': 250, 257
Votes on account: 251–3, 254, 259
Votes, secret: 32–3, 196–7. See also Budget, Elections, Financial matters, Franchise, Polling, Registers *and* Voting
Voting at elections: 27–37; and number of parties, 27; a 'right' or a 'duty', 28–9; optional or compulsory, 29; compulsory, 29–30; sanctions, 29; abstentions, 29–30, 49; by proxy, 30–1; by post, 31; secrecy of, 32–3; voting papers and ballot boxes, 32–5; computers, 33; counting the votes, 35–7
Systems of: 24–7; single ballot, 24–6; two ballots, 25, 27; proportional representation, 24–27; geographical variations, 24–7; election by majority, 24–5, 26, 27; for lists of candidates, 25; single transferable vote, 26; object of, 27; and number of parties, 27. See also Ballot, Elections, Financial matters, Franchise, Polling, Registers *and* Voting in Parliament.

Voting in Parliament, methods of: 196–203; 'public' ,197; oral, 197–8; by show of hands, 198; by sitting and standing, 198; by gathering together, 198; by division, 198–9; by roll call, 199; by voting papers, 199; by electric and electronic devices, 200; by proxy, 200, 201; delegated, 200; 'pairing', 200; majority decisions, 201; quorum and equality of votes, 201; ties, procedure in case of, 201; special majorities, 202–3 (*see also* Majorities); 'without debate' procedure, 165, 180

Ways and Means: Chairman and Deputy Chairman of, 79, 103, 118; Committee of, 112, 149
Whips (and Chief Whips) of political parties: 100–1

Yugoslavia (*See also* People's Democracies): Structure of Parliament: unicameral system in, 6–7 *passim*, 12–13 *passim*; elections and electorate, 14–23 *passim*, 49–52 *passim*; ballots, 23–40 *passim*; Members of Parliament, 40–55 *passim*, 59–77 *passim*
Organisation of Parliament: administration of, 77–88 *passim*; independence of, 88–97 *passim*; parties and groups, 97–102 *passim*; committees of, 102–22 *passim*; sittings of, 122–30 *passim*
Legislative function of Parliament: limitations on, 133–40 *passim*; introduction of bills, 140–51 *passim*; delegated legislation, 151–9 *passim*; making of law, 159–213 *passim*; promulgation of laws, 213–19 *passim*; constitutional validity of laws, 219–24 *passim*
Financial power of Parliament: the budget, 227–41 *passim*, 246–59 *passim*; rights of Members, 241–5 *passim*
Control of Executive by Parliament: appointment of executive officers, 263–75 *passim*; accountability of government, 276–88 *passim*, 304–10 *passim*; machinery of control, 288–304 *passim*; in foreign policy, 310–16 *passim*; judicial function of Parliament, 316–19 *passim*